D1622066

Modern Authentication with Azure Active Directory for Web Applications

Vittorio Bertocci

PUBLISHED BY
Microsoft Press
A Division of Microsoft Corporation
One Microsoft Way
Redmond, Washington 98052-6399

Copyright © 2016 by Vittorio Bertocci. All rights reserved.

No part of the contents of this book may be reproduced or transmitted in any form or by any means without the written permission of the publisher.

Library of Congress Control Number: 2014954517
ISBN: 978-0-7356-9694-5

Printed and bound in the United States of America.

4   18

Microsoft Press books are available through booksellers and distributors worldwide. If you need support related to this book, email Microsoft Press Support at mspinput@microsoft.com. Please tell us what you think of this book at http://aka.ms/tellpress.

This book is provided "as-is" and expresses the author's views and opinions. The views, opinions and information expressed in this book, including URL and other Internet website references, may change without notice.

Some examples depicted herein are provided for illustration only and are fctitious. No real association or connection is intended or should be inferred.

Microsoft and the trademarks listed at www.microsoft.com on the "Trademarks" webpage are trademarks of the Microsoft group of companies. All other marks are property of their respective owners.

Acquisitions and Developmental Editor: Devon Musgrave
Project Editor: John Pierce
Editorial Production: Rob Nance, John Pierce, and Carrie Wicks
Copyeditor: John Pierce
Indexer: Christina Yeager, Emerald Editorial Services
Cover: Twist Creative • Seattle and Joel Panchot

Ai miei carissimi fratelli e sorelle: Mauro, Franco, Marino, Cristina, Ulderico, Maria, Laura, Guido e Mira—per avermi fatto vedere il mondo attraverso altre nove paia d'occhi.

Contents

**Chapter 3   Introducing Azure Active Directory and Active
             Directory Federation Services   51**

Chapter 4   Introducing the identity developer libraries   69

Chapter 9   Consuming and exposing a web API protected by Azure Active Directory   223

Chapter 10   Active Directory Federation Services in Windows Server 2016 Technical Preview 3   273

Foreword

The purpose of an application is to take input from users or other applications and produce output that will be consumed by those same users or applications or by other ones. That's true of a website that gains input from a click on a link and sends back the content of the requested page as output; a middle tier that processes database requests queued from a front end, executing them by sending input to a database; or a cloud service that gets input from a mobile application to look up nearby friends. Given this, a fundamental question faced in the design of every application is, Who is sending the input and should the application process it to produce the resulting output? Put another way: every application must decide on an identity system that represents users and other applications, a means by which to validate an application's or user's claimed identity, and a way to determine what outputs the user or application is allowed to produce.

These decisions will determine how easily users and applications can interact with an application, what functionality they can take advantage of to secure and manage their identities and credentials, and how much work the application developer must do to enable these capabilities, which are known as authentication and authorization. The ideal answers make it possible for users and applications to use their preferred identities, whether from Facebook, Gmail, or their enterprise; for the application to easily configure the access rights for authorized users; and for the application to rely on other services as much as possible to do the heavy lifting. Identity and access control, while key to an application's utility, are not the core value an application delivers, so developers shouldn't spend any more time on this area than they have to. Why create a database of users and worry about which algorithm to use to encrypt the users' passwords if you can take advantage of a service that's built for doing just that, with industry-leading security and management?

Microsoft Azure Active Directory (Azure AD) is arguably the heart of Microsoft's cloud platform. All Microsoft cloud services, including Microsoft Azure, Microsoft Xbox Live, and Microsoft Office 365, use Azure AD as their identity provider. And because Azure AD is a public cloud service, application developers can also take advantage of its capabilities. If an application relies on Azure AD as its identity provider, it can rely on Azure AD APIs to provision users, rely on Azure AD to manage their passwords, and even give users the ability to use multifactor authentication (MFA) to securely authenticate to the application. For application developers wanting to integrate with businesses, including the many that are already using Azure AD, Azure AD has the most flexible and comprehensive support of any service for integrating Active Directory and LDAP identities. Fueled by enterprise adoption of Office 365, Azure AD is already a connection point for hundreds of millions of business and organizational identities, and it's growing fast.

Using Azure AD for the most common scenarios is easy, thanks to the open source developer libraries, tooling, and guidance available on Microsoft Azure's GitHub organization. Going beyond the basics, however, requires a good understanding of modern authentication flows—specifically OAuth2 and OpenID Connect—and concepts such as a relying party and tokens, federation, role-based access control, a provisioned application, and service principles. If you're new to these protocols and terms, the learning curve can seem daunting. Even if you're not, knowing the most efficient way to use Azure AD and its unique capabilities is important, and it's worthwhile understanding what's available to you.

There's no better book than *Modern Authentication with Azure Active Directory for Web Applications* to help you make your application take full advantage of Azure AD. I've known Vittorio Bertocci since I started in Azure five years ago, and I've watched his always popular and highly rated Microsoft TechEd, Build, and Microsoft Ignite conference presentations to catch up with the latest developments in Azure AD. He's a master educator and one of Microsoft's foremost experts on identity and access control.

This book will guide you through the essentials of authentication protocols, decipher the disparate terminology applied to the subject, tell you how to get started with Azure AD, and then present concrete examples of applications that use Azure AD for their authentication and authorization, including how they work in hybrid scenarios with Active Directory Federation Services (ADFS). With the information and insights Vittorio shares, you'll be able to efficiently create modern cloud applications that give users and administrators the flexibility and security of Microsoft's cloud and the convenience of using their preferred identities.

Mark Russinovich
Chief Technology Officer, Microsoft Azure

Introduction

It's never a good idea to use the word "modern" in the title of a book.

Growing up, one of the centerpieces of my family's bookshelf was a 15-tomes-strong encyclopedia titled *Nuovissima Enciclopedia* (Very new encyclopedia), and I always had a hard time reconciling the title with the fact that it was 10 years older than me.

I guarantee that the content in this book will get old faster than those old volumes—cloud and development technologies evolve at a crazy pace—and yet I could not resist referring to the main subject of the book as "modern authentication."

The practices and technologies used to take care of authentication in business solutions have changed radically nearly overnight, by a perfect storm of companies moving their assets to the cloud, software vendors starting to sell their products via subscriptions, the explosive growth of social networks with the nascent awareness of consumers of their own digital identity, ubiquitous APIs offering programmatic access to everything, and the astonishing adoption rate of Internet-connected smartphones.

"Modern authentication" is a catch-all term meant to capture how today's practices address challenges differently from their recent ancestors: JSON instead of XML, REST instead of SOAP, user consent and individual freedom alongside traditional admin-only processes, an emphasis on APIs and delegated access, explicit representation of clients, and so on. And if it is true that those practices will eventually stop appearing to be new—they are already mainstream at this point—the break with traditional approaches is so significant that I feel it's important to signal it with a strong title, even if your kids make fun of it a few years from now.

As the landscape evolves, Active Directory evolves with it. When Microsoft itself introduced one of the most important SaaS products on the planet, Office 365, it felt firsthand how cloud-based workloads call for new ways of managing user access and application portfolios. To confront that challenge Microsoft developed Azure Active Directory (Azure AD), a reimagined Active Directory that takes advantage of all the new protocols, artifacts, and practices that I've grouped under the modern authentication umbrella. Once it was clear that Azure AD was a Good Thing, it went on to become the main authentication service for all of Microsoft's cloud services, including Intune, Power BI, and Azure itself. But the real raison d'etre of this book is that Microsoft opened Azure AD to every developer and organization so that it could be used for obtaining tokens to invoke Microsoft APIs and to handle authentication for your own web applications and web APIs.

Modern Authentication with Azure Active Directory for Web Applications is an in-depth exploration of modern authentication protocols and techniques used to implement sign-on for web applications and to protect web API calls. Although the protocols and pattern descriptions are applicable to any platform, my focus is on how Azure AD, the latest version of Active Directory Federation Services (ADFS), and the OpenID Connect and OAuth2 components in ASP.NET implement those approaches to handle authentication in real applications.

The text is meant to help you achieve expert-level understanding of the protocols and technologies involved in implementing modern authentication for a web app. Substantial space is reserved for architectural pattern descriptions, protocol consider-ations, and other abstract concerns that are necessary for correctly contextualizing the more hands-on advice that follows.

Most of the practical content in this book is about cloud and hybrid scenarios addressed via Azure AD. At the time of writing, the version of ADFS supporting modern authentication for web apps is still in technical preview; however, on-premises-only scenarios are covered whenever the relevant features are already available in the preview.

Who should read this book

I wrote this book to fill a void of expert-level content for modern authentication, Azure AD, and ADFS. Microsoft offers great online quick starts, samples, and reference documentation—check out *http://aka.ms/aaddev*—that are perfect for helping you fulfil the most common tasks as easily as possible. That content covers many scenarios and addresses the needs of the vast majority of developers, who can be extremely successful with their apps without ever knowing what actually goes on the wire, or why. I like to think of that level of operation as the automatic mode for handheld and smart-phone cameras—their defaults work great for nearly everybody, nearly all the time. But what happens if you want to take a picture of a lunar eclipse or any other challenging subject? That's when the point-and-click facade is no longer sufficient and knowing about aperture and exposure times becomes important. You can think of this book as a handbook for when you want to switch from automatic to manual settings. Doing so is useful for developers who work on solutions for which authentication requirements depart from the norm and for the devops who run such solutions.

Developers who worked with Windows Identity Foundation will find the text useful for transferring their skills to the new platform, and they'll pick up some new tricks along the way. The coverage of how the OWIN middleware works is deeper than anything I've found on the Internet at this time: if you are interested in an in-depth case study of ASP.NET's Katana libraries, you'll find one here.

This book also comes in handy for security experts coming from a classic background and looking to understand modern protocols and approaches to authentication—the principles and protocols I describe can be applied well beyond Active Directory and ASP.NET. Security architects considering Azure AD for their solutions can use this book to understand how Azure AD operates. Protocol experts who want to understand how Azure AD and ADFS use OpenID Connect and OAuth2 will find plenty to mull over as well.

Assumptions

This book is for senior professionals well versed in development, distributed architectures, and web-based solutions. You need to be familiar with HTTP trappings and have at least a basic understanding of networking concepts. All sample code is presented in C#, and all walk-throughs are based on Visual Studio. Azure AD and ADFS can be made use of from any programming stack and operating system; however, if you don't understand C# syntax and basic constructs (LINQ, etc.), it will be difficult for you to apply the coding advice in this book to your platform of choice. For good background, I'd recommend John Sharp's *Microsoft Visual C# Step by Step, Eighth Edition* (Microsoft Press, 2015).

Above all, this book assumes that you are strongly motivated to become an expert in modern authentication techniques and Azure AD development. The text does not take any shortcuts: you should not expect a light read; most chapters require significant focus and time investment.

This book might not be for you if...

This book might not be for you if you just want to learn how to use Azure AD or ADFS for common development tasks. You don't have to buy a book for that: the documentation and the samples available at *http://aka.ms/aaddev* will get you up and running in no time, thanks to crisp step-by-step instructions. If there are tasks you'd like to see covered by the Azure AD docs, please use the feedback tools provided at that address: the Azure AD team is always looking for feedback for improving its documentation.

This book is also not especially good as a lookup reference. The text covers a lot of ground, including information that isn't included in the documentation at this time, but the information is unveiled progressively, building on the reader's growing understanding of the topic. The book is optimized as a long lesson, not for looking things up.

Finally, this book won't be of much help if you are developing mobile, native, and rich-client applications. I originally intended to cover those types of applications, too, but the size of the book would have nearly doubled, so I had to cut them from this edition.

Organization of this book

This book is meant to be read cover to cover. That's not what most people like to do, I know: bite-size and independent modules is the way to go today. I believe there are media more conducive to that approach, like video courses or the online documentation at *http://aka.ms/aaddev*. I chose to write a book because to achieve my goal—helping you understand modern authentication principles and how to take advantage of them with Azure AD—I cannot feed you only factlets and recipes. I have to present you with a significant amount of information, highlight relationships and implications for you, and then often ask you to tuck that knowledge away for a chapter or two before you actually end up using it. That's where I believe a book can still deliver value: by giving me the chance to hold your attention for a significant amount of time, I can afford a depth and breadth that I cannot achieve in a blog post. (By the way, did I mention that I do blog a lot as well? See *www.cloudidentity.com* and *www.twitter.com/vibronet*.)

If this book has a natural fault line in its organization, it lies between the first four chapters and the last six. The first group provides context, and the later chapters dive deeply into the protocols, code, libraries, and features of Active Directory. Here's a quick description of each chapter's focus:

- Chapter 1, "Your first Active Directory app," is a soft introduction to the topic, giving you a brief glimpse of what you can achieve with Azure AD. It mostly provides instructions on how to use Visual Studio tools to create a web app that's integrated with Azure AD. Instant gratification.

- Chapter 2, "Identity protocols and application types," is a detailed history of identity protocols. It introduces terminology, topologies, and relationships between standards and helps you understand how modern authentication came to be and why identity is managed the way it is today.

- Chapter 3, "Introducing Azure Active Directory and Active Directory Federation Services," presents basic concepts, terminology, and a list of developer-relevant features for Azure AD and ADFS. The hands-on chapters (Chapters 6-10) provide detailed descriptions of the features of both services that come into play in the scenarios of interest for the book.

- Chapter 4, "Introducing the identity developer libraries," covers basic concepts, terminology, and the features of the Active Directory Authentication Library (ADAL) and ASP.NET OWIN middleware.

- Chapter 5, "Getting started with web sign-on and Active Directory," provides a walk-through of how to create from scratch a web app that can sign in with Azure AD. Starting with the vanilla MVC templates, you learn about the NuGets packages you need to add, what app provisioning steps you need to follow in the Azure portal, and what code you need to write to perform key authentication tasks.

- Chapter 6, "OpenID Connect and Azure AD web sign-on," provides a very detailed description of OpenID Connect and related standards, grounded on network traces of the actual traffic generated by the sample app. This is a very practical way of understanding the underlying protocol and why it operates the way it does. The descriptions of the constellation of ancillary specifications for OpenID Connect and OAuth2 will help you to navigate this rather crowded space, even if you are not planning to use Azure AD at the moment.

- Chapter 7, "The OWIN OpenID Connect middleware," is a detailed analysis of how the authentication pipeline in ASP.NET works—with an emphasis on the OpenID Connect middleware, its extensibility points, and what scenarios these are meant to address.

- Chapter 8, "Azure Active Directory application model," is a deep dive into the Azure AD application model: how Azure AD represents apps and handles consent, and how it deals with app provisioning, multitenancy, app roles, groups, app permissions, and the like.

- Chapter 9, "Consuming and exposing a web API protected by Azure Active Directory," does for web APIs what Chapters 6 and 7 do for web apps—it explains the protocol flows used by web apps for gaining access to a protected API and describes how to use ADAL and the OAuth2 middleware for securely invoking and protecting a web API. This chapter also briefly introduces the Directory Graph API and discusses advanced scenarios such as exposing and securing both the user experience and an API from the same web project.

- Chapter 10, "Active Directory Federation Services in Windows Server 2016 Technical Preview 3," discusses the new modern authentication features in ADFS, showing how to adapt web sign-on, web API invocation, and code protection covered in the earlier chapters to on-premises-only scenarios.

- The appendix, "Further reading," provides you with pointers to online content describing ancillary topics and offerings that are still too new to be fully fleshed out in the book but are interesting and relevant to the subject of modern authentication.

Finding your best starting point in this book

As I mentioned, every chapter in this book builds on the knowledge you acquire in the preceding ones. That makes choosing an arbitrary starting point a tricky exercise. I recommend that you look over the description of the book's chapters in the previous section and decide whether you feel comfortable enough on the matter to choose a specific starting point.

System requirements

You will need the following software if you want to follow the code walk-throughs in this book:

- Any Windows version that can run Visual Studio 2015 or later.

- Visual Studio 2015, any edition (technically, apart from Chapter 1, Visual Studio 2015 isn't a hard requirement; Visual Studio 2013 will work with just a few adjustments).

- A Microsoft Azure subscription and access to the Azure portal.

- Telerik Fiddler v4 (*http://www.telerik.com/fiddler*).

- Internet connection to reach Azure AD during authentication operations and provisioning tasks.

In addition, Chapter 10 requires you to have access to an ADFS instance using Windows Server 2016 Technical Preview 3. Its system requirements can be found at *https://technet.microsoft.com/en-us/library/mt126134.aspx*. For the book, I hosted my own instance in a Hyper-V virtual machine, running on a laptop with Windows 10.

Downloads: Code samples

This book contains a lot of code, and I present some of it in the form of guided walk-throughs. The goal is always to unveil the concepts you need to understand in manageable chunks, as opposed to the classic recipes you get in traditional labs or exercises. Also, I often discuss alternatives in the text, but the code can't always reflect all possible options. Expect the code to demonstrate the mainline approach; where possible and appropriate, alternatives are provided in code comments.

You can find the code I use in the book on my GitHub, at the following address:

http://aka.ms/modauth/files

You will notice a number of repositories with the form <ModAuthBook_Chapter*N*>, *where N* represents the chapter number in which the repository code is described and demonstrated. (Not every book chapter contains code; only the chapters that do have a corresponding repository on GitHub.) If you are not familiar with GitHub, just click the repository name for the chapter you are interested in; somewhere on the page (at this time, at the bottom-right corner of the layout), you'll find the Download ZIP button, which you can use to save a local copy of the code.

Using the code samples

Every repository contains a Visual Studio solution and a readme file. The readme provides a quick indication about the topic covered by the corresponding chapter, prerequisites, and basic instructions on how to provision the sample in your own Azure AD tenant. I'll do my best to keep the setup instructions up to date.

Once again, don't expect too much handholding: the code is provided mostly for reference. (Microsoft's fficial step-by-step samples and quick starts are provided at *http://aka.ms/aaddev*.) If a sample requires extra steps to fully demonstrate a scenario (for example, the presence in your tenant of an admin and at least a nonadmin user), I've assumed that you'll get that information by reading the book and don't repeat it in the sample's readme. The code provided at *http://aka.ms/modauth/files* is meant to support and complement the reading of the book rather than as a standalone asset.

Acknowledgments

We have to go deeper.

—Cobb in *Inception*, a film by Christopher Nolan, 2010

This book has been a labor of love, written during nights, weekends, and occasional time off. I have willingly put that yolk on myself, but my wife, **Iwona Bialynicka-Birula,** did not . . . she endured nearly one year of missed hikes, social jet lag, and a silence curfew "because I have to write." Thank you for your patience, darling—as I promised in the acknowledgments for *Programming Windows Identity Foundation* back in 2011: No more books for a few years!

This book would not have happened at all if **Devon Musgrave**, my acquisitions editor, would not have relentlessly pursued it, granting me a level of trust and freedom I am not sure I fully deserve. Thank you, Devon!

John Pierce has been an absolutely incredible project editor, driving everything from editing to project management to illustrations. He has this magic ability of turning my broken English into correct sentences while preserving my original intent. I wish every technical writer would have the good fortune of working with somebody as gifted as John. **Rob Nance** and **Carrie Wicks** also made significant contributions to producing this book.

I will be forever grateful to **Mark Russinovich** for the fantastic foreword he wrote for the book and for the kind words he offered about me. I am truly humbled to have my book begin with the words of a legend in software engineering.

Big thanks to my management chain for supporting this side project. **Alex Simons, Eric Doerr, Stuart Kwan**—thank you! I never quite managed to write on Fridays, but it was a great attempt.

I need to call out Stuart for a special thanks—from welcoming me to the product team to mentoring me through the transition from evangelism to product management. A large part of whatever success I have achieved is thanks to our work together. Thank you!

Rich Randall, the development lead on the Azure AD developer experience team, is my partner in crime and recipient of my utmost respect and admiration. Without his amazing work, none of the libraries described in this book would be around. And without the contribution of **Afshin Sephetri, Kanishk Panwar, Brent Schmaltz, Tushar Gupta, Wei Jia, Sasha Tokarev, Ryan Pangrle, Chris Chartier,** and

Omer Cansizoglu—developers on Rich's team—those libraries would not be nearly as usable and powerful as they are.

Danny Strockis has been on the PM team for a relatively short time, but his contributions are already monumental. **Ariel Gordon**, responsible for designing many of the experiences that the Azure AD users go through every day, is a source of never-ending insights. **Dushyant Gill** drove the authorization features in Azure AD, and he patiently explained those to me every single time I barged into his office.

Igor Sakhnov, developer manager for Azure AD authentication, and his then-PM counterpart **David Howell** have my gratitude for trusting us on the decision to move the web authentication stack to OWIN. It worked out pretty well!

Speaking of OWIN. **Chris Ross, Tushar Gupta, Brent Schmaltz, Daniel Roth, Louis Dejardin, Eilon Lipton,** and **Barry Dorrans** all did a fantastic job, both in developing and driving the libraries and in handling my mercurial outbursts. Dan, I told you we'd get there! Special thanks to Chris Ross and Tushar Gupta for reviewing Chapter 7 in record time.

I started working with **Scott Hunter** on ASP.NET tooling and templates back in 2012 and loved every second. The man cares deeply about customers, understands the importance of identity, and is a force to reckon with. It is thanks to him and to my good friends **Pranav Rastogi, Brady Gaster,** and **Dan Roth** that web apps in Visual Studio can be enabled for Azure AD in just a few clicks.

In my opinion, Visual Studio 2015 has the most sophisticated identity management features in all of Microsoft's rich clients, and that's largely thanks to the relentless work that **Anthony Cangialosi, Ji Eun Kwon,** and all the Visual Studio and Visual Studio Online gang poured into it. That made it possible for many other teams to build on that core and deliver first-class identity support in Visual Studio for Azure, Office 365, and more. Among others, we have **Chakkaradeep (Chaks) Chinnakonda Chandran, Dan Seefeldt, Steve Harter, Xiaoying Guo, Yuval Mazor, Sean Laberee,** and **Paul Yuknewicz** to thank for that.

The Azure AD authentication service is for developers and maintained by some of the finest developers I know—**Shiung Yong, Ravi Sharma, Matt Rimer,** and **Maxim Yaryn** are the ones patiently fielding my questions and listening to my crazy scenarios. The architects behind the service, **Yordan Rouskov** and **Murli Satagopan**, are an inexhaustible source of insight.

The guys working on the directory data model, portal, and Graph API are also amazing in all sorts of ways: **Dan Kershaw, Edward Wu, Yi Li, Dmitry Pugachev,**

Vijay Srirangam, Jeff Staiman, and Shane Oatman are always there to help. Special mention to Yi Li who reviewed Chapter 8 and deals with my questions nearly every day.

Besides doing a fantastic job with ADFS in Windows Server 2016, Samuel Devasahayam, Mahesh Unnikrishnan, Jen Field, Jim Uphaus, and Saket Kataruka from the ADFS team were of great help for Chapter 10.

The people on the partner teams are the ones who keep things real: they won't be satisfied until the services and libraries address their scenarios, and in so doing they push the services to excellence. Mat Velloso from Evangelism; Rob Howard, Matthias Leibmann, Yina Arenas, and Tim McConnell from Office 365; Shriram Natarajan (Shri) and Pavel Tsurbeleu from Azure Stack; Dave Brankin, David Messner, Yugang Wang, and George Moore from Azure; and Hadeel Elbitar from Power BI are all people who keep asking the right questions and offer priceless insights. Thank you guys!

The contribution from people in the development community is of paramount importance, especially now that our libraries are open source. Dominick Baier and Brock Allen are the most prominent sources of insight I can think of and are a beacon in the world of claims-based identity and modern authentication.

The identirati community plays a key role in moving modern authentication forward, divining what the industry wants and translating it into the form of RFC stone tablets. I am super grateful to John Bradley for our beer-fueled chats every time we meet at the Cloud Identity Summit and to the excellent Brian Campbell and, well, Canadian Paul Madsen for the friendly banter; to Bob Blakley and Ian Glazer for never failing to inspire; and to our own Mike Jones and Anthony Nadalin for being dependable, in-house protocol oracles. Although I cannot stop myself from reminding Tony that it is imperative that he work on his focus—he'll know what that means.

Last but not least, I want to thank the readers of my blog, my Twitter followers, the people I engage with on StackOverflow, and the people I meet at conferences during my sessions and afterward. It is your passion, your desire to know more and be more effective, and, yes, your affection,that made me decide to invest time in writing this book. Thank you for your incredible energy. *This book is for you.*

Errata, updates, & book support

We've made every effort to ensure the accuracy of this book and its companion content. You can access updates to this book—in the form of a list of submitted errata and their related corrections—at:

http://aka.ms/modauth

If you discover an error that is not already listed, please submit it to us at the same page.

If you need additional support, email Microsoft Press Book Support at *mspinput@ microsoft.com*.

Please note that product support for Microsoft software and hardware is not offered through the previous addresses. For help with Microsoft software or hardware, go to *http://support.microsoft.com*.

Free ebooks from Microsoft Press

From technical overviews to in-depth information on special topics, the free ebooks from Microsoft Press cover a wide range of topics. These ebooks are available in PDF, EPUB, and Mobi for Kindle formats, ready for you to download at:

http://aka.ms/mspressfree

Check back often to see what is new!

We want to hear from you

At Microsoft Press, your satisfaction is our top priority, and your feedback our most valuable asset. Please tell us what you think of this book at:

http://aka.ms/tellpress

We know you're busy, so we've kept it short with just a few questions. Your answers go directly to the editors at Microsoft Press. (No personal information will be requested.) Thanks in advance for your input!

Stay in touch

Let's keep the conversation going! We're on Twitter:

http://twitter.com/MicrosoftPress

CHAPTER 1

Your first Active Directory app

To give you a good sense of how modern identity works, this book takes you on a roller-coaster ride, swinging from the heights of highly abstract architectural diagrams down to nitty-gritty details of implementation and protocols. There will be time for all that later, though. In this chapter, I provide some immediate gratification by walking you through the simple task of using Active Directory to protect a web application—without worrying at all about the underlying principles at play or the code necessary to implement them. Later chapters will give you more insights about what's really going on: you'll be able to come back to this example, reinterpret what you see in light of your new knowledge, and tweak things to your specific needs. For now, we'll just have some uncomplicated fun.

The sample application

Here's what I'm going for. I want to create an ASP.NET application that can be accessed only by users from a given organization. Furthermore, I want the application to be able to retrieve data about users and the organization itself at any time during a user's session.

I've assumed that the organization I'm targeting has an instance of Azure Active Directory (Azure AD). The organization could have obtained that instance in a number of ways: for example, having a Microsoft Azure or an Office 365 subscription automatically provides one. I could just as well have picked an on-premises instance of Active Directory and the example would have worked the same, but the setup would have been more laborious.

The application scenario I've described can be achieved by relying on Azure AD for authenticating users to the app and by querying the directory tenant for whatever extra information might be required.

Prerequisites

The use of cloud services and of highly integrated tooling such as Microsoft Visual Studio allows me to keep the list of requirements very short.

Microsoft Azure subscription

The scenario requires a Microsoft Azure subscription to host the Azure AD tenant and allow development against it. In fact, to try the code samples for yourself, you'll use your Azure AD tenant over and over again throughout this book.

Developing against Azure AD is free as long as you stay below 500,000 objects. You can get a Microsoft Azure free trial and, assuming that you don't use any other paid services, you can try everything you'll find in this book without spending a dime—excluding electricity and Internet connectivity bills, of course.

At the time of writing this chapter, you can set up a Microsoft Azure trial by visiting *http://azure .microsoft.com/en-us/pricing/free-trial/*. I won't provide detailed setup instructions here because the process has likely changed since the book went to press. However, setup should be pretty simple. Please note that you must successfully complete the process and have a valid subscription to follow along with the samples. All the other setup steps depend on you having a subscription available, so you need to take care of this right away.

Of course, if you already have a Microsoft Azure subscription, you are most welcome to use it here: there's no need to set up a new one.

Visual Studio 2015

You can choose to develop your app with pretty much any tool you like. To save time, I'll use Visual Studio 2015, which contains wizards and templates that greatly speed up the creation of an Azure AD–protected application.

You can download Visual Studio 2015 from *https://www.visualstudio.com/downloads/download-visual-studio-vs*. Go ahead and install it on your development machine.

Once you are done with the setup, you need to tie the user account associated with your Azure subscription to your Visual Studio instance. This allows Visual Studio to gain access to your Azure assets, including your Azure AD tenant, enabling various tools and wizards in Visual Studio to take care of many configuration steps for you. Later in the book, I walk you through in painstaking detail what happens behind the scenes, but for the time being, abstracting away all those details makes it possible for you to protect applications with Azure AD without having to be a domain expert.

Launch Visual Studio. At the top-right corner of the screen is a Sign In link. Click on it: you'll be presented with a dialog prompting you for your credentials.

If you associated your Azure subscription with a Microsoft account, enter the associated credentials here. Once you successfully sign in, you are done with your setup.

What if your instance of Visual Studio is already tied to a different identity?

If you are already using Visual Studio 2015, chances are that you have entered an account in it. If that account is associated with an Azure subscription, you are all set. If instead you created a different account during your Azure sign-up process, or if your company manages your Azure subscription under your work account, you can simply add that account to Visual Studio as well. Open the drop-down list at the top-right corner and choose Account Settings. You're presented with the dialog shown in Figure 1-1. Click Add An Account, and simply enter your credentials to associate the new account with Visual Studio.

FIGURE 1-1 The account management dialog in Visual Studio 2015.

Creating the application

Let's get started!

1. Open Visual Studio 2015 (if you do not have an instance already running).

2. Go to the File menu. Choose New, Project.

3. In the list of templates on the left, choose Web. From the list of project types in the main area, select ASP.NET Application.

4. Enter a project name of your choice. (I used FirstADWebApp.) Click OK.

5. In the dialog that follows, select MVC (which should be the default). Click the Change Authentication button on the right side of the dialog.

6. In the next dialog, select the Work And School Accounts option. You should see a screen similar to this:

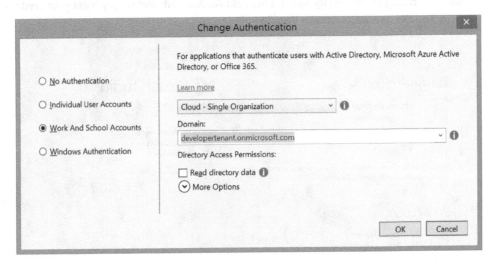

7. Leave the top drop-down with its default value: Cloud—Single Organization. The Domain drop-down will show a list of all the domains available to all the Azure AD tenants associated with the users signed in via Visual Studio. You can leave the default here as well. Leave Read Directory Data cleared.

8. Click OK through all the dialogs to get back to Visual Studio.

9. You're done. After you click OK in the last dialog, Visual Studio reaches out to Azure AD, creates a new entry describing your application, and generates a new project that is already configured to handle authentication to your Azure AD tenant.

Running the application

Visual Studio creates the application already configured to enforce authentication on every request. That means that as soon as you try to access it, you are prompted to authenticate.

Note This is a common setup for line-of-business (LOB) applications, where users normally access the application from their workplace. Chances are that such users are already signed in to their directory, in which case the application authenticates them transparently, without showing any prompt.

Go back to Visual Studio and press F5. The first thing you'll see in the browser is an Azure AD sign-in page prompting you for your Azure AD credentials, as shown in Figure 1-2.

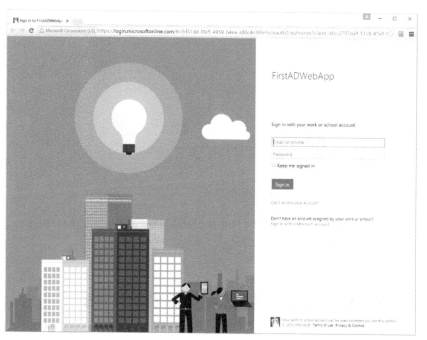

FIGURE 1-2 The Azure AD credentials prompt.

Enter any valid credentials from your Azure AD tenant, and then click Sign In. You are presented with the consent prompt shown in Figure 1-3. Because you are running this application for the first time, Azure AD informs you about the privileges the application needs to acquire in your directory to perform its function. In this case it is requesting the bare minimum—the abilities to sign in the user and gather basic information.

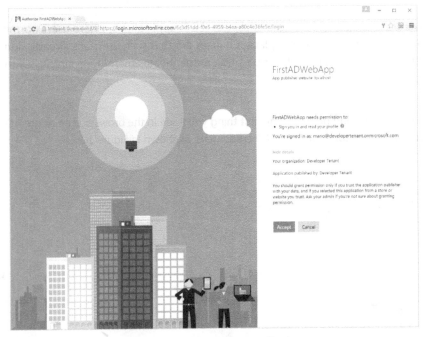

FIGURE 1-3 The Azure AD consent page for the test application.

Click OK. That frees Azure AD to conclude the authentication flow and return the results to the application, which will sign in the user. In Figure 1-4 you can observe the results.

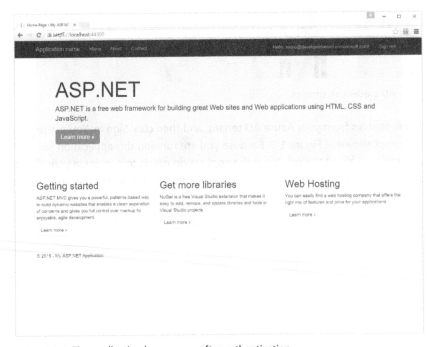

FIGURE 1-4 The application home page after authentication.

This is all very straightforward. When it works well, identity is quite boring and uneventful!

This walk-through demonstrates that you don't need to read an abstruse book cover to cover to take care of the most fundamental authentication scenario. As things become more complicated later on, don't forget that digging deeper is a choice, not a requirement!

ClaimsPrincipal: How .NET represents the caller

The process followed in the preceding section injected some authentication code and configuration settings into the application. That logic ensures that unauthenticated requests are redirected to the intended Azure AD tenant and challenged to authenticate; after that, the same logic ensures that only users from the Azure AD tenant you specified can gain access to the application.

Unless you want to tweak how the default authentication process unfolds, you can happily work on developing your application without ever looking at the code that makes authentication happen.

That said, you will often need to work with at least one aspect of the authentication operation: the authenticated user—or more precisely, the set of attributes that defines the user (whether a him, her, or it) in the context of your application. You might want to display a welcome message including the name of the user, or you might want to authorize an operation only if the caller belongs to a specific role: in both cases, your code needs to gain access to the caller's attributes. For reasons that will become clear in Chapter 2, "Identity protocols and application types," in this context, user attributes are called *claims*.

The .NET Framework features a specific class meant to represent the identity of the authenticated caller: `ClaimsPrincipal`, from the `System.Security.Claims` namespace. Introduced in the Windows Identity Foundation package in 2009, from version 4.5 `ClaimsPrincipal` migrated to mscorlib (the very core of .NET), and all other principal classes have been rebased to derive from `ClaimsPrincipal`. Unless you do some heavy customization, you can be sure that if your application is accessed by an authenticated user, you will find the user represented in a `ClaimsPrincipal`.

As you'll discover later in the book, an application can implement authentication in many ways: different protocols, different token formats, different providers, different consumption models, different development stacks. Every combination comes with its advantages and its quirks, and especially with its own unique implementation details. By representing only the *outcome* of the authentication operation, `ClaimsPrincipal` decouples your code from all the details of present and future authentication mechanisms: the code you write for inspecting the attributes of the caller remains the same regardless of how that information is dispatched to the app and validated.

Gaining access to `ClaimsPrincipal` is easy. Retrieving individual claims is even easier; it's just a matter of querying `ClaimsPrincipal`'s `IEnumerable<Claim>` `Claims` collection. Let's take a quick look at a common task, such as how to retrieve the first and last name of the caller.

Go back to Visual Studio, open the project created in the previous sections, and open Home-Controller.cs from the Controllers folder. Locate the `Index` action and type the following code:

```
public ActionResult Index()
{
    ClaimsPrincipal cp = ClaimsPrincipal.Current;
    string welcome = string.Format("Welcome, {0} {1}!",
                            cp.FindFirst(ClaimTypes.GivenName).Value,
                            cp.FindFirst(ClaimTypes.Surname).Value);
    return View();
}
```

Place a breakpoint on the last line, and run the application. You'll see that you end up with the expected values in your welcome string.

Note The first name/last name sequence won't work for every culture. That does not change the value of the code snippet as a demonstration of the programming model, but I wanted to be sure to point this out.

Here are a couple of important things to observe in that snippet of code:

- **The current *ClaimsPrincipal* can be extracted from the context** `ClaimsPrincipal` contains a static property, named `Current`, that can be used to gain access to the current instance of `ClaimsPrincipal`.

Note Where do the bits of the current `ClaimsPrincipal` actually live? There are two places from which the current `ClaimsPrincipal` is typically sourced: `Thread.CurrentPrincipal` or `HttpContext.Current.User`. `ClaimsPrincipal` also offers a delegate, `ClaimsPrincipalSelector`, that developers of authentication components can use to change where the current `ClaimsPrincipal` is sourced from in case their scenario calls for a different location.

- **The *ClaimTypes* enumeration can be used to inspect *ClaimsPrincipal* for commonly used attributes** Claims are represented by a type, indicating the specific attribute being described, and the attribute's value. In the case of the first-name claim received in our sample application, the type identifier is http://schemas.xmlsoap.org/ws/2005/05/identity/claims /givenname. Not the easiest string to remember! The first-name claim type is hardly alone in its verbosity. Many claim types come from identity protocol specifications such as Security Assertion Markup Language (SAML) and WS-Federation, which define how to represent attributes on the wire. The top concerns in these definitions were uniqueness and consistency rather than ease of coding. In the XML-crazy world that they emerged from, the size overhead that resulted from having a long namespace included in definitions was only a minor concern.

The `ClaimTypes` class was introduced to ease the burden of knowing and entering the exact claim types, and it collects all the most common types of the era. You can still query the `Claims` collection by using an explicit string type, and in fact you have no choice but to do this for custom types, but when applicable, `ClaimTypes` makes things easier.

Today, the pendulum has swung decisively in the other direction. Modern identity protocols go out of their way to be concise. For example, in OpenID Connect, the first-name claim type is simply `given_name`. That's a good name for saving bandwidth and keystrokes, but one possible consequence is that it could invalidate the principle that `ClaimsPrincipal` is independent from whatever authentication mechanism is used. If in my claims collection, first name is represented by a claim of type "given_name", as might be the case if I use OpenID Connect as opposed to SAML or WS-Federation, a query based on `ClaimTypes.GivenName` (which is equivalent to entering the type http://schemas.xmlsoap.org/ws/2005/05/identity /claims/givenname, used by SAML and WS-Federation) won't work.

As you'll discover in later chapters, our validation components do their best to normalize differences such as these. Whenever a modern claim type can be represented by a semantically equivalent member of `ClaimTypes`, the validation pipeline automatically performs the mapping. That allows you to keep using `ClaimTypes.GivenName` for accessing the first name of the caller, no matter what protocol is used.

> **Note** That mapping is not always available; you can expect to occasionally see a mix of long and short claims in your `ClaimsPrincipal` and to have to use explicit strings to reach the latter of these.

Before I close the chapter, there are a couple of other things about user attributes that I want to tell you.

The first is that you should be prepared for every provider to send a different set of claims. If you list the entire content of the claims collection you received in the sample application, you will have an idea of the attributes that Azure Active Directory includes in the context of an authentication operation. Every Azure AD tenant will consistently issue the same set of claims, but that is not true if you are authenticating users directly against their on-premises directory, via Active Directory Federation Services (ADFS) or any other identity product. The set of claims issued by ADFS during an authentication operation is determined by what the directory administrator has decided to share with your application. Although it is plausible to expect that some claims will be present most of the time (UPN, names, and so on), the reality is that what claims are available is a completely arbitrary decision by the administrator, with no defaults you can rely on.

> **Note** This is much to the chagrin of my friends on the ASP.NET team, who would very much like to have some claims that are guaranteed to be present at all times, to be used in the likes of cross-site forgery-request prevention. Unfortunately, there's no such thing.

Getting back to Azure AD. I cover this in depth later in the book, but I want to give you a heads-up at this point: `ClaimsPrincipal` is not the only way of accessing user info in Azure AD. The claims your app receives contextually to an authentication operation are not everything that Azure AD knows about the current user. The directory records a far richer set of user information; however, including all of it at authentication time would be impractical and would waste a lot of bandwidth.

Azure AD provides a specialized API, commonly referred to as the Directory Graph API, for gaining access to extra information after authentication takes place. You'll learn more about this as you go along.

There is more to be said about `ClaimsPrincipal`, in particular about its structure and usage. For the time being, the preceding discussion should be enough to get you going for the most common scenarios.

Summary

This lightweight chapter started our journey into the world of modern authentication. You acquired two of the key assets you'll need through the book, an Azure AD tenant and Visual Studio 2015, and you had a taste of what you can achieve with them. The simple web application protected by Azure AD you created in this chapter will be the backbone of many future explanations.

Finally, you learned the conventional ways in which .NET makes available to you the user identity information acquired during the authentication phase.

The next couple of chapters will be decidedly more abstract. Hang in there. Code-level considerations will return—with a vengeance—in just a couple of chapters.

CHAPTER 2

Identity protocols and application types

If experience serves me well, this chapter and the next will likely cost me one star on Amazon. That's because I'll write quite a bit without showing any code, a mortal sin in a book for developers. Still, I believe that this chapter is the fulcrum around which the entire book turns, especially for readers without a background in identity. I like great reviews, but I like my readers more; hence, I'll go ahead and write this chapter anyway.

> **Note** If you are an industry veteran and already fully acquainted with the modern identity landscape and the road that led to it, feel free to skip this chapter. I assume you are reading this book because you want to learn how Azure Active Directory does things. You'll find plenty of that from Chapter 3 onward.

Today's identity landscape is the result of a couple of decades of market-driven selection, during which time numerous protocols and technologies evolved to address the needs of the application architectures du jour. Interestingly, as new protocols and technologies emerged, they didn't always supplant the old ones. Rather, they often built on their predecessors to reach further and address new scenarios. To offer an analogy: Animals on the earth evolved through a variety of forms, from fish to amphibians, to terrestrial animals and birds. However, the emergence of a new body plan did not necessarily mean the demise of the ones that preceded it, especially when the new form enabled the colonization of yet unexploited environments. Today, the skies are full of birds, but there's still plenty of fish in the sea. You can think of identity protocols in similar terms.

To the newcomer, the world of authentication is a veritable bestiary: seemingly ancient tecnologies, such as passwords and integrated authentication, still play a key role in enabling modern scenarios such as single sign-on from a tablet application, accessing an OAuth2-protected web API via fine-grained delegation, and many others. That makes it hard to understand what's still relevant, what's outdated, and what has changed its role to adapt to a new environment.

The best way I've found for helping people make sense of today's landscape (and maintain my own sanity as I navigate through this industry's nuances every day) is to go through the sequence in which technologies evolved, describing the problems they solved and how and what shortcomings led to the emergence of each new generation. That also happens to be a very natural way to introduce you to the terminology and general concepts I'll use throughout this book, disentangling that from specific development tasks.

You can expect the narration to start light and then dive more deeply into the details as we go along. The first sections will mostly set context. As I get to modern territory, I'll build the scaffolding on which I'll later position Active Directory features and development guidance. That will preempt an untold number of questions you would eventually have—I assure you—if you did not build a solid base from the very start.

Another of the goals of this chapter is to clarify what this book will *not* be about. Many of the protocols and standards I mention here are still widely adopted in the market, hence it is useful for you to know what they are and what they are for. However, they do not qualify as modern protocols in the year 2015. As such, they will be briefly described here but rarely mentioned again through the book.

Pre-claims authentication techniques

Let's start by discussing the very basics of authentication. I'll describe a couple of brute-force approaches to the problem: password-based authentication and integrated authentication. This section might challenge some of the implicit assumptions you have on the topic—a healthy thing to do from time to time.

Passwords, profile stores, and individual applications

For an application, a user is really a collection of attributes that are relevant for the functionality the application provides. Shipping address, name, affiliation with a specific employer, native tongue, spending limit, power of attorney, and birth date are all good examples of attributes.

These attributes, which constitute the *identity* of the user, drive the application's behavior: fetch a specific record, show or hide a certain piece of user interface, pick a certain locale for a string, allow or deny the request to perform a given task. Different applications care about different attributes.

Building on that idea, here's an attempt at an operational definition of authentication:

> *Authenticating a user is the act of recognizing that a certain set of attributes should be used in the context of the current transaction.*

For one application, the brute-force approach to representing a user's identity in those terms is to maintain its own user-profile store listing the attributes of each user. After you have a profile store, the problem is reduced to how to correlate the current request to the correct user profile.

Passwords are the crudest mechanism the industry has devised for dealing with this scenario. At some initial stage, the application and the user (this time, intended as a person) agree on a secret string, entering a contract that establishes that neither will ever reveal that secret to anybody (or anything) else.

> **Note** I mention strings because that's the most common mechanism, but in the end, any type of credentials negotiated between users and apps (certificates, temporary codes, etc.) are architecturally equivalent for the purposes of this chapter—in the sense that they still require the app to keep track of user profiles. The characteristics of different credential types do vary greatly in terms of security assurances and infrastructure costs, of course.

The application associates that secret to the set of attributes defining the user for its purposes. If during a future transaction the user presents that very same secret, the app knows that the identity that should be selected is the one previously associated with that secret—and voilà, that's authentication for you.

> **Note** Although, technically, the scenario described—in which only the password is sent—could work, in a real system it would be impractical to use only the secret to identify the user. As you know, all password-based systems usually also rely on an identifier of some sort (nickname, username, email address, etc.) that is effectively a way of passing an identity by reference. That decouples the handle for the identity from the password itself so that you can change passwords without breaking any reference to any specific user.

If you exclude authentication schemes based on physically accessing resources (for example, sharing time on a mainframe that can be used only by entering the building and the room where it is installed), applications implementing their own username-password-profile schemes represent the earliest authentication strategy that went mainstream.

Today we know that many issues are associated with the use of passwords: they can be cracked, leaked, or lost, and we need to memorize far too many of them. However, most of those problems are felt in large part because of sheer scale and ubiquitous connectivity considerations. If you go back a couple of decades or more, before the advent of local networks, those elements didn't carry the same weight as they do today. Passwords worked great for securing the sparse set of independent, disconnected apps that characterized the early waves of personal computing, as shown in Figure 2-1.

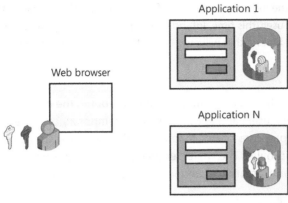

FIGURE 2-1 Applications authenticating users directly via a username and password act as independent entities, each solving credential management and user representation in its own terms.

For many application developers, username-and-password user-store systems remain attractive today. That's thanks to their relative simplicity, and in no small part thanks to the complete control they grant to the relationship with the user. The many technologies created to support the scenario (such as the ASP.NET membership provider, whose recent redesign shows that this approach still has a lot of fight in it) alleviate the most obvious development chores and make it (often deceptively) easy to go that route.

If your solution shares traits with those ancient app topologies, especially in terms of isolation and independence from other systems, implementing a username-and-password profile store as an application feature might still make sense. Both in business and consumer contexts, however, those traits are increasingly rare. If you can't afford to reinvent the wheel, if your users aren't willing to create yet another account and enter their profile data in yet another application, or if you need to integrate with preexisting resources, you might want to read on.

Domains, integrated authentication, and applications on an intranet

One of the strongest influences on today's world of authentication can be traced back to the early 1990s, when businesses started to corral their computers within local networks. An increasing desire to model business processes with the help of nascent IT departments soon exposed the limitations of a model in which every application implemented authentication independently. That was simply not an accurate representation of the life cycle of real-life employees.

The life cycle of a user in a work environment is inherently tied to the user's organization: an account comes into existence as the employee is hired, attribute values are initialized and continuously updated according to job functions for the duration of his or her tenure with the company, and the account is decommissioned when the relationship ends. Projecting that business process in one unified IT system is nearly impossible if authentication is a cacophony of multiple apps maintaining their own view of the user and their own credentials-verification mechanism.

With the advent of Active Directory and analogous offerings, the user-profile storage and credential-verification functions migrated from each individual app to a central position—the fabric of the network itself. In the new approach, users are authenticated as soon as they first touch the IT system when they sit at their workstation. I am sure you are familiar with what that feels like: you sit at your computer in your company's network, you enter your credentials, and bam! All (or at least some) applications on the intranet act like they know who you are and handle access accordingly. In fact, employees aren't the only ones that need to authenticate with the system: to even exist as an entity on the network, computers themselves are required to authenticate at some level (which is basically what you are enabling when you join a machine to a domain). That's why every intranet app acts as though it already knows you.

This new approach was made possible, among other ways, by the introduction of a new artifact: the domain controller (DC), a server machine that plays a special role. The DC knows about everything and everybody on the local network; hence, it can transparently broker secure communications between any two entities.

The value this approach unlocked was nothing short of amazing, and it is still going strong today. (Active Directory was in use in 95 percent of Fortune 500 companies as of March 2014.)[1] Administrators finally had a common repository for modeling their processes and enforcing their policies, while applications were free to focus on their intended function without worrying about authentication or user life-cycle management. And, of course, users enjoyed a much improved and consistent experience.

Describing in detail how Active Directory works from the infrastructural standpoint is well beyond the goals of this book (and, frankly, my own knowledge). When I get questions about domains, forests, and the like, I typically feign ignorance of all things related to IT administration and introduce people to my good friends Dean Wells and Samuel Devasahayam from the Active Directory fabric team. The details of how Kerberos and Windows Integrated Authentication work would also not be very useful here, mostly because they serve no purpose for the apps you'll write throughout this book.

What I do want to be sure I discuss is the value that traditional on-premises Active Directory has for developers—and, along with that, the tradeoffs it carries.

If your application is going to run on a domain-joined machine, accessed by a domain user through the user's home network, authentication is simply a nonissue. The identity of a user is established well before your application is even accessed, and (in the general case—forget delegation for a moment) it is simply available from the environment, just like the IP address of the machine or the file system. The only task left to you is to reach out and cherry-pick the user attributes that are useful to your application. The user changes job role, department, surname? Forgets his or her password? Leaves the company? Not your problem anymore! Of course, this delivers a great experience for your users, too: from their first logon to the workstation in the morning, they have access to every

---

1. Brad Anderson, "Success with Hybrid Cloud: Getting Deep—Azure Active Directory," March 11, 2014, http://blogs .technet.com/b/in_the_cloud/archive/2014/03/11/success-with-hybrid-cloud-getting-deep-azure-active-directory.aspx.

application without any further prompts, interruptions, or passwords to remember. The topology of the solution is presented in Figure 2-2.

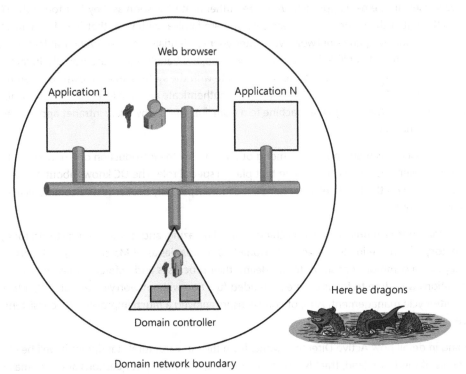

Web browser

Application 1

Application N

Domain controller

Here be dragons

Domain network boundary

FIGURE 2-2 In a canonical on-premises Active Directory (AD) setup, applications can rely on the infrastructure to provide centralized authentication and identity life-cycle management functionalities.

The price to pay for this awesome convenience is that the magic works only within your own infrastructure. Joining a computer to a domain is an important commitment, which makes total sense if that is the reason for which you got the machine (real or virtual) to begin with. Not every machine can be joined to a domain: it might belong to your partner, it might be located in a place where the necessary network infrastructure is not available, it might be shared by different organizations, and—as is often the case with modern devices—its OS might simply lack the capability to do so.

AD on-premises is still fantastically popular today. It remains very well suited for addressing the intranet case. However, it is also constantly adding features for supporting new scenarios: some of those features entail venturing outside the boundaries of the local network and complementing the traditional authentication approaches with something that is not bound by the same infrastructural constraints.

Claims-based identity

No company is an island, as the old adage goes. The need for cross-company collaboration solutions was the natural follow-up to the local network era, but the local authentication solutions that worked so well within the boundaries of one organization were not as effective in addressing the new scenario. Company A and company B could both have well-managed intranets, but company A's domain controller didn't help one bit when one of company A's users wanted to access an app exposed by company B.

Moreover, the increasing appeal of software as a service (SaaS) apps or hosting one's own applications off-premises—hosts at first, cloud providers later on—further exposed the limits of an approach based entirely on network locality. Consider this: if your employees log in to their domain-joined workstation, but the apps they access live on other networks or the public Internet, all the user identity info known by the DC cannot be used as is. Nonetheless, business apps still need the identity of the user, and without a way of making it available via infrastructure, it's back to a cottage industry in which every app reimplements identity management.

The industry did not tolerate for long the inefficiencies of having to reinvent the wheel at every new partnership or purchase of an SaaS app. Although different people place its inception at different historical moments, I think it is safe to say that claims-based identity was born to address these issues. Claims-based identity is not an actual protocol. Rather, it is a set of concepts that is common to many of the identity protocols that emerged in the last decade. In this section I'll sketch its main traits, the ones that—if you squint hard enough—you can find in all modern protocols. The following sections will show how the principles of claims-based identity find application in actual protocols.

Identity providers: DCs for the Internet

That DC idea worked so well on-premises! Couldn't it work outside the boundaries of the local network? As it turns out, it could, albeit with some important revisions.

> **Note** Reusing Kerberos "as is" for cross-collaboration scenarios has been attempted. Ever heard of Kerberos federation? The idea wasn't terribly successful.

The key point is to let go of the idea that you can have a single, omniscient authority that knows every possible actor and can broker all transactions on all possible networks. Such an authority can exist in the limited scope of a local network, but it is simply unfeasible on the Internet. More realistically, we should acknowledge that there are constellations of multiple authorities run by independent business entities, the competence of each scoped to a specific user population. All the Active Directory instances out there are good examples of that: Contoso's AD instance can tell you whether Mario is a Contoso employee, his job title, and so on, but it can't really say much about whether someone works for Fabrikam. There are other user populations that naturally aggregate through different criteria, with different degrees of presence on the Internet: customers of a given company, students of a school, members of a club, citizens of a country, and so on.

In the literature you'll often find that such authorities are referred to as *identity providers*, or IPs (or IdPs). At the level of detail I'm providing at this point in the story, IdP is a fine moniker. However, later in the book, things become more nuanced, and the notion of identity provider will not be general enough for our goals. At that point I will switch to the broader term *authority*. (Be prepared for other terms in this chapter to be renamed or redefined later on, when you'll have more context to build on.)

We say that an application *trusts* a given IdP if the application believes what the IdP has to say about the users the app wants to work with. (An application that trusts an IdP is often referred to as a *relying party*, or RP. I will keep using "application" here, though, given that I feel it is easier to understand in this context, but I wanted to be sure you are aware of the term.)

A trivial case exemplifying the above is the home network of a domain. Each and every application on the intranet that uses integrated authentication trusts the domain controller. If you took one of those applications and lifted it to the public cloud, conceptually it would still trust the domain controller: the business requirements have not changed, and the domain's users remain its intended audience. In its new environment, however, the app can no longer rely on the network infrastructure to find the DC and request its services. The trust is still there, but the infrastructure described so far is no longer enough to express it.

After postulating the existence of the role of the identity provider, the next problem to solve is how to ensure that one IdP's authority is acknowledged by the interested parties in a transaction—without the luxury of operating within a closed network.

Tokens

The details are different for every protocol, but the essence of the solution to the problem of extending one authority's scope beyond infrastructural boundaries is the same across the board:

- Be sure that the IdP can be easily identified by every application. That boils down to describing the IdP through formal means and making that description available for any entity that wants to work with that IdP. Unique string identifiers, specific endpoints, and cryptographic public-private key pairs are the standard arsenal to do that. The set of coordinates formally identifying an IdP are commonly known as *metadata*.

- Represent the outcome of an authentication operation with some artifact that can be unambiguously tied to the IdP that performed the authentication, without relying on any special network infrastructure. The information in the formal IdP description mentioned just above is used to identify such an artifact as coming from that IdP, through mechanisms that I will mention in a moment.

To be more concrete, say that you want to use Contoso as an IdP. You assign to Contoso's DC an X.509 certificate and a unique identifier, something like http://contoso.com—both technologies that do not require any special network settings to function. When Mario, a Contoso employee, authenticates for accessing an app running in the public cloud, the DC produces a string along the lines of "I, http://contoso.com, certify that Mario is an employee and that at 9:05 a.m. he successfully authenticated for accessing application A." The DC uses the private key associated with the X.509

certificate to digitally sign the string. The application receives the string, verifies the digital signature, and confirms it has been performed with Contoso's key. If everything works as expected, the application believes the assertions it finds in the string and lets Mario in.

How did the application know about Contoso's key and identifier? It learned about those values previously in one offline step, from Contoso's metadata. I'll dig into this scenario soon.

Digital signatures

Oversimplifying a bit, a digital signature is an operation that combines a document with a certain string (called a *key*) to generate a third string, called a *signature*. If somebody who knows the key receives the document and its signature, she can repeat the signature operation and verify that the resulting string is exactly the same as the signature. That guarantees that the document was not modified after the original signature was computed.

Signatures are a pretty great technology that makes a lot of today's secure communications possible. However, in the form I've described (where the keys are known as *symmetric*), they have an important shortcoming: given that both the signer and the signature verifier know the signing key, we can't use the knowledge of the key as a way of distinguishing one from the other.

X.509 certificates enable what is known as *public key cryptography*, which uses two keys. Signatures are applied with a private key, known only by the signer. Such signatures are special, as they are meant to be verified by using a different key: that key is called *public* because everybody can know it without compromising the security of the system. I will use public key cryptography all the time throughout the book, but I will rarely point that out. It is mostly an implementation detail, not actionable for you.

Now, everybody (and in particular app A) who has access to Contoso's DC description (and in particular its unique identifier and public key) can verify the signature on that string. A successful verification confirms two important facts:

- The string could have been produced only by Contoso's DC and nothing else, given the assumption that only Contoso's DC has access to the private key that performed the signature.

- The content of the string has not been altered from the moment it was signed onward; hence, what is in there truly represents Contoso's DC's original statement about the user.

In identity parlance, such a string is universally known as a *token*.

Note Tokens come in many formats and variants, almost as many as the protocols that use them in some capacity: SAML and JWT (JSON Web Token) are two examples of token formats you might already have read about. At this point in the story, we don't need to pick a specific format.

Set aside for a moment the mechanics of how a requestor can get a token from an IdP. A token as I've described it is a satisfying representation of the successful outcome of an authentication operation, which can be verified simply by knowing the IdP's coordinates (identifier, signature-verification key) without requiring any special network sauce. In fact, a token can do much more than that.

Trust and claims

In the first section of this chapter, I defined a user's identity as the collection of attributes that are relevant for the application's context. Just a couple of pages ago, I also said that an application *trusts* a given IdP if it believes what the IdP has to say about the users the app wants to work with.

A signed token is a perfect vessel with which an IdP can communicate just in time the relevant user attributes to the application—contextually, to an authentication operation. Given that the token is signed, whatever the IdP claims about the user at the time the token is issued cannot be tampered with without breaking the signature. Once again, applications no longer need to maintain a profile store: they can receive all the user information they need via a token, right at authentication time, while being assured that the token originates from a reputable source.

> **Note** This is an oversimplification that serves us well here but won't hold forever. Later in the book I'll go into details, but I wanted to give you a heads-up: applications will occasionally want to remember things about the user that the IdP can't or won't track.
>
> Think of a hardware vendor that partners with Contoso: that vendor's app can expect to learn from Contoso the name and the shipping address of each user, but if it needs to track the last 10 items a given user bought, the vendor is better served by saving that info in its own app.

After an attribute is serialized into a signed token, it becomes a *claim*. At rest, a string in a database containing the last name of a user is just an attribute. Once the very same string is serialized in a token and signed with the IdP's private key, however, it is augmented by the IdP's credibility. It is the IdP itself that is claiming that the last name of Mario is "Rossi." For every application trusting the IdP, that becomes the Truth.

The concept of claims is so pivotal to nearly everything in modern (and less modern) identity scenarios that it provides the name to the entire approach.

Claims-oriented protocols

Let me summarize the story so far.

An identity solution was needed that would allow applications to run anywhere, without completely giving up on the investment made in DCs and local domains. We recognized that DCs are just concrete instances of a more abstract role, the IdP, which represents an authority that knows about users (attributes and credentials). We devised a mechanism for identifying IdPs via identifiers and keys (metadata), breaking free of the network restrictions of DCs. We invented a new artifact, the token, to make the outcome of an authentication operation verifiable (via signature validation) by any app knowing the IdP's coordinates. Finally, I explained what trust between an app and an IdP means, and how this allows claims (attributes traveling in a signed token) to provide to the application just-in-time user-identity information right at authentication time.

The main concept left to define is how these entities interact with each other—what messages should be exchanged and in what order—to take advantage of all the good properties we identified and that make authentication happen.

As I anticipated a few pages ago, claims-based identity refers to a bunch of different protocols sharing a common undercurrent—they make authentication happen through boundaries. Those protocols differ from one another in various aspects: for example, in the token formats that they mandate or prefer, the exact message shape and sequence, metadata formats, names they assign to the roles that identity-transaction participants can play, and more. Every protocol has its zealots who swear their approach is the best and insist on renaming common concepts using their own terminology—a handbook case of Freud's narcissism of small differences. For now I am going to ignore all that and paint in very broad strokes the main legs that nearly all claims-oriented protocols must specify.

Say that you have Mario, an employee at Contoso, and he wants access to an expense note application from Fabrikam. Fabrikam is a software vendor offering SaaS solutions running in the cloud. Here's how claim-based identity would go. The steps are summarized in Figure 2-3.

1. **The application reads an IdP's metadata**   Typically, this step happens out of band, although there are exceptions. Fabrikam decides that its expense note application should trust Contoso (as a consequence of Contoso buying a few licenses, for example). In concrete terms, this means that the application must access Contoso's IdP metadata and be sure that its content will be available later, at authentication time. That will provide to the application the information it needs to verify whether the incoming token is truly from Contoso.

2. **The user authenticates and obtains a token**   This step will be different depending on the type of application. Good portions of this book will be dedicated to filling in details about how some key protocols perform this task.

   a. **Web applications**   In classic browser-based apps, Mario would type the address of the expense note app and navigate there. The app would detect an access attempt from an unauthenticated requestor. The canonical reaction to that would be to look up its own configuration, find Contoso's metadata, and use it to craft a sign-in message according to the message syntax defined by the protocol of choice. The browser's session would then be transferred to Contoso, which would take the necessary steps to authenticate Mario: showing a credentials-gathering page is a common way of implementing that. Upon successful authentication, Contoso issues a token for Mario in the format that the protocol of choice dictates.

   b. **Native clients and web APIs**   Native clients typically pursue a different strategy. Redirects don't really work when calling an API (usually, there is no browser to execute the redirect); hence, even before attempting to access the API, the client will use a different protocol for asking Contoso for a token for Mario. The sequence is slightly different, and the exchanged messages also differ, but a successful authentication still results in a token issuance.

3. **Client sends the token to the application, and the app validates the token**   The token so obtained is sent to the application according to the protocol of choice. The application (or, more likely, the developer libraries it uses to implement authentication) retrieves the token and verifies whether it is a valid Contoso token. If that's the case, it will extract the claims describing Mario's persona and pass them to the app so that it can do whatever the app needs to do with them: welcome messages, authorization operations, priming of a shopping cart with a shipping address, whatever.

4. **Optional: Application establishes a session**   For applications such as websites, where the user interaction consists of round trips, going through the token-acquisition dance at every request would be fantastically expensive. That is why various web protocols very commonly react to the first successful token validation with the creation of some kind of session— represented by a cookie or similar mechanism—that can be included in every subsequent request. Such a session reminds the application at every round trip that a successful token validation already took place and provides a natural place for holding the claim values of the current user, keeping them available to the app through the lifetime of the session.

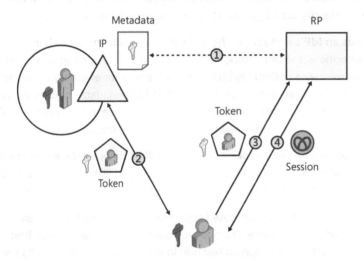

FIGURE 2-3 Entities, roles, and messages come into play in claims-based identity.

Recall that the goal of a claims-oriented protocol is to enable identity transactions to span boundaries, both organizational (Contoso to Fabrikam) and infrastructural (intranet to public Internet). As such, all the messages I enumerated cannot depend on any special network requirement. Rather, they rely on the minimum common denominator of all networks, the public Internet: every claims-oriented protocol with meaningful adoption is built on top of HTTP. In the next sections, you'll see this in more detail.

DCs are just an example of an IdP

The roles I described—IdPs and applications/RPs—reflect the function that each entity performs in the context of an identity transaction, but they don't really say anything about their internal structure or the technology used to implement them. I have been using the DC as a practical example to ground the concept of an IdP, but I want to be extra clear that any entity that is capable of keeping track of user attributes and can authenticate and emit and process protocol messages qualifies. Claims-oriented protocols go to great lengths to define contracts and interfaces that abstract away the details of every provider, exposing only the functionality of the role they take. Fair warning: later in the book, I will routinely go beyond what's specified by the contract to take advantage of AD-specific features.

The pattern described here is very expressive and exceptionally malleable. It can be used to describe almost all the protocols I mention from now on, with only minor variations. As you read through the next section, I recommend that you keep an eye on how the details of every specific protocol ultimately map to this structure.

Round-trip web apps, first-generation protocols

The first protocols that can be classified as claims oriented appeared in the early 2000s. Two of them, SAML and WS-Federation, are still widely used to this day and supported in both Windows Server AD and Azure AD. Both emerged as solutions to cross-domain single sign-on (SSO), a scenario that the authentication systems popular at that time didn't handle well.

The problem of cross-domain single sign-on

The main interaction pattern in traditional web applications is very straightforward. I've shown it in action in the previous section, the last two legs of the diagram in Figure 2-3 being an example. The user points his or her browser to the URL of a resource, the web server receives the request and runs whatever business logic it deems necessary, and then the server proceeds to return HTML describing the experience it intends to present back to the user. The browser simply renders the experience, as described by the HTML it receives. The user interacts with the experience, maybe clicking a link or perhaps pressing a button or triggering a form post. That causes new info to be sent to the web server, and the cycle begins anew.

Per the definition of authentication given earlier in the chapter, at every round trip to the web server, authenticated web applications need to know which user should be considered the current caller. The most classic, pre-claims way to achieve this in apps that use round trips can be broken down into three steps:

1. The application serves to the user some credential-gathering experience. The username and password form is the most recognizable example.

2. After the credentials travel back to the server, the application validates them. If the verification is successful, the application emits a *session cookie,* which represents the successful outcome of the authentication operation. Such a cookie will typically contain some reference to session data, often the identifier of the current user, and will normally be protected in some way (for instance, it might be signed and encrypted so that only the app can read and modify it).

3. From that moment on, every request to the application's domain will carry the session cookie. The application will be able to retrieve the cookie from the request and verify it. The presence of the valid cookie obviates the need to present the username and password every time, allowing the app to maintain the current user in scope for the duration of the session. Cookies will typically have a limited validity window to minimize abuse.

This validate-and-drop-a-cookie approach is an exceptionally common pattern, a fundamental primitive you need to understand as thoroughly as possible. Even if it's very simple, I've gone so far as to put together a diagram for it in Figure 2-4.

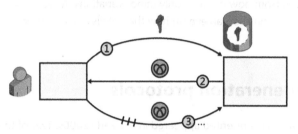

FIGURE 2-4 The credentials validation and session cookie authentication pattern.

Session cookies work pretty well: browsers save cookies per domain and automatically include them whenever a request to the corresponding domain is made. If cookie A has been saved under www.myapp.com, every subsequent request to a URL starting with www.myapp.com will include cookie A. No explicit work by the developer is required. The browser is even going to handle the life cycle automatically, omitting expired cookies from requests.

Things start to get less rad when your solution includes applications hosted on different domains.

> **Note** For simplicity's sake, whenever possible I am going to borrow sample scenarios from the original protocol specifications. I hope this will help you to navigate the specification documents, should you decide to dig deeper.

Consider the following scenario. You developed an application for an airline, hosted at airline.example.com. Say that the application is meant to be used by frequent flyers, who can book flights and manage their benefits with it. The application maintains its own credential-verification system and user-profile store following the session pattern described earlier.

Say that the airline enters into a partnership with a car rental company, which guarantees steep discounts to frequent flyers who achieve the gold level. The car rental company runs its booking site from cars.example.co.uk.

Wouldn't it be awesome if Mario, a gold user who is already signed in to airline.example.com, could simply follow a link to cars.example.co.uk and find himself authenticated, his status acknowledged, and his discounts unlocked?

The session-cookie approach is clearly not going to help here. When Mario authenticated to airline.example.com, he obtained a cookie scoped to airline.example.com, which is useless for requests to cars.example.co.uk. What to do?

SAML

The Security Assertion Markup Language, SAML for short, appeared on the scene mostly for handling this very problem. Its origin dates back to the early 2000s as a concerted effort of various industry players that wanted to establish an interoperable solution to the SSO problem. SAML 2.0 is the most widely adopted version, with some systems (especially those in academia) still on 1.1. Although SAML touches on how to secure web services and lots of other scenarios, its most widely adopted use case is web browser–based SSO, and that's what I'm going to focus on.

Note Although both Azure Active Directory and Active Directory Federation Service (ADFS) (from version 2 onward) support SAML, the .NET Framework does not offer any classes out of the box for building applications that understand the protocol. Developing with the .NET Framework is the main focus of this book, so even if I provided a detailed description of how SAML works, it would not be very actionable for you. However, the importance of SAML as a framing reference for identity problems cannot be overstated. Moreover, a good chunk of the jargon you'll encounter comes straight from SAML. Learning the basics is a good investment for any beginner in this space.

In a nutshell, SAML sidesteps the shortcomings of domain-bound cookies by, you guessed it, adding an extra abstraction layer. Instead of relying on browser automatisms, SAML introduces a sequence of application-level messages that enable an application to send authentication requests and obtain tokens that can be sent across domains. Once those tokens successfully cross domain boundaries, they can be validated by the target app and used to initialize a session with the new domain. I'll unpack the scenario as soon as I define more terminology to work with.

SAML follows precisely the blueprint introduced in the claims-based identity section. Let's draw some correspondences between the abstract entities defined in the general meta protocol and concrete artifacts from SAML.

Roles

I am sure you noticed that the sample scenario I introduced earlier contained one entity playing the role of the IdP (that was airline.example.com and its profile store). The good news is that in SAML, IdPs are called . . . IdPs.

In the terminology of claims-based identity, the cars.example.com.uk application is called an RP. In SAML, it is known as a *service provider*, or SP. Another important role is the *subject*, the entity that is meant to be authenticated. In the vast majority of cases, that's simply the user. SAML also describes other roles, but the ones I've enumerated suffice for the purposes of this book.

Artifacts

SAML is guilty of having introduced not one but two widely successful technologies: the protocol it defines and the specific token format that the protocol's messages exchange. I say "guilty" facetiously: people commonly refer to both technologies with the same term, "SAML," which has caused confusion for the past decade or so. When somebody states, "My app supports SAML," you always have to ask for clarification: "The protocol or the token format?"

In SAML parlance, tokens are called *assertions*. They follow the exact token semantic described in the preceding section: they are a vessel for the IdP's assertions about the user (excuse me), the subject. And they are signed.

The SAML acronym, together with the epoch in which it was conceived, probably already gave away that SAML assertions are based on XML. In fact, the entire specification defines *everything* in terms of XML. That leads to a very expressive, powerful format that can represent pretty much anything. However, all that expressivity comes with various drawbacks. The main one is that XML is very verbose, which leads to big tokens. Furthermore, in XML, the same document can be expressed in multiple equivalent representations, and that flexibility becomes a problem when you need to perform signatures, where two elements listed in a different order can break a signature verification. Those are the main reasons that you won't encounter SAML assertions in modern protocols later in the book, apart from cases in which they are used to bridge existing solutions to new ones.

> **Note** It is tempting for me to use the SAML token structure to start entering into the mechanics of how claims are defined, tokens are scoped, and signatures are applied, but, as I said, SAML is not at the core of the modern protocols that are the main focus of this book. Those explanations will have to wait until a bit later.

Another important artifact defined by SAML is the format of its metadata documents. You already encountered the idea of IdP metadata in the section on claims-based identity. SAML goes well beyond that: it defines an XML-based format that can be used for describing endpoints, identifiers, and keys for IdPs, SPs, and many other entities.

Messages

SAML defines lots of different messages that support various sign-in flows, from the one triggered by an unauthenticated request to an SP (similar to what's described in the claims-identity section), to one in which the IdP itself initiates a sign-on with a given SP. One interesting fact is that besides signing its assertions, SAML often mandates that messages themselves need to be signed as well.

The other interesting category of SAML messages, Single Logout, focuses on providing a mechanism to propagate a sign-out operation to all the applications participating in an SSO session. SAML defines many other messages for various other operations, which I won't mention here.

Status

SAML has had an impressive ride from its first versions in the early 2000s. It's still going strong in many of today's SSO deployments in enterprises, government, and education. SAML is widely supported in SSO products, developer libraries (across platforms and languages), and cloud services. For many of those products, the SAML functionality is the centerpiece of their offering. As I mentioned, Active Directory itself (both ADFS from version 2 onward and Azure AD) supports it. On the software vendor side, many applications in active development today use SAML, including software as a service (SaaS) apps. The protocol is alive and well.

That said, if you are starting to develop a new solution, SAML might not be your best choice. Although really well suited for solving the cross-SSO domain problem and bringing lots of good features to the table, SAML does not offer the flexibility for addressing the challenges of the modern topologies I will introduce later in this chapter. Furthermore, its own richness translates into expensive requirements in term of cryptography and bandwidth that are not proportionate to the actual needs of modern applications. I won't go so far as to say that SAML is dead, as was fashionable to say in identity circles a couple of years ago, but it is certainly no longer the recipient of innovation. I believe it will be around for a long time still, but mostly as a bridge to existing systems.

WS-Federation

Web applications weren't the only type of application that suffered from cross-boundary integration problems back in the early 2000s. Nonbrowser flows between remote components, such as server-to-server requests and calls from rich-client applications to back-end resources, also had to come to terms with the facts that any two entities could be separated by organizational and network boundaries, based on different development stacks, and hosted on different platforms.

That prompted a number of companies to set aside their competitive differences and work together to create a set of protocols, languages, and frameworks that defined how to ensure interoperable, reliable, and secure communications between software components regardless of their location, development stack, hosting platform, and similar factors.

This effort led to the creation of a long list of specifications, collectively known as WS-* (pronounced "WS star," where WS stands for "web services" and the asterisk is a wildcard character). You might have heard the names of some of the most important specifications: WS-ReliableMessaging, WS-Trust, WS-Security, and many others. The idea was to provide different specifications for every aspect of communications so that implementers could pick and choose only the capabilities their system needed. That was in contrast with some earlier efforts, such as CORBA, that were delivered as monolithic, monumental uber-specifications.

What Happened to WS-*?

Today, you don't hear much about WS-* anymore.

Companies poured significant effort into implementing those specifications in their products. Microsoft led the pack, building its remote API stack on it from .NET 3.0 on (Windows Communication Foundation, WCF, is largely based on WS-*) and exposing its server products through those protocols (ADFS 2.0 supports WS-Trust). Other companies, notably IBM and Sun, released products and development stacks based on WS-*. Many of those applications are still around, and, in fact, lots of customers still use WCF for brand-new applications.

However, WS-* lost traction, and nowadays all of our new work relies on more modern, REST-based protocols. One can endlessly speculate on the reasons that led to the demise of WS-*. My read is that WS-* provided very sophisticated features, but the price that this complexity carried was not justified for the kinds of apps most developers wanted to build. For example, WS-* went to great lengths to enable messages to be exchanged securely over insecure channels and maintain integrity also after having exited the channel. Using the feature required rich development stacks on both ends of the channel and elaborate setups, which could be justified only in specific high-value scenarios. Most web apps could live without those high assurances. As a result, the lightweight REST model gained ground, eventually making inroads in the business scenarios and supplanting the old models.

WS-Federation is one of the specifications that was produced as part of the WS-* effort. Its specific role was to define how to make it possible for a user in a given organization to access resources managed by another organization—another form of the same problem covered previously. Unlike the rest of the WS-* specifications, which focused on web services, WS-Federation also covered how to achieve its goals through browser-based applications. Ironically, that relatively minor section of the specification is what most people identify with WS-Federation today because it is the part still widely in use.

WS-Federation addresses many of the same scenarios I described earlier for SAML. However, it does so with a significantly simpler set of messages, which are themselves more straightforward to produce and process than their SAML counterparts (no signatures).

In fact, having the WS- prefix causes WS-Federation to give the wrong impression to the casual observer. Unlike most of the other WS-* specifications, the web browser flows described in WS-Federation are very simple.

Let's take a quick look at how the elements of WS-Federation map to the generic claims-based protocol template.

Roles

In WS-Federation, the IdP role is indicated by the same term, *identity provider*. However, it is abbreviated as IP.

IP and STS

The WS-Federation specification also refers to a Security Token Service, or STS, which represents the concrete software artifact that actually processes authentication requests and issues tokens. In the literature, you will often hear people use IP and STS interchangeably, but that's a slight misnomer: whereas IP indicates a functional role (the job performed by that entity), the STS is a concrete component that is used to express that role (the tool that entity needs to perform its job). Given that every IP must have an STS, one can often confuse the two in a conversation without serious consequences. However, you'll see that there are times when you need to issue tokens without being an IP, in which case you need an STS that is not used to implement an IP.

The other important role defined in WS-Federation is the *relying party* (RP), which you already encountered. It is defined, quoting the specification, as a "web application that consumes [. . .] tokens issued by a Security Token Service." (See the preceding sidebar on IP and STS terminology gotchas.)

Artifacts

In line with WS-* tenets, WS-Federation does not mandate a specific type of token. There are some exceptions in the market today, but for all intents and purposes, you can safely assume that every WS-Federation deployment uses SAML as its token type of choice.

WS-Federation also defines its own metadata document format, which can describe both web apps and web services, plus lots of other concerns (attributes, scopes) of no consequence for our discussion. It serves the same function already described for SAML metadata.

Messages

WS-Federation defines messages supporting standard sign-in and distributed sign-out operations. Those messages are simpler than their SAML counterparts. For starters, they do not require any cryptographic operation at the message level—the only signed (and possibly encrypted) element is the token itself (for the flows that contain one).

All messages exchanged between the RP and IP rely on a combination of 302 redirects and auto-posting forms. You won't ever use WS-Federation directly while developing the apps described in this book. However, WS-Federation is still very much in use as an integration protocol, so you will often see it in action in network traces. For that reason, it's good to have at least an idea of what it looks like. Here's the simplest sign-in flow you can enact in WS-Federation, which is illustrated in Figure 2-5.

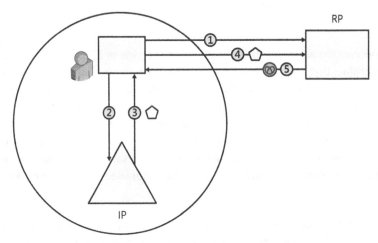

FIGURE 2-5 An example of the basic sign-in flow with WS-Federation.

1. The user navigates to the RP application, performing an HTTP GET of one of its protected pages.

2. The RP (or more likely the development library that sits in front of it and enforces the use of WS-Federation) detects that the request is from an unauthenticated user. Instead of returning the requested resource, it returns a 302 code that redirects the browser to the IP. The query string of the redirect contains various parameters supplying the IP with context about the request: an indication that this is a sign-in request, the identifier with which the RP is known to the IP, and so on.

    The IP does whatever it deems necessary to authenticate the user. In the case depicted in Figure 2-5, the user is accessing the IP within the boundaries of the local network; hence, the request is automatically authenticated via integrated authentication.

3. Upon successful user authentication, the IP sends back a signed token with claims describing the user. The token travels in an HTML form. The response also contains JavaScript code that will automatically post the token back to the RP.

4. The RP receives the IP response; as it renders, it triggers the POST of the token back to the RP.

5. The RP receives the token and validates it. If the verification succeeds, it creates a session cookie to establish a session. From this moment onward, every request coming from the user's browser will carry the session cookie and will be considered authenticated by the RP. The session will terminate once the user explicitly signs out (another WS-Federation flow) or once the session expiration time elapses.

Not especially complicated, right? This simple sample provides two important confirmations:

■   The claims-based identity approach does successfully cross boundaries. Here, the user of a local network gains authenticated access to one RP located outside his or her domain.

- WS-Federation, and claims-based identity in general, work well in collaboration with older protocols. In this case, the user does not experience any explicit authentication prompt in step 2 thanks to the existing local network infrastructure. There is no visible sign that all this dancing is taking place. The user types the address of the RP, and the next thing he or she sees in the browser is what gets rendered after step 5—the authenticated experience of the RP application.

Status

Microsoft bet on WS-Federation as a web sign-on protocol early on, from the very first version of ADFS back in 2005.

That initial choice created ripples through all its offerings. ADFS kept supporting WS-Federation through all subsequent Windows Server versions, including the latest one (Windows Server 2016). WS-Federation was the protocol of choice in the first developer libraries for identity (Windows Identity Foundation 1.0, in 2009), it was the protocol integrated in the .NET Framework from version 4.5 onward, and it is still supported today in the latest ASP.NET OWIN middleware components that I'll cover later in this book. Tools for adding WS-Federation support were included in Visual Studio 2010, 2012, and 2013. In turn, that determined the protocol of choice of a generation of servers and cloud services, from SharePoint 2013 on. Office 365 and Azure AD itself use WS-Federation as the backbone of their on-premises / cloud integration flows. Every day there are new installations appearing, all using WS-Federation under the hood.

With its widespread presence, you can imagine that the protocol will keep being supported for a long time. On the other hand, the same considerations I offered for SAML apply here as well. WS-Federation does a great job of allowing tokens (hence claims) to flow outside the boundaries of a local network, and does solve the cross-domain SSO federation problem. However, WS-Federation is incapable of modeling many of the topologies and relationships that are required for addressing the challenges of modern application architectures. As a result, you can consider WS-Federation "done": it is a mature protocol, safe to be used in production, but is no longer a recipient of innovation. In the next sections, I will finally breach the modern era, introducing the protocols that are best suited for new apps.

Modern apps, modern protocols

This section ushers us to the modern era. As in the earlier sections, I will first present the forces that have created the ideal conditions for a protocol or a topology to arise. Then I will give you a brief introduction to the protocol itself. I won't go very deep, given that each and every one of these flows will be explained in depth in the application development chapters later in the book.

The rise of the programmable web and the problem of access delegation

So far I have focused on the business world and how its authentication requirements evolved. Let's step out for a moment and consider what happened in the public web and the world of consumer-oriented applications.

From its research and business beginnings, the Internet today is a daily fixture for a large percentage of the world population. As I am typing this sentence, it is estimated that more than 40 percent of the world's population uses the Internet. In the United States, that number is 87 percent, and Norway, Netherlands, and Iceland exceed 96 percent.[2] People devote a growing portion of their lives to online activities—from how they get their news to how they learn, from how they do their jobs to how they pay their bills and taxes, from how they organize their holidays to how they congregate in communities and stay in touch with friends. Until a few years ago, my sisters would not have touched a PC in their free time with a 10-foot pole, but now they are more active on Facebook than I am, an Internet user since the early 1990s.

Facebook is a perfect example of why this increased online activity is relevant to our identity discussion. As people spend more and more time online, it becomes natural to try to compose and combine the many different services people use on a daily basis in more complex or efficient work streams. Say that you have a Facebook and Twitter account: you will occasionally want to publish the same status update on both, without having to do a lot of copying and pasting. Say that you are a longtime user of Gmail, where you accumulated a large number of contacts. Wouldn't it be nice if when you sign up for a new service, for example LinkedIn, you could automatically send invitations to connect to all your Gmail contacts, instead of having to type them in LinkedIn all over again?

In the mid-2000s, those new integration flows were all the rage, with web apps frantically trying to grow their user base as fast as possible. The way in which the flow was initially implemented, however, went ahead to become one of the most infamous antipatterns in recent history, shown in Figure 2-6. The idea was very simple. Say that web app A wanted to access the resources that one of its users keeps in web app B. Web app A simply asked its user to reveal to app A his or her credentials for web app B. App A would then use those credentials to access B and somehow retrieve the desired resources, often via brute-force screen scraping.

> **Note** This approach unfortunately survives to this day, although it is much less common. As I am writing this, I visited LinkedIn's section "See what you already know on LinkedIn," and I am given the choice of entering my credentials for Outlook, Comcast, AT&T, and many other providers for the purpose of importing the address book.

That is, of course, all kinds of wrong. Where should I start? Forsaking your credentials gives the recipient too much power. What if instead of simply accessing the resources the recipient declared it wants, it accesses everything else? Changes things? Does bad things on your behalf? And, of course,

---

2. See Internet Live Stats, http://www.internetlivestats.com/internet-users/ (accessed April 23, 2015).

there is the matter of the increased risk. Nothing prevents the recipient from storing your credentials with insufficient care, exposing you to the possibility of leaks and various other disasters. And just to close, even if most apps are honest and perfectly secure, this approach teaches users bad habits, training them to disclose their credentials in multiple contexts, with great risk.

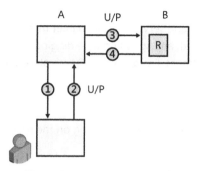

FIGURE 2-6 The password-sharing antipattern: (1) The user navigates through A, landing on a page that needs access to the user's resources in B; (2) A prompts the user to disclose his or her username and password for B; (3) A uses the credentials to establish a session with B as the user and access the targeted resources; and (4) thinking it is dealing with the user directly, B complies and returns the requested resources.

The need for granting access to resources across applications was not going to go away, but the brute-force solution simply could not cut it.

OAuth2 and web applications

Those were the requirements that eventually led to the creation of OAuth, an authorization framework designed to enable those very scenarios while eliminating the need for sharing credentials.

OAuth and OAuth2: A bit of history

OAuth went through a somewhat tormented history. OAuth 1.0 emerged from an early collaboration of individuals coming from Twitter, Ma.gnolia, Google, and Yahoo, beginning around 2006 and leading to an RFC in 2010. The initial formulation owes a lot to the Flickr and the Google authentication API of that time.

OAuth 1.0 solved the delegated-access scenario between web apps but had many shortcomings. For example, it imposed strong cryptographic requirements on clients, it did not support revocation all that well, and its model had important architectural limitations that made it unsuitable for being used outside the web-app-to-web-app-server communications case, which made it hard to generalize the authorization functions outside specific applications. Among other things, those limitations made it hard for OAuth to be applied in many business scenarios.

For that reason, a group of companies (Google, Yahoo, Microsoft) got together and created an alternative OAuth profile, called OAuth WRAP (Web Resource Authorization Profile), which was aimed at eliminating those shortcomings.

The OAuth working group considered the new profile and decided to build the new version of OAuth (OAuth 2) on top of it. OAuth2 is *not* compatible with either OAuth 1 or OAuth WRAP, although it contains elements of both. Its scope ballooned to encompass way more scenarios than the web-app-to-web-app case described in this section.

This context is important. You can still find products and services in the market that support those old versions, but they're definitely on their way out, and spending time digging any further into those versions would not be a good investment. From now on, OAuth always refers to OAuth2 unless I specify otherwise.

The purpose of OAuth can be described in slightly different terms, depending on the role you play in the scenario.

- Say that your web app contains resources that you want to make available programmatically to third parties. OAuth describes an architecture and a protocol to use in your solution that allow such third parties to request and obtain access to your resources, involving your users in the process so that they can grant or deny consent for the operation. In short, OAuth teaches you how to expose your resources for delegated access.

- Say that your web app contains workloads that require access to resources managed by a different web application. OAuth teaches you how you can engage with that web application so that the user (the resource owner) has the opportunity of granting or denying the request—and in case of success, OAuth provides you with the means of securely accessing that resource. In short, OAuth teaches you how to be a client.

Here's a quick, high-level description of the most canonical OAuth2 flow used between web applications to achieve delegated access. The sequence is portrayed in Figure 2-7.

Important For the sake of clarity, I am going to tweak things a little and describe the flow on the basis of a scenario that is *more* restrictive than the protocol's real scope. I will also avoid some of the protocol-specific terminology for now. I will describe the true flow in later parts of the book, when I have more of a foundation to build on.

Our scenario includes the following:

- Web application A

- Web application B

- A user (U) that has accounts with both applications A and B.

- An artifact that I call *Authorization Server* (AS); in this diagram, AS is affiliated with application B.

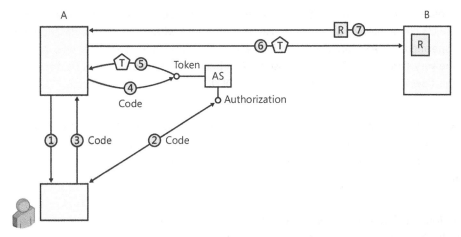

FIGURE 2-7 Simplified OAuth2 authorization and delegated access flow between web applications.

Here how the action unfolds:

1. U navigates to one area of app A that requires access to resources that U maintains in app B.

2. App A triggers a redirect to one endpoint on AS, named the authorization endpoint. App A includes in the redirect information about the resources it needs access to and its identity ("This request is coming from A, and it entails access to resource R"). AS responds to the request by presenting a user experience that authenticates U with his or her account for app B. Once U is successfully authenticated, the AS presents to U some user experience asking for consent ("Do you want to allow A to access R?"). Upon granting consent, the AS returns an authorization code—a string whose content is opaque to everybody but the AS.

3. The browser delivers the code back to app A.

4. App A connects to a different AS endpoint, the token endpoint, sending the code it just received together with some proof of its own application identity ("I am A; here, there's a password to prove that, and here, there's an authorization code you just issued to one of my users").

5. AS validates the request from A. If everything is in order, it returns an *access token* that reflects (directly or indirectly) the delegated permissions granted by the user. In this leg of the sequence, the AS returns lots of other things, including an instance of OAuth's famous *refresh token*, which we will ignore for the time being.

6. A uses the access token to request R from B. B verifies (directly or indirectly) the token, and if everything is in order, it grants access in the terms in which it has been authorized.

7. A delivers to U the experience that required access to R (not shown).

Ta-da! Application A gained access to U's resource in B without ever seeing U's credentials for B. The only time U's credentials for B came into play were in step 2, with the AS. In the description of the sequence, I specified that AS is affiliated with B. In everyday reality on the consumer web, AS and B are in fact the very same entity. That is the case for Facebook and the Facebook Graph, for example. Ergo, with this flow, only B gets to see B's credentials. QED.

> **Note** The sections on modern protocols in this chapter will not include the subsections on roles, artifacts, and messages. The context for describing those, in great detail, will present itself later, when I demonstrate how to use those protocols to develop applications and solutions.

This is profoundly different from what we've been studying so far. Whereas integrated authentication, SAML, WS-Federation, and passwords (in the ways I presented them) were all aimed at establishing the identity of the user, OAuth's chief concern is on determining whether the caller is authorized to perform the operation or access the resource that he, she, or it is requesting. If identity comes into play, it is only as a factor to help make that decision.

The differences don't stop there. All the other protocols included one user performing an authentication to access a resource directly. OAuth operates at multiple levels: there is a phase in which the user is involved to allow for the delegation consent to take place, and another in which web applications talk to one another through server-to-server channels, where the user is no longer directly involved.

OAuth2 and claims

What can I say about OAuth2 and its relationship with the general claims-based identity pattern without going too much into details? Apart from the fact that access to resources is validated by examining a token, rather than raw credentials, not much.

Whereas in claims-oriented protocols, the token was used as a vessel for communicating identity information about the user across boundaries, here the token might not be crossing a boundary at all. Take the sequence in Figure 2-7 and apply it to the case in which B is Facebook and A is a web app trying to write on your Wall. In that case, the AS you need to get tokens from is run by Facebook itself. That means that the AS might record the user's consent in a database and return as an access token a reference to that database row. Once A sends the token back to access the Facebook Graph API for writing on your Wall (R in our diagram), all the Graph needs to do is look up the right row in the database and determine whether the caller is authorized. Note that I am not saying that this is how Facebook implements this flow. I am saying that the topology of the solution makes it possible, whereas in the claims-based scenario, a shared database between an IP and an RP goes against the premise that the two are separate entities.

The OAuth2 specification does not *mandate* that the AS and the application managing the resources must be collocated or owned by the same entity. On the other hand, it does not provide enough information for specifying how things would work in case they do not. To help regulate communications across boundaries, claims-oriented protocols provide artifacts such as metadata documents indicating which token formats to use and how to perform validations. OAuth2 does not regulate those aspects, leaving it to you to decide how to fill in the blanks if your resource and your AS do not live under the same roof.

Without a specification, every vendor filled those blanks in a different way. The end result is that interoperability in OAuth2 is difficult to achieve. You can observe the structure of the most popular OAuth2 developer libraries to get a feeling of the situation: they'll typically have a long collection of modules, one for each provider they work with, each meant to connect with the specific OAuth2 implementation of that provider. Compare that with SAML libraries, which implement the protocol logic and expect every provider and resource to comply with it.

Active Directory, like every other authority wanting to expose its functionality via OAuth2, did have to fill those blanks, and it chose to do so by introducing many claims artifacts, as you'll discover in the later parts of the book.

Status

OAuth2 is now completely mainstream, with widespread support from vendors large and small, ubiquitous presence in cloud and server products, and support in practically every relevant web programming stack. At this point the protocol is stable enough to be confidently used in all kinds of applications, while at the same time it is still evolving for supporting new scenarios. The subtleties about interoperability I mentioned earlier are often a source of confusion and inflated expectations on what it means for an app to support OAuth2—"I know that A and B both speak OAuth2. That means that I can get any OAuth2 library and use it for making A and B communicate right out of the box, right?" Not right out of the box, pal, but close.

All of the developer libraries, tools, services, and server products you'll learn to use in this book make use of OAuth2 in one way or another.

Layering web sign-in on OAuth

The emergence of OAuth offered a great solution for authorizing server-to-server access to resources, but that wasn't the only identity-related issue waiting to be solved: the consumer web was not immune to the cross-domain single sign-on problem.

As web apps proliferated, the desire to reuse the same account for sign-in purposes across multiple apps grew with it. The web community rallied around OpenID, an effort to devise a general protocol to be used across vendors and apps. Despite initial support from multiple important vendors, and peaks of remarkable adoption numbers, the original OpenID formulation and its successor, OpenID 2.0, never managed to tip the scale and become the de facto standard. OpenID was never especially easy to use (it required users to identify themselves with a URL). Moreover, it was conceived to put every provider on equal footing, regardless of size. That approach proved less and less appealing to users as the rise of social networks clustered users around a few big providers that became natural gateways for identity on the web.

There are other reasons that OpenID 2.0 didn't make it, but those that I've mentioned should be enough to give you an idea. Most of the big vendors who did offer OpenID 2.0 implementations are deprecating them and shutting them down. Nowadays, the OpenID foundation backs OpenID Connect, a new protocol that is as backward incompatible with OpenID 2.0 as OAuth2 is incompatible with OAuth1. You won't read anything about OpenID 2.0 in this book from now on. Conversely, I'll describe OpenID Connect in great detail later because it fuels lots of authentication flows in Active Directory.

As committee-driven efforts floundered, the resourceful web community devised ways to go around them. People observed that the providers that were the most attractive identity sources—the major social networks—already offered an API via delegated access, and in particular OAuth, and they figured out a schema to leverage those for a kind of poor-man's sign-in protocol. There are many individual variations, but in broad strokes the schema worked as a variant of the canonical OAuth2 flow shown earlier in Figure 2-7. Say that web application A does not want to maintain its own authentication schema; rather, it wants to allow its users to sign in using the account they have with another application, app B. The flow goes something like this:

> **Note** I will keep using A and B so that my descriptions remain as generic as possible, but whenever you lose track, I encourage you to pick your own concrete example of an app, provider, or resource and make a mental substitution early on. To make things more concrete, when I read through these sequences in my mind, I substitute Facebook for B.

1. When the user tries to sign in to A, A triggers an authorization flow toward B (steps 1 to 5 in Figure 2-7).

2. After A obtains the access token, it uses it to call B's API (step 6). In the ideal case, A will choose to call one of B's APIs that can provide some information about the identity of the user, but that is not strictly necessary.

3. If A successfully calls the API, it deduces that the user is indeed capable of obtaining a valid token from B, indirectly proving that the user is a user of B. If the call carries identity information, all the better. At this point A can create a session (by dropping a cookie or something similar) and declare the user signed in.

Ingenious, right? This is a clever hack, which allows applications to do some form of single sign-on even when the provider does not expose a path specifically meant to enable that. But, alas, a hack it is. Just think of how provider dependent the entire thing is. The API for B that A needs to call to test whether the access token works is an API that B chooses to expose for its own reasons. Facebook exposes its entities via the Graph, 23andMe exposes genome-related APIs, and Eventbrite offers event-organization APIs. That means that the "sign-in" code you write for Facebook cannot work with 23andMe, Eventbrite, or pretty much any other provider.

In turn, this makes it impossible to enshrine an approach in a developer library that works with every provider. Many libraries are in fact thin shells over a vast enumeration of ad hoc adapters that implement each provider's specific flow, vulnerable to changes in APIs that are not bound by any commonly accepted specification.

Although developers targeting consumers and the public web have a higher tolerance for maintaining glue code to integrate things not originally meant to be used together, in the business world, repeatability and predictability are assets that are difficult to renounce. That's why, in hindsight, the next step in this journey was truly the obvious thing to do.

OpenID Connect

The previous section highlighted the misadventures that the original OpenID and OpenID 2.0 went through, just at the same time that OAuth was experiencing its meteoric rise. Oversimplifying things again: the people on the OpenID working group (which, by the way, were in part the same people who were working on OAuth2) decided to formalize the pseudo sign-in pattern in the third generation of the OpenID standard, which they named OpenID Connect.

You'll see all this in much greater detail later in the book, but in a nutshell, OpenID Connect positions itself as an extension to OAuth2, formally adding sign-in capabilities and providing prescriptive guidance on functional areas that the original spec left as exercises for the reader. For what concerns sign-in, OpenID Connect augmented the bare bones OAuth2 specs with various key extensions:

- OpenID Connect explicitly defines an authentication-request message type, layered on top of OAuth2's authorization requests. It includes lots of new parameters meant to allow developers to control important aspects of the authentication experience.

- OpenID Connect extended OAuth2 with a new token, named the ID token, which is meant to communicate *to the client* information about the authentication operation that took place in the context of an OAuth2 grant flow. OpenID Connect is normative about the ID token content, defining a set of claim types that must be present, their semantics, and how to use them for validation. Note that the ID token is often also used to carry information about the user that authenticated and gave consent.

- OpenID Connect defined a formulaic API whose explicit purpose is to obtain information about a subject after the token-acquisition operation takes place. This API is exposed via an endpoint named UserInfo.

- Whereas SAML and WS-Federation emphasized the advertisement of authority coordinates in metadata documents to help apps consume their services, OAuth2 didn't offer direct counterparts. OpenID Connect defines a document format for publishing endpoints, key material, identifiers, and various other information that provides to apps the means to automate trust establishment, automatically keep track of endpoint changes and key rolling, and many of the functions you'd expect from a modern sign-in solution.

OpenID Connect provides alternative paths for authenticating users. Let's take a look at two of them.

> **Note** OpenID Connect specifies lots of other things. Here I am focusing on just two flows to highlight the role the protocol plays in the evolutionary path I've been describing. You'll have opportunities to explore the other aspects soon enough.

Hybrid flow

As you've seen, OAuth2 teaches apps how to be clients—to obtain tokens meant to be consumed by the resources the app wants to access—but the information in those tokens cannot be directly accessed from the app itself. Conversely, sign-in protocols such as SAML or WS-Federation produce tokens meant to be consumed by the app itself so that it can verify that successful authentication took place and extract user information.

In the so-called hybrid flow, OpenID Connect combines these two approaches. It augments the classic OAuth2 flow described in Figure 2-7 by injecting in legs 2 and 3 an extra token (the ID token) specifically meant to deliver to the application verifiable information about the authentication operation that just took place. This allows you to both sign in a user *and* obtain delegated access to a resource, all within the same transaction. Pretty neat.

To make the new flow viable, OpenID Connect had to become prescriptive about the ID token: what format it should be encoded in, the exact information it should carry, what checks should be performed to establish validity, and so on.

SAML tokens, the default currency for the older sign-in protocols, was off the table here. Their size and complex validation rules did not fit the requirements for simplicity and compactness imposed by the OAuth2 portion of the flow. Luckily, there was another, better-fitting token format circulating in the wild: the JSON Web Token, abbreviated JWT (and pronounced "jot"). As you work through the hands-on chapters of this book, you will become intimately familiar with this format. For the time being, it should suffice to say that JWT provides SAML-like expressive power (it's a great vessel for transporting claims; standard signature and encryption algorithms; the usual mechanisms for specifying audience, issuer, and intended validity period; and so on) at a fraction of the size. Just as important, JWT does not require very sophisticated cryptographic capabilities from its producers and consumers.

From SWT to JWT: A brief history of lightweight token formats

Remember OAuth WRAP, the "missing link" protocol that bridged the evolution of OAuth1 through OAuth2, described in the sidebar "OAuth and OAuth2: A bit of history"?

Whereas OAuth1 was largely meant to help companies expose their own APIs—hence coalescing the authorization server and resource roles in a single entity—OAuth WRAP was

---

conceived by companies that acted as custodians of other company's resources. To take a practical example from the modern world, Azure Active Directory can be used to protect calls to the Office 365 API (in which case, the authorization server and resource belong to the same business owner), but it can also be used to protect your own custom web API. (Microsoft provides the authorization server, but the resource is your own.) This is simply another facet of the phenomenon described in the section "OAuth2 and claims."

In their attempt to address this situation and counter the vagueness of the original OAuth, the author of OAuth WRAP introduced an explicit token format as part of the core specification: the Simple Web Token, or SWT. The SWT was indeed exceptionally simple, just a set of HTML form-encoded name/value pairs signed by one simple algorithm.

I use the past tense because today SWT is all but dead. When the OAuth working group decided to take OAuth2 WRAP as the foundation of OAuth2, its members decided that imposing a token format was not in line with the spirit of OAuth (teaching apps how to be clients—and for clients, access tokens are opaque), and SWT missed its opportunity. You can still observe pockets of usage of SWT in the real world (Azure Access Control Service, ACS, uses it for all its management API and REST workflows), but those are all remnants of early implementations, still around for honoring support terms but all unequivocally fading into the sunset.

Naturally, SWT did not make the real-world requirement for a lightweight token format go away. Evolution took its course, and at least two new formats, both based on the lightweight but expressive JSON, independently emerged around 2010. One was the JSON Tokens, from Google's Dirk Balfanz. The other was JWT, from Microsoft's Mike Jones and Yaron Goland. The various parties agreed to unify the efforts, and JWT was picked up by the working group, where it went through multiple drafts and authors from multiple companies (Microsoft, Google, Ping Identity, NRI, Facebook, and many others).

When OpenID Connect needed to specify a token format for its ID token construct, JWT was the obvious choice.

The hybrid flow is represented in Figure 2-8. The sequence is the same as described in the earlier section, with some extra operations.

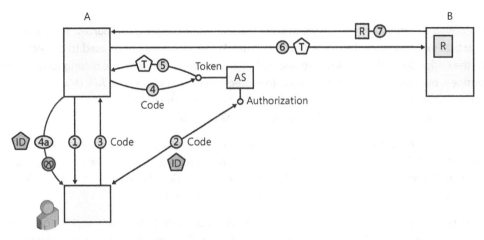

FIGURE 2-8 OpenID Connect hybrid flow.

When the application receives the code and the ID token (leg 3), it can now proceed to validate the incoming token—just like a SAML or WS-Federation app did upon receiving a SAML token. And just as SAML or WS-Federation did not specify how an app should represent its own session, OpenID Connect does not tell you what to do once you are satisfied that the ID token represents a successful authentication—but in practice today that almost always means that you'll drop a session cookie. That is represented in Figure 2-8 by leg 4a.

The operations in leg 4a can take place at the same time as leg 4, before, or after. For example, you'll do it before if you think that receiving a valid ID token means you have a valid session in all cases, even when the authorization code redemption (which in this case would happen after you already created your session) fails for some reason. This discussion brings us into philosophical territory, which I'd rather avoid if I can. But I'll add that, in fact, if you care only about the sign-in capabilities of the protocol, you can opt out from receiving a code, telling the authorization server at sign-in time that you only need the ID token. That brings us full circle, back to the claims-based identity protocols described earlier in the chapter.

To be strict, the specification suggests that the ID token should relay information about the authentication operation rather than the subject itself, with the user information being obtained afterward via the UserInfo endpoint. The UserInfo endpoint is meant to formalize the functionality that concrete OAuth2 implementations obtained by hitting a provider-specific API, like in the Facebook Graph example I discussed in "Layering web sign-in on OAuth." In reality, people aren't always crazy about having to shoot multiple outgoing HTTP connections from their web servers. A large portion of the value proposition of claims was precisely to receive everything in a nice package with no need for follow-ups. That's why in practice the ID token does contain user information as well in most cases. There are cases in which the amount of user information required makes it impractical to put it all in a token, which would become too big to be handled efficiently, and in these cases the UserInfo endpoint comes back in the picture. Note that all this occurs in the context of the authentication phase. Of course, the UserInfo is super useful afterward for obtaining incremental info about the user.

Authorization code flow

The authorization code flow is another variation of the base OAuth2 flow described in Figure 2-7. The difference is that this time the ID token is returned in leg 6, together with the access token. You've got the hang of how it works at this point, so I won't add yet another variation of Figure 2-7 here.

The fact that the app receives the ID token from a server-to-server call makes it possible to dramatically simplify the ID token validation logic. Think about it. In the hybrid flow, the app receives the ID token from a browser. Anybody in the winding road from the authorization server to the app could have tampered with the token or even forged it in its entirety. The application must protect itself from those occurrences, and the way to do so is by verifying that the signature on the token was actually performed by the trusted authority and not compromised.

But when you receive a token directly from a server, you can rely on the security of the channel to guarantee that none of those attacks could take place. As long as you are getting a token from a trusted TLS channel (a channel secured by a certificate issued by a trusted certificate authority, the subject of the certificate matching the hostname of the authorization server you trust, etc.), you know that the token is coming from the intended authority through a direct channel, with no intermediaries. You still need to verify the information inside the token (for example, the audience of the token must indicate that the token was issued for your app), but you are no longer obligated to verify the signature. In turn, this means that setting up an application that supports this OpenID Connect flow requires extremely simple code.

Status

OpenID Connect is the area where most of the innovation is taking place these days, no matter what vendor or platform you pick. Its ability to support both sign-in and API-invocation scenarios in the same application makes it well suited for addressing the requirements of today's solutions. It is the protocol underlying most Active Directory flows, and it's going to be the protocol that fuels all the scenarios I'll walk you through in this book.

I can almost hear you protesting. "Didn't you just say the same about OAuth2?" The fact that OpenID Connect is basically OAuth2 with just a bunch of extra details makes things a bit confusing. In the literature you'll often find that people refer to OpenID Connect when they talk about web scenarios and stick with OAuth2 when referring to server-to-server flows or native applications. In fact, even in the latter scenarios you'll often find that it's almost never classic OAuth2—OpenID Connect fills in the details of so many important functional areas left unaddressed by the original OAuth2 that you'll almost always end up using at least one or two of its extra parameters.

More API consumption scenarios

Let's take a small detour from our history of user-authentication techniques and consider for a moment a couple of resource-consumption patterns that are very common in enterprise scenarios.

Impersonation and acting on behalf of a caller

Chances are that you've heard the term *impersonation* before. Imagine that you are working on an on-premises solution, perhaps using Kerberos as your authentication technology. Say that you have a web app that needs to access some resources and that access to those resources is allowed only to specific users or groups. (Think specific network shares or rows in a database.) When Mario navigates to your app and requests a page that retrieves files from a share he owns, he correctly expects to be authorized to perform the operation. However, Mario is not accessing the share directly: he is accessing the app, which is presumably running on a different box, and in turn the app is accessing the share. At the network layer, the app is not Mario: it is its own process, whose identity (for what Kerberos is concerned about) is determined by the web server settings. Kerberos provides a mechanism, called *constrained delegation*, which allows a web application at deployment time to impersonate its caller; thus, inherit its access rights.

That's pretty neat, but as is common for many of these tricks, this flow is made possible by the nature of the domain controller and its special network requirements—to which everything within a domain network must abide.

On the other hand, this pattern is clearly useful outside a local network, too. If you squint a little, this is something that the authorization code flow in OAuth2 could enable. The main requirement would be that the end user give his or her consent to one specific access right, full impersonation. (The authorization code flow allows for far finer-grained delegation. For example, the app might ask for read-only access for only a specific subset of resources.) The identity experts would be quick to say that this would not be full-blown impersonation—the identity of the app would never disappear here—but as long as it grants the access level requested, who cares about those subtleties?

Another hard requirement would come from the need of the code grant to display a consent prompt, which can happen only if the app has a user interface. But what happens if the app does not have a user interface? Think of a web API meant to be consumed programmatically: the client would simply not know what to do with the HTTP 302 response redirecting to the consent pages. What to do?

Luckily, OAuth2 has one specific flow, described in the OAuth2 Token Exchange extension, that describes how to request a token on behalf of a caller without showing any further prompts. The flow is commonly referred to as the "on-behalf-of" security token request. You can find a simplified diagram in Figure 2-9. The on-behalf-of flow plays an important role in many Active Directory solutions, and I'll cover it in depth later in the book.

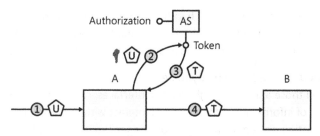

FIGURE 2-9 Simplified diagram of an on-behalf-of token request. A and B are web APIs. (1) A is accessed via a user token U; (2) A requests a token for B from the AS. A presents U and some means for AS to know that the call comes from A, such as a shared secret; (3) AS issues a new token T that allows A to access B with the same rights as the user who originally sent U; (4) A accesses B with T.

No user in sight: Accessing a resource as the application itself

Another common pattern you'll encounter fairly often is one in which an application needs to access one resource independently from whoever is signed in to the application itself. In fact, there are cases in which there is literally nobody signed in, and the application acts in complete independence. Here, you can think of daemon apps or Windows services that start as soon as a server boots, with no need for anybody to log on to the machine or access a web app running on that server.

OAuth2 has a special grant for this very scenario, called the *client credentials grant*. This is probably the simplest grant of all, so I won't illustrate it. The client sends whatever credential or authentication type the authorization server deems appropriate (more often than not, a classic shared secret in a string or a signed token demonstrating ownership of a private key), and if the authorization server considers the credentials valid, it will issue a token to the client. The claims in the token will describe the client application itself.

Single-page applications

Let's resume the narrative arc that brought us through the ever-escalating conflict between evolving authentication requirements and the protocols that emerged to satisfy them.

Although we saw application topologies change a lot from one generation to another, one thing remained the same: the round-trip-based request-response pattern underlying every web application with a user interface. We take that idea for granted, so you might not think about it too often, but it's worth spending a moment teasing it apart.

Web applications run entirely on the server. Their code is expected to implement both the presentation-generation logic and whatever computation (old-fashion professionals like me would be tempted to call this "business logic") is required for performing the function the apps are meant to offer. In practice, the web app you use for your tax-filling duties spends CPU cycles both for sending down the HTML rendering the forms you use to fill in your hard-earned numbers and for crunching the same number according to the tax scheme in fashion for the year.

This mechanism is what made cookie-based sessions so handy for web sign-on. Given that every interaction with the app is actually a full round trip, having a cookie along for the ride is a handy way of reminding the server that it's still you, the authenticated user, at the other hand of the cable.

This pattern does have significant downsides. I am ready to bet that you are no stranger to Facebook, Gmail, or Outlook.com. All those apps have high-density interfaces, crowded with lots and lots of semi-independent pieces of information. Whenever you interact with one element, like expanding a comment thread or selecting one email message, you trigger changes at the local level. The comment thread expands, moving the rest of the content down; the email body appears in the main area, while the email entry shows a "selected" indicator. A large portion of the screen remains the same.

Think of how wasteful it would be to implement this functionality via a classic round trip. As soon as you click, the browser would have to tear down a complex user interface and send a request for the new information and enough data to reconstruct the current state. Once the server is done processing your request, it has to send back all the code the browser needs to reconstruct the entire scene: the parts that changed, but also the parts that did not. The performance of such an app would be pitiful, and the waste of resources criminal.

The last few years have seen the rise of a new approach to web development that provides an elegant and efficient solution for architecting these kinds of applications. The idea is simple: instead of expecting the server to handle both presentation and back-end logic, the architecture separates the two and distributes the work between the browser itself and the server.

Modern browsers are far more than glorified markup renderers. From simple origins, the JavaScript language has evolved into a powerful programming platform that can implement very sophisticated logic entirely on the client. A developer can now code the presentation layer of one app entirely in JavaScript: logic-layout management, data binding, dynamic updates, state changes, and more can now be bundled with one initial HTML page (or a few more) and sent down at the very first request to the application. From that moment on, all the UI behavior can be handled without having to flush the entire browser state and perform a round trip. That's why this app architecture is often referred to as *single-page application*, or SPA. In theory, your whole app can live in one single page, the first one, and all the JavaScript files it references.

That sounds fantastic, but clearly something is missing. Thank you, JavaScript, for having rendered all those tax forms, the experience was amazingly fluid. But now that I have filed my numbers, how am I going to deliver them to the tax-crunching logic on the server side?

Simple. JavaScript also allows you to perform programmatic HTTP requests to the back end. If the back end exposes a web API, the front end can invoke it via JavaScript, read back the results, and use them to selectively update the UI. In the Facebook example, clicking a comment thread can trigger JavaScript logic to perform a request to the server for the text for all those comments, parse them back, and display them on the page, without having to touch the UI elements around it. In the tax-return example, clicking Submit sends all your numbers to the server, which crunches them and sends back to the client a "total due" number, which the same JavaScript logic can display in a new text box, once again without having to do anything with the rest of the UI.

This is a very neat architecture. How do we secure it? Sticking with cookies is tempting. The browser will automatically attach cookies to every request heading to the domain a cookie is associated with, and that holds for JavaScript-generated requests as well. That might work for testing or quick and dirty prototyping, but as soon as you get serious about your app, the limitations of this approach become evident:

- Cookies go only to the domain from where they originated; but technically, your JavaScript code might call any API, including APIs hosted on other domains.

- Cookie-based sessions are really children of round-trip applications. What happens when a cookie expires when working with a web app protected by WS-Federation or SAML? The app deems the caller unauthenticated, so it reacts with an HTTP 302 request and a sign-in message. In a round-trip app, that 302 will be immediately executed by the browser, prompting the user to authenticate. In an SPA, however, that won't happen: a 302 return code is really not actionable for a JavaScript web API call. Sure, you could write more logic that makes the redirection happen, but in the process you'd flush whatever client-side state the app built up to that point. You could prevent that as well by saving everything, but doing so can get messy.

The solution is surprisingly simple. You secure web API calls just as I described for other topologies—with tokens. The missing link here is how do you enable JavaScript to obtain and use tokens? OAuth2 introduced, and OpenID Connect refined, a special grant precisely for this scenario: it's called the *implicit grant*.

In the implicit grant, an application can request an access token directly to the authorization endpoint without any interaction with the token endpoint. The token itself is returned in a URI fragment, which is fancy HTTP jargon to indicate a string in a URI after the # symbol. Such a string is meant to be visible only to the browser itself (and everything that runs within it, like your JavaScript code) and won't be sent to the server. The JavaScript can retrieve the token bits and squirrel them away, typically by saving them in some HTML construct (sessionStorage and localStorage being common favorites). Once the token bits have been obtained, more JavaScript logic can attach them to the requests whenever there's the need to contact a back-end web API. That is a little more work than letting the browser automatically attach cookies, but it grants far more control to the developer. Moreover, nowadays nobody builds a single-page application from scratch: there are multiple excellent JavaScript frameworks (the one in fashion today is AngularJS), and the logic to attach tokens can be easily buried there. No action is required for the application developer.

Azure AD supports the implicit flow, and Microsoft in general exposes many APIs to be consumed from JavaScript clients.

Leveraging web investments in native clients

This book focuses on web applications, so mobile clients and rich applications aren't in scope. However, I'd do you a disservice if I did not cap my story and say a little about the latest step in the evolution of modern authentication methods, one in which the authentication logic leaves the browser to support native apps and then kind of gets cold feet and brings the browser back, albeit in a different guise.

Throughout this chapter I've focused on web applications because they constitute the vast majority of the apps requiring the identity of the user to cross a boundary of some kind. However, the reality is that native applications have been with us every step of the way, although their number and widespread adoption didn't reach today's oceanic proportions until the advent of application stores. What is a native application? It is one application that's meant to be run on a specific platform, intended as an OS or a set of APIs (Windows desktop or iOS; .NET 4.5 or Java), and built with the building blocks that such platforms offer: runtimes, visual components, packaging and deployment technologies, and so on. Microsoft Word, Visual Studio, Adobe Reader, Corel Painter, TurboTax, Flappy Bird, the Facebook and Twitter apps on iOS and Android, and the Kindle reader app are just a few examples of native applications from the devices currently scattered on my desk.

Native applications running within the boundaries of an enterprise have always been able to benefit from the Kerberos infrastructure, just like their web app counterparts in the intranet. In the early 2000s, the WS-* movement introduced new protocols to obtain the same expressive power and cryptographic guarantees across organizational and network boundaries. You know how it went: the people that could cope with the complexity adopted them, but in the wild web the WS-* specs remained underutilized. All this happened at the same time as the rise of the programmable web, when web apps were gearing up to expose (or obtain) delegated access to one another's resources via OAuth2.

In 2008 Apple introduced its App Store on iOS, making it extra easy for end users to acquire native applications on its devices. That marked a turning point in the ease with which a native app could make its way to a device, and in the appeal that the native app format exercised on developers. Suddenly, every website needed to have an app counterpart, and such apps had to offer comparable functionality to their web counterpart. This meant that they needed to have access to the same protected resources—before displaying your pictures, Facebook needs to ascertain that it's really you on the other part of the wire, regardless of whether you're using a browser or an application.

All those applications had just made massive investments in getting their identity story straight: supporting the nascent OAuth, providing authentication experiences, and managing consent-gathering experiences and lots of other tasks tailored to be performed within a browser. Duplicating all that work solely to support a new client type wasn't something anybody looked forward to.

I am not sure who first came out with the following idea, but whoever he or she was, it was a stroke of genius. It goes as follows:

> What if we pretend that native apps are just a special kind of web app? One that cannot have its own credentials, given that we cannot trust a device to keep a secret, but a web app of some sort nonetheless. When the app needs a token for requesting a remote resource, we can use the native UI elements to display a browser surface and host in there the usual OAuth2 code grant dance. That way we can reuse all our existing authentication and consent logic. We just need to be sure the layout of the

page looks good in the form factor of the device. After we get back a code, we hide the browser, redeem the code, and retrieve the access token we need. QED.

Perhaps this is a bit oversimplified, but it's pretty much what happened. Today, when you launch an app from your device, it is very common to be taken to a hosted web experience when you perform tasks that require authentication and authorization. Hosting the prompting logic in a browser is exceptionally flexible. It allows you to change the logic at any time—for example, by inserting an additional step for multifactor authentication—without having to deliver updates to your client code. Throughout this book, you will often use ADAL, Microsoft's library for requesting tokens. When used within a native app, ADAL has built in the ability to display that browser surface, using the primitives that make sense in each of the platforms (modal dialog in Windows desktop apps, full-screen browser experiences on mobile devices, and so on).

Today we are witnessing the emergence of the next step in this evolution: the hero app, or broker. When a native application needs a token, instead of contacting the authorization server directly, it passes the request on to another app installed on the device that is designed specifically to maintain contact with the provider of choice. That app plays the role of the broker. It knows how to talk to a specific authority, it can maintain a cache of tokens to share among apps (which are normally unable to share any context given that every mobile platform sandboxes them), and it can even perform advanced functionality such as proving the identity of the device itself.

The world of modern authentication in native apps is wondrous and extensive, worthy of a book of its own. For this book, the foregoing should give you enough background to put things in perspective.

Summary

This chapter led you through a whirlwind tour, examining how authentication requirements and technologies changed and adapted through two decades of IT history.

I began with a definition of some foundational concepts, such as identity and authentication. You had the opportunity to see those concepts in action right away, observing how the simplest authentication schemes implemented them.

You witnessed the advent of local networks and their influence on authentication artifacts and techniques: the emergence of the domain controller, the advantages and limitations of Kerberos, and so on. I also invested some time introducing claims-based identity as a framework for understanding the intent and scope of modern authentication protocols, without getting sidetracked by individual differences in syntax and terminology.

You applied what you learned by examining SAML and WS-Federation under the claims-identity lenses, acquiring basic terminology and an understanding of how these protocols provided solutions to the main authentication need of that time, cross-domain single sign-on.

I also presented the life-altering changes brought by the programmable web and explained how its widespread adoption created the ideal conditions for the emergence of OAuth2, a delegated authorization protocol. You saw how that seeded spontaneous extensions that repurposed OAuth2 to achieve single sign-on and how those initiatives were soon appropriated by standard bodies and turned into a du jour protocol specification, OpenID Connect.

Finally, you had a taste of how authentication is evolving beyond its traditional browser round-trip origins by leveraging the advanced JavaScript capabilities of modern browsers—or leaving the browser altogether to enable authentication for native applications.

I realize that this is a lot to take in. I don't expect you to retain all the content you read in this chapter right away. Some of it will be repeated later on, when you write apps using the protocols described here. Other content will be there for you as a reference so that if you get lost you can always find refuge back here and refresh your understanding of why things are the way they are today.

You are now equipped with a specific mindset you can use for approaching authentication problems: by knowing what the problem is you're trying to solve, you'll know what to look for in a solution.

Next, you'll become acquainted with the entity that will play the role of the IdP, IP, and AS throughout the book: Active Directory.

CHAPTER 3

Introducing Azure Active Directory and Active Directory Federation Services

In this chapter you make first contact with Azure Active Directory (Azure AD) and Active Directory Federation Services (ADFS), the two authority types that Active Directory offers for protecting your applications.

My goals for this chapter are to inform you about what those services are, how they are structured, and what they can do for you. I'll focus mostly on terminology, components, and functional aspects that you encounter while using those authorities for development-related tasks. You won't find fine details or instructions here—those will be provided in the later chapters of the book, in the context of the scenarios I'll describe there.

I purposely ignore tasks and features that are prevalently administrative in nature, not because they are not important or handy—they are—but because this is a book for developers, and if I don't draw the line somewhere, the size of the book will get out of control.

A warning about content freshness

Azure Active Directory is a cloud service. As such, it evolves at an exceptionally quick pace. New features are added every few weeks, and existing ones are refined and improved all the time. This is a very poor match with the typical time frames of the printed publishing trade. No matter how fast I write, or how promptly the production team sifts through the manuscript and fixes my broken English, you will read those words months from the moment I typed them. To minimize the aging of the text, I avoid as much as I can presenting content that has a high rate of obsolescence, such as screenshots and preview features. Instead, I focus on topics that are slower to change: intended usage, supported scenarios, architectural principles. Those measures notwithstanding, some of my descriptions will inevitably no longer be the latest and greatest at publication time. I'll try to minimize impact by publishing new info online. If you read something that does not seem to perfectly match what you see or experience when using the products, please make sure to check out *http://www.cloudidentity.com/blog/books/book-updates/*.

Active Directory Federation Services

In Chapter 2, "Identity protocols and application types," I introduced the concepts of a domain controller (DC) and Kerberos, and I explored how every aspect of the local network can benefit from their presence and functionality. As I ventured beyond local network scenarios and acquainted you with claims-based identity, you learned about protocols such as SAML and WS-Federation, which are capable of handling authentication and web single sign-on outside the boundaries of a local network.

As out-of-network scenarios became more common, the use of a DC speaking exclusively Kerberos was not going to cut it. Administrators and developers wanted to use their investment in Active Directory also for exposing or accessing partners' and customers' applications. Microsoft addressed that requirement by introducing a new Windows Server role, called Active Directory Federation Services, or ADFS for short. For all intents and purposes, this new role augmented the network capabilities with the following:

- Network endpoints supporting various claims-based identity protocols, which includes metadata endpoints for the protocols that admit them.

- A configuration database for keeping track of applications configured to operate through those protocols (RPs). This database can be sourced from Windows Internal Database (WID) or from a full-flown instance of SQL Server.

- Management tools for turning endpoints on and off and for provisioning and removing RPs. These are mostly a Microsoft Management Console snap-in and a set of Windows PowerShell cmdlets.

- A proxy role for extending the reach of ADFS authentication capabilities to clients operating outside the local network.

- Claim values that are sourced from the local Active Directory and LDAP attributes. These can also be sourced by custom attributes stores.

- A claims rules engine (and associated claims-transformation language) designed to provide maximum flexibility in the issuance of claims in ADFS-produced tokens.

That is not an exhaustive list, but it captures the general intended use of the new service. Figure 3-1 shows the key functional components of ADFS.

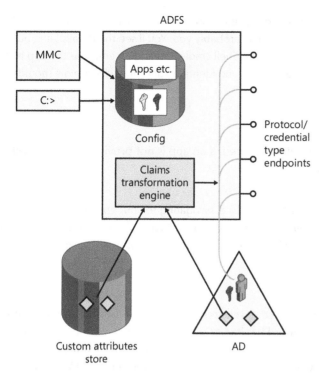

FIGURE 3-1 Main ADFS functional components.

Although the service has evolved significantly from its early days, these components remain the pillars of its functionality. IT administrators are typically in charge of local ADFS instances: they are the ultimate arbiters of which applications can be provisioned, what protocols they should use, and what user attributes (in the form of claims) they should receive. If you consider that an app that is not provisioned in ADFS cannot receive any tokens, you can see how ADFS administrators hold tremendous power over us developers. This power dynamic changed when Azure AD emerged—and you'll see that soon enough.

ADFS and development

Let's get the basics out of the way. Say that you have an application hosted outside your intranet and want to make it available to users from your local AD. Say that your company does have ADFS up and running. How does ADFS enter your life?

- You need to find out which version of ADFS you have, and select a protocol that it supports for protecting your app.

- You need to add code and libraries to your app to support that protocol (which, by the way, is the reason you are holding this book). Note that you'll need to configure the libraries to use the protocol coordinates of your ADFS instance, which means that you'll need to find out what those coordinates are.

- You need to contact the ADFS admin to provision your application. If you work in a small shop or in a test environment, that admin is probably you. You'll see the details later, but in a nutshell this means using the MMC or PowerShell cmdlets to add an entry for the app in ADFS, supplying information such as the app's URL and identifier, deciding what claims should be sent at authentication time, and the like.

 Important This step cannot be skipped. If an app is not provisioned, ADFS will not issue a token for it.

That's pretty much it. After all of this work is in place, navigating to your app will bounce the user to authenticate against the local ADFS pages. Upon successful authentication, a token will be issued and forwarded to your app, which in turn will validate it and sign in the user. All as expected.

Getting ADFS

ADFS is a Windows Server role, its life cycle tied to releases of Windows Server. That means that every Windows Server release from 2003 R2 onward has had its own ADFS version, with its own features. It also means that ADFS versions aren't backported. If you want a certain shiny feature available in a certain ADFS version, you've got to upgrade the entire server OS to the version of Windows that carries that ADFS version with it. After that's done, you can find and turn on the Active Directory Federation Services role in the Server Roles screen or through any other management tool you like. And once that role is turned on, you need to configure it. The good news is that configuration is pretty straightforward; there's a wizard for it, and (if you're okay with the default settings) the biggest task required is that you create and assign a self-signed certificate.

I am not going to give you detailed instructions because those change from version to version. I just want to give you a feeling for what setting up one ADFS instance entails.

There's more. ADFS requires you to have an AD deployment, even if you plan to use functions that in themselves would not seem to require AD. You don't need to turn on ADFS on a domain controller (though lots of demo environments do that for economic reasons), but you do need to use a domain-joined server.

Once ADFS is up, managing it largely boils down to the following:

- Deciding which protocols and credential types endpoints should be active.

- Provisioning applications that should be allowed to receive a token, and specifying what claims such a token should carry.

- Keeping certificates fresh, and performing other administrivia.

I am sure that administrators would add tons of tasks to this meager list, but for developers, I'd say that's as far as most of us would want to go.

Protocols support

ADFS did have a v1, introduced with Windows Server 2003 R2, and a v1.1 shortly after—but they aren't talked about nowadays. From a developer's perspective, ADFS started to get interesting from version 2.0 onward.

Every version of ADFS has interesting features, besides which protocols it supports, but from the perspective of how you can hook up apps to it, the protocol support truly is the higher-order bit.

ADFS v2

ADFS v2 came out in the first half of 2010, as an out-of-band download for Windows Server 2008 R2.

As I write this, ADFS v2 is probably the most commonly deployed ADFS version. It supports the following protocols:

- SAML2

- WS-Federation

- WS-Trust

From the perspective of .NET development, the most interesting of the supported protocols is WS-Federation. That's mainly determined by exclusion: as mentioned earlier, the SAML protocol is not directly supported by .NET libraries, and WS-Trust is on the sunset path together with all its other WS-* friends. ADFS v2 uses SAML tokens in all its protocols.

ADFS "v3"

Some ADFS team members get irked when someone refers to the version of ADFS shipping in Windows Server 2012 R2 as "ADFS v3." These team members would prefer that everyone say "the ADFS version that ships in Windows Server 2012 R2," but they kind of brought this situation on themselves by calling the former versions 1.0, 1.1, 2.0 and 2.1. Also, who has time for that?

ADFS "v3" is a superset of ADFS v2. In particular, it adds the OAuth2 authorization-code grant for public clients. In practice, this means that from this version onward you can write native applications that obtain tokens from ADFS and web APIs that validate tokens from ADFS. That flavor of OAuth2 is not suitable for web applications, however, so no code-behind token-acquisition scenarios are possible with that release.

Apart from the addition of the OAuth2 endpoint, ADFS had to add a couple of other features to support the new flow:

- The ability for issuing and processing JSON Web Tokens (JWTs).

- An extended model for representing applications, augmented by the definition of a client app, which was absent in the protocols supported in v2. ADFS "v3" did not add this to its management UI, though, and only offers PowerShell cmdlets for managing this new type of app.

ADFS "v3" also has some other protocol-related capabilities. In particular, it has its own ceremony for determining whether a device is "workplace joined"—an operation morally similar to joining a domain but with far fewer requirements on the OS and the capabilities of the machine and far less administrative power. ADFS uses that knowledge to decide whether a token should be issued or refused in accordance to it. I am not going to detail this flow any further. There are more modern approaches to this scenario, and I am bringing it up mostly so that you know that it exists and you have one possible culprit when you troubleshoot why you are failing to get a token from an ADFS instance: "Don't tell me it has the workplace join on. . . . Let's check."

ADFS in Windows Server 2016

Now we venture into highly unstable territory. I pledged to minimize the coverage of preview features, but the improvements introduced by ADFS in Windows 2016 are simply too significant and relevant to this book for me to ignore.

At the time of writing, Windows Server 2016 is in preview, and so is its implementation of ADFS. There is no guarantee that some features won't get cut, or at least change, before this book finds its way to your shelf. Here are the protocols currently supported:

- OAuth2 authorization-code grant for protected clients

- OAuth2 client credentials

- OAuth2 on behalf of

- OAuth2 resource owner grant

- OAuth2 implicit grant

- OpenID Connect (various grants and response types)

I haven't introduced some of the protocols in this list yet, so don't worry if you don't recognize them. I'll cover all of them in detail in the hands-on chapters of this book.

Nowadays, software products are released at faster and faster rates, and ADFS is no exception. However, no matter how much agility you pour into the process, innovation will always be slower in a product meant to be distributed and installed on customers' machines than in a service run in the cloud. That's why the features in ADFS will likely always trail a bit behind its big cloud-based sibling, Azure Active Directory. This is also one of the reasons that most of the hands-on chapters will mainly use Azure AD as the reference authority.

Azure Active Directory: Identity as a service

Azure Active Directory is a cloud-based service that is aimed at providing you with all the features you need to handle authentication in your cloud-based workloads. It is designed to do for cloud-based applications what on-premises Active Directory does for traditional intranet applications. Azure AD achieves this by reimagining key aspects of Active Directory, shedding the features that make sense on-premises but don't cut it in the cloud, and adding brand-new features to offer functionality in a platform as a service (PaaS) style.

In the previous section, you learned how ADFS, by teaching the DC how to converse in SAML and WS-Federation, enabled directory users to access apps hosted outside the corporate network. That was a huge step forward toward a true claims-based apps-and-providers ecosystem, but, as usual, it didn't solve every possible problem associated with cross-boundary authentication. Two issues proved to be particularly thorny for cloud applications:

- **Application provisioning**   Consider a developer who is selling to organizations access to his application. Although WS-Federation and SAML establish the roles that each party should play, and define the trust-establishment ceremony (via metadata) as well as the subsequent message exchanges, the process is far from being automatic.

  Think of this as getting married. Your local government establishes a process that should be followed to make marriage happen in valid legal terms, as opposed to the engaged couple just coming up with a private agreement with no rules or guarantees. The existence of that process makes getting married possible, but it still takes quite a lot of paperwork.

  There are multiple elements that conspire to make direct trust establishment an operation that's difficult to generalize. For one, administrators are normally the only entity that can modify ADFS (or any equivalent product) to add an entry for a new application, establish what claims should be sent, and so on. There is no programmatic way out of the box of provisioning an app on the fly. Also, individual users must always depend on administrators if they want to start using a new application. Another issue arises in connection with the wide variety of deployment types you'll encounter. Every administrator decides what attributes define his or her users, groups, and infrastructure, which in turn determines the pool of possible claims that applications can expect to receive. That entails some investigation on the app developer's part, possibly followed by the creation of ad hoc code for handling any impedance mismatch. If your app expects a "street address" claim, but the IP sends you that information in a claim called 街道地址, you might need to work something out before your app can correctly serve that customer.

- **Directory queries**   Claims-based identity provides just-in-time identity information about the currently signed-in user, which in turn unlocks all the goodness we've discussed so far, and—by this property alone—it addresses a very large portion of authentication scenarios. However, that doesn't help when your app needs information held in the directory that is not a direct attribute of the currently signed-in user. Imagine that you are writing a classic expense notes application. Your users can submit expense notes and, when they receive reports from others, approve them. The application needs to know for every user who her manager is and which reports, if any, are his. That information does not typically travel in the form of claims— including a list of reports can rapidly lead to untenable token sizes. Even if such information could go with a claim, where do you draw the line? Say that you need the street address of all users to mail invoices, or that you need to traverse multiple management layers to reach somebody with a purchase limit great enough to approve a particularly large expense note. All that information is stored in the directory. If your app runs within the boundaries of the local network, it can simply reach out and examine the directory. Not so if the app runs in the cloud, because there's a firewall between the app and that information. And even if the app could manage to pierce that firewall, that would mean forsaking operating at cloud scale because it would introduce in the app's critical path a dependency on the performance of individual IdPs.

Microsoft itself felt that pain early on, and very close to home. Its Office 365 services faced the exact problems I just described, with the raging intensity you should expect when you're chartered to deliver a service at mind-boggling scale.

To support Office 365 workloads, Microsoft reimagined Active Directory functionality, creating a brand-new service—Azure Active Directory, as you guessed. Almost immediately, the service was made available for securing a customer's own applications besides Office 365 and others from Microsoft.

The differences between the on-premises approach and the cloud approach are numerous and substantial, but to summarize:

- For organizations already operating an AD instance, Azure AD offers the possibility of *creating a projection of AD in the cloud*. I'll unpack what this means in practice a bit later, but for the time being, this capability allows organizations to continue to manage users and assets in their regular AD, while at the same time gain the ability to perform the cloud-based app workloads I'll describe later.

   For organizations that do not have an on-premises AD deployment, or that want to keep it isolated from their cloud workloads, Azure AD offers the opportunity of *hosting a new directory entirely in the cloud,* with no local footprint whatsoever. Among other advantages, this finally makes it possible for small organizations (or development shops) to make use of sophisticated directory-grade features for a small or at no cost.

- Whereas Active Directory is traditionally a singleton service within its own organization, Azure AD is a *multitenant system*. It is designed to provide authentication and directory functionality to multiple organizations, partitioning the service in such a way that every tenant has complete control over its data, with the illusion of being Azure AD's only beneficiary. However, the fact that every directory tenant shares the same pipes unlocks scenarios that would otherwise be impossible, such as just-in-time provisioning of new apps without any explicit work from administrators or extra integration code necessary on the app side.

- Because Azure AD is a native cloud offering, the authentication mechanisms that it offers cover the *full range of protocols* that have no infrastructural constraints—from the classic SAML and WS-Federation to all the known variations of OAuth2 and OpenID Connect.

- The tokens issued by Azure AD contain claims populated with user attributes maintained in a cloud store. Those values can be cloud-only or a synchronized copy of the corresponding attributes on-premises.

- Traditional on-premises directories offer well-supported querying protocols, such as LDAP. Repurposing such protocols for cloud workloads proved to be difficult given their reliance on complex development stacks (as opposed to the RESTful nature of most decentralized cloud systems nowadays) and their inflexibility in matters of access control. To expand on the last point, granting access to your directory to a third-party expense note app is far riskier than allowing one of your own users to access the same data, because the potential for abuse is far higher for the former. Protocols such as LDAP do not provide the flexibility of modulating access levels very easily.

   Azure AD features a new API, called the *Directory Graph API*, that allows developers to query and manipulate directory entities by using simple REST operations. The access control for these operations is implemented through Azure AD's own OAuth2 features, making it possible for application developers and administrators alike to request and grant fine-grained permissions, to everybody's satisfaction.

- Given that Azure AD focuses on enabling cloud-based workloads, in its current form it sheds much of the functionality that was instead a staple of its on-premises origins. You will not use Azure AD for finding the printers available on your office floor, and (at least for now) you will not join a machine to an Azure AD domain. Those functionalities are not entirely outside the scope of Azure AD, but they are not as relevant to cloud workloads, so they'll come in later (if ever).

Apart from those changes, Azure AD contains pretty much what you'd expect from a directory: a store for users with their own schema, groups, ways of representing applications, and so on.

Figure 3-2 schematizes Azure AD's main functional components. Please note that some of these components will be described later in this chapter. Also, all the components below the cloud/on-premises interface are optional. Later in the chapter, I'll describe the difference between managed and federated tenants.

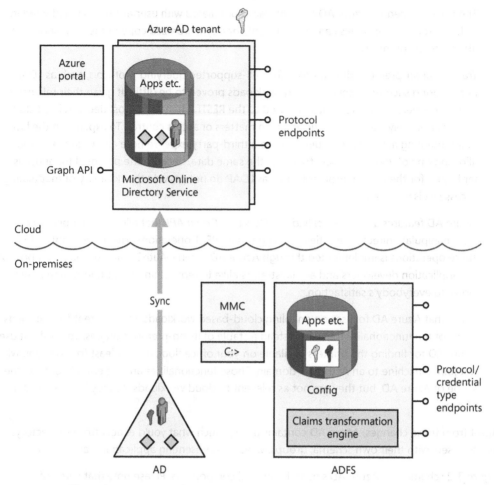

FIGURE 3-2 The main components of an Azure AD tenant.

Azure AD and development

How does Azure AD enter into your daily development chores? Say that you have an app that you want to protect with Azure AD. Also assume that you already have access to one Azure AD tenant. There are many different ways in which you can get to the same result: an app protected by Azure AD. The least sophisticated way goes as follows:

- Navigate to the Microsoft Azure portal, and go to the Azure AD section. Select the tenant you want to use, and then go to the Applications section. Click Add Application. That will help you add an entry for the app in Azure AD. Like the corresponding step in the case of ADFS, this step is not optional. Those instructions might change as the service evolves, but the intent remains the same.

- Add to the app support for your protocol of choice (among the ones Azure AD supports), and configure the app with the protocol coordinates indicating your Azure AD tenant and your app entry in it.

I say this is the "least sophisticated" way because it forces you to do all the steps by hand. There are speedier ways, the Visual Studio wizard you encountered in Chapter 1 being one of them. However, it's useful to remember that behind the scenes, this is what always has to happen for every application.

Azure AD tokens are Microsoft cloud services' currency

Accessing custom applications is not the only reason for requesting Azure AD tokens. Services such as the Azure management API, Office 365 API, and Intune API all trust Azure AD: if you want to invoke any of those APIs, you have to obtain an Azure AD token first.

Getting Azure Active Directory

Getting an Azure Active Directory tenant is very easy. Chances are that you already have one and you don't even know yet!

At the time of writing, there are three main ways of obtaining an Azure Active Directory tenant.

Important Below I state that Azure AD "developer features" are free to use. That's a pretty broad definition written at a specific point in time. To know for sure what is and isn't covered by the free offering, please check out the latest pricing documentation at *http://azure.microsoft.com/en-us/services/active-directory/.*

- **Buy a Microsoft cloud service** When you acquire a Microsoft cloud service such as Office 365, Microsoft Azure, or Intune, you get an Azure AD tenant in the so-called Azure AD Free tier as part of the deal. Such services need an underlying directory to deliver the functionality they are meant to perform, hence there's not a lot of choice in the matter. Whether you use that directory exclusively as a piece of infrastructure for the services you purchased, or if you also make use of it for protecting applications you develop, is of course completely up to you. Again, as is the case today, *all development features offered by Azure AD are free to use.* There are some (very generous) usage thresholds, and there's no enforced service-level agreement, but in practice you'll find that the reliability and performance you get is far superior to many (most?) on-premises systems.

  And here's a small note: when you already have an Azure AD tenant, you can subscribe to new services that leverage that tenant. The act of activating a service subscription does not necessarily mean creating a new tenant; it just requires the existence of one tenant, and if one is already available, that's great as well.

- **Create new directory tenants as part of your Microsoft Azure subscription** Creating a new Azure AD Free tier tenant is as easy as opening the Azure portal, navigating to the Directory section, and clicking a button that says Add. In mere seconds, you'll get a full-featured directory that you can use for whatever purpose you decide: managing user populations, as a development or staging environment, and so on. Considering that you can get a free trial of Microsoft Azure and that Azure AD development features are free, that is a pretty sweet deal.

- **Buy an Azure AD edition through an Enterprise Agreement** This is one way in which large companies get Microsoft software. You can also get one via a reseller.

In this book I almost always use the Azure AD Free tier, given that practically all authentication features used in development are available with it. Azure AD comes in two other editions: Azure AD Basic and Azure AD Premium, which offer SLAs, superior administrative features (such as multifactor authentication and reporting), and much more. Those are offerings you pay for, so they are available through the last two channels I mentioned.

Directories, tenants, domains. What should I call this thing?

Blogs, articles, and even official documentation can't seem to agree on a definitive term for indicating what one should call "the thing that you get when you subscribe to Azure AD." The challenge here is that all the candidates are already overloaded terms and often have a firm meaning in the on-premises world that only partially holds in the cloud case. I am personally a fan of "tenant," not because it is especially apt, but thanks to the fact that it carries less baggage.

Saying "directory" is odd for concordance reasons: the name of the service itself is Azure Active Directory, hence calling a part of it a directory is weird—even ignoring the potential for confusion with on-premises directories that might be involved in the federated case.

Saying "domain" is also problematic: every tenant must have at least one domain, which is why it is assigned one at creation time (the famous something.onmicrosoft.com). Seeing two phenomena always occurring at the same time might lead you to believe that they are one and the same. But correlation is not causation! After creation, you can register in your tenant any extra domains you own. Cases in which a tenant has hundreds of domains are not unheard of.

But "tenant" is not perfect. For example, if you are writing a multitenant application, "tenant" is polysemic. Sometimes it means your customer, a tenant of your application, and sometimes it means your own tenant in Azure AD, the artifact in which you developed and published your Azure AD app entry. But the multitenant case is somewhat advanced and comes into play when you are already partially familiar with Azure AD basics. Thus, it is more likely that you'll be able to deal with those subtleties at that point—or at least that's what I am counting on.

Azure AD for developers: Components

In this section I'll enumerate the main functional components of Azure AD that you, as a developer, will have to touch or otherwise leverage while building and running your apps. At the cost of being pedantic, I'll stress that at this level I am only introducing those artifacts and associated terminology. The features mentioned in this section are the ones you'll need hands-on experience with—experience that you will gain in the later chapters of the book.

Protocol endpoints

The most tangible manifestation of your Azure AD tenant from an app's standpoint is the endpoints it exposes. Every Azure AD tenant comes into existence with a comprehensive collection of tenant-specific endpoints. Those are the network-addressable endpoints that apps trusting your tenant need to engage with to complete the protocol dance of choice.

As discussed earlier, when you get a new tenant, you are assigned a default domain, commonly of the form of *tenantname.onmicrosoft.com*. The tenant also receives a unique, immutable, nonreassignable identifier, called *tenantID*, in the form of a GUID. The default domain, any domains you add afterward, and the tenantID itself are used to generate protocol URLs that are specific to your tenant. Using <tenant> to indicate any of those identifiers, a protocol URL template looks like the following:

```
https://<instance>/<tenant>/<protocol-specific-path>
```

To make a practical example: here are three equivalent ways of indicating the OAuth2 authorization endpoint of one of my tenants:

```
https://login.microsoftonline.com/9fc82e9f-7e34-4522-9146-cb065e1d0046/oauth2/authorize
```

```
https://login.microsoftonline.com/vittoriobertocci.onmicrosoft.com/oauth2/authorize
```

```
https://login.microsoftonline.com/cloudidentity.net/oauth2/authorize
```

These are all equivalent because even though they use different identifiers, they all refer to the same tenant. There are tradeoffs. The domain-based identifiers are easier to remember but aren't set in stone: I might not renew my custom domain cloudidentity.net, and eventually somebody else might reclaim it for their own tenant. The URL based on the tenantID is the most reliable, but it is not the easiest to type from memory or to recognize while you scan the config files of an old project.

The "login.microsoftonline.com" portion of the URL goes under the name of "instance." That represents the Azure AD service deployment in which your tenant is provisioned. If you are working in a Western country, in the large majority of cases you will see "login.microsoftonline.com" (or its predecessor, "login.windows.net"), which represents the public cloud instance of Azure AD. There are other deployments: for example, in China, the Azure AD instance is indicated by "login.partner.microsoftonline.cn". Azure AD instances are isolated from each other and operate in complete independence.

You'll get to know the OAuth2 (hence OpenID Connect) endpoints very well. The other ones (SAML sign-on and sign-out, WS-Federation, and metadata for both) won't be covered in any details because those protocols aren't the focus of this book. However, you should have no difficulty leveraging them: they are just standard implementations.

Azure portal

Today, the main user experience for getting settings into and out of your Azure AD tenant is the Azure management portal (https://manage.windowsazure.com/). This might, and likely will, change in the future, but wherever the component itself is hosted, the function it performs will remain available.

Today's Azure AD portal extension offers features for both developers and administrators. From a developer's perspective, the main reason you use the portal is to provision new apps, tweak the settings of apps in development, and manage apps that are further along in their life cycle.

Admin operations you might catch yourself performing have to do with creating test users and groups, creating brand-new tenants for development and staging, assigning users and groups to app roles, and so on.

Application model

Azure Active Directory represents applications following a specific model designed to fulfill two main functions:

- **Identify the application in terms of the authentication protocols it supports**   In practice, this means enumerating all the identifiers, URLs, secrets, and similar information that play a role at authentication time. In this, Azure AD is quite similar to ADFS—at least in terms of intent.

- **Handle user consent at token-request time, and facilitate the dynamic provisioning of applications across tenants**   In practice, when a user requests a token for a given application and no one has told Azure AD yet that it is okay to issue a token in that context, Azure AD will ask the user to consent to the operation. If the consent is successful, the decision will be recorded so that the next time the token will be issued right away. There's more! If the application was originally defined in a different tenant, perhaps by an ISV, Azure AD takes care of creating one entry for the app in the user's tenant, automating a provisioning operation that on other systems (think of ADFS) would have required administrative involvement and action.

These two functions shape the way in which Azure AD models applications and the relationships tying them to one another. The application model does more than that, but I don't want to go too much into the details before you are in the position of actually using those features in practice. Chapter 8 will describe the Azure AD application model in great detail.

Directory Graph API

The previously mentioned Graph API is the programmatic interface of Azure AD. This is an OData3-compliant set of entities that you can use to manipulate nearly all aspects of your Azure AD tenant: users, groups, and applications are the ones you will most often deal with. Like all the other endpoints discussed so far, the Graph API is exposed through a tenant-specific endpoint of the form https://<instance>. You can access the API by using good old REST, or you can use the client libraries that Microsoft provides. In both cases, calls are authorized through OAuth2 bearer tokens issued by the same Azure AD tenant. Chapter 9, "Consuming and exposing a web API protected by Azure Active Directory," will provide some practical examples demonstrating how to invoke the Graph API.

Notable nondeveloper features

Just like AD, Azure AD is, first of all, a directory. As such, most of its surface is really meant to be used by administrators: developers are mostly along for the ride.

Here I review a selection of interesting features that aren't directly actionable for you but can influence in one way or another the behavior of your apps or create expectations about what your apps can or can't do.

Directory sync

Earlier I mentioned that an Azure AD tenant can be either standalone and cloud-only or be a projection of an on-premises AD deployment. How does such projection work?

Simple. On a local machine, the administrator installs a tool that takes care of synchronizing users and groups to the Azure AD tenant in the cloud. As I write this, the recommended tool for performing this function is Azure Active Directory Connect. Before Azure Active Directory Connect, a progression of different tools was used to perform that function: the Azure Active Directory Synchronization Tool (DirSync), the Azure Active Directory Synchronization Services (Azure AD Sync), and even the familiar Forefront Identity Manager 2010 R2 (FIM). I mention them all here in case you stumble onto them in the literature. Azure Active Directory Connect supersedes them all.

Now, how that synchronization takes place is a fascinating subject. Administrators can elect to synchronize from single or multiple forests, consider or ignore custom attributes, filter depending on specific values, and so on. Beyond the Free tier feature set, other editions add advanced features such as the ability to write back into the on-premises directory changes that occurred on the cloud data set. I personally try to stay away from admins when they set these things up, coming back into the picture when things are ready to consume my apps.

The most important aspect of a sync deployment that a developer should know is whether it includes the users' credentials or relies on federation. An administrator can elect to sync users but keep all credentials-verification operations on-premises. This is achieved by federating the Azure AD endpoints of a given tenant with an ADFS deployment on the corresponding on-premises AD. Applications trusting a tenant configured that way will send sign-in requests to Azure AD endpoints as usual, but Azure AD will bounce those requests to the local ADFS. A successful authentication will yield an ADFS-issued token, which will be forwarded to Azure AD and exchanged for the usual Azure AD token. This arrangement decouples the app from the tenant settings—it's always an Azure AD token no matter who checks credentials—which leaves admins free to pursue whatever policy they prefer.

Tenants configured as I've just described are often referred to as *federated tenants* (tenants configured to operate exclusively in the cloud are known as *managed tenants*). Federated tenants have the advantage of immediately reflecting in the system on-premises changes: if a user is deprovisioned on-premises, he won't be able to sign in anymore right away. This won't rely on a timely sync. Moreover, federated tenants preserve in the authentication process whatever customization an ADFS deployment might have. This topology does have some disadvantages: it requires an ADFS deployment, which not everybody has, and its SLA is tied to the SLA of the same ADFS, so if ADFS is down, no one can access apps even if Azure AD and the apps themselves are up.

For that reason, admins can decide to also sync credentials to the cloud. In that case, users can get an Azure AD token by entering their credentials directly in the pages served by cloud endpoints, guaranteeing service continuity even in the case of downtime of the on-premises systems.

Application access enhancements

This feature is often confused with the Azure AD developer capabilities you've learned about so far.

Azure AD maintains a list of popular SaaS and consumer web apps that are integrated with the directory out of the box. This means that one administrator can offer to his or her users the chance to access those applications directly through their Azure AD accounts—without needing to memorize extra credentials or worry about application provisioning. At the same time, this allows the administrator to exercise control over what applications can be accessed, in what terms, and by whom. It even allows provisioning of users in the app so that the app's life cycle can be tied to the user account in the directory—and automatically deprovisioned when the user leaves the company, along with his main account. Admins can set all this up by using the Azure portal. Users have a dedicated landing page (myapps.microsoft.com) where they can discover and reach all the apps they have been granted access to.

Note that Azure AD–app integration is not necessarily (in fact, it usually isn't) based on federation protocols such as the ones you encountered in Chapter 2. In this scenario, Azure AD works behind the scenes doing whatever it takes to talk to those applications in their own terms. For example, in many cases Azure AD uses a browser plug-in to perform just-in-time injection of credentials as soon as the app's login form appears. Some apps will indeed use federation for integrating with Azure AD— Salesforce being a good example of that—in which case the admin setup experience for the app will be different. The user is none the wiser, of course: the experience is "I browse to the app I want, and then I am signed in." How that happens doesn't really matter.

This is a pretty awesome administrative feature, but it is not very actionable for developers. The code to perform that magic is part of Azure AD itself rather than an extensibility point one can latch on to.

Beyond the Free tier

Azure AD Basic and Azure AD Premium add lots of advanced admin features: advanced reporting, more sophisticated synchronization options, many more self-service features for users, and so on. Some of those features will have an impact on the apps you write. For example, in those tiers an admin will be able to customize the pages used for gathering credentials and consent to reflect a specific corporate look and feel or specific policies. Those pages are the ones that are used in your apps, too. Another good example is the suite of multifactor authentication features: those don't really change the way in which you write your apps—that's one of the advantages of claims-based identity, in fact—but they do change the experience of your app's users.

Another notable feature in those tiers is the Application Proxy. In a nutshell, this feature allows admins to expose intranet apps to be consumed by clients running outside the network—all protected by Azure AD. Application Proxy is notable because it offers an infrastructural alternative to using claims-based identity to cross a boundary, and this comes in handy when you are working with legacy apps whose source has been lost or is as brittle as a reliquary. The use of the Application Proxy solves the issue without having to touch the code.

I should again warn you that Azure AD adds features at a crazy pace, so now that you have this book in your hands, I am sure this list will already be incomplete. But I hope this will be enough to give you at least an idea of the kinds of features you should keep an eye out for so that you don't risk diving headfirst into implementing custom features at the app level if they are already present out of the box.

Summary

In this chapter I introduced the sources of user identities that we'll be working with, ADFS and Azure AD. For the most part, both authority types share the same goals, but the way in which they pursue those goals varies according to the workloads they were designed to support: on-premises direct federation for ADFS, multiorganization identity as a service for Azure AD.

This chapter touched on many features you'll never see mentioned again in this book, notably all the admin features that can influence the behavior of your apps but that are usually managed by an administrator. All the other features introduced here are instead meant to be directly exercised during the app development life cycle. Later chapters will revisit them, complementing the information you learned here with hands-on examples.

CHAPTER 4

Introducing the identity developer libraries

In this chapter you'll become acquainted with the collection of developer libraries maintained by the Azure Active Directory team. These libraries are meant to help you take advantage of claims-based identity, and specifically Active Directory, in your applications.

I'll begin by identifying the tasks that, if you coded them from scratch, would require a great deal of in-depth knowledge of authentication protocols. Those tasks are the best candidates to be packaged in reusable libraries.

I will proceed from there to enumerate the developer libraries that the AD team offers as of spring 2015, outlining their intended use. The list includes libraries that you'll use throughout the book and ones that you won't touch again.

Finally, I'll describe some Visual Studio features meant to enable identity workloads in your apps that under the hood take advantage of the same libraries.

Token requestors and resource protectors

If you think back to the discussion of protocols in Chapter 2, "Identity protocols and application types," you might realize that in terms of identity tasks, all apps can be classified by using two coarse roles: applications that need to securely access resources, and applications that play the role of the resource itself.

Those two categories don't really have official names. The need for a taxonomy arises somewhat artificially by the fact that I am writing a chapter about libraries meant to help applications fulfill such roles, and highlighting that fact makes it easier for me to talk about the big picture. Normally, you just use those libraries to accomplish the task at hand without thinking all that much about whether the library as a whole fits a specific role. But for the sake of classification, I'll use the monikers *token requestors* and *resource protectors*. I do not foresee using those terms much outside this chapter.

Token requestors

The token-requestor category includes all the applications that act as the client for some remote resource—think of Outlook consuming an Exchange API, a web application querying the directory for a listing of all the reports of the currently signed-in user, a Twitter native client sending a new tweet to be published, and so on.

All those client-resource interactions have to be secured with a token, which must be acquired, used, and presumably stored. More specifically, what logic do you have to add to your application to have it act as a client when it's accessing an Active Directory–protected resource? The following list summarizes the logic you need, and Figure 4-1 illustrates the concepts.

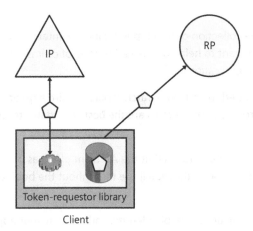

Client

FIGURE 4-1 The key responsibilities of a library enabling an app to play the token-requestor role. From the top, in counterclockwise order: acquire tokens, store them and manage session-related tasks, and attach them to requests.

■ **Token acquisition** Your app needs to request a token from AD. That entails crafting a request in the correct format for the chosen protocol and specifying all the entities involved: the client application, the target resource, which directory should be used, and so on. If the authentication process for your kind of client app requires the display of user experience (UX) elements, you need to take care of that aspect as well. And, of course, you need to find the token within a response or handle and interpret errors that might have prevented a successful issuance operation.

■ **Token inclusion in requests whenever the client accesses a resource** Inclusion has to take place in accordance with whatever protocol the resource supports, which might or might not be the same as the protocol used for acquiring the token. Note that this entails selecting the right token for the resource if the client uses more than one.

■ **Session management and token caching** Acquiring a token anew every time the app needs to access a resource would be unfeasible for performance and usability reasons. You would not want to prompt the user for his or her credentials multiple times. This means that you need logic for storing tokens and for retrieving them when you need them. In fact, this task is even more complicated. As you will see in detail later, protocols such as OAuth2 include special mechanisms for renewing access tokens without prompting the user again, and such mechanisms require explicit implementation of renewal operations, which go beyond the simple act of storing away access tokens for later use.

Why libraries?

Technically, it is perfectly possible to code all of these token-requestor tasks directly in your application. That is the case especially for OAuth2 and OpenID Connect because their crypto-graphic and message-exchange requirements are relatively easy. However, unless some special circumstances exist (for example, you need to write an app on a development stack that does not offer any library for the protocol of choice), you will rarely want to do that.

- All of the token-requestor tasks, and the ones listed in the next section, remain largely unchanged across applications. Rewriting the same logic from scratch every time does not make sense, and using a library is a great way to avoid that.

- Writing custom security code is dangerous. It requires you to have deep knowledge of the protocols involved and to operate at a low level. Knowing how the protocol solves your specific scenario is not enough; you also need to be cognizant of the many possible threats the protocol can suffer from and include appropriate mitigations in your code. Given that authentication is on the critical path to accessing precious resources, a bug can be very costly. Libraries aren't perfect, but they are usually written by domain experts, and they offer you a programming model that's much simpler than tackling things at the protocol level. Their large circulation ensures that lots of bugs are identified and weeded out quickly.

- Writing custom security code is not fun. It takes a very special mindset to enjoy menial and repetitive tasks, obscure cryptographic references, absurdly fine-grained nitpicking, and outlandish what-if attack scenarios—all part of the daily diet of the people writing identity libraries.

In a nutshell, that's why the AD team pours so much effort into offering identity libraries for development, and on as many platforms as it can. Doing so just makes a lot of sense. All these tasks are fully dependent on the specific protocols used to acquire and use tokens: those determine message formats, sequences, the artifacts used to shuffle things around, and the like. Of course, they are also largely dependent on the development stack that's used. Every platform will have its own calling pattern, its own storage model for persisting data, its own ways of performing HTTP requests.

I want to give you a heads-up here. The identity libraries for token requestors offered for Active Directory help you with the first and third tasks (token acquisition and session management) but not the second (token inclusion in requests). The main reason is that resources often offer client libraries of their own, and if AD offered an identity library for consuming resources, you'd be confronted with a difficult choice: use the AD classes or the client libraries of your target resource. In the time frame of the Windows Communication Foundation, Microsoft chose to offer specialized channels and learned a painful lesson. In this generation of its libraries, the AD team helps you acquire and maintain tokens, but it stays out of the way of any operation using tokens.

Note The only exception at this time is ADAL JS. In that case, the AD team knows how resources are going to be consumed, hence that library can efficiently inject tokens in the process.

Access tokens are opaque for token requestors

The relationship that a token requestor has to an access token is a frequent source of serious issues, so I feel it's wise to point your attention to the problem early on. When a client requests a token for a target resource, it does so for the purpose of accessing that resource. What goes into the token and the format in which it is encoded is a contract between the resource itself and the IdP: *the client is not part of that contract* and is not supposed to attempt parsing the access token.

Between two requests that look exactly alike from a client's standpoint, the IdP might decide to start sending different data or to change the token format. If your client code has a dependency on the content of the access token, those changes will likely break it, forcing you to discover why, fix the issue, and worst of all, redistribute updated bits to all clients. Note that some of those changes might actually make it impossible for your client to peek into the access token. If the IdP starts encrypting tokens, for example, only the resources will be able to open them. An architecture that relies on the client being able to read such tokens would be irredeemably broken by such a change. Bottom line: resist the temptation of peeking inside access tokens on the client.

Note Client is, unfortunately, an overloaded term. In the context of identity matters, a client is usually a token-requestor application. But in general IT parlance, a client is a workstation—or, in general, a device meant to be directly operated by a user. That is the antonym of a server, a machine meant to serve content back to remote consumers.

When the discussion is about a client app running on a client machine, there is little chance for confusion. Common cases are a rich client app running on a desktop and a native app running on a tablet or a phone. The discussion becomes trickier when you have a client application running on a server computer, like the middle tier of one distributed app accessing a remote resource, hence playing the role of the token requestor.

No matter what magic terminology guidance I come up with, I guarantee that the conversation will eventually lead to the use of the word "client" to indicate both the app's role and the machine. It will be up to you to always be sure that you understand each time which meaning the term *client* refers to.

Resource protectors

Think of any piece of software that can be consumed by a remote client: web applications serving UX elements to a browser, a web API consumed by mobile apps or server processes, and so on. If you want to restrict access to those resources, you need some component that enforces the necessary checks whenever a request is made.

To learn what tasks are necessary for protecting a resource, all you need to do is leaf back a few pages to the section "Claims-oriented protocols" in Chapter 2. There you will find a list of the steps that need to happen for an app to authenticate an incoming request. You can read the complete description there: for convenience, I'll repeat the highlights here:

- The resource app reads an IdP's metadata to configure itself.

- In web apps, in the event of an unauthenticated request, the app must generate a sign-in message and send it to the IdP of choice.

  In a web API, the resource does not (usually) actively involve itself in the token-acquisition process; rather, it relies on the client to act as a token requestor before attempting access to the resource.

- The client sends the token to the resource app. The resource finds the token in the incoming message, extracts it, and attempts validation.

- In web apps, the resource app marks a successful token validation with the creation of a session—for example, by issuing a cookie.

- Every request carrying the session cookie must also be validated. If the cookie represents a valid session, the request is considered authenticated.

These tasks are illustrated in Figure 4-2. The library is represented as middleware in the diagram—a rectangle that intercepts and filters requests to the relying party (RP), which is represented by the circle. The tasks performed by the library are, from top to bottom: interception of requests and enforcement of the protocol implemented (for example, intercepting unauthenticated requests and responding with a sign-in message to the IdP of choice); validation of tokens; emission of session artifacts (such as cookies); and session validation. Figure 4-2 also shows a store for holding the protocol coordinates defining the desired behavior—for example, the trusted identity provider, the application IDs, and so on.

That's quite a few tasks. Moreover, some of these tasks are quite complicated: token validation requires cryptographic logic, sign-in request generation requires the use of techniques that prevent numerous attacks—techniques that can become quite intricate at times. The reasons for using a library instead of coding all of these tasks into your apps from scratch are generally the same as the ones listed in the previous section.

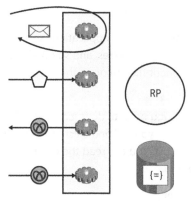

FIGURE 4-2 The responsibilities of a library providing resource-protector functionality.

Whereas you might be required to use token-requestor logic at almost any point during your app's activities, the instant in which you need to apply resource-protection logic is very well defined: it has to happen at resource access time, of course. That marks an important difference between the two libraries' roles. Although a library implementing token-requestor tasks will offer you primitives that you can access from your code at any time, resource protectors will tend to be packaged as interceptors—software that sits between the requestor and the resource the protectors are meant to protect (hence the use of the term *middleware*) and triggers automatically when a request arrives. That has advantages: your code does not have to change as much, you usually just need to opt in for the portions of the resource you want to protect, and the protection will happen automatically. It also carries its own challenges, however: the need for the middleware to latch on to an existing request-processing pipeline makes it heavily dependent on the development stack of choice.

Hybrids

Very commonly, a web application plays both the role of the protected resource and of the token requestor. The classic example of this I can think of is Twitter. Twitter has protected resources of its own, like the web API you use for publishing new tweets. On the other hand, if you associate your Facebook account with Twitter, any new tweet will also appear as a status update on your Facebook timeline. That means that the body of the Twitter web API that publishes tweets must also contain token-requestor code, which is used to gain access to Facebook's API.

Most of the time, this dual behavior is achieved simply by composing different library types within the same application. There are occasions in which those combinations are frequent enough to warrant a higher degree of integration between scenarios at the library level. At those times, the line between token-requestor and resource-protector libraries becomes blurred.

The Azure AD libraries landscape

The Active Directory team wants to make it as easy as possible for you to take advantage of AD from your applications. One of the ways the team tries to do that is by offering you a comprehensive set of developer libraries that can help you with your token-requestor and resource-protection tasks, on as many platforms and development stacks as it can.

Given the number of development stacks you can target nowadays, the complete offering is an intimidating sprawl of libraries, packages, and versions, as shown in Figure 4-3.

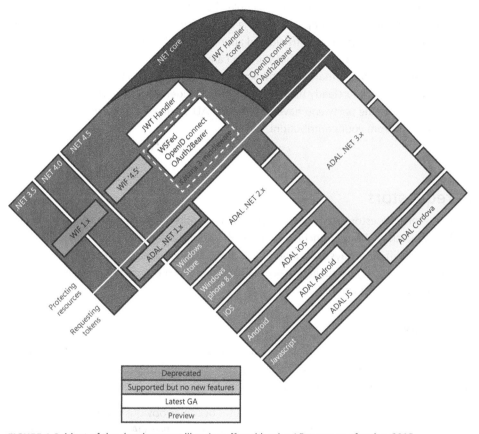

FIGURE 4-3 Most of the development libraries offered by the AD team as of spring 2015.

A slanted line partitions the diagram into two main areas, gathering together the libraries that fulfill the roles of resource protectors and token requestors. The backdrop of the diagram represents the various operating systems and development platforms targeted by the libraries. Finally, each box in the foreground stands for a particular version of a library, targeting all the platforms it overlaps.

The next section introduces each library from a functional perspective: you'll learn what libraries are for. In Chapter 5 on, you will finally start using them. Many of the libraries discussed here are meant to be used in native applications. Given that in this book I focus on web applications, such libraries won't be discussed further after this chapter. The same can be said for libraries that are now superseded by newer technologies. I mention these libraries here so that you can correctly position them if you encounter them in web searches, conversations, and specifications.

All modern AD developer libraries are open source

Back in 2013, the AD team decided that all the developer libraries it published should be open source and that its development should happen in the open. At any time, you can navigate to *https://github.com/AzureAD* and see what the team is working on. It releases binaries whenever it makes sense for the target platform. For example, the .NET libraries are regularly released in the form of fully supported NuGet packages. The availability of the source code and the opportunity to contribute to it extends the traditional approach to releases; it is not a substitute for it. The approach has several advantages, but the one I am most fond of is that it allows a level of collaboration with developers that was unthinkable before opening up the libraries. If you spent money to get this book, you clearly have a deep interest in identity and development: I warmly encourage you to join the party and have fun with the AD team—these are your libraries and can greatly benefit from your contribution!

Token requestors

Currently, the token-requestor category is composed in its entirety by instances of the ADAL (Active Directory Authentication Library) franchise. In some philosophical sense, there is only one ADAL, manifesting itself in different ways according to the characteristics of each of the targeted platforms. However, philosophy is rarely useful in practice, so I am going to present each different package and platform as a standalone deliverable.

The ADAL vision

As its name implies, ADAL is meant to help your apps act as token requestors against Active Directory, either in its on-premises or Azure flavor. The library is not designed to get tokens from any other authority type. You cannot point ADAL to Salesforce or Ping and get a token from them.

The reason for this is not immediately intuitive, but it becomes obvious if you think about it for a moment. The main protocol that teaches apps how to act as clients is OAuth2. OAuth2 leaves large areas of functionality unspecified. A library implementing only the common denominator between all existing OAuth2 providers would not be able to take care of a lot of functionality, leaving to you the burden of supplying extra logic in your apps. That logic would be necessary to bridge the gap between the theoretical OAuth2 and the reality of a provider choosing its own token formats, credential types, addresses, parameters, and refresh token strategies. I won't name names, but there are various libraries like that in the market. The only other alternative is to embed in a library an enumeration of provider-specific modules implementing the quirks and peculiarities of every provider. In a sense, that's what ADAL is doing, but just for Azure AD and Active Directory Federation Services (ADFS).

The goal with ADAL is to make it as easy as possible for you to obtain and use tokens from AD. As the library was being designed, the AD team realized that it would be better able to achieve that goal by letting go of the idea of a protocol library. A traditional protocol library is a library that provides artifacts representing protocol constructs in the programming language of choice, forcing you to be an expert in the use of said protocol.

The AD team decided to go for the polar opposite. ADAL is not a protocol library. ADAL provides you with primitives that are designed to help you perform the token-requestor tasks I listed earlier in the chapter, without exposing to you which protocol is actually used to make things happen. Sure, as of today, that protocol is largely OAuth2, and the AD team is not immune from the occasional abstraction leak, but the point is that you don't need to know what protocols the library uses to successfully take advantage of ADAL.

In fact, if you squint hard enough, every token acquisition in ADAL can be modeled by the first leg of the diagram in Figure 4-4.

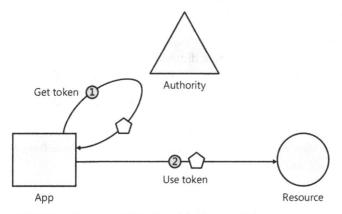

FIGURE 4-4 The main ADAL token-acquisition pattern.

The actors are all well known. There's the application that needs access, the target resource, and the authority that takes care of handling token requests. ADAL provides a primitive that implements the first leg of the diagram—a function call that accepts as input everything you know about your scenario (authority, application identifier, resource identifier, and more) and returns to you a token satisfying those constraints. Once you get it, you can use that token to access the targeted resource.

This simple pattern can be applied in a staggering number of variants. Applications might be native clients or web apps. The token might be requested acting as a user or as an application. The targeted authority might support or require different protocols. The credential types coming into play can vary. The token requested might be already cached, or it might be obtainable without prompting the user again. And, of course, there are lots of platforms you might want to target, all with their peculiarities and limitations. The need to support such a wide range of combinations translates into quite a lot of complexity that's bottled right beneath the library's surface: support for different protocol variants, cryptography, validations, smart caching, and much more. The libraries can't always isolate you completely from complexity. For example, if your subscenario requires a certain key to function, your app does need to somehow pass those key bits in, but this approach does simplify things quite a lot.

ADAL .NET

ADAL .NET was the first library in the franchise to be released. It created the blueprint for all the others, and as of today it remains the one that supports the widest range of scenarios. That's mainly for two reasons.

First, applications written in .NET can be both desktop apps (think of Outlook, Excel, or Visual Studio itself) and web apps (ASP.NET, Web Forms, etc.). In terms of OAuth2, those are public clients and protected clients, respectively. Both support their own set of scenarios, and both sets are supported in ADAL .NET. Neither are sandboxed in app stores of any kind.

Second, applications written in .NET historically run on Windows, which means that apps can take advantage of special infrastructure features (such as integrated authentication) and need special logic to do so (for example, current machine domain-join detection).

You can find the ADAL .NET source in the GitHub repo *https://github.com/AzureAD/ azure-activedirectory-library-for-dotnet*. The library itself is distributed as a NuGet package. You can find its entry at *https://www.nuget.org/packages/Microsoft.IdentityModel.Clients.ActiveDirectory/*.

As I write this chapter, the AD team has worked through three major versions of ADAL .NET.

ADAL .NET version 1.x The first version of ADAL .NET was released in September 2013, in the form of a NuGet package. That version is based on .NET 4.0, and it supports obtaining tokens from Azure AD, ADFS in Windows Server 2012 R2, and the Access Control Service 2 (ACS).

What is (was) the Access Control Service (ACS)?

The Access Control Service, ACS for short, is (was) the first Azure offering in the identity space. In a nutshell, ACS is a Security Token Service (STS) designed to sit between your applications (mostly web) and the IdPs you want to work with: ADFS, Google, Facebook, and Yahoo! were among the choices. ACS decouples your app from the different protocol requirements that each IdP has: your app only accepts tokens from ACS, hence it only needs to work with the protocol that ACS supports (mostly WS-Federation). As part of the process of issuing such tokens, ACS takes care of authenticating the user against the IdPs you want to work with, without exposing any of those details to your apps.

ACS was a breakthrough product when it first came out, and its features are still super useful today. However, it was kind of a local maxima, with some intrinsic limitations (no georeplication, no disaster recovery) that did not fit well when Azure AD came to be. As a result, ACS as a service is being discontinued, but (most) of its features will resurface as part of Azure AD. Given the current estimates, I don't believe that those new features will emerge fast enough for me to be able to describe them in this book. But I wanted to at least give you a heads-up about this, as I guarantee that sooner or later ACS will come up in your conversations.

ADAL .NET version 1 was a release meant mostly to enable the development of .NET native clients on Windows desktop. It offers mechanisms for acquiring tokens by displaying a browser dialog for the authentication and consent experience. It has a customizable token cache that automates session management and greatly reduces the number of times it is necessary to prompt users for credentials.

ADAL .NET v1 also helps with some flows more typically found on the server side, such as the client-credential and the confidential-client authorization-code grant. Those flows are somewhat limited in the version 1 release, as they don't use the cache (which is not designed to operate at web scale in version 1), and they work only against Azure AD authorities.

The main reasons you might consider using ADAL v1 these days are platform constraints (your app cannot be moved to .NET 4.5.x) or if you are still using ACS.

ADAL .NET version 2.x　ADAL .NET v2 was released in September 2014. Currently, version 2.x is the latest stable, production-ready release.

The new version brought a very significant expansion in scope. The changes can be summarized as follows:

- Multitargeting NuGet. ADAL .NET v2 goes beyond .NET, supporting multiple platforms:

    - Any .NET 4.5+ project, desktop or web

    - Windows Store projects for tablets/PCs in any Windows Store language, from Windows 8 onward

    - Windows Store projects for Windows Phone 8.1

    - Windows Silverlight projects for Windows Phone 8.1

- Out-of-the-box persistent cache for all project types targeting a sandboxed app's platform (Windows Store, Windows Phone)

- Moving from .NET 4.0 to .NET 4.5.x, and the introduction of async primitives

- Discontinuation of the ACS 2 support in ADAL

- New authentication flows

    - Direct use of username-password credentials for .NET native clients

    - Windows Integrated Authentication (WIA) for federated tenants and .NET native clients

    - On behalf of—a new flow allowing the user identity to flow through tiers (for example, user1 calling service1, which in turn calls service2 on behalf of user1)

- Better support for middle-tier workloads. ADAL .NET v2 is more server-side friendly. A newly redesigned cache makes it easier to meet the demands of web-scale scenarios, and all the primitives are aimed at grants more typically used on the server side.

All the Windows Store libraries for Windows and Windows Store in ADAL 2.x are compiled as Windows Runtime Components (extension .winmd). This allows you to write apps using any of the languages Windows Store supports—C#, JavaScript, and C++. In fact, all the samples the AD team provides are in C#, so targeting the other platforms might not be as easy, but it is definitely possible.

ADAL .NET 2.x ships in a large number of Microsoft products and is used in almost all Azure services that need tokens for accessing Azure AD–protected resources.

ADAL .NET version 3.x   Currently, the AD team is working on the third refresh of the preview of ADAL .NET v3. ADAL .NET v3 expands its reach further by adding support for more platforms. From this version on you can use ADAL for writing multitarget applications with Xamarin: namely, you can write C# apps and deploy them on iOS and Android devices. Furthermore, ADAL .NET v3 adds support for the brand-new .NET core.

ADAL .NET v3 drops support for Windows Phone Silverlight and discontinues the use of winMD files. As a result, you no longer can use ADAL .NET in JavaScript apps. You can, however, use the ADAL JavaScript versions described later in the chapter.

ADAL .NET and this book   This book focuses on the development of web applications, in particular on the .NET platform. Whenever the scenarios described require the app to act as a client, I will use ADAL .NET to implement the tasks that role entails.

The ADAL features used for requesting and handling access tokens from the server portion of a web application are a small subset of all the things that ADAL .NET can do. For more details on ADAL and native clients, please refer to the product documentation. Moreover, I blog about this topic quite often at *www.cloudidentity.com*. I hope to eventually follow up this book with a second on native clients, but the documentation and samples should be more than enough to get you going.

ADAL libraries targeting native apps–only platforms

Many of the most interesting development platforms can run only native applications. Examples include all mobile operating systems: iOS, Android, and Windows Phone. That holds for both native development stacks (Objective-C and Java apps for iOS and Android, respectively) and multitarget stacks (such as Cordova). The AD team maintains a number of ADAL libraries that target such platforms. I won't discuss any of these libraries in detail, but I want to be sure you are aware of them.

ADAL iOS and OS X   ADAL iOS is an Objective-C library designed to help you enhance your iOS and OS X apps with token-requestor capabilities. You can find it in the repo *https://github.com/AzureAD/ azure-activedirectory-library-for-objc*.

ADAL iOS follows the general ADAL franchise tenet that requires all platform-specific libraries to be good citizens of the stack they target. In this case that means that ADAL iOS, although featuring all the ADAL primitives for native clients common to all ADAL flavors, strictly follows the Objective- C naming and calling conventions you would expect in a native Objective-C library. Furthermore, it takes advantage of the platform-specific features offered by iOS. For example, all method names end with the suffix "with<FirstParameter>", tokens are persisted on the device's keychain, and so on.

ADAL Android ADAL Android is a Java library designed to help you enhance your Android apps with token-requestor capabilities. You can find it in the repo *https://github.com/AzureAD/azure-activedirectory-library-for-android.*

Pretty much everything I mentioned about ADAL iOS applies here, translated for the target platform: same primitives as all other ADALs, but coding conventions and affordances that are 100 percent native to Android.

ADAL Cordova ADAL Cordova is a framework meant to enable you to write one application in JavaScript and execute it as a native app on multiple platforms. That's the old idea of "write once, run everywhere"—historically, that did not work too well, but the conditions have never been better for making that motto a reality. You can find ADAL Cordova in the repo *https://github.com/AzureAD /azure-activedirectory-library-for-cordova.*

ADAL Cordova is a Cordova plug-in that wraps the ADAL native libraries on iOS, Android, Windows Store, and Windows Phone and exposes the main token-acquisition primitives through a JavaScript layer. The advantage of using the native libraries on each target platform—instead of implementing the token-acquisition code in JavaScript—is that this allows you to pierce the sandbox that typically isolates web apps from the client environment, and thus take advantage of device-specific features. For example, on iOS, that would give you access to the tokens stored in the keychain.

ADAL libraries targeting mostly midtier clients

Some platforms are traditionally used for developing software running on a server. You can put in that category most web frameworks: PHP, Java Server Pages (JSP), and the like.

To this point, the AD team has released two ADAL libraries targeting such platforms: one for Java (ADAL4J) and one for Node.JS. They both cover the basics well, though currently they don't offer the same exhaustive list of features you can find on the confidential client portions of ADAL .NET.

You can find ADAL4J on GitHub at *https://github.com/AzureAD/azure-activedirectory-library-for-java,* and ADAL for Node.JS at *https://github.com/AzureAD/azure-activedirectory-library-for-nodejs.*

Resource protectors

Microsoft has been in the business of offering development libraries for resource protectors much longer than it has for token requestors. That is the natural consequence of two main factors. The first lies in how natural it is to provide a resource protector—which can simply be a piece of middleware that intercepts requests without really disturbing the logic it is trying to protect—and the mission-critical nature of enforcing access restrictions to resources. The second is that the claims-based protocols were initially used mostly on web applications, where there's not much to be developed on the client (or at least that was the case before Web 2.0 and JavaScript).

For the sake of brevity, I won't dig too deeply into the history of resource-protector libraries, leaving ancient artifacts like the Web Services Enhancements (WSE) library and Windows Communication Foundation (WCF) to rest in peace. Rather, I'll cover the mainstream libraries in use today.

Windows Identity Foundation

Windows Identity Foundation (WIF) was the first developer library entirely devoted to identity tasks. WIF is a collection of classes meant to provide common language runtime (CLR) representations of protocol artifacts (WS-Federation messages, SAML tokens, session cookies, and so on) and HTTP modules meant to easily weave claims-based identity support to ASP.NET applications. For the first time, a developer could take advantage of those new protocols without having to code everything from scratch, paving the way for claims-based identity to reach the mainstream status it enjoys today. Moreover, WIF offered a rich extensibility model, which the community used to handle scenarios that were far from the basic ones, including entirely new products, such as custom STSs.

The first WIF version was an out-of-band release based on .NET 3.5. That release has special sentimental value to me, because at that time I was the identity developer evangelist at Microsoft and I finally had a toy to play with. Between 2008 and 2012, I spent a lot of time producing lots of samples, videos, hands-on labs, training events, even a book (*Programming Windows Identity Foundation*, Microsoft Press) to kick-start the claims-based identity development movement.

In 2012, clams-based identity (and the cloud scenarios it enabled) reached such an importance that Microsoft decided to take all the identity classes from WIF and embed them in the next version of the .NET Framework, 4.5. That was also the time at which I decided to join the engineering team, to contribute all the feedback I had gathered in years of evangelizing identity to developers. The process was already in flight, hence there wasn't much latitude for big changes. Those came later, with the OWIN wave that I'll introduce in the next section.

The .NET Framework 4.5 was reengineered to root all identity representations to a base class, `ClaimsPrincipal`, centered on the idea of claims. That class went all the way to mscorlib.dll, the core assembly of .NET. All other classes were scattered through various .NET namespaces. Visual Studio 2012 was extended with specific tools to facilitate the use of WIF in .NET applications.

Both versions of WIF share a common feature set and only differ in the degree of integration they offer with the .NET Framework versions they target. The most common reason for which WIF is used is to secure an ASP.NET app with WS-Federation. That is achieved by adding in the ASP.NET pipeline a series of `HttpModules` and adding to the app's config file a special section capturing the protocol coordinates of both the application and the STS it wants to trust. The developer does not need to understand any of the intricacies of the protocols and token formats, and the config file is generated automatically via tools. However, customizations and troubleshooting quickly raise the level of proficiency required to operate the library.

The WIF classes in the .NET Framework are still supported today, in the same way in which the framework itself is supported, and they are used in Visual Studio 2013 tools to this day. However, WIF is no longer the recipient of innovation, and all efforts and new features are concentrated on a new generation of libraries (described in the next section). Although WIF proved to be an excellent product—ferrying an entire generation to the claims-based identity era is no small feat—its extensibility model and configuration mechanisms were too rooted to its XML legacy. Proper modern protocols support required some backtracking and a fresh start.

OWIN middleware for .NET 4.5.x, or "Katana" 3.x

If WIF's approach is not fully suitable for implementing modern protocols, what should be used? The answer the AD team gave to that question is "OWIN."

OWIN stands for Open Web Interface for .NET. It is a community-driven specification meant to encourage the creation of highly portable HTTP processing components that can be used and reused on any web server, hosting process, or even OS—as long as .NET is available on the target platform in some capacity. This is openly in contrast with the approach that was popular when WIF was first conceived: the main HTTP processing primitive was the `HttpModule`, a construct tied to ASP.NET and Internet Information Services (IIS). OWIN sheds many other aspects of old-guard ASP.NET programming that WIF depended on. One glaring example is the web.config file—a mandatory artifact in the old ASP.NET approach rendered clunky and inadequate by the new cloud deployment technologies—which is completely optional in OWIN.

In ASP.NET 4.6 the Web tools team rewrote most of ASP.NET request processing in OWIN style. The AD development experience team decided to latch on to that initiative and package all of its resource-protector components as OWIN middlewares. I will cover all those components very thoroughly in the hands-on parts of the book. Here I just want to introduce terminology and provide a basic orientation.

The OWIN components offered by the AD team continue the tradition introduced by WIF to isolate you and your application from the details of the protocol being used. In fact, in OWIN even the identity extracted by incoming tokens is represented by a `ClaimsPrincipal`—you can keep your business logic completely unchanged, change protocol, or even switch WIF to OWIN and things should keep working as usual. What did change is the development surface exposed by the libraries. Whereas WIF was designed for a cast of administrators-developers who were rather well versed in protocol configuration, the OWIN middlewares for claims-based identity require an absolutely minimal amount of input to do their job—while gracefully increasing the sophistication that's needed as you choose to work with more advanced features.

The source code for all ASP.NET OWIN components is available under *http://katanaproject .codeplex.com/.* "Katana" is the original code name of the project. It should have been superseded by the official name, ASP.NET OWIN Components, but you can see how Katana wins hands down against that any day of the week.

The AD team contributed three assemblies to the project, available as NuGet packages:

- **Microsoft.Owin.Security.OpenIdConnect** Contains middleware for protecting web apps with OpenID Connect.

- **Microsoft.Owin.Security.WsFederation** Contains middleware for protecting web apps with WS-Federation.

- **Microsoft.Owin.Security.ActiveDirectory** Contains middleware for protecting web APIs as prescribed in the OAuth2 bearer token usage specification.

These assemblies contain the OWIN-specific logic that is necessary for implementing the protocols mentioned. There is a number of lower-level components not tied to OWIN that model protocol-specific artifacts such as messages or token formats. Those are mostly packaged in two assemblies also available on NuGet—Microsoft.IdentityModel.Protocol.Extensions and System.IdentityModel .Tokens.Jwt. We keep the source for both assemblies in *https://github.com/AzureAD/azure -activedirectory-identitymodel-extensions-for-dotnet*.

> **Important** At the time of writing, Katana 3.x is the recommended library for modeling protected resources in .NET. Unless you are dealing with special constraints, you should always consider Katana 3.x as your first choice for securing your web apps and web API on .NET with claims-based identity.

One level below: The JSON Web Token (JWT) handler

Katana 3.x depends on an assembly that predates it, what is commonly known as the .NET JWT handler (the NuGet package is at *https://www.nuget.org/packages/System.IdentityModel.Tokens.Jwt/*, and the source is at *https://github.com/AzureAD/azure-activedirectory-identitymodel-extensions-for-dotnet*).

As its name implies, the JWT handler offers classes designed to work with JWT tokens: it offers primitives to parse, validate, and manufacture them. This class has been widely used by developers who for one reason or another did not use higher-level constructs such as OWIN middlewares. If you decide to handle protocol messages yourself, you can identify a JWT token in a request and feed it to the JWT handler, and with the proper configuration, it will be able to validate it for you.

That came in very handy in the past, before OWIN middleware was even available. In fact, versions 1.x to 3.x of the JWT handler also work within the WIF request pipeline.

OWIN middleware for .NET core, or "Katana" vNext

The year 2015 brought unprecedented changes in the .NET Framework. The introduction of .NET core, a version of the .NET Framework that allows deployment scoped to individual apps, counting only the assemblies that are needed for the task at hand, marks a turning point in what it means to develop for .NET.

The ability to obtain tokens and validate incoming requests is, if possible, even more on the critical path for those new scenarios. The OWIN components mentioned earlier are being ported to the new framework, including the OpenID Connect and the OAuth2 middlewares.

> **Note** WS-Federation support requires advanced XML cryptography capabilities, which are not part of the first wave of .NET core assemblies. For that reason, WS-Federation is lagging a bit behind the other protocols.

Currently, as I write this chapter, .NET core (and the stacks that rely on it, such as ASP.NET 5) is in developer preview. I expect some important news to be added to the new middlewares, so I will cover some aspects of Katana vNext in the pages ahead.

Hybrids

Applications are often not easily classified as pure resources or pure token requestors. You have seen that in many occasions they play a bit of both roles. This is normally addressed by using more than one library in the same app: an ASP.NET web application can be protected by OpenID Connect middleware and use ADAL to acquire the access tokens it needs to use external APIs. However, there are some hybrid situations where the library itself can be seen as enabling both approaches. As of today, the collection of ADAL libraries counts only one such artifact, ADAL JS.

ADAL JS

In Chapter 2, I described single-page applications (SPA), a web application development pattern that distributes app functionality between a JavaScript front end and a web API back end. From a purely mechanical perspective, the front end in an SPA acts as a token requestor. But that said, the front end also works in a way with resources—it is natural for the developer to treat as resources the routes and views accessed by the end user, although the actual resource to protect is the web API that such routes need to access.

ADAL JS is a JavaScript library meant to help SPA developers add logic to their front ends that acquires, stores, and uses tokens for accessing web APIs, both those in its own back end and any other web API that can be called from JavaScript (via CORS or an equivalent mechanism). That falls squarely in the token-requestor camp.

The library also includes primitives for indicating that a certain route requires the use (hence the presence) of a token, making it also a sort of resource protector. Note that this is mostly a convenient model for the front-end developer: ultimately, somebody must validate the token after acquisition, and today that's done on the service side. That means that a complete SPA solution would include ADAL JS on the front end and perhaps the OWIN middleware for OAuth2 on the web API back end.

ADAL JS is also open source, of course. Source and instructions are available at *https://github.com/ AzureAD/azure-activedirectory-library-for-js*. The library proper is split into two files—a core JS file containing all the low-level primitives, and an AngularJS module that makes it extra easy to hook up identity features without disturbing the usual Angular application structure.

Visual Studio integration

Visual Studio has a rich tradition of identity-integration features, dating back to the first WIF SDK in Visual Studio 2010. In this last section I will list the identity features you are most likely to encounter while using Visual Studio to develop apps that leverage AD. I won't go back further than Visual Studio 2013.

It's worth stressing that none of the tools I discuss here are strictly necessary to successfully add AD authentication to your apps. Nowadays, cloning a sample from GitHub and doing some cutting and pasting takes you a long way. The value of Visual Studio integration lies in its ability to automate menial tasks such as app provisioning in Azure AD, the inclusion of identity libraries' NuGet packages, injection of boilerplate code, and various other activities that are not rocket science per se but can occupy your time and focus.

AD integration features in Visual Studio 2013

In the Visual Studio 2013 time frame, the collaboration between the AD and the ASP.NET teams marked an important milestone. Visual Studio 2013 shipped with a new unified ASP.NET project templates dialog, which included a section dedicated to creating new ASP.NET projects (Web Forms and MVC projects) already configured to outsource authentication to AD from the get-go. The project template instantiation includes a wizard that gathers basic info about your authentication requirements (which Azure AD tenant you want to work with, for example) and also does the following:

- Automatically provisions one entry in Azure AD for your app, customized for your project: the name derives from the project name, the URL is the one assigned by IIS express, and so on.

- Adds references to the necessary assemblies and injects config elements that point to the target tenant and the newly created app entry.

In Visual Studio 2013, the identity library used in the templates is WIF, specifically the WIF classes from .NET 4.5.x. The only exception to this is the Web API templates, which use an early version of the OWIN middleware for OAuth2 bearer token authorization.

The templates allow for few application variants, the main one being Web API (as in web apps meant to be accessed programmatically) versus Web UX (as in apps with a user interface served via a browser) and the choice of Azure AD and ADFS.

AD integration features in Visual Studio 2015

In the development of Visual Studio 2015, the level of collaboration between teams has reached a new level. Every Thursday morning since the summer of 2014, I have run a v-team meeting with participants from Visual Studio IDE, Visual Studio Online, ASP.NET, and Visual Studio tools for connected services (Azure and Office 365). Our goals are to ensure that Visual Studio 2015 minimizes the number of authentication prompts and that every feature offers a consistent identity experience by augmenting every other feature's functionalities instead of stepping on one another's metaphorical toes.

Here's a summary of the most recognizable features you'll encounter.

Visual Studio 2015 keychain

In Visual Studio 2015 you can associate directly to the IDE users from all your tenants—or, more precisely, the IDE will save the users' tokens in a persistent cache and make them available to all the other Visual Studio features when they need them. That greatly reduces the need for prompts and improves discoverability—you always know which directories you can work with.

ASP.NET templates and Azure Web Sites publishing

The ASP.NET templates in Visual Studio 2015 are entirely based on OWIN. The wizard experience has been designed to take advantage of the keychain and make it easy to select which Azure AD tenant should be used. The generated project templates follow a structure that was agreed upon across all identity features in Visual Studio so that every tool working on the same project can successfully modify it. Another improvement in Visual Studio 2015 is that any user can create applications in Azure AD, including users with a Microsoft account; in Visual Studio 2013, the identity templates are restricted to admin directory users.

Azure AD connected services

Visual Studio 2015 introduces a feature that allows you to configure Azure AD authentication for a project after creation time. The experience is very similar to the ASP.NET New Project wizard, with provisions made for a reentrant experience.

Office 365 tools

Visual Studio 2013 already features tools for adding to a Web application the ability to invoke the Office 365 API. However, the tool isn't very sophisticated. It creates the entries in Azure AD for you, but it doesn't emit the code necessary to leverage it, leaving many developers stranded. The version in Visual Studio 2015 is vastly superior, building on the Visual Studio keychain and emitting project code along the same lines as the ASP.NET and connected services features.

Summary

This chapter unfolded before you the full range of the developer libraries maintained by the AD team. Above all, it introduced the idea of token-requestor and resource-protector libraries, highlighting differences and the combined effect of the two.

Many of the libraries I've mentioned in this chapter are covered just for exhaustiveness and for preempting questions you might have about their relevance to Web application scenarios. The libraries that do not play a role in Web app development scenarios will not be mentioned again in this book.

Well, that's it for the pure theory. The remaining chapters in this book will keep telling you what goes on under the hood, but I'll always do so in the context of trying to accomplish something in code. Now the fun begins!

CHAPTER 5

Getting started with web sign-on and Active Directory

This chapter opens the hands-on portion of this book, where all the theory you've been absorbing until now will help you to be a more effective developer for identity-related tasks.

The first task I'll cover is the most common you will ever encounter: you will learn how to use Active Directory to sign in users to a web application. I will focus on the libraries required, the structure you need to use to organize your project, and the (largely boilerplate) code you need to add. I will show you how to set an entry for your application in Azure AD by using the technologies available today. Finally, I'll walk you through a test run of the project to ensure that you've achieved the results you aimed for.

Literally all of these steps can be easily automated by using the web project templates in Visual Studio 2015. I am describing how to do everything by hand because that gives you great insights about the moving parts and project structure—insights that you'll need when you find yourself troubleshooting more complex scenarios.

After the binge of theory in the first four chapters, I'll let your brain take a break . . . and avoid discussing protocol details, object model elements beyond the ones necessary for the task at hand, and the Active Directory application model. There will be time for that in the subsequent chapters.

The web app you build in this chapter

The app I want you to build in this chapter is pretty much the same app that you created in Chapter 1, "Your first Active Directory app." It's a minimal ASP.NET 4.6 web application, which makes use of Azure AD for authenticating users from an Azure AD tenant of choice. The app will also reprise details from Chapter 1 about how to access user attributes from the claims in the incoming token. Finally, you will learn how to implement basic sign-out functionality.

In Chapter 1, Visual Studio did all the heavy lifting for you, but here you will manually add all the identity logic. Furthermore, you'll explicitly provision the app in Azure AD via the Microsoft Azure portal. In this section, I outline the prerequisites and break down into functional steps the task of adding authentication logic to the app.

Prerequisites

The prerequisites here are even more relaxed than the ones you encountered in the "Prerequisites" section in Chapter 1.

You still need a Microsoft Azure subscription: please refer to the aforementioned section in Chapter 1 for details.

Here you can use any version of Visual Studio you like, from Visual Studio 2013 on. You don't need any special tooling or automation. I'm using Visual Studio Enterprise 2015, but as long as you account for small differences in the user interface, you can easily apply the same instructions in whichever version you have.

ASP.NET 4.6 vs. ASP.NET 5

I am purposely choosing to focus on ASP.NET 4.6 for all the code samples in the book. ASP.NET 5 has some awesome features, and giving them up here is not an easy choice. However, what you can do in terms of identity does not change much, hence what you'll learn here will be applicable to ASP.NET 5 with just some small adjustments in syntax and NuGet versions. Furthermore, ASP.NET 4.6 is mature, stable, and enjoys widespread adoption—and while I write this chapter, the ASP.NET 5 bits are still a moving target.

Steps

Here's the sequence of steps I'll walk you through:

1. Create a basic project as a starting point.

2. Add references to the NuGet packages you need.

3. Create the app's entry in the Azure AD tenant of choice.

4. Write the code that initializes the OWIN pipeline and the OpenID Connect middleware.

5. Add logic for triggering authentication and access claims and initiating sign-out

That should all be very straightforward.

The starting project

Your starting point is one of the simplest ASP.NET project templates, the MVC project type with no authentication. The template bits are largely unchanged from Visual Studio 2013.

Start Visual Studio, and open the New Project dialog via the File menu. (I like the keyboard shortcut Ctrl+Shift+N.)

Under Templates > Visual C# > Web, select ASP.NET Web Application. I named my project WebAppChapter5. Click OK.

Among the ASP.NET 4.6 templates, choose MVC. That done, click the Change Authentication button. In the dialog that appears, select No Authentication. Click OK here and again in the first dialog. Visual Studio mulls over what you asked for and then opens your newly created project.

The first time I use a new installation, I normally hit F5 at this point to verify that nothing is wrong with the Visual Studio setup. If you do this, you should see a rendering of the usual ASP.NET Bootstrap-based template—a basic home page with tabs for Home, About, and Contact, all corresponding to basic actions and views in the project.

Before going any further, you should set up the project to operate on HTTPS instead of the default HTTP. From the earlier chapters you know that the security in OpenID Connect is predicated on the ability to use opaque channels. Furthermore, you might encounter providers (such as Active Directory Federation Services) that will simply refuse to have anything to do with your app if they do not sit at one end of a secure HTTPS pipe.

Visual Studio and IIS Express make it super easy to set that up. In Solution Explorer, select your project. On the Properties page, you will find a property dubbed SSL Enabled, with a default value of False. Flip it to True.

Notice that the property SSL URL, previously empty, now has a local-host-based value (along the lines of https://localhost:44300/), indicating the HTTPS URL on which your app will listen. Select that value, and copy it to the Clipboard.

In Solution Explorer, right-click the project and choose Properties. Select the Web tab. In the Servers section, find the Project URL field. You'll see that it contains the old HTTP URL for the project. Replace this with the HTTPS URL you copied, save your work (press Shift+Ctrl+S), and then close the Properties page.

Press F5 again to verify that everything went as expected and that the project does indeed start on HTTPS. If this is the first time you've used HTTPS with IIS Express, you might be prompted to trust the development certificate. Doing so will make development tasks much easier, especially when it comes to web API development.

 Important This is also a great place to remind you that development should be done on machines that do not run production code or perform any critical tasks for your business. Development often calls for relaxing security constraints that would not be advisable to weaken on production iron or boxes hosting critical resources.

At this point your starting project is ready to be enhanced with Azure AD authentication capabilities.

NuGet packages references

The first step toward enabling Azure AD authentication is to add references to the libraries that will take care of implementing the resource protector functionality. As explained in Chapter 4, "Introducing the identity developer libraries," in the section "Resource protectors," you can choose from a number of OWIN middleware packages. There isn't really a fixed order to follow when adding packages: I'll follow a sequence that makes functional sense according to the features each package provides.

Open the Package Manager Console by clicking Tools > NuGet Package Manager > Package Manager Console. That done, enter the following command:

```
install-package Microsoft.Owin.Host.SystemWeb
```

We aren't in Identity Land yet. The SystemWeb package pulls down the assemblies required to host an OWIN middlewares pipeline in an ASP.NET application. At this time, the version you get is 3.0.1: the version might be higher in the future, and this holds for all the OWIN packages covered in this chapter.

The command also pulls down as a dependency Microsoft.Owin, the package containing all the OWIN base classes and primitives.

Percolating up through functionality layers, you'll add the cookie middleware next. Enter the following command:

```
install-package Microsoft.Owin.Security.Cookies
```

Recall from Chapter 3, "Introducing Azure Active Directory and Active Directory Federation Services," that most redirect-based web apps request a token only for the initial authentication and rely on a cookie-based session for all subsequent interactions. The job of the cookie middleware is to generate and track such a session. Note that the package brings down Microsoft.Owin.Security as a dependency—this is a repository of classes and primitives that constitute the building blocks of security-related middlewares.

Finally, it's time to add the package implementing OpenID Connect web sign-on. Enter the following:

```
install-package Microsoft.Owin.Security.OpenIdConnect
```

This package contains the OpenID Connect middleware proper. It pulls down as dependencies the JWT handler (System.IdentityModel.Tokens.Jwt, which you already encountered in Chapter 4) and Microsoft.IdentityModel.Protocol.Extensions, a package of classes representing OpenID Connect constructs (messages, constants, etc.). These two packages are purposely separate and distinct from the OWIN packages because they implement concepts and protocol artifacts that can come in handy even if you decide to build a stack that has no dependency on OWIN itself.

That's it. All the packages you need are onboard.

Registering the app in Azure AD

Before you do more work on the project, this is a good time to step out of Visual Studio and use the Microsoft Azure portal for provisioning the application in Azure AD.

Like creating the package references described in the previous section, this is a task that in Chapter 1 was performed automatically by Visual Studio, via an API. That is not meant to hide complexity (as you will see, the registration steps are trivial); the convenience offered by the tools lies in sparing you yet another menial task.

> **Warning** Given how frequently the portal experience goes through iterative improvements, providing screenshots here would be a sure way of confusing you if things change after the book is printed. The same level of volatility should be expected for any detailed instructions based on today's experiences. I invite you to keep an open mind as you try to reproduce the steps I describe here. The high-level goals remain the same; hence, if you grasp the intent, you should be able to adapt in case any UI elements move around and no longer match the instructions here.

As articulated in the prerequisites, you need to have an active Microsoft Azure subscription. Open a browser, navigate to *https://manage.windowsazure.com/*, and sign in with the account (organizational or Microsoft account) associated with that Azure subscription.

Once in, scroll through the leftmost list of services until you find the entry for Active Directory, and then click it.

The main area will list all the Azure AD tenants you can work on with your subscription. There are a couple of common cases:

- If you have an individual subscription rooted to a Microsoft account, you will likely find a single entry—this is the directory tenant automatically generated for you by Azure. Your current user is a global administrator in that directory. This will be the case also if you signed up for Azure on your own and chose the organizational path.

- If your Azure subscription is associated with your company, here you will likely see your company's directory tenant. Unless you work in the IT department or your company isn't big enough to justify a strong separation of roles, chances are that your current user is not an administrator in that directory. Don't worry! By default, any user can provision one app by using the steps described in this section.

It is also possible to find more than one directory tenant listed here. That's the case if you created test tenants or if your user is a guest administrator in multiple tenants.

Choose the Azure AD tenant that gathers the users you want to be able to authenticate from your app, and then click its entry. In the tabs list on the top row, choose Applications. You will be presented with the list of all the apps that are being developed within that tenant.

At the bottom of the screen, you'll find the Add button. Click it to start the provisioning of your new application.

At the time of writing, the first dialog you encounter asks whether you are adding an application you are developing or choosing a preconfigured app from the gallery. You'll want to select the first option.

The next screen prompts you to name your application. I tend to use the same name I have in the Visual Studio project, so in this case I would enter WebAppChapter5.

The same screen asks you to specify whether your app is a web app or a native client. That is an important decision, which will determine what your application can and cannot do in terms of authentication flows. A web application can be the recipient of tokens issued via redirect-based protocols like SAML and OpenID Connect, but a native client cannot do that; a web app can be assigned a secret, whereas a native client cannot be trusted to protect it; and so on. As you already guessed, we want to provision a web application here, so choose the corresponding option and click Next.

On the next screen you are asked to provide the URL of your application. Azure AD will not send tokens to URLs that aren't registered. Remember the URL you obtained earlier, in the section "The starting project," when you enabled SSL, along the lines of https://localhost:44300/? Retrieve that from Visual Studio, and paste it in the Sign-On URL field.

The next field, App ID URI, requests that you provide a unique resource identifier. That identifier is used for protocols like SAML, WS-Federation for web sign-on, and OAuth2 for a web API. You don't need this identifier for the app you're developing (given that we plan to use OpenID Connect for web sign-on), but you need to provide a value nonetheless. I won't go into the details of how to choose that value here: for your purposes it should be enough to say that you need to choose a valid URI that is unique within the tenant. A common choice is the app URL concatenated to the project name, as in https://localhost:44300/WebProjectChapter5.

Click the button that indicates the conclusion of the wizard. The portal immediately provisions a new entry for your app and selects that entry. From the top tabs row, choose Configure.

On this page you can see all of the app entry's settings, and you have the chance to modify them. For the time being, you can ignore everything else and focus on a single field, client ID. Client ID is an identifier generated by Azure AD at application-provisioning time. It is used to identify this app to Azure AD in the context of an OpenID Connect authentication transaction so that the authentication flow can unfold as configured. For example, tokens issued for the app with this client ID will be delivered to the sign-on URL specified at the time the app was provisioned.

You need to plug the client ID value into the configuration of the OpenID Connect middleware in your app so that it can be used at the appropriate time when the middleware generates and processes protocol messages. Keep the browser open on this page because you will need it for the steps in the next section.

OpenID Connect initialization code

Let's get back to the app's code. To enable the app to make use of OpenID Connect, you need to perform two small tasks:

- Add an OWIN pipeline in front of the app.

- Add and initialize the appropriate middlewares in the pipeline.

As you know by now, this is normally done for you by Visual Studio. I am walking you through a manual process so that you can understand what makes the scenario tick.

Host the OWIN pipeline

Like many other things in the ASP.NET world, OWIN pipeline initialization relies on naming conventions. You will add the initialization logic in a .cs file, called Startup.cs, at the root of the project.

In Project Explorer, right-click the project, choose Add New Item, select the Web node in the list at the left, and scroll through the various item types until you find the entry for OWIN Startup class. Select it, be sure you change the proposed file name to Startup.cs, and then click Add.

Visual Studio opens the new file for you. Edit the class declaration to include a `partial` keyword, as you have to complement it soon. The resulting file should look like the following:

```
using System;
using System.Threading.Tasks;
using Microsoft.Owin;
using Owin;
[assembly: OwinStartup(typeof(WebAppChapter5.Startup))]
namespace WebAppChapter5
{
    public partial class Startup
    {
        public void Configuration(IAppBuilder app)
        {
            // For more information on how to configure your application, visit http://
go.microsoft.com/fwlink/?LinkID=316888
        }
    }
}
```

In Chapter 7, "The OWIN OpenID Connect middleware," you'll learn how the OWIN pipeline works in detail. Here it suffices to say that the `OwinStartup` attribute causes the `Configuration` method to be invoked at assembly load time—that is to say, when the app first wakes up. That means that you can use that method to run all the initialization code you need.

Technically, you could just add the code for initializing the identity protocols middleware in line here, in `Configuration`. However, it's traditional in ASP.NET 4.6 to include the initialization code for each functional area in a separate file and to invoke it from the OWIN Startup class.

Initialize the cookie and OpenID Connect middlewares

Let's add the identity pipeline init code in its own file. In Solution Explorer, right-click the App_Start folder and choose Add New Item > Class. Name the file Startup.Auth.cs.

Replace all the using directives with the following:

```
using Owin;
using Microsoft.Owin.Security;
using Microsoft.Owin.Security.Cookies;
using Microsoft.Owin.Security.OpenIdConnect;
```

Get rid of the trailing .Startup from the namespace:

```
namespace WebAppChapter5
```

Change the class declaration to public and partial:

```
public partial class Startup
```

Finally, you get to the identity-initialization code. Add to the Startup class the method shown here:

```
public void ConfigureAuth(IAppBuilder app)
{
    app.SetDefaultSignInAsAuthenticationType(CookieAuthenticationDefaults.AuthenticationType);
    app.UseCookieAuthentication(new CookieAuthenticationOptions());
    app.UseOpenIdConnectAuthentication(
        new OpenIdConnectAuthenticationOptions
        {
            ClientId = "c3d5b1ad-ae77-49ac-8a86-dd39a2f91081",
            Authority = "https://login.microsoftonline.com/DeveloperTenant.onmicrosoft.com"
        }
    );
}
```

Those 10 lines of code (barely) are enough to initialize the entire OpenID Connect pipeline. The best part is that they are almost pure boilerplate.

As I mentioned, Chapter 7 will delve into the details of the OWIN mechanics. Here I'll just say that the UseXXX extension methods push middleware elements onto a stack, passing initialization data when necessary. UseCookieAuthentication adds an instance of the cookie middleware in the pipeline. UseOpenIdConnectAuthentication does the same with the OpenID Connect middleware.

> **Note** The order is important! The first middleware you add will be the first to be invoked when a suitable request is invoked. The response will travel through the middleware pipeline in the opposite order; the last middleware you add will be the first to have a chance to work on the response.

The OpenID Connect middleware allows you to control nearly every aspect of how the authentication flow takes place, by accepting as the initialization parameter an `OpenIdConnectAuthenticationOptions` instance.

If you are okay with the default settings, however, you need only to provide a couple of values:

- `Authority`   This is the complete URL of the Azure AD tenant you want your app to accept users from. If you are following along, you should substitute the value here with the URL of the tenant in which you provisioned your app.

- `ClientId`   This is the already-mentioned identifier that Azure AD assigned to your app at provisioning time. Retrieve that value from the Azure portal, and paste it in here. You can refer to the earlier section, "Registering the app in Azure AD," if you've forgotten where to find it exactly.

You are almost done! This is all the init code that's required. All that's left to do is to ensure that the code is called at load time. Back in Startup.cs, add a call to `ConfigureAuth` from the `Configuration` method:

```
public void Configuration(IAppBuilder app)
{
    ConfigureAuth(app);
}
```

Your app is now configured to use OpenID Connect against your Azure AD tenant of choice whenever authentication is necessary. What does that mean, exactly?

[Authorize], claims, and first run

The section you just read showed you how to set up OpenID Connect support in your application. However, the sheer presence of the appropriate middlewares in the pipeline does not automatically determine when the protocol enforcement should kick in. The authentication performed via OWIN middlewares is activated just like any other authentication technology in ASP.NET—by introducing authentication and authorization requirements on the app, on individual resources served by the application, or on both.

Adding a trigger for authentication

The project template you used as a starting point is devoid of any authentication elements, hence the app and all its resources are accessible anonymously by default. Say that you want to maintain anonymous access to the entire app apart from one specific action. For example, working with the resources already present in the project template, let's imagine that you want to restrict access to the `Contact` action from the `HomeController` so that only authenticated users can access it. You can do so with the same technique you've been using for more than half a decade: simply decorate the action with the `[Authorize]` attribute.

```
[Authorize]
public ActionResult Contact()
{
    //...
```

That attribute will ensure that the resource is returned only to authenticated users and will trigger a 401 upon receiving unauthenticated requests. Here's the important point: by default, the OpenID Connect middleware is configured to react to outgoing 401s by intercepting and transforming them in authentication requests. In this specific case, this means generating an OpenID Connect authorization request message and sending it back to Azure AD in the form of an HTTP 302, which the requesting browser will receive and promptly bounce toward Azure AD's authorization endpoint. As I mentioned previously, you'll find out in detail how this all unfolds in Chapter 7.

In this example, I am instructing you to protect just one action, but in fact you can extend the mechanism to whatever scope best fits the business goals of your app. If you want to protect all the actions in the controller, place [Authorize] at the class level; if you prefer to work with the web.config file, feel free to use the good old <authorization> element. In general, anything that will generate a 401 will be a trigger for authentication.

Showing some claims

At this point you might be ready to give the app a first run, but before you do, I'd like to add a bit of code that shows in the app's UI some tangible sign that a successful authentication operation took place. Modify the Contact method as follows:

```
[Authorize]
public ActionResult Contact()
{
    string userfirstname = ClaimsPrincipal.Current.FindFirst(ClaimTypes.GivenName).Value;
    ViewBag.Message = String.Format("Welcome, {0}!", userfirstname);

    return View();
}
```

> **Note** As you type this code, Visual Studio shows wiggly red lines under ClaimsPrincipal and ClaimTypes. That's because you are missing the necessary using directives, hence the types are not available in the current scope. From now on I will no longer explicitly instruct you to add using directives unless it serves to clarify a concept. I will assume that every time you encounter those wiggly lines, you will just position the cursor on the offending term, press CTRL+. (a period), and pick the appropriate using directive that Visual Studio helpfully offers in a context menu.

The effect of this code should already be clear to you. I already covered how claims are handled in .NET in Chapter 1, in the section "*ClaimsPrincipal*: How .NET represents the caller." If you find that you need a refresher, I recommend leafing back to that section to bring this to mind.

Running the app

Time to give the app a spin!

Press F5. The app should open just like it did earlier. But the story should change when you click Contact. The browser should redirect to the Azure AD authentication pages, and upon successful authentication redirect back to the Contact view—where your "Welcome, <firstname>!" message should demonstrate that the user was correctly authenticated.

Voilà. You have a web app that can authenticate users from an Azure AD tenant.

Quick recap

Let's take a moment to summarize what we have done so far:

Starting from a simple project, with no authentication logic whatsoever, you

- Added three NuGet references.

- Stepped through a brief wizard on the Azure portal to provision the app.

- Enabled the OWIN pipeline in your app with less than 10 lines of boilerplate code.

- Configured the OpenID Connect middleware by adding another 10 lines (more or less) of boilerplate code, customizing the values of a couple of strings: Authority and ClientId.

- Added an [Authorize] attribute on the action you wanted to protect.

And that's all that's required for setting up a quick web app for users in one organization, without taking advantage of any of the tools that Visual Studio offers for automating all this.

Sure, there's more to do to have a full-featured system—I will add a few extra details in the following sections—but I wanted to be sure to highlight the minimal set of actions. If you have been working with enterprise-grade authentication for web apps in the past, I am sure you appreciate how much simpler things have become.

Sign-in and sign-out

Although triggering authentication by protecting individual assets is a fine mechanism, you will at times want to offer to the user an explicit sign-in link. And, of course, most apps need an affordance for signing out.

> **Note** The only common exception to the sign-out requirement is the class of apps that are designed to run exclusively on an intranet, where an authenticated user is always present and signing out cannot really take place until the user logs out of his or her workstation.

The OWIN infrastructure itself offers two methods, `Challenge` and `SignOut`, that can be used to message the middlewares in the pipeline to trigger a sign-in and a sign-out flow, respectively. What that means in practice will be determined by each middleware. For the OpenID Connect middleware, signing out means sending a message to Azure AD to cancel a session; for the cookie middleware, it means dropping its session tracking cookie; and so on.

The ASP.NET Visual Studio templates already come with sign-in and sign-out logic wired in, but just for kicks let's add that functionality manually to our web app.

In Project Explorer, right-click the Controllers folder, choose Add New Item, pick Controller, select MVC 5 Controller—Empty, click Add, and then name the controller `AccountController`.

Sign-in logic

Let's start by adding the sign-in functionality. Delete the `Index` method from the controller, and add the following:

```
public void SignIn()
{
    // Send an OpenID Connect sign-in request.
    if (!Request.IsAuthenticated)
    {
        HttpContext.GetOwinContext().Authentication.Challenge(new AuthenticationProperties {
RedirectUri = "/" },
            OpenIdConnectAuthenticationDefaults.AuthenticationType);
    }
}
```

`HttpContext.GetOwinContext().Authentication` exposes the authentication functions of the OWIN pipeline. The `Challenge` method accepts input references to the middlewares that should be involved in generating the sign-in action.

`AuthenticationProperties` is a general-purpose group of settings that are independent from the specific protocol implemented by the middlewares in the pipeline. For example, `RedirectUri` here represents the *local* address in the application to which the browser should ultimately be redirected once the authentication operations conclude. In this case, it's the root of the app: that's because I plan to place the sign-in link on the home page, so I expect the user to be brought back there once the authentication dance is done. You have already seen in the previous section that a similar behavior occurred automatically when the authentication was triggered by clicking a specific action: clicking Contacts triggered the authentication flow, and you ended up back on the Contact view.

> **Note** It is an unfortunate coincidence that the `RedirectUri` property just described happens to be named exactly the same as an OAuth2/OpenID Connect protocol parameter. The value passed in `Challenge` is *not* sent to Azure AD and used as part of the protocol dance: it is a local value that is used *after* the authentication dance takes place. All redirect URIs used by Azure AD must be explicitly registered for security reasons, and it is clearly

not feasible to register all possible controller actions as return URIs. That's why Azure AD normally associates only a few return URIs with each app (typically one for every deployment root) and the middleware itself takes care of performing local redirects without involving the IdP to ensure that requests land on the correct resource. Clear as mud? Don't worry. I will expand on this in Chapter 7.

That's it for the sign-in feature.

Sign-out logic

Implementing sign-out requires a similar method. Add the following code to HomeController:

```
public void SignOut()
{
    HttpContext.GetOwinContext().Authentication.SignOut(
                OpenIdConnectAuthenticationDefaults.AuthenticationType,
                CookieAuthenticationDefaults.AuthenticationType);
}
```

In this case, you are telling OWIN that you want both the OpenID Connect and the cookie middlewares to act on the sign-out request. As mentioned earlier, that will cause the OpenID Connect middleware to emit a sign-out message to Azure AD and the cookie middleware to drop the local app's session cookies.

Important As I write this, the OpenID Connect middleware for ASP.NET 4.6 (that is to say, the one with package version 3.x.x) does not support *distributed* sign-out. Say that you have a user signed in to both apps A and B with an account from the same Azure AD tenant. Now you trigger a sign-out from A. As a result, the user will no longer be signed in either in A or the Azure AD tenant; however, the user will still be signed in to B. That is not the case, for example, if A and B implement WS-Federation using Windows Identity Foundation (WIF): in that case, B would automatically sign the user out as a consequence of the sign-out triggered by A. You'll learn more about this in Chapter 6, "OpenID Connect and Azure AD web sign-on," but for the time being—long story short—OpenID Connect handles sessions via a combination of iframes and JavaScript client-side logic, making it pretty hard to package automatic support for it in a general-purpose development library. The AD team is looking to improve things for ASP.NET 5.

If you leave things as they are right now, you will implement sign-out, but the experience won't be great. After performing the sign-out, the browser will remain stuck on a nondescript page served by Azure AD. A quick fix to that would be to specify in the OpenID Connect middleware initialization an app resource you want to land on after a successful sign-out. (It is usually a good idea to pick a resource that does not trigger an automatic redirect to the authentication pages, or your user might be up for a confusing experience.)

It's easy to do that. Go back to Startup.Auth.cs, and modify the `OpenIdConnectAuthentica-tionOptions` init logic so that it looks like the following:

```
new OpenIdConnectAuthenticationOptions
{
    ClientId = "c3d5b1ad-ae77-49ac-8a86-dd39a2f91081",
    Authority = "https://login.microsoftonline.com/DeveloperTenant.onmicrosoft.com",
    PostLogoutRedirectUri = "https://localhost:44300/"
}
```

Here I am hardcoding the root of my app, but I am sure that in your apps you will be far more elegant. It's important to note that the `PostLogoutRedirectUri` property is sent to Azure AD as part of the sign-out request and must correspond to one of the app URLs you registered. If for some reason you need to pick a more precise app URL as a landing point, you can pass it via `Authentica-tionProperties` in the call to `SignOut`.

At this point the app has its sign-out logic, too. Now you just need to add some controls on the app's surface to activate the two new features.

The sign-in and sign-out UI

You need to expose some controls so that the user can sign in and sign out with your brand-new methods.

> **Note** Some of the development tasks I need to walk you through have nothing to do with the API surface of the AD identity libraries, and this section falls under that category. I do need to write something so that you are able to see the identity features in action, but I want to be sure you realize that if you want to write different code for that, you absolutely can. There is no hard requirement to do things the way I suggest in this section.

I'll do that by adding in line some basic UI elements in the default view. In Project Explorer, navigate to the folder View/Shared and open _Layout.cshtml.

Locate the `<div>` element containing all the links to the `HomeController` actions; it's the one with the style `navbar-collapse collapse`. Right below the `</ul>` closing tag of that list, paste the following code:

```
@if (Request.IsAuthenticated)
{
    <text>
        <ul class="nav navbar-nav navbar-right">
            <li class="navbar-text">
                Hello, @User.Identity.Name!
            </li>
            <li>
                @Html.ActionLink("Sign out", "SignOut", "Account")
            </li>
        </ul>
```

```
        </text>
}
else
{
    <ul class="nav navbar-nav navbar-right">
        <li>@Html.ActionLink("Sign in", "SignIn", "Account", routeValues: null, htmlAttributes:
new { id = "loginLink" })</li>
    </ul>
}
```

The code is straightforward. If there is no authenticated user, it displays a Sign In `ActionLink` that triggers the corresponding action on the `AccountController`.

If there is a signed-in user, the code displays a greeting (note that it accesses claims values through another property, which shows that the preclaims ASP.NET identity code is compatible with the new protocols) and a link bound to the `SignOut` method of the `AccountController`.

Running the app

To double-check that everything works as expected, press F5. Depending on the browser you are using or whether you closed the browser after the last run or not, you might or might not still be signed in with the account you used earlier. If you are, you will see in the top-right corner a greeting and the sign-out link. If you aren't, you will see the sign-in link: click it, and you'll have the same experience as in the earlier run.

Once you've done that, click the sign-out link and verify that you do get signed out of the app and brought back to its home page.

Using ADFS as an identity provider

In an ideal world, in this section I would tell you that if you want to authenticate users coming directly from your on-premises Active Directory, all you need to do is change the Authority value in Startup.Auth.cs to point to your local ADFS instance, provision your app there, and you'll be good to go. But, alas, this is not an ideal world.

ADFS in Windows Server 2016 is the first version of ADFS that supports OpenID Connect. As I write this, the functionality is still in technical preview and very rough around the edges. Setting up ADFS in Windows Server 2016 to handle OpenID Connect would require me to take a long detour to describe how the new system works, and I don't want to do that here. All of Chapter 10, "Active Directory Federation Services in Windows Server 2016 Technical Preview 3," will focus on taking advantage of ADFS in the Windows Server 2016 preview to handle modern authentication in web applications.

I won't leave you without anything at all on the topic, though. ADFS has supported WS-Federation since version 2.0. It just so happens that the ASP.NET 4.6 collection of OWIN middlewares includes one that implements WS-Federation, and its usage is remarkably similar to the one for OpenID Connect. In fact, if you were to modify your app to connect to an ADFS instance, you would have just a couple of places to touch.

You would touch up Startup.Auth.cs as follows:

```
app.UseCookieAuthentication(new CookieAuthenticationOptions());
    app.UseWsFederationAuthentication(
        new WsFederationAuthenticationOptions
        {
            Wtrealm = "http://myapp/whatever",
            MetadataAddress =
                "https://sts.contoso.com/federationmetadata/2007-06/federationmetadata.xml"
        }
```

In this specific case, Wtrealm is the moral equivalent of ClientID—the identifier you would assign to your app when provisioning it in ADFS.

MetadataAddress would point to the metadata document of the ADFS instance you want to target, performing a function similar to Authority.

You would, of course, have to change the sign-in and sign-out logic in AccountController, but just for retargeting which protocol middleware is involved:

```
public void SignIn()
{
    // Send an OpenID Connect sign-in request.
    if (!Request.IsAuthenticated)
    {
        HttpContext.GetOwinContext().Authentication.Challenge(new AuthenticationProperties {
RedirectUri = "/" },
            WsFederationAuthenticationDefaults.AuthenticationType);
    }
}
public void SignOut()
{
    HttpContext.GetOwinContext().Authentication.SignOut(
            WsFederationAuthenticationDefaults.AuthenticationType,
            CookieAuthenticationDefaults.AuthenticationType);
}
```

For what concerns the code, that's pretty much it!

You would also need to provision your app in ADFS before being able to run this code. I won't include the instructions here because supporting WS-Federation is not much in line with the "modern" moniker in the book's title, but this has been a common task for the last half decade, and you can easily find a lot of content online that will walk you through the process.

Once again, if you are interested in using OpenID Connect and OAuth2 with ADFS in Windows Server 2016 preview, please be sure to check out Chapter 10. However, I would recommend doing so only after you go through the other chapters to gain in-depth understanding of how the protocol and OWIN middleware work, as Chapter 10 heavily relies on you being familiar with those concepts.

Summary

In this chapter you discovered what it takes to add web sign-on capabilities to an ASP.NET app from scratch, without any assistance from tools and wizards.

You wrote your first identity code, familiarizing yourself with the libraries required, the absolutely essential set of parameters required to configure meaningful support for web sign-in via OpenID Connect, and the rudiments of using OWIN for handling session management.

You also took your first steps with app provisioning in Azure AD via the Microsoft Azure management portal.

At this point, you know enough to understand the code that Visual Studio and the ASP.NET project templates generate automatically when you use the organizational identity features, which puts you already one step above a general developer who just needs to add authentication to an app and is happy with the defaults.

The next proficiency level entails being able to manipulate how the protocol middleware operates by changing its defaults and injecting your own custom logic. But before you can get there, you must first learn in more detail how the OpenID Connect protocol operates for making web sign-on happen and what parameters you can use to influence its course. That's the subject of the next chapter.

CHAPTER 6

OpenID Connect and Azure AD web sign-on

In this chapter you'll take a closer look at OpenID Connect. Specifically, I'll describe how Azure Active Directory and its libraries use the protocol to power the sign-in flow you implemented in Chapter 5, "Getting started with web sign-on and Active Directory."

I pick up again on some of the ideas that were introduced in Chapter 2, "Identity protocols and application types," going into greater detail on terminology, message exchanges, concepts, and artifacts that come into play when you use OpenID Connect. Understanding how the basic building blocks are used in the default case will help you to troubleshoot when something goes wrong. It also equips you with the knowledge you need for customizing the default behavior to fit the requirements of your specific scenarios.

My goal is not to write an annotated version of the entire specification; the specs themselves are readable enough. Rather, I focus on the aspects that are directly involved in the default flow that Azure AD and associated libraries implement for achieving web sign-on. This is not to say that the rest of the specification is not useful, or that Azure AD supports only the flows described here. My focus is mostly to keep the size of the book (and the time it takes to write it) under control. If you want to dig deeper into other aspects, you will find plenty of material online that expands beyond the basics.

The protocol and its specifications

In Chapter 2 I introduced OpenID Connect's role in the sequence of protocols that led authentication into the modern era. In the same chapter I also described the exchanges that define two of its main authentication flows, the hybrid flow and the authorization-code flow. In this chapter I assume that you have read and internalized that description. If your recollection of it is less than perfect, I recommend that you go back a few pages and reread that section before going any further.

Figure 6-1 shows the specifications that are relevant for the flow you'll study in this chapter. I'll describe them briefly here, and in the next section, "OpenID Connect exchanges signing in with Azure AD," I'll go into the details. For now, this will provide you with a map should you choose to match what you read about here to the formal specifications.

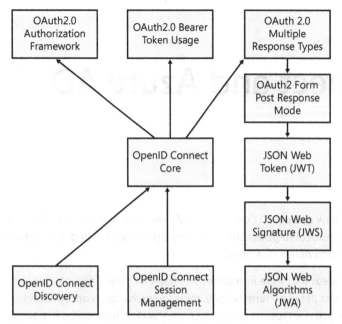

FIGURE 6-1 The specifications mentioned in this chapter and their dependency relationships.

OpenID Connect Core 1.0

By default, the OpenID Connect OWIN middleware uses the hybrid flow to implement sign-on. That flow is described in the OpenID Connect Core specification, which at the time of writing is in its 1.0 version. You can find it at *http://openid.net/specs/openid-connect-core-1_0.html*.

The OpenID Connect Core specification prescribes in detail the format of authentication request and response messages for the hybrid, authorization-code, and implicit flows (also described in Chapter 2, in the context of single-page applications). It also describes in detail the format of the id_token, the criteria that should be applied for validating it in different contexts, and a list of canonical claim types that OpenID Connect providers and clients can use to transmit common attributes.

The Core spec describes lots of other things, such as the UserInfo endpoint, but those don't come into play in this chapter.

OpenID Connect Discovery

Throughout Chapter 2 I discussed how claims-identity protocols describe ways for identity providers (IdPs) to advertise their metadata—endpoints, identifiers, signing keys, and the like—so that relying parties (RPs) can acquire the information they need to generate authentication requests and validate responses according to the protocol of choice.

OpenID Connect provides such a mechanism, too. You can find all the details in the OpenID Connect Discovery 1.0 specification, available at *http://openid.net/specs/openid-connect-discovery-1_0 .html*.

Azure AD advertises its OpenID Connect endpoints in accordance with the Discovery specs. The OpenID Connect OWIN middleware leverages that mechanism to minimize the configuration burden on the developer and to ensure that the validation info stays as fresh as possible.

OAuth 2.0 Multiple Response Type, OAuth2 Form Post Response Mode

The Multiple Response Type and Post Response Mode specs (available at *http://openid.net/specs/ oauth-v2-multiple-response-types-1_0.html* and *http://openid.net/specs/oauth-v2-form-post-response- mode-1_0.html*) provide normative guidance on how to control which tokens should be returned in response to an authentication request and the HTTP mechanism that should be used to carry them.

In particular, the OpenID Connect middleware asks by default for tokens to be returned to the RP via form POST, making it easy to work with the big token sizes that are common in business scenarios.

OpenID Connection Session Management

This specification, available at *http://openid.net/specs/openid-connect-session-1_0.html*, describes how an RP can inquire about the sign-in status of a user with the IdP and how to manipulate sessions— most notably, how to handle distributed sign-out.

Azure AD supports this specification, which works great for JavaScript apps. However, I am person- ally not very fond of this spec in the context of server-based web applications, given that it relies on a hidden iframe and splits functionality between JavaScript and server-side logic, which makes it really complicated to package this functionality in a easy-to-use server-side authentication library.

Another draft spec, available at *http://openid.net/specs/openid-connect-logout-1_0.html*, imple- ments sign-out through a more traditional mechanism, one that's far easier to package in a library. It shows great promise, but it's still a draft at this point, so I'll ignore it.

Other OpenID Connect specifications

The family of OpenID Connect specifications has lots of other members, but they describe aspects of the protocol that don't come into play in this book. For example, there is a spec that describes how to dynamically register clients with IdPs (available at *http://openid.net/specs/openid-connect- registration-1_0.html*), which is not a great match for the scenarios that Azure AD supports today.

Supporting specifications

OpenID Connect as a whole is a high-level specification that relies on lower-level building blocks for essential functionality such as token formats, cryptographic operations, and the like.

As you know from Chapter 2, OpenID Connect extends OAuth2 to add support for authentication. The fundamental OAuth2 specifications are the core OAuth2 Authorization Framework (available at *https://tools.ietf.org/html/rfc6749*) and the OAuth2 Bearer Token Usage (you can find it at *https://tools.ietf.org/html/rfc6750*).

Besides those two essential specifications, you will encounter JSON Web Token (JWT, *https://tools.ietf.org/html/rfc7519*), JSON Web Signature (JWS, *https://tools.ietf.org/html/rfc7515*), and JSON Web Algorithms (JWA, *https://tools.ietf.org/html/rfc7518*). If you dig deep enough, you can reach all the way to RSA cryptography and encoding specifications.

I will mention the relevant tidbits from each of these whenever the need arises. You don't need to go into any of these in any level of detail, but it is useful to know where a given concept comes from so that in case an issue or ambiguity arises, you can zero in on it instead of playing the whack-a-mole game specs sometimes like to trick you into.

OpenID Connect exchanges signing in with Azure AD

I want to tell you more about the protocol, but I also want to keep things concrete. Here is what we will do. We will capture a network trace of the traffic generated as you sign in and sign out from the vanilla app you developed in Chapter 5. After we have that trace, I'll walk you through it, highlighting the crucial protocol exchanges.

Capturing a trace

Let's start by capturing a network trace of the flows we want to examine.

You have numerous options for capturing a trace. However, they boil down to two alternatives:

- You can use a proxy, which intercepts and saves traffic. The canonical example of this approach on Windows is Fiddler, a free web-debugging proxy utility.

- You can use the network tracing features in the development tools of your web browser of choice (the classic F12 option). Alternatively, you can use a plug-in such as HttpWatch. The advantage here is that the plug-in operates at the end of the HTTPS tunnel, hence you don't need to make any special provisions to decrypt traffic.

I will use Fiddler in this example, mostly because I am used to it (it was around well before browsers had decent dev tools) and allows me to give consistent instructions no matter which browser you're using. That said, during development I normally use Chrome. If you use another browser and something does not look right even when you follow the instructions to the letter, I recommend that you try it with Chrome before despairing.

Setting up Fiddler

You can download Fiddler from *http://www.telerik.com/download/fiddler*. I highly recommend that you choose the option Fiddler for .NET4.

Launch the setup. Once that's done, run Fiddler. When it first runs, the app appears as shown in Figure 6-2.

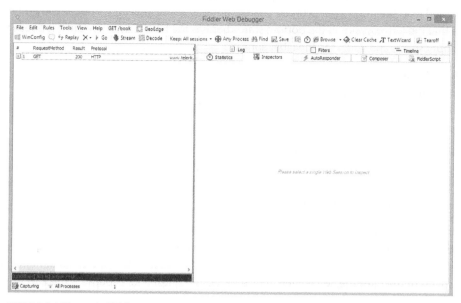

FIGURE 6-2 The main Fiddler screen.

As soon as Fiddler opens, it starts to capture traffic. The left pane contains the list of captured frames, requests, and responses. The right pane shows details of the selected frame or more general options.

The first thing you need to do is turn on HTTPS decryption, given that all the flows we'll use will be on HTTPS. Do this by going to the Tools, Fiddler Options menu and selecting the HTTPS tab. As soon as you check the Decrypt HTTPS traffic check box, you're prompted to trust a certificate that Fiddler generates for its own HTTPS tunnel. Assuming that you are working on a development machine that does not run any critical services for your business, click through the many confirmation dialogs to set up the certificate as trusted.

Finally, Visual Studio 2015 can be quite chatty with its debug-related messages, so it's easy for the messages you care about to be drowned in a sea of unrelated frames. Luckily, Fiddler provides a superhandy filtering feature that can clean up the list. Select the Filters tab in the right pane, check the Use Filter check box, check Hide If URL Contains, and enter the following in the corresponding text box: **SignalR browserLink google visualstudio.com.** By the time this book goes to press, there might be additional sessions you will want to hide. Just apply the same trick on the appropriate search term.

The trace

Now we are ready to capture the trace of a sign-in and sign-out to our application. Open Visual Studio 2015 and load the project you worked on in Chapter 5. Start Fiddler if it's not already running, and ensure that the leftmost slot in the bottom status bar has the label Capturing On. If it doesn't, click that empty space, and you'll see the label appear.

Go back to Visual Studio and press F5. When the application appears in the browser, click the Sign In link. Sign in with your test user account, and observe that the app correctly shows the user principal name (UPN) of the user in its top-right corner. Hit the Sign Out link and confirm that you successfully sign out.

Switch back to Fiddler and switch off the Capturing label. If you want to read this chapter in multiple takes, you can save the current capture by selecting File, Save, All Sessions. That way, you will always be able to reload the same session and keep following the discussion without having to capture the trace every time you pick up the book.

Examining individual frames is easy, as demonstrated in Figure 6-3. Just select the frame you want in the left pane. In the right pane, choose the Inspectors tab. You will be presented with a split view representing the request and the response messages. You can choose different views that highlight different aspects of the message. My default choice for both request and response is the Raw view, which shows what you would see on the wire.

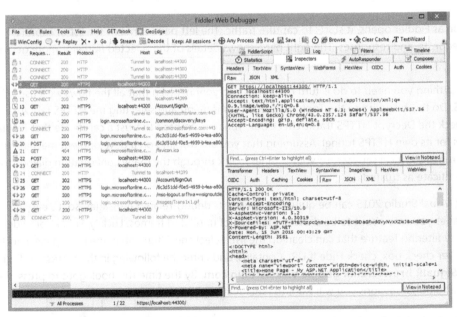

FIGURE 6-3 The trace of the sign-in and sign-out flows. One frame is selected on the left; the details of the request and response are shown in the inspector views on the right.

Now that we have the trace, let's dive in.

Authentication request

Scan the list of frames from top to bottom. Search for requests that aim for your app: given that it is running on IIS Express, you can expect the host to be something like `localhost:44300`.

The first one you'll encounter is the request to your home page—that is to say, to the URL /. Just to warm up, select that frame. You will see on the right side the bits of the request, a simple GET, and the HTML constituting the response.

If you followed the proposed sequence, the next frame aimed at your app should be a GET to `/Account/SignIn`, triggered by clicking the Sign In link. You know that the `Account/SignIn` route activates the code that generates an authentication request. In fact, if you deselect the frame and examine its response, you will find a 302 redirect toward Azure AD, carrying the OpenID Connect authentication request message. It looks like the following:

```
HTTP/1.1 302 Found
Cache-Control: private
Location: https://login.microsoftonline.com/6c3d51dd-f0e5-4959-b4ea-a80c4e36fe5e/
oauth2/authorize?client_id=c3d5b1ad-ae77-49ac-8a86-dd39a2f91081&response_mode=form_
post&response_type=code+id_token&scope=openid+profile&state=OpenIdConnect.Auth
enticationProperties%3dMw7NzZk2Eu7JttOTRIcYEs-O81rWJcYNRXUeoAOAO4eu2v7W8KIfE-
zf7fabTD-NVnmGNKb5F4jN1-F1GYmTj6MfpMexQnrMuc8s1pU5qzU&nonce=635699258270224980.
MGFhMDg1OGQtOGY2Yy0O0GJlLThmOGEtODFhMmNhZDJhOWZjYTQxNTlmNDMtYjU3MC00MTQzLTkzYjMtMDdmNzRlZWY1NWY4
Server: Microsoft-IIS/10.0
X-AspNetMvc-Version: 5.2
X-AspNet-Version: 4.0.30319
Set-Cookie:
OpenIdConnect.nonce.NtAEBISzI9Su4nompbFjAZLP30DDfgVO9WcjUtrNdqM%3D=RkhuWmpsYlREMFJodm1zQkxIcFZ5X
25MWGNfZllWOWlBTUF3eTdBdk1ZMzl1cjU1REtiTGJiZEhmeFNDbDY3MFp4aV9KRXVyNm9hWUVDMjAtXy14a0wwdncteEV5N
UpJSGsxMk9YdmZBQjE5ZOQ5cDkyNOE4VmgyZzJxTGhjWDBBV3RUUjY4d1JUZTZVTWdBQ2JXZE5a3RGdlp4Q3RwUVVBLVR5c
W4xUUZGRkQOVOw1dUt6Tks3LUZJbm5Bd2FraUJCUnhPcUpwT3dtTE1zLS1rcks3Q3VqqN19aR1JkWGFINEk3Y3hyUDZOaw%3D
%3D; path=/; secure; HttpOnly
X-SourceFiles: =?UTF-
8?B?QzpcQm9va1xXZWJBcHBDaGFwdGVyNVxXZWJBcHBDaGFwdGVyNVxBY2NvdW50XFNpZ25Jbg==?=
X-Powered-By: ASP.NET
Date: Mon, 15 Jun 2015 00:43:47 GMT
Content-Length: 0
```

Note Because this is the first frame I present in the text, I have preserved all its parts, including those that are not directly relevant to OpenID Connect. From now on I will edit down the information to highlight only that which plays a direct role in the use of the protocol.

The Location header is the most important piece, as it contains the sign-in message that the browser will send to Azure AD as soon as it executes the 302. The default behavior of the OpenID Connect OWIN middleware is to initiate a *hybrid flow*, though here I will ignore the authorization code redemption part and focus only on sign-in functionality and authorization endpoint traffic. Let's break the message down to its fundamental components and examine how the protocol is being used.

Authorization endpoint

Each Azure AD tenant exposes endpoints for the protocols it supports. The message here is sent to the authorization endpoint of the tenant in which we configured the app:

```
https://login.microsoftonline.com/6c3d51dd-f0e5-4959-b4ea-a80c4e36fe5e/oauth2/authorize
```

The authority part of the URL indicates the Azure AD instance, in this case the public cloud. The GUID following that represents the tenant identifier of the directory tenant of choice.

That GUID could be replaced by one of the domains associated with the tenant, such as `developertenant.onmicrosoft.com`, to the same effect. But using the tenant identifier is preferable because it can't be reassigned, whereas a domain could be decommissioned and acquired by a different organization later.

The last portion of the path simply tells Azure AD which protocol should be used. If you were using SAML, for example, the authority and tenant part of the URL would be the same, but the last portion of the path would be `/saml2`.

client_id

The first parameter you encounter in the message is `client_id`. This is the same value you encountered while configuring the OpenID Connect middleware. It's the ID that allows Azure AD to correlate the request to the app's entry in the tenant.

response_mode, response_type

The next two parameters are especially interesting.

The `response_type` parameter indicates which artifacts your app wants as the outcome of this authentication operation. The value you observe here is the default because the sample from Chapter 5 did not specify any custom value for this parameter. The default `response_type` for the OWIN OpenID Connect middleware is `code+id_token`. In fact, in this particular scenario we ignore code. It would be useful if we had invoked a web API from our app, but given that we're interested just in sign-on, we end up consuming just the `id_token`. (That means that if we had sent a value of `id_token`, we would have achieved the goals of this scenario just as well.)

The `response_mode` parameter indicates the way in which we want the authorization server (that is, Azure AD) to return the requested artifacts to the application. In this case the trace reports a value of `form_post`, which means that Azure AD is supposed to return the `id_token` in a POST. Once again, that's the middleware's default behavior. This is just like how WS-Federation and SAML return their tokens—by sending back to the browser some simple JavaScript that autoposts the token to the application. The main advantage of this approach lies in the fact that big tokens can be handled easily, whereas other methods (such as those embedding tokens in a URL) suffer from stringent size limitations. Another advantage is that token validation can take place entirely on the server.

Important The response parameters discussed here are all meant to be sent to a specific URL that Azure AD knows is assigned to the app identified by the `client_id` you are sending. However, note that the request does not include the `redirect_uri` parameter, which the OpenID Connect specification indicates as the parameter that's used to communicate which URI should be used for that purpose. You can definitely specify such a value via the OWIN middleware, and Azure AD will understand that: in fact, you must do so when your apps have multiple registered URLs. If you don't specify it, as is the case in this trace, Azure AD automatically uses the URL you provided at registration time.

More *response_mode, response_type* values OpenID Connect relies on (and Azure AD supports) various other `response_type` values. You can find the complete list in the previously mentioned "OAuth 2.0 Multiple Response Type Encoding Practices" specification, which extends the canonical OAuth2 code and token with `id_token` and combinations.

The same spec defines two `response_mode` values:

- `fragment`, which establishes that the response parameters should be returned in a URL fragment. A fragment is the portion of a URL following the # symbol. Its defining characteristic is that it is not sent to the server when used in HTTP verbs. An authorization server uses a fragment when it wants to return values to JavaScript code running in a browser and ensure that the same values aren't seen by the server side of that app.

- `query`, which returns the response parameters in the query string. `query` is the Cinderella of `response_mode` values. It is used only when returning a code, which is supposed to be mostly single use anyway, but its use is discouraged for pretty much all other cases. That's mostly because of its nasty habit of remaining available in the browser history and for other possible attacks.

What about `form_post`? That's actually defined in an extra specification, the previously mentioned "OAuth 2.0 Form Post Response Mode."

Each `response_type` value has a default `response_mode`, which kicks in in case no overriding value is specified. Table 6-1 shows the complete list of values at the time of writing. The table is mostly self-explanatory if you remember that *token* stands for access token and *none* is just an artifact for triggering consent without returning anything. Also note that some `response_type` values explicitly disallow the use of `query`. The table reports on that, too.

TABLE 6-1 `response_type` and corresponding default `response_mode`

response_type	Default response_mode
code	query
token	fragment
id_token	fragment, query disallowed
none	query

response_type	Default response_mode
code token	fragment, query disallowed
code id_token	fragment, query disallowed
id_token token	fragment, query disallowed
code id_token token	fragment, query disallowed

scope

Just like in OAuth2.0, the scope parameter indicates which things (resources and permissions/actions) an app is requesting access to.

If my mention of access control and authorization at this point confuses you, remember what you read in Chapter 2: OpenID Connect layers sign-in on top of OAuth2, which remains fundamentally a means for obtaining authorization. In OAuth2 the scope applies only to the access token, whereas in OpenID Connect it also affects the id_token, the main artifact making the sign-in portion of the flow possible.

In our example, scope has two values, openid and profile.

- openid is a conventional scope value, used to indicate to the authorization server (Azure AD, that is) that the client intends to use OpenID Connect as opposed to vanilla OAuth2. Let me stress this: a request that does not include a scope parameter that includes the value openid is not an OpenID Connect request.

- profile is one of four special scope values (profile, email, address, phone) that OpenID Connect defines as a mechanism for requesting access to a specific set of predefined claims. That access is expressed in different ways depending on the artifact requested via response_type. An access token will carry permission to access that particular claim set, and id_token might include such claim values directly. You will see in this case that the id_token you get back will indeed contain some claims from the profile set (name, given_name, family_name).

state

The client uses the state parameter for preserving state throughout the authentication flow. Whatever information the app needs to remember after the user comes back with the requested token (and/or code) can be squirreled away here: the authority (Azure AD) has the responsibility of reattaching the state parameter, unchanged, to its eventual response.

From the trace, you can see that this parameter can be rather beefy. The canonical function of the state parameter as envisioned by the specification's authors is to supply a mechanism for averting forgery attacks from cross-site requests. The OpenID Connect OWIN middleware goes a bit further and uses state to remember important information, such as whether the authentication request was triggered by a specific route (as happened in Chapter 5 when you clicked the Contact action). If that's the case, after the authentication exchange concludes later on, the middleware can unpack from the state the original path and perform an internal redirect to dispatch the browser to the requested resource.

nonce

The nonce parameter is a hard-to-guess value that OpenID Connect introduced for mitigating token replay attacks. Here's how it works.

The client generates a nonce value and includes it in the request. Furthermore, it saves that value somewhere—in the case of Azure AD, it's saved in a cookie with a unique name—so that the original nonce value will be available later, during the last leg of the authentication flow. If you examine the request trace, you will find the `set-cookie` directive for the `OpenIdConnect.nonce.NtAEBISzI 9Su4nompbFjAZLP30DDfgVO9WcjUtrNdqM%3D` cookie. That cookie is protected by server-driven cryptography and cannot be forged or tampered with by a client.

When the app eventually receives an `id_token`, it searches among its claims for a nonce claim and verifies that it contains the original nonce value communicated in the request. For the middleware, that's an easy task, given that the same value is available in the aforementioned cookie. An attacker who somehow stole an `id_token` would not be able to pass this test, given that he or she would not be able to craft the corresponding cookie.

This is a nice and necessary security measure. However, be warned that it will occasionally give you pain. Any scenario in which cookies are somehow deleted or otherwise altered in the time between the sign-in request and the response will cause the authentication to fail, given that the nonce check relies on them. There are various solutions to this, up to and including saving the nonce reference values on the server side. I will get back to that later in the book when I focus on libraries and the object model.

Parameters omitted in the default request

The parameters described so far are the ones in use in the request generated in the default configuration of the OWIN OpenID Connect middleware. Besides the previously mentioned `redirect_uri`, OpenID Connect includes many other very useful parameters that can help you to influence the way in which a request is handled. Here's a quick list of the most notable ones. They'll come in handy when I cover middleware customizations in later chapters.

- `login_hint` This parameter is used for prepopulating the username text box in the credential-gathering experience with the identifier of a particular user. For Azure AD, the identifier must be the UPN of the desired user.

- `prompt` This is my favorite parameter!

  Say that you want to guarantee that the end user is prompted for credentials, regardless of whether the user is already signed in with Azure AD. Send `prompt=login` along with your request, and that will do the trick.

  Now say that you want the exact opposite. Maybe you want to renew the user session without affecting the user experience, hence you want to drive an authentication request via a hidden iframe. Sending `prompt=none` with your request guarantees that Azure AD will do whatever it can to authenticate the user without showing any UI. If that isn't possible, Azure AD will send a failure message right away.

Another interesting option is sending `prompt=select_account`. If the user is signed in to Azure AD with multiple accounts at the same time, this parameter ensures that the user has the opportunity to choose which account he or she wants to use for signing in to the application.

■ `domain_hint`   This parameter is not part of the OpenID Connect standard. Azure AD introduced it to allow you to specify which IdP you want users to authenticate with. Say that your app trusts a federated Azure AD tenant. With the default request, users would first see the Azure AD authentication pages and be redirected to the federated ADFS only after they type their username in the text box. If you send the `domain_hint` parameter set to the federated domain, the Azure AD page is skipped, and the request goes straight to the ADFS associated with the tenant. If the user is accessing your app from an intranet, and is thus already authenticated with ADFS, this can actually enable a seamless single sign-on experience.

■ `resource`   The `resource` parameter is another Azure AD–specific parameter, which is used even in vanilla OAuth2 flows. Explaining what this parameter does requires a bit of a detour, which ties in to the limitations of OAuth2 that I described in the section "OAuth2 and claims" in Chapter 2.

In a nutshell, the `resource` parameter tells Azure AD which resource you want an access token for (or a code that is eventually redeemed for an access token). The resource can be a Microsoft API (Office 365, Azure management, etc.), a third-party web API, or your own web API registered as an app in Azure AD. Concretely, this means that the access token you get back will contain a claim stating that its intended audience is the resource it has been issued for. This provides resources with a mechanism to verify whether the incoming token is truly meant for them, as opposed to a token being stolen or reused from a different resource transaction.

In canonical OAuth2, you indicate the target you are requesting access to via the `scope` parameter. However, that usually refers to portions of an implied resource or to specific actions one can perform. When you are getting a token from Facebook, the only resource you can spend it on is the Facebook Graph. The same holds for all other big OAuth2 providers: they issue tokens for themselves, so there's never a need to specify a resource. On the other hand, Azure AD is a generic authority that can issue tokens for different resources, owned by multiple tenants—with strong business reasons to maintain independence and isolation. That calls for a token-validation strategy that can be applied by third parties as described in Chapter 2. The use of the `resource` parameter is part of that.

At this point, I'll summarize what you've learned about the request message. It's a 302 redirect toward an Azure AD tenant endpoint, and specifically the authorization endpoint. It contains the `client_id` of the requestor, it specifies which kind of tokens you are requesting (via `response_type`) and how you want to receive them (via `response_mode`). It uses `scope` to indicate that you want to talk OpenID Connect (as opposed to vanilla OAuth2) and what resources you want to access. Finally, it uses some tricks for protecting the request (state, nonce).

The browser will receive the 302 and honor it, sending the request to Azure AD. Before getting to that point, though, there's more interesting traffic we need to examine.

Discovery

The OpenID Connect OWIN middleware can automatically consult the metadata published by Azure AD to acquire up-to-date information on how to validate incoming tokens. (Please refer to Chapter 2 for an introduction to metadata consumption and token validation.) Given that in this specific flow we are using OpenID Connect, the metadata document being consulted is the so-called discovery document—described in the homonymous specification mentioned earlier in this chapter.

If you scan the trace shown earlier, you will eventually find a request to login.microsoftonline.com that looks like the following:

```
GET https://login.microsoftonline.com/DeveloperTenant.onmicrosoft.com/.well-known/openid-
configuration HTTP/1.1
Host: login.microsoftonline.com
Connection: Keep-Alive
```

The URL path being requested is actually normative—OpenID Connect mandates that if you want to support discovery from your issuer, you better publish the corresponding document under /.well-known/openid-configuration. And, of course, this exchange *must* take place over a trusted HTTPS connection. Here's the discovery document, taken from the body of the response to the previous request:

```
{
    "authorization_endpoint" : "https://login.microsoftonline.com/6c3d51dd-f0e5-4959-b4ea-
a80c4e36fe5e/oauth2/authorize",
    "check_session_iframe" : "https://login.microsoftonline.com/6c3d51dd-f0e5-4959-b4ea-
a80c4e36fe5e/oauth2/checksession",
    "claims_supported" : [
        "sub",
        "iss",
        "aud",
        "exp",
        "iat",
        "auth_time",
        "acr",
        "amr",
        "nonce",
        "email",
        "given_name",
        "family_name",
        "nickname"
    ],
    "end_session_endpoint" : "https://login.microsoftonline.com/6c3d51dd-f0e5-4959-b4ea-
a80c4e36fe5e/oauth2/logout",
    "id_token_signing_alg_values_supported" : [ "RS256" ],
    "issuer" : "https://sts.windows.net/6c3d51dd-f0e5-4959-b4ea-a80c4e36fe5e/",
```

```
    "jwks_uri" : "https://login.microsoftonline.com/common/discovery/keys",
    "microsoft_multi_refresh_token" : true,
    "response_modes_supported" : [ "query", "fragment", "form_post" ],
    "response_types_supported" : [ "code", "id_token", "code id_token", "token id_token", "token"
],
    "scopes_supported" : [ "openid" ],
    "subject_types_supported" : [ "pairwise" ],
    "token_endpoint" : "https://login.microsoftonline.com/6c3d51dd-f0e5-4959-b4ea-a80c4e36fe5e/
oauth2/token",
    "token_endpoint_auth_methods_supported" : [ "client_secret_post", "private_key_jwt" ],
    "userinfo_endpoint" : "https://login.microsoftonline.com/6c3d51dd-f0e5-4959-b4ea-
a80c4e36fe5e/openid/userinfo"
}
```

Now, aren't you glad this document is not really meant for human consumption and is mostly read by software?

But, in fact, if you give it a second glance, it's not that bad. The document provides all the information that a client needs to know to consume Azure AD (and more specifically, this tenant of Azure AD) as an OpenID provider. It lists all the relevant endpoints (authorization, token, UserInfo, and session-related endpoints, including end_session_endpoint, which I have not covered yet), specific claim types it supports, values of response_type and response_mode that it accepts, and so on.

The reason that the OWIN middleware reaches out to this document, however, is to discover what criteria to use for validating incoming tokens. To that end, there are two crucial pieces of information:

- The issuer value, which in this case is:

  https://sts.windows.net/6c3d51dd-f0e5-4959-b4ea-a80c4e36fe5e/.

  This is the value that applications should expect to find in the iss claim of all tokens issued by this particular Azure AD tenant. The OpenID Connect middleware will automatically enforce that the incoming token complies with this condition and refuse all others, ensuring that only users from the target tenant are granted access.

- The keys to use for validating token signatures, provided by reference by jwks_uri. The way keys are handled warrants more discussion, which I provide in the next section.

You might have noticed that the issuer value contains a GUID, which happens to be the same GUID value that appears in all endpoints. That value is the identifier that Azure AD assigned to the tenant.

Signing keys

The discovery document does not supply raw key values. Rather, it points to a different document—https://login.microsoftonline.com/common/discovery/keys—indicated by the value of jwks_uri, which the middleware must retrieve as well. Sure enough, in the neighborhood of the frame retrieving the discovery document, you will find another request of the following form:

I will discuss at length the strange properties of /common later in the book, but for the time being it's enough to observe that its appearance here breaks the pattern of using the tenant ID GUID in endpoint paths. Despite the fact that we are inquiring about the metadata of one specific tenant, the keys are kept at a URL that is not tied to any tenant.

This has a very important implication: *all Azure AD tenants issue tokens signed by the same keys.*

A corollary is that *the only way of determining whether a token comes from a given tenant is to check its* iss *value.* I found this to be counterintuitive for people familiar with "traditional" federation, where every Security Token Service (STS) has its own keys, which is why I am emphasizing this here.

Back to the keys. Let's take a look at the body of the response:

Important For the sake of readability, I will abbreviate long encoded values. I've used [...SNIP...] in the text as a placeholder for content I edited out. I will use the same approach in later chapters as well.

```
{
    "keys" : [
        {
            "e" : "AQAB",
            "kid" : "kriMPdmBvx68skT8-mPAB3BseeA",
            "kty" : "RSA",
            "n" : "kSCW[...SNIP...]enufuw",
            "use" : "sig",
            "x5c" : [
                "MIID[...SNIP...]LAIarZ"
            ],
            "x5t" : "kriMPdmBvx68skT8-mPAB3BseeA"
        },
        {
            "e" : "AQAB",
            "kid" : "MnC_VZcATfM5pOYiJHMba9goEKY",
            "kty" : "RSA",
            "n" : "vIqz-4-[...SNIP...]gelixLUQ",
            "use" : "sig",
            "x5c" : [
                "MIIC4j[...SNIP...]KvJQ=="
            ],
            "x5t" : "MnC_VZcATfM5pOYiJHMba9goEKY"
        }
    ]
}
```

I don't think it would be terribly useful if I were to go into the details of all the parameters you see here. You can find a detailed reference in the JSON Web Key specification at *https://tools.ietf.org/html/rfc7517.*

But at a high level, what you have here is a set of two keys, which happen to be RSA (suited for asymmetric cryptography) and, specifically, packaged in X.509 certificates. Those keys are used by Azure AD for signing tokens. I can tell this by the mix of identifiers and cryptographic parameters in the key declarations. The middleware will parse this response and keep the keys handy, using them to verify signatures whenever a token arrives.

Why two keys? This is part of Azure AD's key-rolling strategy. At any given time, the metadata contains both the key currently in use and the one that will take over once the first is rolled. As a result, planned key rolls can take place without affecting the business continuity of the apps that rely on those values for verifying token signatures.

Authentication

As you keep scanning down the frames list, you will soon encounter the GET that honors the 302 with the authentication request. That triggers the authentication experience for the user.

The details of how that takes place depend on many factors. Here are few common cases:

- Users who are already authenticated will have a session cookie, which is sent along with the first request. This tells Azure AD that the user is already authenticated. Hence, if the requested token does not require any consent, the request will be granted without displaying any user experience.

- If user interaction is required for authenticating the request, you can observe several subcases:

  - Managed tenants will handle the full credential-gathering experience directly.

  - Federated tenants will redirect the browser to the on-premises IdP, typically ADFS, which will then have full control over the credential-gathering experience and any customizations that might have been applied.

  - Guest Microsoft account (MSA) users will be redirected to the Microsoft account pages for authentication.

  - In all cases, the authentication process can be affected by extra elements such as a requirement for multiple authentication factors (MFAs) or the presence of Windows Integrated Auth, and so on.

To make things even more interesting, different releases of the service might handle the details of authentication differently. For example, about one year ago a trace of the authentication phase of the OpenID Connect flow would have shown some extra redirects to an internal STS endpoint based on WS-Federation. Today, such extra redirects are no longer in place. Tomorrow others might be introduced. The bottom line is that how authentication takes place is up to the authority you are working with, in this case Azure AD. The OpenID Connect protocol does not specify what should be done to authenticate the user; it only regulates how to format requests and responses without worrying too much about what happens between the two.

That doesn't mean that you can afford to ignore the authentication phase, though. Very often, issues in the authentication flows take place in this phase—misconfigured ADFS, network restrictions, and DNS errors are all examples of such potential issues. It is useful to know that the solution to those issues is usually independent from how OpenID Connect is set up for the application.

For the sake of simplicity, I assume here that you are in a situation in which you are working with a managed tenant, your user does not have an existing session, and you do not have any MFA setup in place.

Important I also assume that Azure AD will be using the same logic for handling credential gathering, which might not be the case by the time you read this. Don't take any of this too literally, and keep your eyes open for functional equivalents.

Search the trace for the first POST after the discovery frames that targets `https://login` `.microsoftonline.com/6c3d51dd-f0e5-4959-b4ea-a80c4e36fe5e/login`, where the GUID is the ID of your tenant. The body of that POST will contain, among lots of other things, your username and password. (This is a good opportunity for me to remind you to be very careful with your traces, especially if you save them, as they can contain very sensitive information, such as passwords.)

The response to that POST is the OpenID Connect response we were waiting for.

Response

Let's examine the bits of the Azure AD response. Here's a dump of it, edited for clarity:

```
HTTP/1.1 200 OK
[…SNIP…]
Set-Cookie: ESTSAUTHPERSISTENT=AAA[…SNIP…]LIcgiAA; expires=Sat, 12-Dec-2015 00:43:56 GMT;
path=/; secure; HttpOnly
Set-Cookie: ESTSAUTH=QUFBQ[…SNIP…]kNBQQ==; domain=.login.microsoftonline.com; path=/; secure;
HttpOnly
Set-Cookie: ESTSAUTHLIGHT=+93dba92a-90d2-4f97-801b-a64a3b320f28; path=/; secure
Set-Cookie: PPAuth=AW4[…SNIP…]HSvk; domain=login.microsoftonline.com; path=/; secure; HttpOnly
Set-Cookie: ESTSSC=01; path=/; secure; HttpOnly
Set-Cookie: SignInStateCookie=QUFB[…SNIP…]ySUFB; path=/; secure; HttpOnly
[…SNIP…]

<html>
  <head>
    <title>Working...</title>
  </head>
  <body>
    <form method="POST" name="hiddenform" action="https://localhost:44300/">
      <input type="hidden" name="code" value="AAA[…SNIP…]jyAA" />
      <input type="hidden" name="id_token" value="eyJ0[…SNIP…]zLUWB1Q" />
      <input type="hidden" name="state" value="OpenIdConnect.AuthenticationProperties=[SNIP]" />
      <input type="hidden" name="session_state" value="93dba92a-90d2-4f97-801b-a64a3b320f28" />
      <noscript>
        <p>Script is disabled. Click Submit to continue.</p>
        <input type="submit" value="Submit" />
```

```
      </noscript>
    </form>
    <script language="javascript">window.setTimeout('document.forms[0].submit()', 0);

    </script>
  </body>
</html>
```

> **Note** In this chapter, the term *response* is a bit overloaded. There are the HTTP requests and responses you find in each frame of the trace we are examining, and there are the requests and responses intended as OpenID Connect messages (which are implemented as HTTP request and responses as well). There isn't much risk of confusion, but I wanted to stress this just in case you were wondering.

This response might look intimidating at first glance, but in fact the message follows a very simple structure. The first thing to notice is that Azure AD saves a number of cookies on the user's browser at this point. Some of them are persistent; others are session bound. These cookies keep track of the fact that the user now has an authenticated session with Azure AD. Subsequent requests for tokens will carry these cookies, influencing the experience in a variety of ways. For example, an already-authenticated user who requests a token that does not require any other interaction (such as consent) gets back the requested token without seeing any user experience. Another example is that requests carrying prompt=select_account will now list the currently signed-in account as one of the options, as recorded in one of these cookies.

Knowing the details of what each cookie does won't be of much help to you. The lineup of cookies is not part of the contract of Azure AD and the application; hence, Azure AD can change these cookies or the function they perform at any time, without notice. They truly are an implementation detail, and as such, creating a dependency on their behavior leads to brittle solutions that can break at any time, possibly with no recourse. It's best to stick with the knowledge that Azure AD sessions are represented via cookies, without going into the details of which individual cookies are used.

The body of the response is the interesting part. Remember how the request included a response_mode=form_post? Azure AD is complying with the request, returning the requested response_type in a hidden form: it contains an id_token, a code, and even the state parameter, with the exact value provided in the request.

The HTML that's returned also contains a line of JavaScript that is meant to automatically submit the form (POSTing it to the app, as codified by the form method and action attributes) as soon as the browser loads that HTML.

You should be able to locate the subsequent POST request to the app a bit later in the list of frames. Here an edited dump of it:

```
POST https://localhost:44300/ HTTP/1.1
[...SNIP...]
Cookie: OpenIdConnect.nonce.NtAE[...SNIP...]yUDZOaw%3D%3D
```

```
code=AA[...SNIP...]AA&id_token=eyJ[...SNIP...]B1Q&state=OpenIdConnect[...SNIP...]&session_
state=93d[...SNIP...]28
```

The content of the body should not be surprising. It's just the execution of the form_post we just examined. The only thing I want to highlight is that the request includes the cookie tracking the nonce value, just as intended when it was generated together with the request. If something between the request and the response messes with that cookie—say, an antivirus or a global cookie-cleanse operation—the authentication will fail.

Here's the response to that POST:

```
HTTP/1.1 302 Found
[...SNIP...]
Set-Cookie: OpenIdConnect.nonce.NtAEBISzI9Su4nompbFjAZLP30DDfgVO9WcjUtrNdqM%3D=; path=/;
expires=Thu, 01-Jan-1970 00:00:00 GMT
Set-Cookie: .AspNet.Cookies=UhJY[...SNIP...]ZlhlA; path=/; secure; HttpOnly
[...SNIP...]
```

The first Set-Cookie invalidates the nonce value tracker, which at this point has performed its function and is no longer useful.

The second Set-Cookie establishes a local session, in line with the description of redirect-based sign-on protocols from Chapter 2.

What might surprise you is that the response to that request is a 302. There are two main reasons why it's not a 200. One reason is to enforce logical separation between the management of normal authenticated traffic and the establishment of a session. The other lies in the fact that the requested resource might live at a route that is different from the redirect_uri registered with Azure AD. Just a few pages ago I described the mechanism of saving in the state parameter the local URL of the requested resource: this 302 is where that mechanism comes into play. Note that in this example the requested resource is /, which happens to correspond to the exact value of redirect_uri, hence the 302 ends up taking place against the app's landing page itself.

The subsequent GET shows the blueprint of all authenticated resource requests from now until the session expires:

```
GET https://localhost:44300/ HTTP/1.1
Host: localhost:44300
Connection: keep-alive
Cache-Control: max-age=0
Accept: text/html,application/xhtml+xml,application/xml;q=0.9,image/webp,*/*;q=0.8
User-Agent: Mozilla/5.0 (Windows NT 6.3; WOW64) AppleWebKit/537.36 (KHTML, like Gecko)
Chrome/43.0.2357.124 Safari/537.36
Referer: https://login.microsoftonline.com/6c3d51dd-f0e5-4959-b4ea-a80c4e36fe5e/login
Accept-Encoding: gzip, deflate, sdch
Accept-Language: en-US,en;q=0.8
Cookie: .AspNet.Cookies=Uh [...SNIP...] lhlA
```

Every request includes the session cookie, which is validated by the OWIN cookie middleware.

And just like that, you have followed a full web sign-on journey down to the HTTP messages level! This already makes you far more of an expert than the vast majority of developers. There's just a couple of other aspects I want to cover to complete the journey: the content of the id_token and the simplest form of sign-out. But first, take a moment to step back from the nitty-gritty details and look at the sign-in flow sequence as a whole.

Sign-in sequence diagram

Figure 6-4 summarizes the sequence of messages you've observed as the sign-in operation unfolded.

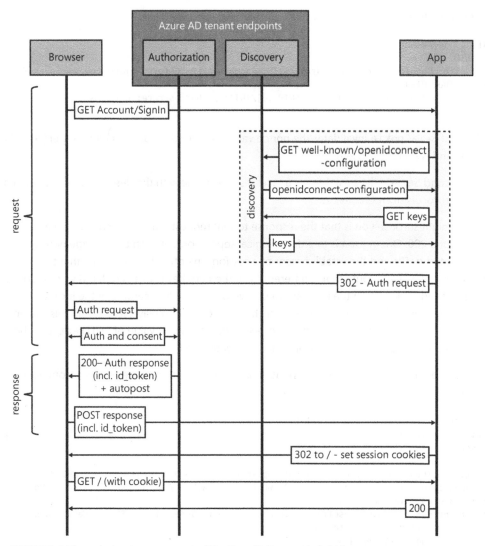

FIGURE 6-4 The web sign-in component of the OpenID Connect hybrid flow.

It took 20 pages to describe that flow, but only because I used it as an excuse to illustrate OpenID Connect in detail. When stripped of all its syntactic sugar, the sequence of messages becomes truly trivial. There's a request phase, where the app sends an authentication request to Azure AD's authorization endpoint. Azure AD then walks the user through the authentication and consent experience and returns the requested token following the method demanded by the app at request time.

The first request also includes a discovery step, where the app (in our case, through the OpenID Connect OWIN middleware) acquires the information required to validate tokens issued by the Azure AD tenant of choice.

The response is straightforward. The last 302 is left out of the bracket because it's not really OpenID Connect; it's more a service offered to developers by the libraries for handling local redirects and sessions.

Now that you've gained a bit of perspective on the process as a whole, let's dive back to the level of the protocol and specs one last time to learn about the all-important JSON Web Token (JWT) format and its role in OpenID Connect.

The ID token and the JWT format

The presence of the id_token is one of the key differentiators that makes OpenID Connect a viable sign-on protocol. It is worth spending some time exploring its structure, content, and function.

I'll start by extracting the token bits from the response and decoding them. There are various tools you can use to help you with this task. For example, you can find a Fiddler inspector at *https://github .com/vibronet/OInspector/tree/dev* that will do this for you. However, the goal of this chapter is to help you understand the low-level details of the protocol and messages. Hence, I will go about it in organic fashion, without any tools other than vanilla Fiddler.

Go back to the POST we examined earlier in the "Response" section. Locate the id_token="[... SNIP...]" part, and copy the string within the quotation marks. You will notice that the actual trace is not as neatly formatted as the dump I've pasted here, making the task of selecting the correct string a bit of a challenge. Feel free to click the View In Notepad button in Fiddler and select the string directly from the Notepad window.

The string should look like the following:

eyJ0eXAiOiJKV1QiLCJhbGciOiJSUzI1NiIsIng1dCI6Ik1uQ19WWmNBVGZNNXBPWW1KSE1iYT1nb0VLWSIsImtpZCI6Ik1u
Q19WWmNBVGZNNXBPWW1KSE1iYT1nb0VLWSJ9.eyJhdWQiOiJjM2Q1YjFhZC1hZTc3LTQ5YWMt0GE4Ni1kZDM5YTJmOTEwODE
iLCJpc3MiOiJodHRwczovL3N0cy53aW5kb3dzLm5ldC82YzNkNTFkZC1mMGU1LTQ5NTktYjR1YS1hODBjNGUzNmZ1NWUvIiw
iaWF0IjoxNDM0MzI4NzM2LCJuYmYiOjE0MzQzMjg3MzYsImV4cCI6MTQzNDMzMjYzNiwidmVyIjoiMS4wIiwidG1kIjoiNmM
zZDUxZGQtZjB1NS000TU5LWI0ZWEtYTgwYzR1MzZmZTV1Iiwib21kIjoiMTNkMzEwNGEtNjg5MS00NWQyLWE0YmUt0DI10DF
hOGU0NjViIiwidXBuIjoibWFyaW9AZGV2ZWxvcGVydGVuYW50Lm9ubW1jcm9zb2Z0Lm5vbSIsInN1YiI6Im9DeXF0M0tIa1B
ELVZiaVNhUnBhQUhQU2k5V2EyZVhmLVdhV0Y2WEozQTgiLCJnaXZlb19uYW11IjoiTWFyaW8iLCJmYW1pbH1fbmFtZSI6I1J
vc3NpIiwibmFtZSI6Ik1hcmlvIFJvc3NpIiwiY1yIjpbInB3ZCJdLCJibm1xdWVfbmFtZSI6Im1hcm1vQGR1dmVsb3B1cnR
1bmFudC5vbm1pY3J3c29mdC5jb20iLCJub25jZSI6IjYzNTY50TI10DI3MDIyNDk4MC5NR0ZoTURhMU9HHUXRPR1kyWXkwME9
HSmxMVGhtT0dFdFE9ERmhNbU5oWkRKaE9XWmpZVFF4T1RsbU5ETXRZalUzTUMwME1UUXpMVGt6WWppNdE1EZG1oelJsW1dZMU5
XWTQiLCJjX2hhc2giOiJ3cTddZbVU1QVBmZjhMZWMtazEtdVRnIiwicHdkX2V4cCI6IjMxMzcwMjkiLCJwd2RfdXJsIjoiaHR
0cHM6Ly9wb3J0YWwubWljcm9zb2Z0b25saW5lLm5vbS9DaGFuZ2VQYXNzd29yZC5hc3B4In0.TXo2700Ww6qD72MH9P23IfU
FRcqNOLmZy18D494pROE9em8QHrRStLvJJ6JjwFfaRBwYWPSBDrjqDrk2FtjOxLWzoAEcujdGQxwkPg030H-
YLsaIygDXAPJg_Khn19SwVP-wdiG-XYKQcIdfMnmrXK8nfajC4R7uP63agy1F2gK38Jgw3-JC_o-9IUoOP-
7YYFM8Kq0fwdHqLpqqxB51T_CWs9pq2uyk0WLe0fbh7GzGdDUebAc7JnVgUH91G1xWJGH_8mljJ7qzfA6o3DHk7GAHzdFXfC
PxQ8bKQp_18f1-I1Wd_KXcKgBFx0P47jq24CTFXAePdvqtp8DzLUWB1Q

You are almost certain not to notice this at first glance, but if you observe the string carefully, you will see that it is partitioned in three segments, each separated by a dot (.) character. Each segment is a Base64 encoded string. To reveal the actual content of the string, you need to decode it. There are plenty of decoders online, but Fiddler includes one out of the box. Search for TextWizard on the main menu, and click it. Paste the string into the top pane. Select From Base64 from the Transform drop-down list. Figure 6-5 gives you an idea of the result.

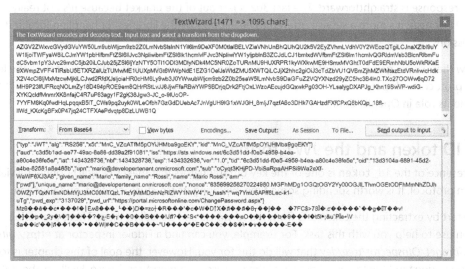

FIGURE 6-5 Using Fiddler's TextWizard to decode the id_token.

Here's the decoded `id_token`, formatted for ease of reference.

```
{
    "alg" : "RS256",
    "kid" : "MnC_VZcATfM5pOYiJHMba9goEKY",
    "typ" : "JWT",
    "x5t" : "MnC_VZcATfM5pOYiJHMba9goEKY"
}
{
    "amr" : [ "pwd" ],
    "aud" : "c3d5b1ad-ae77-49ac-8a86-dd39a2f91081",
    "c_hash" : "wq7YmU5APff8Lec-k1-uTg",
    "exp" : 1434332636,
    "family_name" : "Rossi",
    "given_name" : "Mario",
    "iat" : 1434328736,
    "iss" : "https://sts.windows.net/6c3d51dd-f0e5-4959-b4ea-a80c4e36fe5e/",
    "name" : "Mario Rossi",
    "nbf" : 1434328736,
    "nonce" : "635699258270224980.MGFhMDg1OGQtOGY2Yy000GJlLThmOGEtODFhMmNhZDJhOWZjYTQxNTlmNDMtYjU
3MC00MTQzLTkzYjMtMDdmNzRlZWY1NWY4",
    "oid" : "13d3104a-6891-45d2-a4be-82581a8e465b",
    "pwd_exp" : "3137029",
    "pwd_url" : "https://portal.microsoftonline.com/ChangePassword.aspx",
    "sub" : "oCyqt3KHjPD-VbiSaRpaAHPSi9Wa2eXf-WaWF6XJ3A8",
    "tid" : "6c3d51dd-f0e5-4959-b4ea-a80c4e36fe5e",
```

```
      "unique_name" : "mario@developertenant.onmicrosoft.com",
      "upn" : "mario@developertenant.onmicrosoft.com",
      "ver" : "1.0"
}
```
Mz6♦♦ê♦♦c♦[...SNIP...]

As you know by now, the id_token is in JWT format—the lightweight JSON format for tokens that I introduced in Chapter 2. That alone would be enough to make JWT a very important artifact for you to grok, but there's more: in Azure AD, every access token is also a JWT. As such, it's worth investing some time to understand the format in detail.

The JWT format

You read about the history of JWT in Chapter 2, in the sidebar "From SWT to JWT: A brief history of lightweight token formats." Standardized by the Internet Engineering Task Force (IETF) in May 2015 (the spec is available at *https://tools.ietf.org/html/rfc7519*), the JSON Web Token specification defines a compact token format capable of transporting claims in HTTP headers and URI query parameters. JWT relies on a lower-level spec, the JSON Web Signature (JWS; see *https://tools.ietf.org/html/rfc7515* for the spec), which describes ways of digitally signing a JSON payload and attaching to it all the info that is necessary for validating such a signature.

> **Note** JWT also relies on JSON Web encryption (JWE, spec at *https://tools.ietf.org/html/ rfc7516*) for defining how to encrypt tokens, but Azure AD does not support JWE at this time (so I won't explore it further in this edition of the book).

The specs are very comprehensive—and surprisingly readable. I invite you to check them out if you want to learn about the true extent of the format's expressive power. Here, I just want to give you enough terminology and understanding of the features used in the context of Azure AD to allow you to competently troubleshoot and customize solutions.

The three parts we identified in the token we captured correspond to three canonical components of a JSON payload and an accompanying signature, as defined by JWS:

- **JWS Protected Header** This part contains information about the other parts: the token format (for our scenarios, it's JWT), what algorithm was used to compute the digital signatures, and various ways of referring to the key that should be used for verifying such a signature. The header must be a UTF8 string. As you have seen from the trace, it is Base64 encoded—in fact, to be super precise, it is Base64*url* encoded—that is to say, encoded with a URL and a filename-safe alphabet as defined in *https://tools.ietf.org/html/rfc4648#section-5*. A good trick to recognize it at a glance? There is no trailing equal sign (=) in Base64url encoding.

- **JWS Payload** This is the actual content we want to transmit. For JWS, the payload can be pretty much whatever, but for JWT, it is the set of claims we want to transport. As such, in JWT this portion is the JWT claim set. This portion also travels in Base64url encoded format.

- **JWS Signature** This part carries the bits of the signature proper, performed on the concatenation of the encoded JWS Protected Header plus the dot (.) character, plus the encoded JWT Payload. The signature is calculated with the algorithm and key specified in the header, is Base64url encoded, and concatenated (via the usual ".") to the other parts. As you might have noticed from the funny characters in the decoded output in Figure 6-5, this portion is actually binary.

The JWT structure is summarized in Figure 6-6.

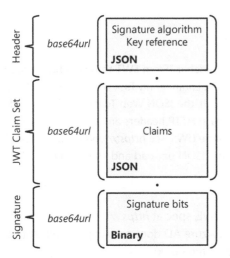

FIGURE 6-6 Functional components of a JWT.

In a nutshell, a resource receiving a JWT will parse the header to confirm that it's a JWT, resolve the key references to retrieve the actual key bits (and take issue if the key cannot be retrieved), and learn which algorithm should be used to check the signature. It will calculate the signature of the combined header and payload bits, comparing the value with the one traveling in the JWT Signature portion. A successful match will indicate that the content has not been tampered with.

> **Important** One subtlety that is not immediately evident to everybody is that a successful signature check is only the beginning of the validation process. It just means that the token has not been modified in transit, but per se it does not say whether the key that was used for signing is one of the keys of the IdP you trust. Remember in the "Discovery" section, where the middleware acquired the keys of our target Azure AD tenant? Not only must the key indicated by the JWT header successfully compute the signature, it also needs to be one of the keys we discovered.

Please remember that developers will rarely, if ever, operate at this level. Libraries and middleware are the natural consumers of this information, taking care of all the cryptography and distilling data away in more abstract form for the application layer. As usual, knowing what's going on below the surface is useful mostly for troubleshooting and customization purposes. The JWS/JWT parts that hold some actionable value for you are the header and the JWT claim set, the latter more than the former.

JWS Header For convenience, here again are the JWT header bits of the decoded `id_token` from the trace:

```
{
    "alg" : "RS256",
    "kid" : "MnC_VZcATfM5pOYiJHMba9goEKY",
    "typ" : "JWT",
    "x5t" : "MnC_VZcATfM5pOYiJHMba9goEKY"
}
```

The JWS spec lists a number of registered header parameter names and details the possible values they can assume. In so doing it relies on yet another specification, JSON Web Algorithms (JWA, see *https://tools.ietf.org/html/rfc7518*), which provides a registry of well-known values and a central place for future extensions. If you are wondering how deep this specifications rabbit hole runs, don't worry: it does go deeper, but this level is as deep as I will go in the context of this book.

The easiest header parameter to describe is typ, indicating the media type of the bits being signed. For us, this will always be JWT, but JWT can be used for signing pretty much anything you'll find listed at *http://www.iana.org/assignments/media-types/media-types.xhtml*.

The alg header gets funnier. A signature operation can be performed through multiple algorithms. The aforementioned JWA spec lists a bunch of well-known ones, with detailed guidance on what identifier to use and how to apply the operation on the bits.

The value we have here, RS256, indicates a signature performed with an RSA key using the SHA-256 hashing function. I might point you to the RFC 3447 specification to expand on what that exactly means, but I promised I wouldn't go any further. Suffice to say that RS256 uses public key cryptography and, in the case of Azure AD, the keys are handled via X.509 certificates.

You should not be surprised that the `id_token` we received from Azure AD was signed using RS256. If you turn back to the "Discovery" section and take a look at the .well-known/OpenId-Configuration document, you will notice that it contains `"id_token_signing_alg_values_supported" : [ "RS256" ]`. Now you know what that means.

The kid header carries an identifier for the key used for performing the signature. If you go back to the "Signing keys" section and take a look at the keys-definition document, you will notice that the value of the kid header here matches exactly the one for the second key on file. That means that the key used actually belongs to Azure AD, as expected.

The x5t header can be used in case the key is stored as a X.509 certificate—it represents the certificate's thumbprint. It is still an identifier, but given that it is computed from the certificate bits themselves, it carries cryptographic strength. You might have noticed that in this case its value is the same as for kid.

There are various other header types, but you'll encounter them more rarely in Azure AD. (Look them up in the specification if you need to.)

JWT Claim Set JWT defines a number of registered claim names that represent common ground for all implementers. These are mostly claims that are useful for validating the incoming token. Here's a list of the intersection between the claims registered by the JWT specification and the ones actually present in the id_token from the trace you captured.

- **iss** This claim represents the identity of the issuer of the token. In this case that's the Azure AD tenant where you provisioned the application.

    If you examine the value of the iss claim in the captured token (in my case it's https://sts .windows.net/6c3d51dd-f0e5-4959-b4ea-a80c4e36fe5e/) and compare it with the issuer value in the discovery method, you will see that they are the same.

    The OpenID Connect OWIN middleware validates the issuer by default, comparing what it finds in iss with what it read in issuer from the discovery document—and refusing any token that does not comply. You will see later in the book that you will want to relax this behavior at times, especially when your app needs to accept tokens from multiple Azure AD tenants, each with its unique issuer value.

- **sub** The sub is an identifier of the subject that went through the authentication process—in this case, the user. Azure AD guarantees that the value of sub is unique and not reassignable.

- **aud** This claim indicates the audience of the token; that is to say, its intended recipient. The captured token bits will show that in this case the value of aud is exactly the client_id that was assigned by Azure AD to your application. You can think of the audience claim as what's written for "pay to the order of" on a bank check. If somebody tries to pay you with a check, but that check indicates someone else as the payee, you are not going to accept the check no matter how legitimate it appears. The same goes with tokens. If your application receives a token with an aud that is different from the app's identifier, that token does *not* prove that the caller successfully obtained a token for your app from Azure AD. The caller might have stolen that token from a transaction with a different app, for example.

    The OpenID Connect OWIN middleware validates the audience by default, comparing what it finds in aud with the client_id value you provide in the middleware initialization.

- **exp** This claim indicates the expiration time of the token. If the token is received an instant later than this value, it must be refused. Typically, the request-issuance-validation chain introduces small clock discrepancies, which our libraries try to account for by introducing some tolerance, so don't expect checks to be too strict here.

- **nbf** nbf ("not before") is the partner of exp. Tokens received at a time that predates nbf must be refused.

- **iat** This claim represents the instant at which the JWT was issued. This can come in handy in case you want to know how old the token really is.

id_token validation

OpenID Connect establishes that the id_token is in JWT format and then proceeds to describe in detail how to validate it. That mostly boils down to mandating the presence of specific claims and describing what criteria they must meet for each of the flows it defines—hybrid, authorization code, and implicit.

The hybrid flow, chosen by default by the OpenID Connect OWIN middleware, is the flow with the most requirements. I won't repeat them verbatim here. The protocol's spec is very clear and easy to consult for this information. I just want to point out the validations that are most likely to provoke failures on real solutions so that you have a starting point.

- The signature must be validated.

- The iss, sub, aud, exp, and iat claims from the canonical claims list in the JWT spec must all be present and validated as I described in their definitions, including all the ties to the discovery constraints (for example, the iss value must match the identifier in issuer from the discovery document).

- The id_token must contain a nonce claim, whose content must match the content provided in the request (in our case, saved in a cookie).

- This does not really come into play in this chapter, given that in this scenario we ignore the authorization code returned alongside the id_token, but per the specification, the id_token must contain a claim c_hash that is derived from the value of the authorization code. In practice, if an attacker would substitute the code in the response message, the c_hash claim would no longer correspond to the code value and would make the validation fail.

Other claims in Azure AD's id_token

As I write, Azure AD's id_tokens come with a number of other claims that aren't strictly used for validation, but they come in handy in describing the subject and piggyback extra functionality on top of the authentication flow. (Again, there is no guarantee that this list will be the same by the time you have this book in your hands, but it probably won't be completely different.)

- auth_time   This claim captures the time at which the user was authenticated.

- acr   This claim, short for authentication context class reference, expresses the level of assurance associated with the authentication method that was used for issuing the token.

- amr   amr represents the authentication method (or methods) that was used to authenticate the user. The captured token actually includes this claim, with the value ["pwd"]—that is to say, an array with one single element, indicating that the user authenticated via a password.

- email   The email address of the user. The temptation to use this claim as an identifier is strong, but it would be a mistake because an email address is not guaranteed to be unique.

- given_name, family_name, name, nickname   These are all mnemonic identifiers. They mean what you think they mean, but if you want to be certain . . . check the OpenID Connect Core specification.

- oid   Short for Object ID, this claim contains the unique, nonreassignable identifier that Azure AD uses for identifying the caller within the tenant. Management operations on the caller (creation, update, modification) can all use this identifier to indicate which entity should be modified.

- pwd_exp   This claim indicates the moment at which the password for the current user will expire.

- pwd_url   Traveling in tandem with pwd_exp, pwd_url indicates the URL to which the user can navigate to access pages providing password-change functionality.

- tid   tid stands for tenant identifier. If you compare its value in the captured token with the GUID in all the endpoints and the issuer value advertised in the discovery document, you'll find that they are the same.

- upn   This is the usual user principal name. It's a bit better than email as an identifier but still not perfect, given that it can be reassigned. Also, not every authentication flow leads to a UPN.

- unique_name   This is a (somewhat) human-readable identifier that is guaranteed to be present for users, even when upn is not. In cases in which upn is present, unique_name has the same value.

- groups, roles   These multivalue claim types are used to transmit role and group membership information about the user. Groups are represented as the object IDs of the groups in the directory. I will have more to say about these claims when I discuss the Azure AD application model in later chapters.

OpenID Connect exchanges for signing out from the app and Azure AD

You have learned how to establish a session, so it seems only fair to conclude by studying how to end one as well.

Assuming that you captured the trace according to the instructions, scroll down the frames list to find a GET of Account/SignOut. This is the action you implemented in Chapter 5 that triggers the HttpContext.GetOwinContext().Authentication.SignOut code against the OpenID Connect and cookie middlewares. Select the frame and inspect the response. It should look like the following:

```
HTTP/1.1 302 Found
[...SNIP...]
Location: https://login.microsoftonline.com/6c3d51dd-f0e5-4959-b4ea-a80c4e36fe5e/oauth2/
logout?post_logout_redirect_uri=https%3a%2f%2flocalhost%3a44300%2f
[...SNIP...]
Set-Cookie: .AspNet.Cookies=; path=/; expires=Thu, 01-Jan-1970 00:00:00 GMT
[...SNIP...]
```

The Set-Cookie operation gets rid of the app's own session cookie. That alone would not be much of a sign-out because at this point the user is still signed in with Azure AD. That is, there is still a cookie tied to the Azure AD domain, which would allow the user to get a new token for the app without any prompt—signing right back in.

Cleaning the session with Azure AD is the purpose of that 302 message returned in the Location header. The sign-out request syntax is described in the OpenID Connect Session Management specification (available at *http://openid.net/specs/openid-connect-session-1_0.html*—at this time it is still an implementers' draft). Here are a few observations:

- The target endpoint, `https://login.microsoftonline.com/6c3d51dd-f0e5-4959-b4ea-a80c4e36fe5e/oauth2/logout`, was advertised by the discovery document under the property `end_session_endpoint`.

- The parameter `post_logout_redirect_uri` instructs Azure AD to redirect the browser to the indicated URI once the sign-out operation concludes.

- Although the default logout logic does not use it, you can use the `state` parameter to preserve state between the request and response, just as you've seen for the sign-in flow.

- It is possible for one user to be signed in to Azure AD with more than one account simultaneously. What should Azure AD do upon receiving a sign-out request? The protocol helps to solve the ambiguity by providing a parameter, `id_token_hint`, which can be used for indicating which account should be signed out. In this case, you would simply provide the id_token you received at authentication time.

The frames that follow show how Azure AD reacts to the request. I won't include the detailed traces here. The implementation details (endpoints, cookies, messages) aren't part of the contract and are likely to change. However, the gist of it is that Azure AD updates its tracking cookies (like the one listing the currently signed-in accounts) and cleans up the ones containing details of the account session.

That done, Azure AD redirects back to the address specified by `post_logout_redirect_uri`, which in our case is the app's root. The user is now signed out: access to the protected portions of the app will require a new sign-in operation.

Figure 6-7 summarizes the flow.

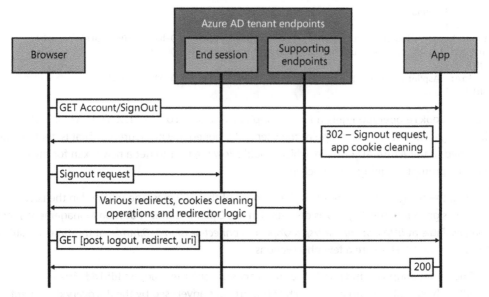

FIGURE 6-7 The sign-out flow sequence.

Summary

This chapter offered you an in-depth look at how Azure AD uses OpenID Connect to implement web sign-on. I did not leave any stone unturned, examining the meaning of every parameter on the wire and even mentioning values that the specs define and that could have been used to customize the sign-in flow. Although the content of the chapter was undoubtedly biased toward Azure AD and its defaults, most of what you learned about OpenID Connect and JWT applies to any service using those specs.

Now that you are aware of what goes on at the wire level, you are ready to go beyond the basics and customize default request generation, response processing, and validation to fit your scenarios. The next chapter examines the OpenID Connect OWIN middleware and supporting classes (such as those handling the JWT format), showing you what settings and extensibility points you can use to leverage your newfound protocol knowledge.

CHAPTER 7

The OWIN OpenID Connect middleware

In this chapter I focus on the OpenID Connect middleware and supporting classes. These are the cornerstones of ASP.NET's support for web sign-on.

As you saw in Chapter 5, "Getting started with web sign-on and Active Directory," in the most common case, the OpenID Connect middleware requires very few parameters to enable web sign-on. Beneath that simple surface, however, are knobs for practically anything you want to control: protocol parameters, initialization strategies, token validation, message processing, and so on. This chapter will reveal the various layers of the object model for you, showing how you can fine-tune the authentication process to meet your needs.

OWIN and Katana

When I wrote *Programming Windows Identity Foundation* (Microsoft Press) in 2009, I didn't have to spend much time explaining HttpModule, the well-established ASP.NET extensibility technology on which WIF was built. This time around, however, I cannot afford the luxury of assuming that you are already familiar with OWIN and its implementation in ASP.NET—this is the foundational technology of the new generation of authentication libraries.

OWIN is a stable standard at this point, but its implementations are still relatively new technologies. You can find plenty of information online, but the details are rapidly changing (as I write, ASP.NET vNext is in the process of renaming lots of classes and properties), and you need to have a solid understanding of the pipeline and model underlying the identity functionality.

In this section I provide a quick tour of OWIN (as implemented in Katana 3.0.1) and the features that are especially relevant for the scenarios I've described throughout the book. For more details, you can refer to the online documentation from the ASP.NET team.

What is OWIN?

OWIN stands for Open Web Interface for .NET. It is a community-driven specification: Microsoft is just a contributor, albeit a very important one. Here's the official definition, straight from the specifications' home page at *http://owin.org/*.

OWIN defines a standard interface between .NET web servers and web applications. The goal of the OWIN interface is to decouple server and application, encourage the development of simple modules for .NET web development, and, by being an open standard, stimulate the open source ecosystem of .NET web development tools.

In essence, OWIN suggests a way of building software modules (called *middlewares*) that can process HTTP requests and responses. It also describes a way in which those modules can be concatenated in a processing pipeline and defines how that pipeline can be hosted without relying on any specific web server or host or the features of a particular development stack.

The core idea is that, at every instant, the state of an HTTP transaction and the server-side processing of it is represented by a dictionary of the following form:

```
IDictionary<string, object>
```

This is commonly known as the *environment dictionary*. You can expect to find in it the usual request and response data (host, headers, query string, URI scheme, and so on) alongside any data that might be required for whatever processing an app needs to perform. Where does the data come from? Some of it, like the request details, must eventually come from the web server. The rest is the result of the work of the middleware in the pipeline.

Oversimplifying, a middleware is a module that implements the following interface:

```
Func<IDictionary<string, object>, Task>;
```

I am sure you have already guessed how things might work. The middleware receives the environment dictionary as input, acts on it to perform the middleware's function, and then hands it over to the next middleware in the pipeline. For example, logging middleware might read the dictionary and pass it along unmodified, but an authentication middleware might find a 401 code in the dictionary and decide to transform it into a 302, modifying the response to include an authentication request. By using the dictionary as the way of communicating and sharing context, as opposed to calling each other directly, middlewares achieve a level of decoupling that was not possible in older approaches.

How do you bootstrap all this? At startup, the middleware pipeline needs to be constructed and initialized: you need to decide what middlewares should be included and in which order and ensure that requests and responses will be routed through the pipeline accordingly. The OWIN specification has a section that defines a generic mechanism for this, but given that you will be working mostly with the ASP.NET-specific implementation, I won't go into much detail on that.

I skipped an awful lot of what the formulaic descriptions of OWIN normally include (like the formal definitions of application, middleware, server, and host), but I believe that this brief description should provide you enough scaffolding for understanding Katana, ASP.NET's implementation of OWIN.

Katana

Katana is the code name for a set of Microsoft's .NET 4.5–based components that utilize the OWIN specification to implement various functionalities in ASP.NET 4.6. It's what you used in Chapter 1 and Chapter 5 and includes base middleware classes, a framework for initializing the pipeline, pipeline hosts for ASP.NET, and a large collection of middlewares for all sorts of tasks.

Katana != OWIN

OWIN is an abstract specification. Katana is a set of concrete classes that implement that spec, but it also introduces its own implementation choices for tasks that aren't fully specified or in scope for the OWIN spec. In giving technical guidance, it's easy to say something to the effect "in OWIN, you do X," but it is often more proper to say "in Katana, you do X." I am sure I will be guilty of this multiple times: please accept my blanket apologies in advance.

In Chapter 5 you encountered most of the Katana NuGet packages and assemblies that appear in common scenarios. You also successfully used them by entering the code I suggested. Here I'll reexamine all that, explaining what really happens.

Startup and *IAppBuilder*

In Chapter 5, in the section "Host the OWIN pipeline," you created a `Startup` class and decorated its source file with the `assembly:OwinStartup` attribute. The function of `Startup` is to initialize the OWIN pipeline by having its `Configure` method automatically invoked at initialization. To follow current practices, I instructed you to make `Startup` partial and to put the actual pipeline-building code in another file—but you could have just as well added the code in line in `Startup`.

Using the attribute is only one of several ways of telling Katana which class should act as `Startup`. You can also do the following:

- Have one class named `Startup` in the assembly or the global namespace.

- Use the `OwinStartup` attribute. The attribute wins against the naming convention (using `Startup`): if both techniques are used, the attribute will be the one driving the behavior.

- Add an entry under `<appSettings>` in the app config file, of the form

  `<add key="owin:appStartup" value=" WebAppChapter5.Startup" />`.

  This entry wins over both the naming convention and the attribute.

Fun times! I've listed these alternatives so that you know where to look if your app appears to magically pick up code without an obvious reason. I used to feel like that all the time when I first started with Katana.

Let's now turn our attention to `Startup.Configure`. Observe the method's signature:

```
public void Configure(IAppBuilder app)
```

`IAppBuilder` is an interface designed to support the initialization of the application. It looks like this:

```
public interface IAppBuilder
{
    IDictionary<string, object> Properties { get; }

    object Build(Type returnType);
    IAppBuilder New();
    IAppBuilder Use(object middleware, params object[] args);
}
```

The `Properties` dictionary is used in turn by the server and host to record their capabilities and initialize data, making it available to the application's initialization code—that is to say, whatever you put in `Configure`. In the case of our sample app, the server is IIS Express and the host is the SystemWeb host we referenced when adding the NuGet package with the same name.

> **Note** That host is actually an `HttpModule` designed to host the OWIN pipeline. That's the trick Katana uses to integrate with the traditional `System.Web` pipeline.

The `Build` method is rarely called in your own code, so I'll ignore it here. The `Use` method enables you to add middleware to the pipeline, and I'll get to that in a moment.

To prove to you that the host does indeed populate app at startup, let's take a peek at the app parameter when `Configure` is first invoked. Open Visual Studio, open the solution from Chapter 5, place a breakpoint on the first line of `Configure`, and hit F5. Once the breakpoint is reached, navigate to the Locals tab and look at the content of app. You should see something similar to Figure 7-1.

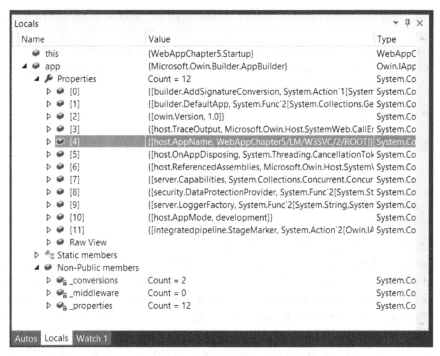

FIGURE 7-1 The content of the app parameter at `Configure` time.

Wow, we didn't even start, and look at how much stuff is there already!

Katana provides a concrete type for `IAppBuilder`, named `AppBuilder`. As expected, the `Properties` dictionary arrives already populated with server, host, and environment properties. Feel free to ignore the actual values at this point. Just as an example, in Figure 7-1 I highlighted the `host.AppName` property holding the IIS metabase path for the app.

The nonpublic members hold a very interesting entry: `_middleware`. If you keep an eye on that entry as you go through the pipeline-initialization code in the next section, you will see the value of Count grow at every invocation of `Use*`.

Middlewares, pipeline, and context

Stop the debugger and head to Startup.Auth.cs, where you will find the implementation of `ConfigureAuth`. This is where you actually add middleware to the pipeline, through the calls to `UseCookieAuthentication` and `UseOpenIdConnectAuthentication`. Those are convenience extension methods. `UseCookieAuthentication` is equivalent to this:

```
app.Use(typeof(CookieAuthenticationMiddleware), app, options);
```

The effect of Use is to add the corresponding middleware to the pipeline in AppBuilder—as you can observe by watching the aforementioned _middleware. Although technically a middleware might simply satisfy the Func interface mentioned at the beginning, Katana offers patterns that are a bit more structured. One easy example can be found by examining OwinMiddleware, a base class for middlewares. It's super simple:

```
public abstract class OwinMiddleware
{
    protected OwinMiddleware(OwinMiddleware next)
    {
        Next = next;
    }
    protected OwinMiddleware Next { get; set; }
    public abstract Task Invoke(IOwinContext context);
}
```

Every middleware provides an Invoke method, accepting an IOwinContext, which is a convenience wrapper of the environment dictionary from the OWIN specs. In addition, every middleware can hold a pointer to the next entry in the pipeline. The idea is that when you call a middleware's Invoke method, the middleware can do its work on the context (typically, the request part of it), await the Invoke call of the next middleware in the pipeline, and do more work (this time on the response) once the Invoke method of the next middleware returns. As mentioned earlier, middlewares communicate via shared context: each middleware can examine the IOwinContext instance to find out what the preceding middleware did. You can see a diagram of this flow in Figure 7-2. The diagram is specific to the sample application scenario—hence IIS and the System.Web model—to make things as concrete as possible. However, I want to stress that the middleware activation sequence would remain the same even if it were hosted elsewhere.

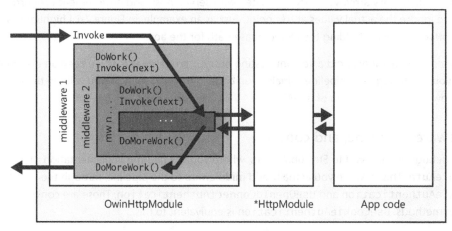

FIGURE 7-2 The OWIN pipeline as implemented by Katana in the sample application scenario: an HttpModule, hosting a cascade of middlewares.

Note that one middleware can always decide that no further processing should happen. In that case the middleware will not call the Invoke method of the next middleware in the sequence, effectively short-circuiting the pipeline.

Note `OwinMiddleware` is great for explaining the base functionality of the middleware, but in practice it raises interop issues. If you plan to build your own middleware (which is far outside the scope of this book), you should consider achieving the same behaviors without using it.

There's a neat trick you can use for observing firsthand how the middleware pipeline unfolds. You can interleave the Use* sequence with your own debug middlewares, and then place strategic breakpoints or debug messages. Here's the pattern for a minimal middleware-like debug implementation:

```
app.Use(async (Context, next) =>
{
    // request processing - do something here
    await next.Invoke();
    // response processing - do something here
});
```

That's pretty easy. Here's the sequence from the sample app, modified accordingly:

```
app.SetDefaultSignInAsAuthenticationType(CookieAuthenticationDefaults.AuthenticationType);
app.Use(async (Context, next) =>
{
    Debug.WriteLine("1 ==>request, before cookie auth");
    await next.Invoke();
    Debug.WriteLine("6 <==response, after cookie auth");
});

app.UseCookieAuthentication(new CookieAuthenticationOptions());

app.Use(async (Context, next) =>
{
    Debug.WriteLine("2 ==>after cookie, before OIDC");
    await next.Invoke();
    Debug.WriteLine("5 <==after OIDC");
});

app.UseOpenIdConnectAuthentication(
    new OpenIdConnectAuthenticationOptions
    {
        ClientId = "c3d5b1ad-ae77-49ac-8a86-dd39a2f91081",
        Authority = "https://login.microsoftonline.com/DeveloperTenant.onmicrosoft.com",
        PostLogoutRedirectUri = https://localhost:44300/
    }
);

app.Use(async (Context, next) =>
{
    Debug.WriteLine("3 ==>after OIDC, before leaving the pipeline");
    await next.Invoke();
    Debug.WriteLine("4 <==after entering the pipeline, before OIDC");
});
```

The numbers in front of every debug message express the sequence you should see when all the middlewares have a chance to fire. Any discontinuity in the sequence will tell you that some middleware decided to short-circuit the pipeline by not invoking its next middleware buddy.

Run the sample app and see whether everything works as expected. But before you do, you need to disable one Visual Studio feature that interferes with our experiment: it's the Browser Link. The Browser Link helps Visual Studio communicate with the browser running the app that's being debugged and allows it to respond to events. The unfortunate side effect for our scenario is that Browser Link produces extra traffic. In Chapter 6, "OpenID Connect and Azure AD web sign-on," we solved the issue by hiding the extra requests via Fiddler filters, but that's not an option here. Luckily, it's easy to opt out of the feature. Just add the following line to the <appSettings> section in the web.config file for the app:

```
<add key="vs:EnableBrowserLink" value="false"></add>
```

That done, hit F5. As the home page loads, the output window will show something like the following:

```
1 ==>request, before cookie auth
2 ==>after cookie, before OIDC
3 ==>after OIDC, before leaving the pipeline
'iisexpress.exe' (CLR v4.0.30319: /LM/W3SVC/2/ROOT-1-130799278910142565): Loaded 'C:\windows\
assembly\GAC_MSIL\Microsoft.VisualStudio.Debugger.Runtime\14.0.0.0__b03f5f7f11d50a3a\Microsoft.
VisualStudio.Debugger.Runtime.dll'. Skipped loading symbols. Module is optimized and the
debugger option 'Just My Code' is enabled.
4 <==after entering the pipeline, before OIDC
5 <==after OIDC
6 <==response, after cookie auth
```

You can see that all the middlewares executed, and all in the order that was predicted when you assigned sequence numbers. Never mind that this doesn't appear to do anything! You'll find out more about that in the next section.

Click Contact or Sign In on the home page. Assuming that you are not already signed in, you should see pretty much the same sequence you've seen earlier (so I won't repeat the output window content here), but at the end of it your browser will redirect to Azure AD for authentication. Authenticate, and then take a look at the output window to see what happens as the browser returns to the app. You should see something like this:

```
1 ==>request, before cookie auth
2 ==>after cookie, before OIDC
5 <==after OIDC
6 <==response, after cookie auth
1 ==>request, before cookie auth
2 ==>after cookie, before OIDC
3 ==>after OIDC, before leaving the pipeline
4 <==after entering the pipeline, before OIDC
5 <==after OIDC
6 <==response, after cookie auth
```

This time you see a gap. As the request comes back with the token, notice that the first part of the sequence stops at the OpenID Connect middleware—the jump from 2 to 5 indicates that the last debug middleware was not executed, and presumably the same can be said for the rest of the following stages.

What happened? Recall what you studied in the section "Response" in Chapter 6: when the OpenID Connect middleware first receives the token, it does not grant access to the app right away. Rather, it sends back a 302 for honoring any internal redirect and performs a set-cookie operation for placing the session cookie in the browser. That's exactly what happens in the steps 1, 2, 5, and 6: the OpenID Connect middleware decides that no further processing should take place and initiates the response sequence. The full 1–6 sequence that follows is what happens when the browser executes the 302 and comes back with a session cookie.

That's it. At this point, you should have a good sense of how middlewares come together to form a single, coherent pipeline. The last generic building block you need to examine is the context that all middlewares use to communicate.

Sign out of the app and stop the debugger so that the next exploration will start from a clean slate.

IIS integrated pipeline events and middleware execution

By now you know that Katana runs its middleware pipeline in an `HttpModule`, which participates in the usual IIS integrated pipeline. If you are familiar with that, you also know that `HttpModule`s can subscribe to multiple predefined events, such as `AuthenticateRequest`, `AuthorizeRequest`, and `PreExecuteRequestHandler`.

By default, Katana middleware executes during `PreExecuteRequestHandler`, although there are exceptions. There is a mechanism you can use for requesting execution of given segments of the middleware pipeline at a specific event in the IIS integrated pipeline, and that's by using the extension method `UseStageMarker`.

Adding `app.UseStageMarker(PipelineStage.Authenticate)` tells Katana to execute in the `AuthenticateRequest` IIS event all the middlewares registered so far, or as far as the first preceding `UseStageMarker` directive.

This is not the whole story: for example, it's possible to use stage markers for requesting sequences that are incompatible with the natural sequencing of events in the IIS pipeline. There are a number of rules that determine Katana's behavior in those cases. Please refer to the ASP.NET documentation for details.

Context Before getting to the specifics of authentication, let's invest a few moments to get to know the OWIN context better.

Place a breakpoint in the first diagnostic middleware, on the line that writes the message marked with 1. Hit F5, and once the execution reaches your breakpoint, head to the Locals tab and take a look at the content of the Context parameter. You should see what's depicted in Figure 7-3.

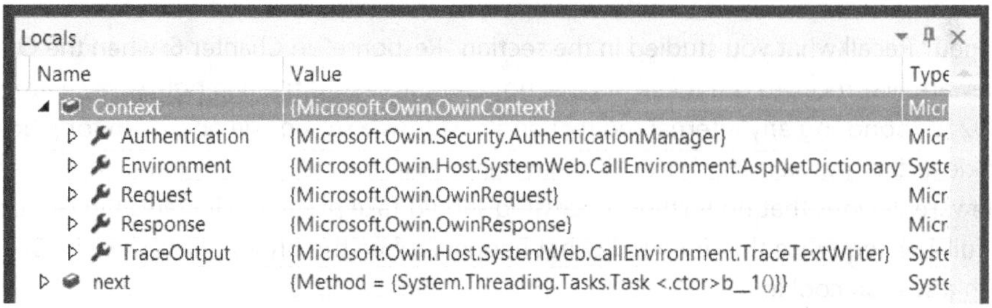

FIGURE 7-3 The structure of the Katana context.

Let's cover each of the entries here.

- *Authentication* The Authentication property is used for exposing authentication capabilities of the current pipeline. You saw this in action when you implemented the sign-in and sign-out features in Chapter 5, via the Challenge and SignOut methods, respectively.

  Authentication is also used by authentication middlewares for communicating with one another, as you will see in the next section. As Figure 7-4 shows, when the request first enters the pipeline, Authentication is empty. You will learn about this property in detail when we focus on the authentication middleware.

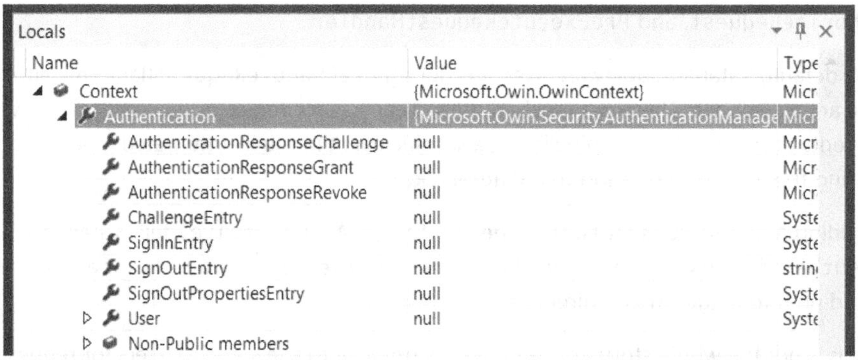

FIGURE 7-4 The Context.Authentication property content upon receiving the first unauthenticated request.

- *Environment* As the OWIN specification states, the core status of an OWIN pipeline is captured by the environment dictionary. Figure 7-5 shows how the Katana implementation features all the values prescribed by the OWIN specification, plus a few more.

FIGURE 7-5 The content of the OWIN environment dictionary on first request.

- *Request* and *Response* If you are familiar with HTTP request and response manipulation in traditional ASP.NET, you should be quite comfortable with their similarly named Context properties in Katana. Figure 7-6 shows an example.

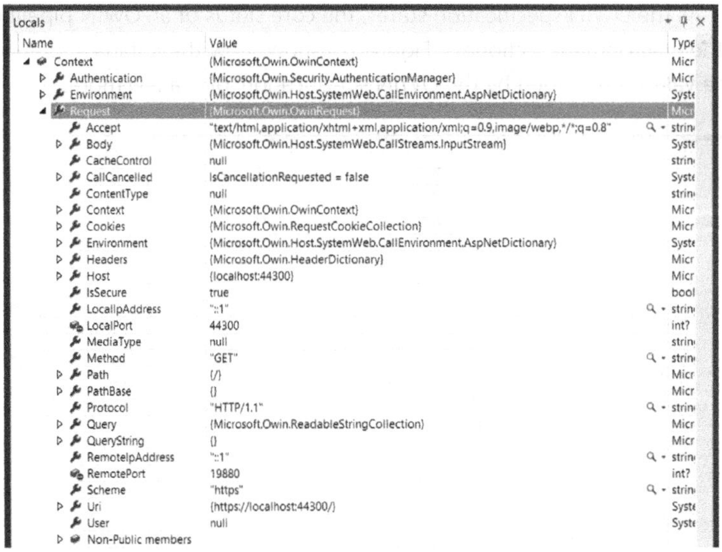

FIGURE 7-6 The first request, represented by the `Context.Request` property.

- *TraceOutput* This property is mainly a clever way of exposing a standard trace at the OWIN level, regardless of the specific host used to run the pipeline.

Add more breakpoints for the other debug middlewares and see how `Context` changes as the execution sweeps through the pipeline. After you have experimented with this, head to the next section, where I review the authentication flow through the OWIN pipeline in detail.

Authentication middleware

The authentication functionality emerges from the collaboration of a protocol middleware (like those for OpenID Connect or WS-Federation) and the cookie middleware. The protocol middleware reacts to requests and responses by generating and processing protocol messages, with all that entails (token validation and so on). The cookie middleware persists sessions in the form of cookies at sign-in and enforces the presence and validity of such cookies from the instant of authentication onward. All communication between the two middlewares takes place via the `AuthenticationManager` instance in the `Context`. Let's break down the sign-in flow we captured earlier into three phases: generation of the sign-in challenge, response processing and session generation, and access in the context of a session.

Sign-in redirect message Assume that you triggered the sign-in flow by clicking Contact. As you observed, this action results in all the middlewares firing in the expected order, and it concludes with the redirection of the browser toward Azure AD with an authorization request message.

If you go through the flow while keeping an eye on `Context.Response`, you will notice that after the request leaves the OWIN pipeline (after the debug message marked 3), something changes the Response's `StatusCode` to 401. In this case, that was the good old [`Authorize`], which does its job to enforce authenticated access regardless of the presence of the OWIN pipeline.

If you go beyond the breakpoint on debug message 4 and let the OpenID Connect middleware execute, you will observe that `Response.StatusCode` changes again, this time to 302. If you dig into the `Response.Headers` collection, you will notice a new entry, Location, containing the OpenID Connect authorization request. Moreover, you will find a new Set-Cookie entry for saving the OpenID Connect nonce.

Walking through the rest of the breakpoint, you will see the response message go unmodified through the remainder of the pipeline and back to the browser.

In Katana parlance, the OpenID Connect middleware is Active by default. That means that its options class's `AuthenticationMode` property is set to `Active`, which makes it react to 401 responses by generating its sign-in challenge message. That is not always what you want: for example, if you have multiple protocol middlewares configured to talk to different IdPs, you will want explicit control (via calls to `Authentication.Challenge`) over what middleware should be in charge to generate the sign-in message at a given moment.

Figure 7-7 displays the steps in the sequence of the sign-in message generation phase.

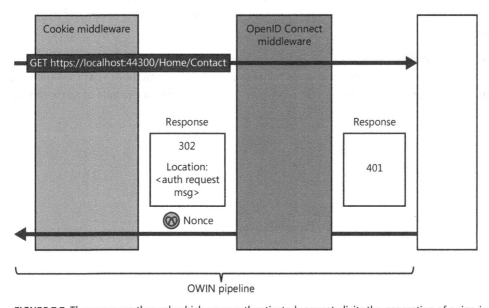

FIGURE 7-7 The sequence through which an unauthenticated request elicits the generation of a sign-in message.

Token validation and establishment of a session   The sequence that processes the Azure AD response carrying the token (characterized by the debug sequence 1, 2, 5, 6 earlier) is the one requiring the most sophisticated logic.

The request goes through the cookie middleware (breakpoints on messages 1 and 2) unmodified. However, as soon as you step over the `Invoke` call in the diagnostic middleware that calls the OpenID Connect middleware, you'll observe that the execution goes straight to the breakpoint on debug message 5, skipping the rest of the pipeline and the app itself and initiating the response.

Once again, the Response object carries a 302. If you recall the explanations in the earlier section, you know that this 302 means that the middleware successfully validated the token received and is now using a redirect operation to perform any local redirect and persist the session cookie in the client browser. If you take a look at the `Response.Header` collection, you will find a Location entry redirecting to "https://localhost:44300/Home/Contact", which is the route originally requested. You will also find a Set-Cookie entry meant to delete the nonce, which is no longer necessary at this point. However, you will not find any Set-Cookie for the session cookie. Where is it?

Saving the session is the job of the cookie middleware, which at this point has not yet had a chance to process the response. In fact, saving a session might be a far more complicated matter than simply sending back a Set-Cookie header. For example, you might want to save the bulk of the session on a server-side store: the cookie middleware provides that ability as a service so that any protocol middleware can leverage it without having to reinvent the process every time.

The OpenID Connect middleware uses `Context.Authentication` to communicate to the cookie middleware the content of the validated token to be persisted as well as other session-related details, such as duration. Right after the OpenID Connect middleware processes the request, you'll see the `Authentication` properties `AuthenticationResponseGrant`, `SignInEntry`, and `User` populated.

The cookie middleware is mostly interested in `AuthenticationReponseGrant`. When its turn comes to process the response, the cookie middleware will find the `AuthenticationReponseGrant` and use its content to generate a session. In Figure 7-8 you can see an example of `Authentication-ResponseGrant` content.

Name	Value
▲ ✦ ((Microsoft.Owin.OwinContext)Context).Authentication	{Microsoft.Owin.Security.AuthenticationManager}
✦ AuthenticationResponseChallenge	null
▲ ✦ AuthenticationResponseGrant	{Microsoft.Owin.Security.AuthenticationResponseGrant}
▲ ✦ Identity	{System.Security.Claims.ClaimsIdentity}
▷ ✦ Actor	null
✦ AuthenticationType	"Cookies"
✦ BootstrapContext	null
▷ ✦ Claims	{System.Security.Claims.ClaimsIdentity.<get_Claims>d__1}
✦ CustomSerializationData	null
✦ IsAuthenticated	true
✦ Label	null
✦ Name	"mario@developertenant.onmicrosoft.com"
✦ NameClaimType	"http://schemas.xmlsoap.org/ws/2005/05/identity/claims/name"
✦ RoleClaimType	"http://schemas.microsoft.com/ws/2008/06/identity/claims/role"
▷ ✦ Static members	
▷ ● Non-Public members	
▷ ✦ Principal	{System.Security.Claims.ClaimsPrincipal}
▲ ✦ Properties	{Microsoft.Owin.Security.AuthenticationProperties}
✦ AllowRefresh	false
▷ ✦ Dictionary	Count = 6
▷ ✦ ExpiresUtc	{7/19/2015 11:45:38 PM +00:00}
✦ IsPersistent	false
▷ ✦ IssuedUtc	{7/19/2015 10:40:38 PM +00:00}
✦ RedirectUri	"https://localhost:44300/Home/Contact"
▷ ✦ Static members	
▷ ● Non-Public members	

FIGURE 7-8 The AuthenticationResponseGrant content right after the OpenID Connect middleware successfully validates a sign-in response from Azure AD.

`Properties` refers to generic session properties, such as the validity window (derived from the validity window of the token itself, as declared by Azure AD). `Identity`, as you guessed, is the

`ClaimsIdentity` representing the authenticated user. The most important thing to notice at this point is the `AuthenticationType` value that's shown: that's a hint left by the OpenID Connect middleware for the cookie middleware, indicating that the `ClaimsIdentity` instance should be persisted in the session. Recall that when the pipeline is initialized in Startup.Auth.cs, you started the method with the following line:

```
app.SetDefaultSignInAsAuthenticationType(CookieAuthenticationDefaults.AuthenticationType);
```

That told the protocol middlewares in the pipeline that in the absence of local overrides, the identifier to use for electing an identity to be persisted in a session is `CookieAuthentication-Defaults.AuthenticationType`, which happens to be the string "Cookies". When the OpenID Connect middleware validates the incoming token and generates the corresponding `ClaimsPrincipal` and nested `ClaimsIdentity`, it uses that value for the `AuthenticationType` property. When the cookie middleware starts processing the response and finds that `ClaimsIdentity`, it verifies that the `AuthenticationType` it finds there corresponds to the `AuthenticationType` value it has in its options. Given that here we used the defaults everywhere, it's a match; hence, the cookie middleware proceeds to save the corresponding `ClaimsPrincipal` in the session.

If you examine the `Response.Headers` collection after the cookie middleware has a chance to execute, you will see that the Set-Cookie value now includes a new entry for an .Asp.Net.Cookies, which contains the `ClaimsPrincipal` information. Figure 7-9 summarizes the sequence.

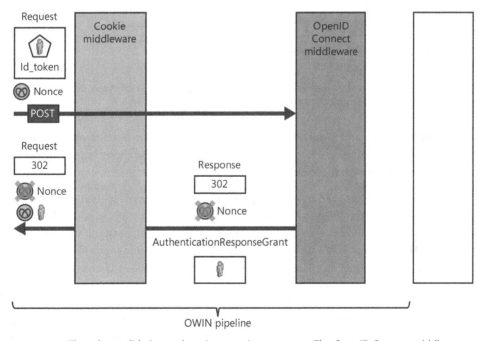

FIGURE 7-9 The token-validation and session-creation sequence. The OpenID Connect middleware processes the incoming token, passing the user identity information it carries to the cookie middleware. In turn, the cookie middleware saves the user identity information in a session cookie.

Authenticated access as part of a session Once the session has been established, all requests within its validity window are handled in the same way: as soon as the request is processed by the cookie middleware (between debug messages marked with 1 and 2), the incoming cookie is retrieved, validated, and parsed. The `ClaimsPrincipal` it carries is rehydrated, as shown by the value of `Authentication.User` being populated with a `ClaimsPrincipal`; the rest of the pipeline just lets the message through without further processing.

Figure 7-10 shows how this all plays out through the middleware pipeline.

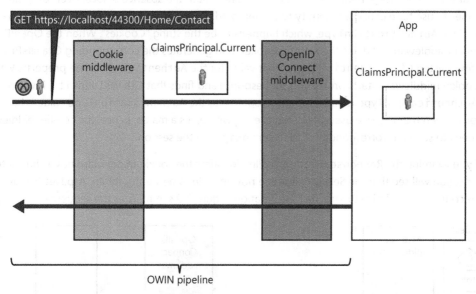

FIGURE 7-10 During a session, every request carries the session token, which is validated, decrypted, and parsed by the cookie middleware. The user claims are made available to the application.

Explicit use of *Challenge* and *SignOut* The explicit sign-in and sign-out operations you implemented in the `AccountController` of the sample app also use the `Authentication` property of `Context` to communicate with the middleware in the pipeline.

If you want to see how `Challenge` works, repeat the sign-in flow as described earlier, but this time trigger it by clicking Sign In. Stop at the breakpoint on debug message 4. You will see that the response code is a 401, just like the case we examined earlier. However, here you will also see populated entries in `Authentication`, in particular `AuthenticationResponseChallenge`. If you peek into it, you'll see that `AuthenticationResponseChallenge` holds the `AuthenticationType` of the middleware you want to use for signing in ("OpenIdConnect") and the local redirect you want to perform after sign-in (in this case, the root of the app). If the OpenID Connect middleware is set to Passive for `AuthenticationMode`, the presence of the 401 response code alone is not enough to provoke the sign-in message generation, but the presence of `AuthenticationResponseChallenge` guarantees that it will kick in. Other than that, the rest of the flow goes precisely as described.

The sign-out flow is very similar. Hit the Sign Out link. Stopping at the usual breakpoint 4, you'll observe that `Authentication` now holds a populated `AuthenticationResponseRevoke` property, which in turn contains a collection of `AuthenticationTypes`, including "OpenIdConnect" and "Cookies". When it's their turn to process the response, the middlewares in the pipeline check whether there is a nonnull `AuthenticationResponseRevoke` entry containing their `Authenti-cationTypes`. If they find one, they have to execute their sign-out logic. As you advance through the breakpoints in the response flow, you can see that behavior unfolding. The OpenID Connect middleware reacts by changing the return code to 302 and placing the sign-out message for Azure AD in the Location header. The cookie middleware simply adds a Set-Cookie entry that sets the session cookie expiration date to January 1, 1970, invalidating the session. Figure 7-11 provides a visual summary of the operation.

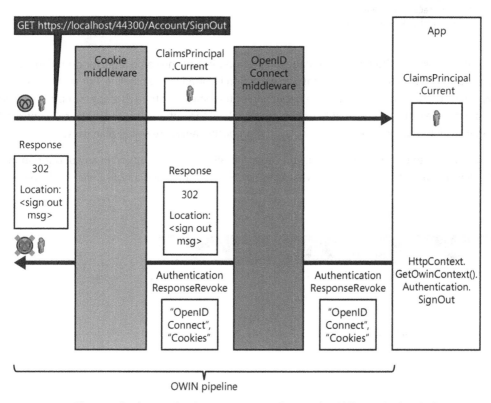

FIGURE 7-11 The contributions to the sign-out sequence from each middleware in the pipeline.

Diagnostic middleware

When something goes wrong in the OWIN pipeline, finding the culprit is often tricky. Adding breakpoints to an "in line" middleware, as I have done in this chapter to highlight how the pipeline works, is definitely an option. Alternatively, Katana offers a specialized diagnostic middleware that can render useful debugging information directly in the browser when an unhandled exception occurs in the pipeline. Setting it up is super easy.

Add a reference to the NuGet package Microsoft.Owin.Diagnostics. In your Startup.Auth.cs, add the associated using directive. Right on top of your main configuration routine (in our sample, ConfigureAuth), add something along the lines of the following:

```
app.UseErrorPage(new ErrorPageOptions()
{
    ShowCookies = true,
    ShowEnvironment = true,
    ShowQuery = true,
    ShowExceptionDetails = true,
    ShowHeaders = true,
    ShowSourceCode = true,
    SourceCodeLineCount = 10
});
```

The extension method UseErrorPage injects into the pipeline some logic for dumping diagnostic information on the current page in case an exception is raised in the pipeline. For that reason, it's important to place this method at the beginning of the pipeline (otherwise, any exceptions occurring before it has a chance to fire would not be captured). All the options you see in the call control what diagnostic information you want to display; the property names are self-explanatory.

If you want to test the contraption, you can artificially raise an exception in any of our debugging middlewares, and then hit F5 to see what happens. Figure 7-12 shows a typical diagnostic page.

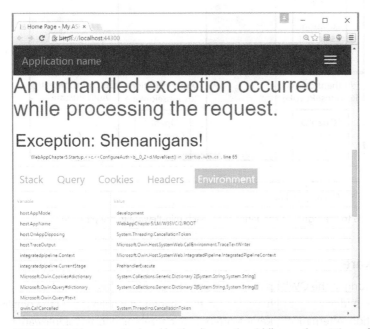

FIGURE 7-12 The page displayed by the diagnostic middleware from Microsoft.Owin.Diagnostics.

Important You should never use this middleware in production applications, as it might reveal information you don't want an attacker to obtain. Please use this only for debugging. Moreover, this middleware will not help in the case of exceptions raised in the application itself. It is really specialized for handling issues occurring in the OWIN pipeline.

OpenID Connect middleware

With the exception of the cookie tracking the nonce, all the considerations so far apply to the OpenID Connect middleware as well as the WS-Federation middleware. In this section I dive deeper into the features and options of the OpenID Connect middleware.

OpenIdConnectAuthenticationOptions

The options you pass in at initialization are the main way that you control the OpenID Connect middleware. The Azure AD and ASP.NET teams have taken a lot of care to ensure that only the absolute minimum amount of information is required for the scenario you want to support. The sample app you have studied so far shows the essential set of options: the ClientId (which identifies your app in your requests to the authority) and the Authority (which identifies the trusted source of identities and, indirectly, all the information necessary to validate the tokens it issues). If you want to exercise more fine-grained control, you can use the middleware initialization options class to provide the following:

- More protocol parameters that define your app and the provider you want to trust.

- What kind of token requests you want the app to put forth.

- What logic you want to execute during authentication, choosing from settings offered out of the box and from custom logic you want to inject.

- The usual array of choices controlling all Katana middleware mechanics.

In this section I describe the most notable categories. Two special properties, Notifications and TokenValidationParameters, are so important that I've dedicated sections to them.

For your reference, Figure 7-13 shows the default values in OpenIdConnectAuthentication-Options for our app, right after initialization.

FIGURE 7-13 The values in OpenIdConnectAuthenticationOptions after a typical initialization sequence.

Application coordinates and request options

Besides the already-mentioned ClientId, you can supply the following application details.

> **Note** Parameters in the options class corresponding to OpenID Connect protocol parameters have the same name, with the notation adjusted to match .NET naming conventions. In early iterations, the Active Directory team tried to use the protocol names verbatim—lowercase, underscore, and all—but the community staged an uprising, and the team quickly settled on the format you see today.

- **RedirectUri** This controls the value of redirect_uri included in the request, corresponding to the route in your app through which you want Azure AD to return the requested token. As I noted in Chapter 6, if you don't specify any value, the parameter will be omitted and Azure AD will pick the one registered at registration time. That's handy, but you should watch out for two possible issues. First, you might register multiple redirect_uri values for your app, in which case Azure AD will choose which one to use in a semirandom fashion (it always looks like it chooses the first one you registered, but you cannot count on that). Second, if you are connecting to providers other than Azure AD, they might require the request to comply with their spec and include a redirect_uri.

  This setting is ingested at the time the app is initialized and won't change later on. In the section about notifications, you will learn ways of overriding this and other parameters on the fly in the context of specific requests and responses.

- **PostLogoutRedirectUri**   You have seen this in use in Chapter 5. It determines where to redirect the browser in your app once the authority concludes its sign-out operations.

- **ClientSecret**   This represents the **client_secret**, which is required when redeeming an authorization code. I covered this at a high level in Chapter 2, in the context of OAuth2, but did not look at it at the trace and code level. I'll do so later in the book.

Here are a few other parameters that control what's going to be sent in the request.

- **ResponseType**   Maps to the OpenID Connect parameter of the same name. Although you can assign to it any of the values discussed in Chapter 6, only "id_token" and "code id_token" (the default) lead to the automatic handling of user sign-in. If you want to support other response types, such as "code", you need to inject custom code in the notifications described later in this chapter.

- **Resource**   In case you are using "code id_token", you can use this parameter to specify what resource you want an authorization code for. If you don't specify anything, the code you get back from Azure AD will be redeemable for an access token for the Graph API. As mentioned in Chapter 6, **resource** is a parameter specific to Azure AD.

- **Scope**   Maps to the OAuth2/OpenID Connect scope parameter.

Barring any custom code that modifies outgoing messages on the fly, the settings described here are the ones used in every request and response.

Authority coordinates and validation

The functional area of validation is one of the toughest to explain. It was one of the main pain points of working with WIF, where the object model expected all validation coordinates to be passed by value. Although Microsoft provided tools that generated those settings automatically from metadata, the obscurity and sheer sprawl of the resulting configuration settings came across as a bogeyman that kept the noninitiated at bay.

In the new middlewares, the default behavior is to obtain (most of) the validation coordinates by reference. You provide the authority from which you want to receive tokens, and the middleware takes care of retrieving the token validation coordinates it needs from the authority's metadata.

In Chapter 6 you saw how that retrieval operation takes place when you pass an Azure AD authority. If you want to customize that behavior, there is a hierarchy of options you can use. From accommodating providers that expose metadata differently from how Azure AD does, to supplying each and every setting for providers that don't expose metadata at all, these options cover the full spectrum.

Here's how it works.

The **ConfigurationManager** class is tasked to retrieve, cache, and refresh the validation settings published by the discovery documents. That class is fed whatever options you provide at initialization. There is a cascade of options it looks for:

- If the options include an `Authority` value, it will be used as you saw in Chapter 6.

- If you are working with a provider other than Azure AD, with a different URL structure, or if you prefer to specify a reference to the actual discovery document endpoint, you can do so by using the `Metadata` property.

- If your provider requires special handling of the channel validation, like picking a well-known certificate instead of the usual certification authority and subject matching checks, you can override the default logic via the properties `BackchannelCertificateValidator`, `BackchannelHttpHandler`, and `BackchannelTimeout`.

- If you acquire the token-issuance information—such as the authorization endpoint, the issuer value, the signing keys, and the like—out of band, you can use it to populate a new instance of `OpenIdConfiguration` and assign it to the `Configuration` property.

- Finally, if you need to run dynamic logic for populating the `Configuration` values, you can completely take over by implementing your own `IConfigurationManager` and assigning it to the `ConfigurationManager` property in the options.

The issuer coordinates are only part of the validation story. Following is a miscellany of options that affect the validation behavior, and there will be more to say about validation in the section about `TokenValidationParameters`.

- `SecurityTokenHandlers` This property holds a collection of `TokenHandlers`, classes that are capable of handling token formats. By default, the collection includes a handler capable of dealing with the JSON Web Token (JWT). You can take control of the collection and substitute your own implementation if you so choose.

- `RefreshOnIssuerKeyNotFound` The practice of publishing in metadata documents both the currently valid and next signing key should guarantee business continuity in normal times. In case of emergency key rolls, however, the keys you have acquired in your `Configuration` and the ones used by the provider might end up out of sync. This flag tells the middleware to react to a token signed with an unknown key by triggering a new metadata acquisition operation so that if the mismatch is the result of stale keys, it is fixed automatically.

- `CallbackPath` If for some reason (typically performance) you decide that you want to receive tokens only at one specific application URL, you can assign that URL to this property. That will cause the middleware to expect tokens only in requests to that specific URL and ignore all others. Use this with care because embedding paths in your code often results in surprise 401s when you forget about them and deploy to the cloud without changing the value accordingly.

- `ProtocolValidator` By default, this property contains an instance of `OpenIdConnect-ProtocolValidator`, a class that performs various static verifications on the incoming message to ensure that it complies with the current OpenID Connect specification. Besides those validations, the class gives you the option of adding extra constraints, like mandating the presence of certain claim types.

Middleware mechanics

Finally, here's a list of options that are used for driving the general behavior of the middleware in the context of the Katana pipeline:

- `SignInAsAuthenticationType`   This value determines the value of the `Authentication-Type` property of the `ClaimsPrincipal`/`ClaimsIdentity` generated from the incoming token. If left unspecified, it defaults to the value passed to `SetDefaultSignInAsAuthenticationType`. As you have seen earlier in the section about authentication middleware, if the cookie middleware finds this in an `AuthenticationResponseGrant`, that's what the cookie middleware uses to determine whether such `ClaimsPrincipal`/ `ClaimsIdentity` should be used for creating a session.

- `AuthenticationType`   This property identifies this middleware in the pipeline and is used to refer to it for authentication operations—think of the `Challenge` and `SignOut` calls you have seen in action earlier in this chapter.

- `AuthenticationMode`   As discussed earlier, when this parameter is set to Active, it tells the middleware to listen to outgoing 401s and transform them into sign-in requests. That's the default behavior: if you want to change it, you can turn it off by setting `Authentication-Mode` to Passive.

- `UseTokenLifetime`   This property is often overlooked, but it's tremendously important. Defaulting to true, `UseTokenLifetime` tells the cookie middleware that the session it creates should have the same duration and validity window as the `id_token` received from the authority. If you want to decouple the session validity window from the token (which, by the way, Azure AD sets to one hour), you must set this property to false. Failing that, all the session-duration settings on the `CookieMiddleware` will be ignored.

- `Caption`   This property has purely cosmetic value. Say that your app generates sign-in buttons for all your authentication middlewares. This property provides the label you can use to identify for the user the button triggering the sign-in implemented by this middleware.

Notifications

Just like WIF before them, the Katana middlewares implementing claims protocols offer you hooks designed for injecting your own custom code to be executed during key phases of the authentication pipeline. Through the years, I have seen this extensibility point used for achieving all sorts of customizations, from optimized sign-in flows, where extra information in the request is used to save the end user a few clicks, to full-blown extensions that support entirely new protocol flavors.

Whereas in old-school WIF those hooks were offered in the form of events, in Katana they are implemented as a collection of delegates gathered in the class `OpenIdConnectNotifications`. The `OpenIdConnectAuthenticationOptions` class includes a property of that type, `Notifications`.

`OpenIdConnectNotifications` can be split into two main categories: notifications firing at sign-in/sign-out message generation, and notifications firing at token/sign-in message validation. The former category counts only one member, `RedirectToIdentityProvider`; all the other notifications are included in the latter.

Here is some code that lists all the notifications. You can add it to the initialization of the OpenID Connect middleware in the sample application.

```
app.UseOpenIdConnectAuthentication(
    new OpenIdConnectAuthenticationOptions
    {
        ClientId = "c3d5b1ad-ae77-49ac-8a86-dd39a2f91081",
        Authority = "https://login.microsoftonline.com/DeveloperTenant.onmicrosoft.com"
        PostLogoutRedirectUri = "https://localhost:44300/",
        Notifications = new OpenIdConnectAuthenticationNotifications()
        {
            RedirectToIdentityProvider = (context) =>
            {
                Debug.WriteLine("*** RedirectToIdentityProvider");
                return Task.FromResult(0);
            },
            MessageReceived = (context) =>
            {
                Debug.WriteLine("*** MessageReceived");
                return Task.FromResult(0);
            },
            SecurityTokenReceived = (context) =>
            {
                Debug.WriteLine("*** SecurityTokenReceived");
                return Task.FromResult(0);
            },
            SecurityTokenValidated = (context) =>
            {
                Debug.WriteLine("*** SecurityTokenValidated");
                return Task.FromResult(0);
            },
            AuthorizationCodeReceived = (context) =>
            {
                Debug.WriteLine("*** AuthorizationCodeReceived");
                return Task.FromResult(0);
            },
            AuthenticationFailed = (context) =>
            {
                Debug.WriteLine("*** AuthenticationFailed");
                return Task.FromResult(0);
            },
        },
    }
);
```

I'll discuss each notification individually in a moment, but before I do, give the app a spin so that you can see in which order the notifications fire. When you click the Sign In link, you can expect to see something like this in the output window:

```
1 ==>request, before cookie auth
2 ==>after cookie, before OIDC
3 ==>after OIDC, before leaving the pipeline
4 <==after entering the pipeline, before OIDC
*** RedirectToIdentityProvider
5 <==after OIDC
6 <==response, after cookie auth
```

This shows that RedirectToIdentityProvider runs in the context of the OpenID Connect middleware, as expected.

Once you sign in with Azure AD and are redirected to the app, you can expect to see the following sequence:

```
1 ==>request, before cookie auth
2 ==>after cookie, before OIDC
*** MessageReceived
*** SecurityTokenReceived
*** SecurityTokenValidated
*** AuthorizationCodeReceived
5 <==after OIDC
6 <==response, after cookie auth
1 ==>request, before cookie auth
2 ==>after cookie, before OIDC
3 ==>after OIDC, before leaving the pipeline
4 <==after entering the pipeline, before OIDC
5 <==after OIDC
6 <==response, after cookie auth
```

This is the same token-processing and cookie-setting sequence you encountered earlier in this chapter. This time, you can see the other notifications fire and the order in which they execute. Figure 7-14 summarizes the sequence in which the notifications fire.

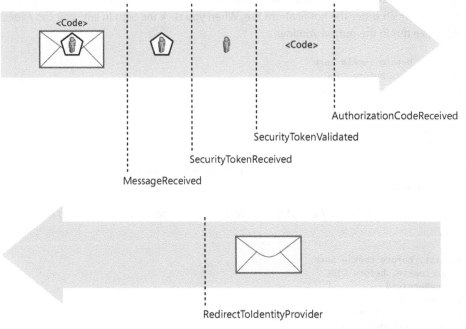

FIGURE 7-14 The notifications sequence.

If you trigger a sign-out, you will see the usual sequence, but look between messages 4 and 5, and you will find that RedirectToIdentityProvider fires on sign-out as well.

Keep in mind also that notifications derive from a BaseNotification class from which they inherit a couple of methods exposing two fundamental capabilities. The first, HandleResponse, signals to the middleware pipeline that whatever logic has been executed in the notification concludes the processing of the current request, hence no other middleware should be executed. A notification calling this method has the responsibility of having everything in the context tidied up, including writing the full response. The second, SkipToNextMiddleware, signals to the middleware pipeline that whatever logic has been executed in the notification concludes the work that the current middleware should do on the request. Hence, any other request-processing code in the current middleware should not be executed, and the baton should be passed to the next middleware in the pipeline as soon as the notification concludes its work.

Now let's look at each notification in more detail.

RedirectToIdentityProvider

This is likely the notification you'll work with most often. It is executed right after the OpenID Connect middleware creates a protocol message, and it gives you the opportunity to override the option values the middleware uses to build the message, augment them with extra parameters, and so on. If you place a breakpoint in the notification and take a look at the context parameter, you'll see something like what's shown in Figure 7-15.

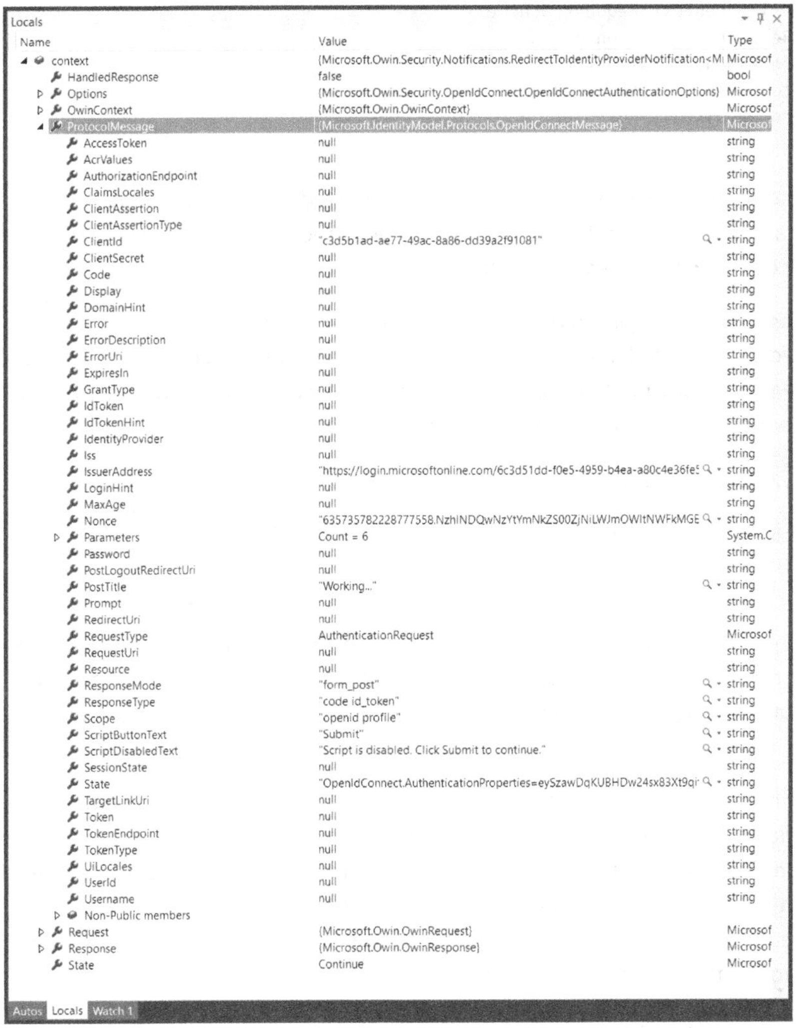

FIGURE 7-15 The content of the context parameter on a typical `RedirectToIdentityProvider` notification execution.

I expanded the `ProtocolMessage` in Figure 7-15 so that you can see that it already contains all the default parameters you have seen in the request on the traces in Chapter 6. There are a number of fun and useful things you can do here, so let's examine a couple of examples.

Say that my app is registered to run both on my local dev box (hence, on a localhost address) and on an Azure website (hence, on something like myapp.azurewebsites.net). That means that depending on where my app is running at the moment, I have to remember to set the correct `RedirectUri` and `PostLogoutRedirectUri` properties in the options right before deploying. Or do I? Consider the following code:

```
RedirectToIdentityProvider = (context) =>
{
```

```
    string appBaseUrl = context.Request.Scheme + "://"
        + context.Request.Host + context.Request.PathBase;
    context.ProtocolMessage.RedirectUri = appBaseUrl + "/";
    context.ProtocolMessage.PostLogoutRedirectUri = appBaseUrl;
    return Task.FromResult(0);
},
```

Here I simply read from the Request the URL being requested, indicating at which address my app is running at the moment and using it to inject the correct values of RedirectUri and PostLogoutRedirectUri in the message. Neat!

Or consider a case in which I want to guarantee that when an authentication request is sent, the user is always forced to enter credentials no matter what session cookies might already be in place. In Chapter 6 you learned that OpenID Connect will behave that way upon receiving a prompt=login parameter in the request, but how do you do it? Check out this code:

```
RedirectToIdentityProvider = (context) =>
{
    context.ProtocolMessage.Prompt = "login";
    return Task.FromResult(0);
},
```

That's it. From this moment on, every sign-in request will prompt the user for credentials. Easy. Now is the time to reap the benefits of having gone through all those nitty-gritty protocol details in Chapter 6; you can use this notification to control every aspect of the message to your heart's content. Of course, this applies to sign-out flows, too.

But before moving on to the next notification, I want to highlight that you don't have to put the code for your notifications in line. If you have notification-handling logic you want to reuse across multiple applications, you can put it in a function, package it in a class, and reuse it as you see fit. Explicitly creating a function is also indicated when the amount of code is substantial, or when you want to enhance readability. As a quick demonstration of this approach, let's rewrite the latest sample in an explicit function at the level of the Startup class:

```
public static Task RedirectToIdentityProvider(RedirectToIdentityProviderNotification<OpenIdConne
ctMessage, OpenIdConnectAuthenticationOptions> notification)
{
    notification.ProtocolMessage.Prompt = "login";
    return Task.FromResult(0);
}
```

Assigning it back in the Notifications is straightforward:

```
//...
Notifications = new OpenIdConnectAuthenticationNotifications()
{
    RedirectToIdentityProvider = Startup.RedirectToIdentityProvider,
// ...
```

I also like the aspect of this approach that makes more visible which parameters are being passed to the notification, which in turns makes it easier to understand what the notification is suitable for.

The `OpenIdConnectMessage` passed to `RedirectToIdentityProvider` is an excellent example of that.

MessageReceived

This notification is triggered when the middleware detects that the incoming message happens to be a known OpenID Connect message. You can use it for a variety of purposes; for example, for resources you want to allocate just in time (such as database connections), stuff you want to cache in memory before the message is processed further, and so on. Alternatively, you might use this notification for logging purposes. However, the main use I have seen for `MessageReceived` occurs when you want to completely take over the handling of the entire request (that's where `HandleResponse` comes into play, by the way). For example, you might use `MessageReceived` for handling `response_types` that the middleware currently does not automatically process, like a sign-in flow based on authorization code. That's not an easy endeavor, and as such not very common, but some advanced scenarios will sometimes require it, and this extensibility model makes doing so possible.

SecurityTokenReceived

`SecurityTokenReceived` triggers when the middleware finds an `id_token` in the request. Similar considerations as for `MessageReceived` apply, with finer granularity. Here, the entity being processed is the token, as opposed to the entire message.

SecurityTokenValidated

At the stage in which `SecurityTokenValidated` fires, the incoming `id_token` has been parsed, validated, and used to populate `context.AuthenticationTicket` with a `ClaimsIdentity` whose claims come from the incoming token.

This is the right place for adding any user-driven logic you want to execute before reaching the application itself. Common scenarios include user-driven access control and claims augmentation. Here are examples for each case.

Say that I run a courseware website where users can buy individual subscriptions for gaining access to training videos. I integrate with Azure AD, given that business users are very important to me, but my business model imposes on me the need to verify access at the user level. That means that the token validations you have studied so far aren't in themselves sufficient to decide whether a caller can gain access. Consider the following implementation of `SecurityTokenValidated`:

```
SecurityTokenValidated = (context) =>
{
    string userID = context.AuthenticationTicket.Identity.FindFirst(ClaimTypes.NameIdentifier).
Value;
    if (db.Users.FirstOrDefault(b => (b.UserID == userID)) == null)
        throw new System.IdentityModel.Tokens.SecurityTokenValidationException();
    return Task.FromResult(0);
},
```

The notification body retrieves a user identifier from the claims of the freshly created AuthenticationTicket. That done, it verifies whether that identifier is listed in a database of subscribers (whose existence I am postulating for the sake of the scenario). If the user does have an entry, everything goes on as business as usual. But if the user is not listed, the app throws an exception that creates conditions equivalent to the ones you would experience on receiving an invalid token. Simple!

Consider this other scenario. Say that your application maintains a database of attributes for its users—attributes that are not supplied in the incoming token by the identity provider. You can use SecurityTokenValidated to augment the set of incoming user claims with any arbitrary value you keep in your local database. The application code will be able to access those values just like any other IdP-issued claims, the only difference being the issuer value. Here's an example.

```
SecurityTokenValidated = (context) =>
{
    string userID = context.AuthenticationTicket.Identity.FindFirst(ClaimTypes.NameIdentifier).
Value;
    Claim userHair = new Claim("http://mycustomclaims/hairlength", RetrieveHairLength(userID),
ClaimValueTypes.Double, "LocalAuthority");
    context.AuthenticationTicket.Identity.AddClaim(userHair);
    return Task.FromResult(0);
},
```

Here I assume that you have a method that, given the identifier of the current user, queries your database to retrieve an attribute (in this case, hair length). Once you get the value back, you can use it to create a new claim (I invented a new claim type on the spot to show you that you can choose pretty much anything that works for you) and add that claim to the AuthenticationTicket's ClaimsIdentity. I passed "'LocalAuthority" as the issuer identifier to ensure that the locally generated claims are distinguishable from the ones received from the IdP: the two usually carry a different trust level.

Now that the new claim is part of the ticket, it's going to follow the same journey we have studied so far for normal, nonaugmented identity information. Making use of it from the app requires the same code you already saw in action for out-of-the-box claim types.

```
public ActionResult Index()
{
    var userHair = ClaimsPrincipal.Current.FindFirst("http://mycustomclaims/hairlength");
    return View();
}
```

This is a very powerful mechanism, but it does have its costs. Besides the performance hit of doing I/O while processing a request, you have to keep in mind that whatever you add to the AuthenticationTicket will end up in the session cookie. In turn, that will add a tax for every subsequent request, and at times it might even blow past browser limits. For example, Safari is famous for allowing only 4 KB of cookies/headers in requests for a given domain. Exceed that limit and cookies will be clipped, signature checks will fail, nonces will be dropped, and all sorts of other hard-to-diagnose issues will arise.

AuthorizationCodeReceived

This notification fires only in the case in which the middleware emits a request for a hybrid flow, where the id_token is accompanied by an authorization code. I'll go into more details in a later chapter, after fleshing out the scenario and introducing other artifacts that come in handy for dealing with that case.

AuthenticationFailed

This notification gives you a way to catch issues occurring in the notifications pipeline and react to them with your own logic. Here's a simple example:

```
AuthenticationFailed = (context) =>
{
    context.OwinContext.Response.Redirect("/Home/Error");
    context.HandleResponse();
    return Task.FromResult(0);
},
```

In this code I simply redirect the flow to an error route. Chances are you will want to do something more sophisticated, like retrieving the culprit exception (available in the context) and then log it or pass it to the page. The interesting thing to notice here is the use of HandleResponse. There's nothing else that can make meaningful work in the pipeline after this, hence we short-circuit the request processing and send the response back right away.

TokenValidationParameters

You think we've gone deep enough to this point? Not quite, my dear reader. The rabbit hole has one extra level, which grants you even more control over your token-validation strategy.

OpenIdConnectAuthenticationOptions has a property named TokenValidationParameters, of type TokenValidationParameters.

The TokenValidationParameters type predates the RTM of Katana. It was introduced when the Azure AD team released the very first version of the JWT handler (a .NET class for processing the JWT format) as a general-purpose mechanism for storing information required for validating a token, regardless of the protocol used for requesting and delivering it and the development stack used for supporting such protocol. That was a clean break with the past: up to that moment, the same function was performed by special XML elements in the web.config file, which assumed the use of WIF and IIS. It was soon generalized to support the SAML token format, too.

The OpenID Connect middleware itself still uses the JWT handler when it comes to validating incoming tokens, and to do so it has to feed it a TokenValidationParameters instance with the desired validation settings. All the metadata inspection mechanisms you have been studying so far ultimately feed specific values—the issuer values to accept and the signing keys to use for validating incoming tokens' signatures—in a TokenValidationParameters instance. If you did not provide any values in the TokenValidationParameters property (I know, it's confusing) in the options, the values from the metadata will be the only ones used. However, if you do provide values directly in TokenValidationParameters, the actual values used will be a merger of the TokenValidation-Parameters and what is retrieved from the metadata (using all the options you learned about in the "Authority coordinates and validation" section).

The preceding mechanisms hold for the validation of the parameters defining the token issuer, but as you know by now, there are lots of other things to validate in a token, and even more things that are best performed during validation. If you don't specify anything, as is the case the vast majority of the time, the middleware fills in the blanks with reasonable defaults. But if you choose to, you can control an insane number of details. Figure 7-16 shows the content of TokenValidationParameters in OpenID Connect middleware at the initialization time for our sample application. I am not going to unearth all the things that TokenValidationParameters allows you to control (that would take far too long), but I do want to make sure you are aware of the most commonly used knobs you can turn.

Autos	
Name	Value
◢ 🔎 TokenValidationParameters	{System.IdentityModel.Tokens.TokenValidationParameters}
🔧 AudienceValidator	null
🔧 AuthenticationType	null
▷ 🔧 CertificateValidator	null
▷ 🔧 ClientDecryptionTokens	Count = 0
▷ 🔧 ClockSkew	{00:05:00}
🔧 IssuerSigningKey	null
🔧 IssuerSigningKeyResolver	null
🔧 IssuerSigningKeyValidator	null
🔧 IssuerSigningKeys	null
🔧 IssuerSigningToken	null
🔧 IssuerSigningTokens	null
▷ 🔧 IssuerValidator	{Method = {System.String <ConfigureAuth>b__0_7(System.String, System.IdentityMo<
🔧 LifetimeValidator	null
🔧 NameClaimType	"http://schemas.xmlsoap.org/ws/2005/05/identity/claims/name" 🔍 ▾
🔧 NameClaimTypeRetriever	null
🔧 RequireExpirationTime	true
🔧 RequireSignedTokens	true
🔧 RoleClaimType	"http://schemas.microsoft.com/ws/2008/06/identity/claims/role" 🔍 ▾
🔧 RoleClaimTypeRetriever	null
🔧 SaveSigninToken	false
🔧 TokenReplayCache	null
🔧 ValidAudience	null
🔧 ValidAudiences	null
🔧 ValidIssuer	null
🔧 ValidIssuers	null
🔧 ValidateActor	false
🔧 ValidateAudience	true
🔧 ValidateIssuer	true
🔧 ValidateIssuerSigningKey	false
🔧 ValidateLifetime	true

FIGURE 7-16 The TokenValidationParameters instance in OpenIdConnectAuthenticationOptions, as initialized by the sample application.

Valid values

As you've learned, the main values used to validate incoming tokens are the issuer, the audience, the key used for signing, and the validity interval. With the exception of the last of these (which does not require reference values because it is compared against the current clock values), Token-ValidationParameters exposes a property for holding the corresponding value: ValidIssuer, ValidAudience, and IssuerSigningKey.

What is less known is that `TokenValidationParameters` also has an `IEnumerable` for each of these—`ValidIssuers`, `ValidAudiences`, and `IssuerSigningKeys`—which are meant to make it easy for you to manage scenarios in which you need to handle a small number of alternative values. For example, your app might accept tokens from two different issuers simultaneously. Or you might use a different audience for your development and staging deployments but have a single codebase that automatically works in both.

Validation flags

One large category of `TokenValidationParameters` properties allows you to turn on and off specific validation checks. These Boolean flags are self-explanatory: `ValidateAudience` turns on and off the comparison of the audience in the incoming claim with the declared audience (in the OpenID Connect case, the `clientId` value); `ValidateIssuer` controls whether your app cares about the identity of the issuer; `ValidateIssuerSigningKey` determines whether you need the key used to sign the incoming token to be part of a list of trusted keys; `ValidateLifetime` determines whether you will enforce the validity interval declared in the token or ignore it.

At first glance, each of these checks sounds like something you'd never want to turn off, but there are various occasions in which you'd want to. Think of the subscription sample I described for `SecurityTokenValidated`: in that case, the actual check is the one against the user and the subscription database, so the issuer check does not matter and can be turned off. There are more exotic cases: in the Netherlands last year, a gentleman asked me how his intranet app could accept expired tokens in case his client briefly lost connectivity with the Internet and was temporarily unable to contact Azure AD for getting new tokens.

There is another category of flags controlling constraints rather than validation flags. The first is `RequireExpirationTime`, which determines whether your app will accept tokens that do not declare an expiration time (the specification allows for this). The other, `RequireSignedTokens`, specifies whether your app will accept tokens without a signature. To me, a token without a signature is an oxymoron, but I did encounter situations (especially during development) where this flag came in handy for running some tests.

Validators

Validation flags allow you to turn on and off validation checks. Validator delegates allow you to substitute the default validation logic with your own custom code.

Say that you wrote a SaaS application that you plan to sell to organizations instead of to individuals. As opposed to the user-based validation you studied earlier, now you want to allow access to any user who comes from one of the organizations (one of the issuers) who bought a subscription to your app. You could use the `ValidIssuers` property to hold that list, but if you plan to have a substantial number of customers, doing that would be inconvenient for various reasons: a flat lookup on a list might not work too well if you are handling millions of entries, dynamically extending that list without recycling the app would be difficult, and so on. The solution is to take full control of the issuer validation operation. For example, consider the following code:

```
TokenValidationParameters = new TokenValidationParameters
{
    IssuerValidator = (issuer,token,tvp) =>
    {
        if(db.Issuers.FirstOrDefault(b => (b.Issuer == issuer)) == null)
            return issuer;
        else


            throw new SecurityTokenInvalidIssuerException("Invalid issuer");
    }
}
```

The delegate accepts as input the issuer value as extracted from the token, the token itself, and the validation parameters. In this case I do a flat lookup on a database to see whether the incoming issuer is valid, but of course you can imagine many other clever validation schemes. The validator returns the issuer value for a less-than-intuitive reason: that string will be used for populating the Issuer value of the claims that will ultimately end up in the user's ClaimsPrincipal.

All the other main validators (AudienceValidator, LifetimeValidator) return Booleans, with the exception of IssuerSigningKeyValidator and CertificateValidator.

Miscellany

Of the plethora of remaining properties, I want to point your attention to two common ones.

SaveSignInToken is used to indicate whether you want to save in the ClaimsPrincipal (hence, the session cookie) the actual bits of the original token. There are topologies in which the actual token bits are required, signature and everything else intact: typically, the app trades that token (along with its credentials) for a new token, meant to allow the app to gain access to a web API acting on behalf of the user. This property defaults to false, as this is a sizable tax.

The TokenReplayCache property allows you to define a token replay cache, a store that can be used for saving tokens for the purpose of verifying that no token can be used more than once. This is a measure against a common attack, the aptly called *token replay attack*: an attacker intercepting the token sent at sign-in might try to send it to the app again ("replay" it) for establishing a new session. The presence of the nonce in OpenID Connect can limit but not fully eliminate the circumstances in which the attack can be successfully enacted. To protect your app, you can provide an implementation of ITokenReplayCache and assign an instance to TokenReplayCache. It's a very simple interface:

```
public interface ITokenReplayCache
{
    bool TryAdd(string securityToken, DateTime expiresOn);
    bool TryFind(string securityToken);
}
```

In a nutshell, you provide the methods for saving new tokens (determining for how long they need to be kept around) and bringing a token up from whatever storage technology you decide to use. The cache will be automatically used at every validation—take that into account when you pit latency and storage requirements against the likelihood of your app being targeted by replay attacks.

More on sessions

Before I close this long chapter, I need to spend a minute on session management. You already know that by default, session validity will be tied to the validity specified by the token itself, unless you decouple it by setting the option UseTokenLifetime to false. When you do so, the Cookie-AuthenticationOptions are now in charge of session duration: ExpireTimeSpan and Sliding-Expiration are the properties you want to keep an eye on.

You also know that the cookie middleware will craft sessions that contain the full ClaimsPrincipal produced from the incoming token, but as mentioned in discussing the use of SaveSignInToken, the resulting cookie size can become a problem. This issue can be addressed by saving the bulk of the session server-side and using the cookie just to keep track of a reference to the session data on the server. The cookie middleware allows you to plug in an implementation of the IAuthenticationSessionStore interface, which can be used for customizing how an AuthenticationTicket is preserved across calls. If you want to provide an alternative store for your authentication tickets, all you need to do is implement that interface and pass an instance to the cookie middleware at initialization. Here's the interface:

```
public interface IAuthenticationSessionStore
{
    Task<string> StoreAsync(AuthenticationTicket ticket);
    Task RenewAsync(string key, AuthenticationTicket ticket);
    Task<AuthenticationTicket> RetrieveAsync(string key);
    Task RemoveAsync(string key);
}
```

That's pretty much a CRUD interface for an AuthenticationTicket store, which you can use for any persistence technology you like. Add some logic for cleaning up old entries and keeping the store size under control, and you have your custom session store.

Considerations about I/O and latency are critical here, given that this guy will trigger every single time you receive an authenticated request. A two-level cache, where most accesses are in-memory and the persistence layer is looked up only when necessary, is one of the solutions you might want to consider.

Summary

This chapter explored in depth what happens when the OpenID Connect middleware and its underlying technologies process requests and emit responses. You learned about the main functional components of the request-processing pipeline, how they communicate with one another, and what options you have to change their behavior.

The complexity you have confronted here is something that the vast majority of web developers will never have to face—or even be aware of. Even in advanced cases, chances are that you will always use a subset of what you have read here. Don't worry if you don't remember everything; you don't have to. After the first read, this chapter is meant to be a reference you can return to whenever you are trying to achieve a specific customization or are troubleshooting a specific issue. Now that you've had an opportunity to deconstruct the pipeline, you'll know where to look.

The next chapter will be significantly lighter. You'll learn more about how Azure AD represents applications.

CHAPTER 8

Azure Active Directory application model

It's time to take a closer look at how Azure AD represents applications and their relationships to other apps, users, and organizations.

You got a brief taste of the Azure AD application model in Chapter 3, "Introducing Azure Active Directory and Active Directory Federation Services." Later on you experienced firsthand a couple of ways to provision apps and use their protocol coordinates in authentication flows. Here I will go much deeper into the constructs used by Azure AD to represent apps, the mechanisms used to provision apps beyond one's own organization, and the consent framework, which is the backbone of pretty much all of this. I'll also touch on roles, groups, and other features that Azure AD offers to grant fine-grained access control to your application.

The application model in Azure AD is designed to sustain many different functions:

- It holds all the data required to support authentication at run time.

- It holds all the data for deciding what other resources an application might need to access and whether a given request should be fulfilled and under what circumstances.

- It provides the infrastructure for implementing application provisioning, both within the app developer's tenant and to any other Azure AD tenant.

- It enables end users and administrators to dynamically grant or deny consent for the app to access resources on their behalf.

- It enables administrators to be the ultimate arbiters of what apps are allowed to do and which users can use specific apps, and in general to be stewards of how the directory resources are accessed.

That is A LOT more than setting up a trust relationship, the basic provisioning step you perform with traditional on-premises authorities like ADFS. Remember how I often bragged about how much easier it is to provision apps in Azure AD? What makes that feat possible is the highly sophisticated application model in Azure AD, which goes to great lengths to make life easy for administrators and end users. Unfortunately, the total complexity of the system remains roughly constant, so somebody must work harder to compensate for that simplification, and this time that somebody is the developer. I could work around that complexity and simply give you a list of recipes to follow to the letter for the most common tasks, but by now you know that this book doesn't work that way. Instead, we'll dig deep to understand the building blocks and true motivation of each moving part—and once we emerge, everything will make sense. Don't worry, the model is very manageable and, once you get the hang of it, even easy, but some investment is required to understand it. This chapter is here to help you do just that.

The building blocks: *Application* and *ServicePrincipal*

Since Azure AD first appeared on the market, a lot of content has been published about its application model. A large part of that content was produced while the application model had not yet solidified in its current form. To avoid any confusion, I am going to open this section with a bit of history: by understanding how we got to where we are today, you won't risk getting confused if you happen to stumble on documentation and samples from another epoch.

In traditional Active Directory, every entity that can be authenticated is represented by a *principal*. That's true for users, and that's true for applications—in the latter case, we speak of *service principals*. In traditional Kerberos, service principals are used to ensure that a client is speaking to the intended service and that a ticket is actually intended for a given service. In other words, they are used for any activity that requires establishing the identity of the service application itself.

Although Azure AD has been designed from the ground up to address modern workloads, it remains a directory. As such, it retains many of the concepts and constructs that power its on-premises ancestor, and service principals are among those. If you use the Internet time machine and fish out content from summer 2012, describing the very first preview of Azure AD development features, you'll see that at that time, provisioning an application in Azure AD was done by using special Windows PowerShell cmdlets, which created a new service principal for the app in the directory. Even the format of the service principal name was a reminder of its Kerberos legacy, following a fixed schema based on the app's execution environment. Disregarding the protocols it enabled, that service principal already had all the things we know are needed for supporting authentication transactions: application identifiers, a redirect URI, and so on.

Service principals are a great way of representing an application's instance, but they aren't very good at supporting the development of the application itself. Their limitations stem from two key considerations:

- Applications are usually an abstract entity, made of code and resources: the service principal represents a concrete instance of that abstract entity in a specific directory. You will want that abstract entity to have many concrete instances, especially if you build and sell software for a living: one or more instances for each of your customers' organizations. Even if you are building applications for your own organization, to be used by your colleagues, chances are that you'll want to work with multiple instances—for example, development, staging, and production. If the only building block at your disposal were app instances, development and deployments would be unnatural, denormalized, and repetitive. For one thing, every time you changed something, you'd have to go chase all your app instances and make the same change everywhere.

- Although so far we have seen applications mostly as resources one user gains access to, a directory sees applications as clients, which need to access resources under the control of the directory. Even the act of a user requesting a token for accessing an application is seen by the directory as the application itself gaining access to the user's identity information. Through this optic, you can see how some applications can be pretty powerful clients, performing functions that range from reading users' personally identifiable information (PII) to modifying the directory itself: deleting users, creating groups, changing passwords—the works. Application instances are normally put in operation by administrators, who enjoy those powers themselves. Hence, they have the faculty to imbue applications with such capabilities. If your company is big enough for employees not to have to juggle multiple hats, however, developers are traditionally not administrators. If service principals were the only way to create an application, very few employees in a company would have the power to develop apps. It gets worse: in today's software as a service (SaaS) push, it is in the developer's best interest that end users be empowered to elect to start using applications, but most users aren't administrators either. Even more than in the development case, this exposes the limits of perpetrating the service principal model "as is" in the cloud.

Given this, and for various other reasons, Azure AD defines a new entity, the `Application`, which is meant to describe an application as an abstract entity: a template, if you will. As a developer, you work with `Applications`. At deployment time a given `Application` object can be used as a blueprint to create a `ServicePrincipal` representing a concrete instance of an application in a directory. It's that `ServicePrincipal` that is used to define what the app can actually do in that specific target directory, who can use it, what resources it has access to, and so on.

Bear with me just a little longer, the abstract part is almost over. The main way through which Azure AD creates a `ServicePrincipal` from an `Application` is *consent*. Here's a simplified description of the flow: Say that you create an `Application` object in directory A, supplying all the protocol coordinates we've discussed so far in earlier chapters. Say that a user from tenant B navigates to the app's pages and triggers an authentication flow. Azure AD authenticates the user from B against its home directory, B. In so doing, it sees that there is no `ServicePrincipal` for the app in B; hence, it prompts the user about whether he or she wants to consent for that app to have access to the directory B (you'll see later in what capacity). If the user grants consent, Azure AD uses the `Application` object in A as a blueprint for creating a `ServicePrincipal` in B. Along with that, B records that the current user consented to the use of this application (expect lots of details on this later on). Once that's done, the user receives a token for accessing the app . . . and provisioning magically happens. No lengthy negotiations between administrators required. Isn't Azure AD awesome? Figure 8-1 summarizes the process.

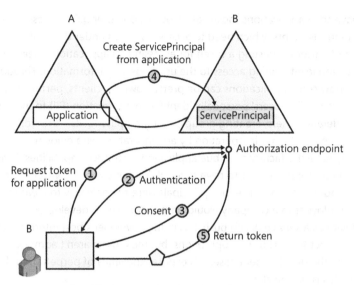

FIGURE 8-1 Simplified provisioning flow driven by consent: 1) a user from B attempts to sign in with the app; 2) the user credentials are acquired and verified; 3) the user is prompted to consent for the app to gain access to tenant B; the user consents; 4) Azure AD uses the `Application` object in A as a blueprint for creating a `ServicePrincipal` in B; 5) the user receives the requested token.

You can iterate the process shown in Figure 8-1 as many times as you want, for directory C, D, E, and so on. Directory A retains the blueprint of the app, in the form of its `Application` object. The users and admins of all the directories where the app is given consent retain control over what the application is allowed to do (and a lot more) through the corresponding `ServicePrincipal` object in each tenant.

A special case: App creation via the Azure portal and Visual Studio

As I write, both of the application provisioning techniques you've experienced so far (using the Azure portal and using Visual Studio) assume that you want to run your application in the same tenant in which you are creating it. Hence, these techniques create both the `Application` and the `ServicePrincipal` objects. The presence of a `ServicePrincipal` right after creation time in the home tenant will cause differences in behavior in respect to what happens when the application is consumed through different tenants. That is especially true for native applications, which are out of scope for this book, but in general this is something you need to be aware of. Note that the current behavior is not set in stone and not part of any explicit contract. I cannot guarantee that it will not change after this book goes to the printer.

In the next two subsections, you'll take a look at the content of the `Application` and `ServicePrincipal` objects. This will give me an opportunity to introduce lots of new directory artifacts, which in turn will refine your understanding of what an application is for Azure AD and what it can do for you.

Note Your hands-on experience so far has been limited to implementing web sign-on to applications with a web interface, rendering their own user experience (UX) in a browser. The Application and ServicePrincipal objects are also used to model web APIs, which follow a different set of protocols. I am going to show you how to write web API projects in the next chapter, but I cannot wait until then to describe those concepts—they play such a central role in the Azure AD application model, in consent, and in provisioning that everything would sound weird without them. This is just to ensure that you know what's coming and don't get confused when I suddenly start to talk about OAuth and exposing scopes.

The *Application*

The Application object in Azure AD is meant to describe three distinct aspects of an application:

- The identifiers, protocol coordinates, and authentication options that come into play when a token is requested for accessing the application.

- The resources that the application itself might need to access, and the actions it might need to take, in order to perform its functions. For example, an application might need to write back to the directory, or it might need to send email via Exchange as the authenticated user. You'll have to wait until the next chapter to learn how to actually perform these actions in code, but it's important to understand in this context the provisioning and consent mechanisms underpinning this aspect.

- The actions that the application itself offers. For example, an application representing a facade for a data store might allow for read and write operations—and make it possible for the directory to decide whether to grant a client permission to do only read operations, or both read and write, depending on the identity of the client. This feature is used when the application is a web API, but it rarely comes into play when doing web sign-on, so I won't spend much time on it in this chapter.

So far you've acted directly only on the first aspect. You indirectly took advantage of the defaults in the second point—every web app is configured to ask for permissions to sign in and access the user's profile. You have not interacted with the third aspect yet, but you will in Chapter 9, "Consuming and exposing a web API protected by Azure Active Directory."

Mercifully, neither the Azure portal or the Visual Studio ASP.NET project templates wizards ask you to provide values for all the properties that constitute an Application object. The vast majority of those properties are assigned default values that work great for most of the populace, who can get their web sign-on functionality by providing just a handful of strings (as you have seen, mainly name and redirect_uri) without ever being aware that there are customizations available.

That said, if you do want to know what's available in the Application object, how would you go about it? You have three strategies to choose from:

- Head to the Azure portal (https://manage.windowsazure.com), go to the Azure AD section, select the Applications tab, search for your app, select it, then click Configuration. You'll see far more info there than you provided at creation time. One example you are already familiar with is the client_id, which is assigned by Azure AD to your app when it's created.

  The information shown there is what you would probably customize to meet the requirements of the most common scenarios. However, not all the application features are exposed there.

- Still in the Azure portal, with your app selected, you can use a link at the bottom of the page, Manage Manifest, to download a JSON file that contains the verbatim dump of the corresponding Application entity in the directory. You can edit this file to change whatever you want to control, then upload it again (through the same portal commands) to reflect your new options in the directory.

- Finally, you can use the Directory Graph API (mentioned in Chapter 3) to query the directory and GET the Application object, once again in JSON format.

The first method goes against the policy I am adopting in the book—the portal UX can change far too easily after the book is in print, so including screenshots of it would be a bad idea. Also, it does not go nearly deep enough for my purposes here.

The second method, the manifest, would work out well—and is the method I advise you to use when you work with your applications. However, there is something that makes it less suitable for explaining the anatomy of the Application object for the first time: the manifest is a true object dump from the directory, and for pure inheritance reasons it includes lots of properties that aren't useful or relevant for the Application itself.

To keep the signal-to-noise ratio as crisp as possible, the JSON snippets I'll show you here will all be obtained through the third method, direct queries through the Graph. I am using a very handy sample web app (which you can find at *https://graphexplorer.cloudapp.net*), which provides an easy UI for querying the graph. I cannot guarantee that the app will still be available when you read this book, but performing those queries through code, or with curl or via Fiddler, is extremely easy. In the next chapter you'll learn how.

Following is a dump of the Application object that corresponds to the sample app we've been working with so far. The query I used for obtaining it is as follows:

```
https://graph.windows.net/developertenant.onmicrosoft.com/
applications?$filter=appId+eq+'e8040965-f52a-4494-96ab-0ef07b591e3f'&api-version=1.5
```

You'll likely recognize the typical OData '$' syntax. The GUID you see there is the client_id of the application. Here's the complete JSON from the result:

```
{
  "odata.metadata": "https://graph.windows.net/developertenant.onmicrosoft.
com/$metadata#directoryObjects/Microsoft.DirectoryServices.Application",
  "value": [
    {
      "odata.type": "Microsoft.DirectoryServices.Application",
      "objectType": "Application",
```

```
      "objectId": "c806648a-f27d-43fd-9f18-999f7708fcfc",
      "deletionTimestamp": null,
      "appId": "e8040965-f52a-4494-96ab-0ef07b591e3f",
      "appRoles": [],
      "availableToOtherTenants": false,
      "displayName": "WebAppChapter5",
      "errorUrl": null,
      "groupMembershipClaims": null,
      "homepage": "https://localhost:44300/",
      "identifierUris": [
        "https://localhost:44300/WebProjectChapter5"
      ],
      "keyCredentials": [],
      "knownClientApplications": [],
      "logoutUrl": null,
      "oauth2AllowImplicitFlow": false,
      "oauth2AllowUrlPathMatching": false,
      "oauth2Permissions": [
        {
          "adminConsentDescription": "Allow the application to access WebAppChapter5 on behalf
of the signed-in user.",
          "adminConsentDisplayName": "Access WebAppChapter5",
          "id": "00431d04-5334-4da6-8396-0e6f54631f10",
          "isEnabled": true,
          "type": "User",
          "userConsentDescription": "Allow the application to access WebAppChapter5 on your
behalf.",
          "userConsentDisplayName": "Access WebAppChapter5",
          "value": "user_impersonation"
        }
      ],
      "oauth2RequirePostResponse": false,
      "passwordCredentials": [],
      "publicClient": null,
      "replyUrls": [
        "https://localhost:44300/"
      ],
      "requiredResourceAccess": [
        {
          "resourceAppId": "00000002-0000-0000-c000-000000000000",
          "resourceAccess": [
            {
              "id": "311a71cc-e848-46a1-bdf8-97ff7156d8e6",
              "type": "Scope"
            }
          ]
        }
      ],
      "samlMetadataUrl": null
    }
  ]
}
```

Feel free to ignore anything that starts with "odata" here. Also, some properties listed are for internal use only or are about to be deprecated, so I won't talk about those.

The most "meta" properties here are `objectId` and `deletionTimestamp`.

- `objectId` is the unique identifier for this `Application` entry in the directory. Note, this is *not* the identifier used to identify the app in any protocol transaction—you can think of it as the ID of the row where the `Application` object is saved in the directory store. It is used for referencing the object in most directory queries and in cross-entity references.

- `deletionTimestamp` is always null, unless you delete the `Application`, which in that case it records the instant in which you do so. Azure AD implements most eliminations as soft deletes so that you can repent and restore the object without too much pain should you realize the deletion was a mistake.

Properties used for authentication

The bulk of the properties of the `Application` object control aspects of the authentication, specifying parameters that define the app from the protocol's perspective, turning options on and off, and providing experience customizations.

Property naming galore

One important thing to keep in mind: Although in this book I am focusing on OAuth2 and OpenID Connect, the `Application` object must support all the protocols that Azure AD implements. As you have seen in previous chapters, all claims-oriented protocols share some common concepts—issuer, audience, URLs to receive returned tokens, and so on. That helps to keep the list of properties short, given that you need to specify the URL where you want to get the tokens back only once and use it with all protocols. However, it also creates a problem: If WS-Federation calls that URL *wsreply*, and OAuth2 calls it *redirect_uri*, what should the corresponding property in the `Application` object be called? You'll see that the question has been answered in many different ways through the object model, largely driven by historical circumstances (for example, which protocols were implemented first). That has led to some confusion, which prompted remediation attempts by surfacing those properties in the Azure portal UX under different labels . . . which led to further confusion. This is just a heads-up to highlight the importance of being very precise when you reason about Applications and protocol literature.

Here's the complete list:

- `appId`   This corresponds to the client_id of the application.

- `replyUrls`   This multivalue property holds the list of registered redirect_uri values that Azure AD will accept as destinations when returning tokens. No other URI will be accepted. This property is the source of some of the most common errors: even the smallest mismatch (trailing slash missing, different casing) will cause the token-issuance operation to fail.

    Although at creation time the only URL in the collection is the one you specified, as is the case with the localhost-based URL in the sample here, you'll often find yourself adding more URLs as your app moves past the development stage and gets deployed to staging and production. If you want to achieve complete isolation between application deployments, you can always create an entirely new Application for every environment, each with its own client_id.

- identifierUris This multivalue property holds a collection of developer-assigned application identifiers, as opposed to the directory-assigned client_id.

  These values are used to represent the application as a resource in protocols such as SAML and WS-Federation, where they map to the concept of realm. The URIs are also used as audience in access tokens issued for the app via OAuth2, when the app is consumed as a web API (as opposed to a web app with an HTML UX). This often generates confusion, given that this scenario can also be implemented by using the app's client_id instead of one identifier URI. More about this in Chapter 9.

- publicClient In the current Azure AD model, applications can be either confidential clients (apps that can have their own credentials, usually run on servers, etc.) or public clients (mobile and native apps running on devices, with no credentials, hence no strong identity of their own). The security characteristics of the two app types are very different, and so is the set of protocols that the two types support. For example, a native client cannot obtain a token purely with its app identity because it has no identity of its own; and a confidential client cannot request tokens with user-only flows, where the identity of the app would not play a role.

  This book focuses on web apps; hence, confidential clients. That means that the apps discussed here will always have the publicClient property set to null.

- passwordCredentials, keyCredentials These properties hold references to application-assigned credentials, string-based shared secrets and X.509 certificates, respectively. Only confidential clients can have nonempty values here. Those credentials come into play when requesting access tokens—in other words, when the app is acting as a client rather than as a resource itself. You'll see more of that in the next chapter.

- displayName This property determines how the application is called in interactions with end users, such as consent prompts. It's also the mnemonic moniker used to indicate the application for the developer in the Azure management portal. Given that the display name has no uniqueness requirements, it's not always a way to conclusively identify one app in a long list.

- Homepage The URL saved here is used to point to the application from its entry in application portals such as the Office 365 application store. It does not play any role in the protocol behavior of the app; it's just whatever landing page you want visitors, prospective buyers, and corporate users (who might get there through the list of applications their company uses) to use as an entry point. At creation time, the Homepage value is copied from the replyUrls property. A common bit of advice to software developers from Office is to ensure that the URL in Homepage corresponds to a protected page/route in your application so that if visitors are already authenticated when they click the link, they'll find themselves authenticated with the same identity in your app as well.

- **samlMetadataUrl** In case you are implementing SAML in your app, this property allows you to specify where your app publishes its own SAML metadata document.

- **oauth2AllowImplicitFlow** This flag, defaulting to false, determines whether your app allows requests for tokens for the app via implicit flow.

- **oauth2AllowUrlPathMatching** By default, Azure AD requires all redirect_uris in a request to be a perfect match of any of the entries in replyURLs. This is a very good policy, designed to mitigate the open redirector attack—an attack in which appending extra parameters to one redirect_uri might lead to the resulting token being forwarded to a malicious party. However, there are situations in which your app might need to have more flexibility and use return_uris that do have a tail of extra characters that aren't part of the registered values. Setting this property to true tells Azure AD that you want to relax the perfect match constraint, and allows you to use URLs that are a superset of the ones you registered. Before changing this value, make sure you truly need it and that you have mitigations in place.

- **oauth2RequirePostResponse** Azure AD expects all requests to be carried through a GET operation. Setting this property to true relaxes that constraint.

- **groupMembershipClaims** If you want to receive group membership information as claims in the tokens issued for your user, you can use this property to express that requirement. Setting groupMembershipClaims to SecurityGroup results in a token containing all the security group memberships of the user. Setting it to All results in a token containing both security group and distribution list memberships. The default, null, results in no group information in the token. Note that the group claims do not include the group name; rather, they carry a GUID that uniquely identifies the group within the tenant. I'll spend more time on this topic later in the chapter.

- **appRoles** This property is used for declaring roles associated with the application. I provide a complete explanation of this property in later sections of this chapter.

- **availableToOtherTenants** This property deviates from the strictly protocol-related functionalities: it's more about controlling the provisioning aspect. Every confidential client application starts its existence as an app that can be accessed only by accounts from the same directory tenant in which the application was created. That's the typical line-of-business application scenario, where the IT department of one company develops an app to be used by their fellow employees. Any attempt to get tokens for the app from a different tenant will not work (excluding guest scenarios, which will be mentioned later).

  However, that clearly does not work if your intent is to make the application available across organizations: that is the case for SaaS scenarios, naturally. If you are in that situation, you can flip availableToOtherTenants to true. That will make Azure AD allow requests from other tenants to trigger the consent flow I described briefly earlier instead of carrying out the default behavior, in which the request would be rejected right away.

  Applications available across tenants (what we commonly call "multitenant apps") have extra constraints. For example, whereas identifierURIs can normally be any URI with no restrictions, for multitenant apps those URIs must be proper URLs and their hostname must match a domain that is registered with the tenant. Also, only tenant administrators can promote an app to be multitenant. The consent for a multitenant app clearly identifies the tenant as the publisher of the app to potentially every other organization using Azure AD—with important repercussions on reputation should something go south.

> **Note** Flipping this switch only tells Azure AD that you want your app to behave as a multitenant app. Actually promoting one application from line of business to multitenant requires some coding changes, which I'll discuss later on.

- knownClientApplications   The last property listed here is also about provisioning. You have seen how consenting for one application to have access to your own directory results in the creation of a ServicePrincipal for the app in the target directory. To anticipate a bit the upcoming discussion on permissions, the idea is that the ServicePrincipal will also need to record the list of resources and actions on those resources that the user consented to. This is possible only if the requested resources are already present with their own ServicePrincipal entries in the target directory. That is usually the case for first-party resources: if your app needs access to the Directory Graph or Exchange online, you can expect those to already have an entry in the directory. It will occasionally happen that your solution includes both a client application and one custom web API application. You'll want your prospective customers to have to consent only once, when they first try to get a token for the client application. If consent can happen only when all the requested resources are present as a ServicePrincipal in the target directory, and one of the resources you need is your own API, you have a problem. It looks like you have to ask your user to first consent to the web API so that it can create its ServicePrincipal in the target directory, and only after that ask the user to go back and consent to the client application.

  Well, this property exists to save you from having to do all that work. Say that the application you are working on is the web API project. If you save in knownClientApplications the client_id (the appId, that is) of the client application you want to use for accessing your API, Azure AD will know that consenting to the client means implicitly consenting to the web API, too, and will automatically provision ServicePrincipals for both the client and web API at the same time, with a single consent. Handy!

  The main catch in all this is that both the client and the web API application must be defined within the same tenant. You cannot list in knownClientApplications the client_id of a client defined in a different tenant.

oauth2Permissions: What actions does the app expose?

The oauth2Permissions collection publishes the list of things that client applications can do with your app—the scopes the app admits, mostly, but that comes into play only in case your app is a web API. If your app is a web application with a UX, the expectation is that browsers will request tokens for your app with the goal of signing in. That does not require any entry for web sign-on, the scenario considered in this chapter, so I thought of deferring coverage of this property until I get to exposing your own web API, but some of the concepts will come in handy sooner than that, so I'll give you a bit of background now. Let's take a closer look at the only entry in the oauth2Permissions collection for the sample application:

```
{
    "adminConsentDescription": "Allow the application to access WebAppChapter5 on behalf of the
signed-in user.",
    "adminConsentDisplayName": "Access WebAppChapter5",
    "id": "00431d04-5334-4da6-8396-0e6f54631f10",
    "isEnabled": true,
    "type": "User",
    "userConsentDescription": "Allow the application to access WebAppChapter5 on your behalf.",
    "userConsentDisplayName": "Access WebAppChapter5",
    "value": "user_impersonation"
}
```

Where does the default *oauth2Permissions* entry come from?

Answering this question requires a bit of history. For the way in which Azure AD is organized, a token obtained by a client for accessing a web API must contain at least a scope—which is, as you have seen, an action that the client obtains permissions to perform. An application representing a web API but not defining any scopes would be impossible to access because any token request would not have any scope to prompt consent for. That wasn't always the case! This constraint was added a few months after Azure AD was released, creating a lot of confusion for developers who were now expected to manually add at least one oauth2Permission entry before being able to use their API. This also influenced all the walk-through and sample readme files at the time, making it necessary to add instructions on how to add that entry. I am happy to report that such manual steps are no longer necessary. Every Application is created with one default permission, user_impersonation, so that if you want to implement your app as a web API you don't need any extra configuration step, and you can begin development right away. I am telling you all this because some of the walk-throughs from that phase are still around. Now you know that you don't need to follow them to the letter on this.

The schema is pretty straightforward:

The ID uniquely identifies the permission within this resource.

Each property ending in "description" or "name" indicates how to identify and describe this permission in the context of interactive operations, such as consent prompts or Application configuration at development time.

The type property indicates whether this permission can be granted by any user in the directory (in which case it is populated with the value User) or is a high-value capability that can be granted only by an administrator (in which case, the value is Admin).

The `value` property represents the value in the scope claim that a token will carry to signal the fact that the caller was granted this permission by the directory. That is what the app should look for in the incoming token to decide whether the caller should be allowed to exercise the function gated by this permission.

I'll come back to this collection in Chapter 9.

requiredResourceAccess: What resources the app needs

This is one of the most powerful entries in the `Application` object, which can lead to utter despair when things go wrong:

```
"requiredResourceAccess": [
  {
    "resourceAppId": "00000002-0000-0000-c000-000000000000",
    "resourceAccess": [
      {
        "id": "311a71cc-e848-46a1-bdf8-97ff7156d8e6",
        "type": "Scope"
      }
    ]
  }
}
```

You can think of `requiredResourceAccess` as the client-side partner of `oauth2Permissions`. The `requiredResourceAccess` entry lists all the resources and permissions the application needs access to, referring to the entries each of those resources expose through their own `oauth2Permissions` entries. For each resource, `requiredResourceAccess` specifies:

- The appId of the requested resource, via the `resourceAppId` property

- Which specific permissions it is after, via the `resourceAccess` collection, which contains

  - The permission ID—the same ID the resource declared (in its own `Application` object) for the permission in its own corresponding `oauth2Permission` entry

  - The type of access it intends to perform: possible values are Scope and Role.

In our sample, the resource we need access to is the directory itself, in the form of the Graph API—the identifier 00000002-0000-0000-c000-000000000000 is reserved for the Graph in all tenants. The permission we are requesting, of ID 311a71cc-e848-46a1-bdf8-97ff7156d8e6, corresponds to "sign in and access the user's profile." I know it doesn't sound that easy to remember . . . but it is not supposed to be. The Azure portal or the Visual Studio project wizards normally take care of putting those values there for you when you select the human-readable counterparts in their UIs.

The type of access Scope determines that the app request the permission in delegated fashion; that is to say, as the identity of the user who's doing the request. Whether an admin user is required for successfully obtaining this permission at run time, or a normal user can suffice, is determined by the Type declared in the corresponding `oauth2Permission` entry—found in the `Application` object of the resource exposing the permission. As you have seen in the preceding section, the possible values are User and Admin. If the permission declares the latter, only an administrator can consent to it.

A requiredResourceAccess entry with a Type of value Role indicates that the application requires that permission with its own application identity, regardless of which user identity is used to obtain the token (if any—there are ways for an app to get tokens with no users involved, and I'll talk about that in the "Application permissions" section toward the end of this chapter). This option does require consent from an administrator.

Now here is a super important concept; put everything else down and read very carefully. In the current Azure AD model, one application must declare in advance *all* resources it needs access to, and *all* the associated permissions it requires. At the first request for a token for that app, that list will be presented to the user in its entirety, regardless of what resources are actually needed for that specific request. Once the user successfully grants consent, a ServicePrincipal will be provisioned, and that consent will be recorded in the target directory (you'll see later how that happens in practice) for all the requested resources. This makes it possible to prompt the user for consent only once.

The side effect of this approach is that the list of consented permissions is static. If you decide to add a new permission request to your application after a customer of yours already consented to it in its own directory, your customer will not be able to obtain the new permission for your app in the customer's own tenant until he or she revokes consent in its entirety and then grants it again. This can sometimes be painful. In version 2 of Azure AD, we are working hard to eliminate this constraint, but in version 1, that is the way it is today.

Figure 8-2 summarizes the main functional groups the Application object's properties fall into. Sure, there are a lot of details to keep in mind, but at the end of the day, more often than not, this simple subdivision will help you to ignore the noise and zero in on the properties you need for your scenario.

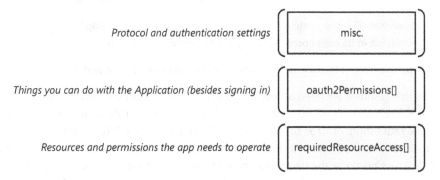

Protocol and authentication settings — misc.

Things you can do with the Application (besides signing in) — oauth2Permissions[]

Resources and permissions the app needs to operate — requiredResourceAccess[]

FIGURE 8-2 A functional grouping of the properties of the Application object in Azure AD.

The *ServicePrincipal* object

In later sections you will study in detail how an app goes from one `Application` object in one tenant to one or more `ServicePrincipals` in one or more tenants. In this section, I've assumed that such provisioning has already happened and will focus on the properties of the resulting `Service-Principal`: what properties are copied as is from the `Application`, what doesn't make it through, and what's added that is unique.

Following is the `ServicePrincipal` for our sample app. It is deployed on the same tenant as the `Application`, but for our analysis that doesn't matter. At first glance, it does look a lot like the `Application` itself, but it is in fact quite different.

```
{
    "odata.type": "Microsoft.DirectoryServices.ServicePrincipal",
    "objectType": "ServicePrincipal",
    "objectId": "29f565fd-0889-43ff-aa7f-3e7c37fd95b4",
    "deletionTimestamp": null,
    "accountEnabled": true,
    "appDisplayName": "WebAppChapter5",
    "appId": "e8040965-f52a-4494-96ab-0ef07b591e3f",
    "appOwnerTenantId": "6c3d51dd-f0e5-4959-b4ea-a80c4e36fe5e",
    "appRoleAssignmentRequired": false,
    "appRoles": [],
    "displayName": "WebAppChapter5",
    "errorUrl": null,
    "homepage": "https://localhost:44300/",
    "keyCredentials": [],
    "logoutUrl": null,
    "oauth2Permissions": [
      {
        "adminConsentDescription": "Allow the application to access WebAppChapter5 on behalf
of the signed-in user.",
        "adminConsentDisplayName": "Access WebAppChapter5",
        "id": "00431d04-5334-4da6-8396-0e6f54631f10",
        "isEnabled": true,
        "type": "User",
        "userConsentDescription": "Allow the application to access WebAppChapter5 on your
behalf.",
        "userConsentDisplayName": "Access WebAppChapter5",
        "value": "user_impersonation"
      }
    ],
    "passwordCredentials": [],
    "preferredTokenSigningKeyThumbprint": null,
    "publisherName": "Developer Tenant",
    "replyUrls": [],
    "samlMetadataUrl": null,
    "servicePrincipalNames": [
      "https://localhost:44300/WebProjectChapter5",
      "e8040965-f52a-4494-96ab-0ef07b591e3f"
    ],
    "tags": [
      "WindowsAzureActiveDirectoryIntegratedApp"
    ]
  }
```

I am sure you are not surprised to find objectId and deletionTimestamp here, too.

Notably missing are all the flags determining protocol behaviors at run time: availableTo-OtherTenants, groupMembershipClaims, oauth2AllowImplicitFlow, oauth2AllowUrlPath-Matching, oauth2-RequirePostResponse, and publicClient. Other properties that don't directly make it in the form of properties in ServicePrincipal are knownClientApplications and requiredResourceAccess, both of which are properties that influence the consent process and the very creation of this ServicePrincipal. As you will see later on, requiredResourceAccess gets recorded in a different form—one that makes it easier for the directory to track down who in the tenant has actually been granted the necessary permissions to use the app.

Properties that do transfer as is from the Application to its corresponding ServicePrincipal are the appId (containing the all-important client_id), various optional URLs (errorUrl, logoutUrl, samlMetadata-Url), the settings used when listing the app in some UX (displayName, homepage), the exposed appRoles and oauth2Permissions, and finally the credentials keyCredentials and passwordCredentials. The presence of the credentials in the ServicePrincipal has important implications: it means that your code can use the same credentials defined in the Application and those will work on every ServicePrincipal in every tenant.

Here's a list of the brand-new properties:

- appOwnerTenantId   This property carries the tenantId of the tenant where you'll find the Application object that was used as a blueprint for creating this ServicePrincipal—in this case, developertenant.onmicrosoft.com. If you search Chapter 6 for the GUID value shown in our example's ServicePrincipal, you'll find it everywhere.

- publisherName   Another property meant to be used for describing the app in user interactions, publisherName stores the display name of the tenant where the original Application was defined. This represents the organization that published the app.

- servicePrincipalNames   This property holds all the identifiers that can be used for referring to this application in protocol flows: as you might have noticed in the sample, it contains the union of the values in the identifierUris collection and the appId value from the Application object. The former is used for OAuth2 and OpenID Connect flows, the latter for WS-Federation, SAML, or OAuth2 bearer token resource access requests.

- appRoleAssignmentRequired   Administrators can decide to explicitly name the user accounts that they want to enable for the user of the app and gate the token issuance on this condition. If appRoleAssignmentRequired is set to true, only the token requests coming from explicitly assigned users will be fulfilled. I'll talk more about this later in the chapter.

- tags   This property is used mostly by the Azure portal to determine the type of application and how to present it in the administrative interface. Without going into fine detail, an empty tag collection results in the corresponding ServicePrincipal not being shown as one of the resources that can be requested by other applications.

Consent and delegated permissions

Now that you know what application aspects are defined in the `Application` and `Service-Principal` objects, it's time to understand how these two entities are used in the application provisioning and consent flows.

You have learned that all it takes for provisioning an app in a tenant (creating a `ServicePrincipal` for that app in the tenant) is one user requesting a token by using the app coordinates defined in the `Application` object, successfully authenticating, and granting to the app consent to the permissions it requires. To get to the next level of detail, you must take into account what kind of user created the application in the first place, what permissions the applications requires, and what kind of user actually grants consent to the app and in what terms. There is an underlying rule governing the entire process, but that's pretty complicated. Instead of enunciating it here and letting you wrestle with it, I am going to walk you through various common scenarios and explain what happens. Little by little, we'll figure out how things work.

Initially, I'll scope things down to the case in which you are creating line-of-business apps—applications meant to be consumed by users from the same directory in which they were created. If your company has an IT department that creates apps for your company's employees, you know what kind of apps I am referring to. Once you have a solid understanding of how consent works within a single directory, I'll venture to the multitenant case, where you'll see more of the provisioning aspect. I'll stick to delegated permissions, but there are other kinds of permissions, like the things that an app can do independently of which user is signed in at the moment, but I'll defer coverage of those and describe the basics here.

Application created by a nonadmin user

In Chapter 5 you followed instructions to create an application in Azure AD via the Azure portal. Did you create it while being signed in with a user who is a global administrator in your tenant? If not, that's perfect—the app you have is already in the state I'll describe in this section. If you did, you can choose to believe that my description is accurate—or you can create a new app, following the same instructions (very important!) but using a nonadmin user. Note: to be able to sign in with that account in the Azure portal, you might need to promote that user to coadmin of your Azure subscription.

As you have seen in the preceding section, creating one app via the Azure portal has the effect of creating both the `Application` object and the corresponding `ServicePrincipal`. What you haven't seen yet is how the directory remembers what permissions have been granted to the `ServicePrincipal` and to which user. The `Application` object enumerates the permissions it needs in the `requiredResourceAccess` collection, but those aren't present in the `Service-Principal`. Where are they?

Azure AD maintains another collection of entities, named `oauth2PermissionGrants`, which records which clients have access to which resources and with what permissions. Critically, `oauth2PermissionGrants` also records which users that consent is valid for.

For example, when you created the sample app in the Azure portal, Azure AD automatically granted consent for that app on behalf of your user. Alongside the `Application` and `ServicePrincipal`, the process also created the following `oauth2PermissionGrants` entry:

```
{
  "odata.metadata": "https://graph.windows.net/developertenant.onmicrosoft.com/$metadata#oauth2
PermissionGrants",
  "value": [
    {
      "clientId": "29f565fd-0889-43ff-aa7f-3e7c37fd95b4",
      "consentType": "Principal",
      "expiryTime": "2015-11-21T23:31:32.6645924",
      "objectId": "_WX1KYkI_OOqfz58N_2VtEnIMYJNhOpOkFrsIuF86Y8",
      "principalId": "13d3104a-6891-45d2-a4be-82581a8e465b",
      "resourceId": "8231c849-844d-4eea-905a-ec22e17ce98f",
      "scope": "UserProfile.Read",
      "startTime": "0001-01-01T00:00:00"
    }
  ]
}
```

Note The query I used for retrieving this result was `https://graph.windows.net/developertenant.onmicrosoft.com/oauth2PermissionGrants?$filter=clientId+eq+'29f565fd-0889-43ff-aa7f-3e7c37fd95b4'`.

Let's translate that snippet into English. It says that the `User` with identifier 13d3104a-6891-45d2-a4be-82581a8e465b (the `PrincipalId`) consented for the client 29f565fd-0889-43ff-aa7f-3e7c37fd95b4 (the `clientId`) to access the resource 8231c849-844d-4eea-905a-ec22e17ce98f (the `resourceId`) with permission `UserProfile.Read` (the `scope`). Resolving references further, the client is our sample app, and the resource is the directory itself—more precisely, the Directory Graph API. Figure 8-3 shows how the consent for the first application user is recorded in the directory; Figure 8-4 shows how the `oauth2PermissionGrants` table grows as more users give their consent.

Important All the identifiers here refer to the `objectId` property of the respective entity they refer to. Given that `clientId` and `resourceId` ultimately refer to `ServicePrincipals`, it's easy to get confused and expect those values to represent the `appId`. But nope, it's the `objectId`. The `principalId` is the `objectId` property of the `User` object representing the user account used for consenting.

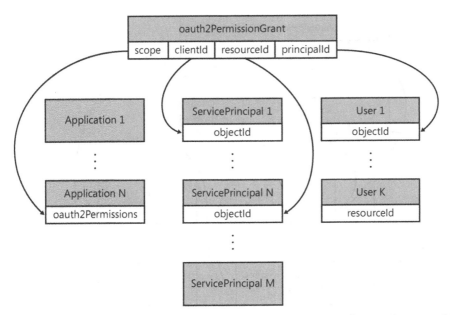

FIGURE 8-3 The oauth2PermissionGrant recording in the directory that user 1 consented for the app represented by ServicePrincipal 1 to access ServicePrincipal N with the permission stored in the property scope, in itself picked from one of the permissions exposed by the original Application N oauth2Permissions section.

When Azure AD receives a request for a token to be issued to the application defined here, it looks in the oauth2PermissionGrants collection for entries whose clientId matches the app. If the authenticated user has a corresponding entry, she or he will get back a token right away. If there's no entry, the user will see the consent prompt listing all the requiredResourceAccess permissions from the Application object. Upon successful consent, a new oauth2PermissionGrant entry for the current user will be created to record the consent. And so on and so forth.

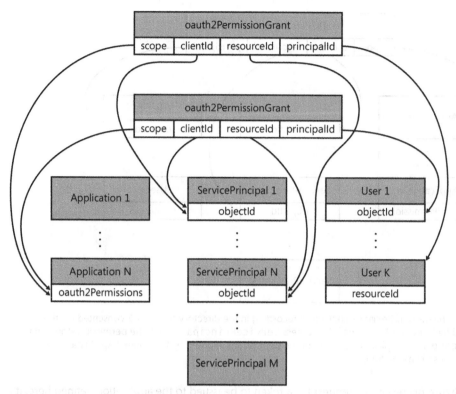

FIGURE 8-4 Subsequent consent operations create more `oauth2PermissionGrant` entries in the directory, one for each new user consenting for the application.

If you want to try, go ahead and launch the sample app again, but sign in as another user. This time, you will be presented with the consent page. Consent and then sign out. Sign in again with the new user: you will not be prompted for consent again. If you queried the directory (in the next chapter you'll learn how) to find all the `oauth2PermissionGrants` whose `clientId` matches the sample app, you'd see that there are now two entries, looking very much alike apart from the `principalId,` which would point to different users. Note that it doesn't matter whether your second user is an administrator or a low-privilege user; the resulting `oauth2PermissionGrant` will look just like the one described earlier when following this flow.

Interlude: Delegated permissions to access the directory

One of the things you have learned in this chapter is that applications can declare the permissions that a client can request of them, via `oauth2Permissions`, as a way of partitioning the possible actions a user can perform over the resource represented by the app and to provide fine-grained access control over who can do what. As I've mentioned, in the next chapter you will learn how clients can actually take advantage of gaining such permissions; here, you're just studying how requesting and granting such permissions takes place.

Each and every resource protected by Azure AD works by exposing permissions—the Office 365 API, Azure management API, and any custom API all work that way. Covering all those would be a pretty hard task. Even ignoring the enormous surface I'd have to cover, chances are that the details would change multiple times from the time I'm writing and when you have this book in your hands. That said, I am going to describe in detail at least one resource: the directory itself. Like any other resource, Azure AD exposes a number of delegated permissions, which determine what actions your application is allowed to perform against the data stored in the directory. Such actions take the form of requests to embed information in issued tokens (what we have been working with until now) and reading or modifying directory data via API calls to the Graph API (what you'll see in the next chapter). You will likely have to deal with directory permissions in practically every app you write; hence, they're a great candidate for showing you how to deal with permissions in depth—well, except for the fact that they feature lots of exceptions, but you need to be aware of these anyway.

As of today, the directory itself is represented by a `ServicePrincipal` in your tenant. You already know both the `AppId` and the `ObjectId` of that principal, given that our sample app had to request at least the permission `UserProfile.Read` in order to sign users in. The `AppId`, 00000002-0000-0000-c000-000000000000, comes from the `requiredResourceAccess` in the `Application` object representing our sample. The `ObjectID` of the `ServicePrincipal`, 8231c849-844d-4eea-905a-ec22e17ce98f, comes from the `oauth2PermissionGrant` tracking the consent to our sample. The `objectId` is enough for crafting the resource URL referring to the Graph API `ServicePrincipal`: it's https://graph.windows.net/developertenant.onmicrosoft.com/servicePrincipals/8231c849-844d-4eea-905a-ec22e17ce98f.

I won't show the entire JSON for the `ServicePrincipal` here, as it contains a lot of stuff I want to cover later. But take a look at the `oauth2Permissions`, the collection of delegated permissions one client can request for interacting with the directory:

```
"oauth2Permissions": [
    {
      "adminConsentDescription": "Allows the app to create groups on behalf of the signed-in
user and read all group properties and memberships. Additionally, this allows the app to update
group properties and memberships for the groups the signed-in user owns.",
      "adminConsentDisplayName": "Read and write all groups",
      "id": "970d6fa6-214a-4a9b-8513-08fad511e2fd",
      "isEnabled": true,
      "type": "User",
      "userConsentDescription": "Allows the app to create groups on your behalf and read all
group properties and memberships. Additionally, this allows the app to update group properties
and memberships for groups you own.",
      "userConsentDisplayName": "Read and write all groups",
      "value": "Group.ReadWrite.All"    },
    {
      "adminConsentDescription": "Allows the app to read basic group properties and memberships
on behalf of the signed-in user.",
      "adminConsentDisplayName": "Read all groups",
      "id": "6234d376-f627-4f0f-90e0-dff25c5211a3"
      "isEnabled": true,
      "type": "User",
      "userConsentDescription": "Allows the app to read all group properties and memberships on
your behalf.",
```

```
        "userConsentDisplayName": "Read all groups",
        "value": "Group.Read.All"
      },
      {
        "adminConsentDescription": "Allows the app to read and write data in your company or
school directory, such as users and groups. Does not allow user or group deletion.",
        "adminConsentDisplayName": "Read and write directory data",
        "id": "78c8a3c8-a07e-4b9e-af1b-b5ccab50a175",
        "isEnabled": true,
        "type": "Admin",
        "userConsentDescription": "Allows the app to read and write data in your company or school
directory, such as other users, groups. Does not allow user or group deletion on your behalf.",
        "userConsentDisplayName": "Read and write directory data",
        "value": "Directory.Write"
      },
      {
        "adminConsentDescription": "Allows the app to have the same access to information in the
directory as the signed-in user.",
        "adminConsentDisplayName": "Access the directory as the signed-in user",
        "id": "a42657d6-7f20-40e3-b6f0-cee03008a62a",
        "isEnabled": true,
        "type": "User",
        "userConsentDescription": "Allows the app to have the same access to information in your
work or school directory as you do.",
        "userConsentDisplayName": "Access the directory as you",
        "value": "user_impersonation"
      },
      {
        "adminConsentDescription": "Allows the app to read data in your company or school
directory, such as users, groups, and apps.",
        "adminConsentDisplayName": "Read directory data",
        "id": "5778995a-e1bf-45b8-affa-663a9f3f4d04",
        "isEnabled": true,
        "type": "Admin",
        "userConsentDescription": "Allows the app to read data in your company or school
directory, such as other users, groups, and apps.",
        "userConsentDisplayName": "Read directory data",
        "value": "Directory.Read"
      },
      {
        "adminConsentDescription": "Allows the app to read the full set of profile properties of
all users in your company or school, on behalf of the signed-in user. Additionally, this allows
the app to read the profiles of the signed-in user's reports and manager.",
        "adminConsentDisplayName": "Read all users' full profiles",
        "id": "c582532d-9d9e-43bd-a97c-2667a28ce295",
        "isEnabled": true,
        "type": "Admin",
        "userConsentDescription": "Allows the app to read the full set of profile properties of
all users in your company or school on your behalf.  Additionally, this allows the app to read
the profiles of your reports and manager.",
        "userConsentDisplayName": "Read all users' full profiles",
        "value": "User.Read.All"
      },
      {
        "adminConsentDescription": "Allows the app to read a basic set of profile properties of
all users in your company or school on behalf of the signed-in user. Includes display name,
first and last name, photo, and email address. Additionally, this allows the app to read basic
```

```
info about the signed-in user's reports and manager.",
    "adminConsentDisplayName": "Read all users' basic profiles",
    "id": "cba73afc-7f69-4d86-8450-4978e04ecd1a",
    "isEnabled": true,
    "type": "User",
    "userConsentDescription": "Allows the app to read a basic set of profile properties of
other users in your company or school on your behalf. Includes display name, first and last
name, photo, and email address. Additionally, this allows the app to read basic info about your
reports and manager.",
    "userConsentDisplayName": "Read all user's basic profiles",
    "value": "User.ReadBasic.All"
},
{
    "adminConsentDescription": "Allows users to sign in to the app, and allows the app to read
the profile of signed-in users. It also allows the app to read basic company information of
signed-in users.",
    "adminConsentDisplayName": "Sign in and read user profile",
    "id": "311a71cc-e848-46a1-bdf8-97ff7156d8e6",
    "isEnabled": true,
    "type": "User",
    "userConsentDescription": "Allows you to sign in to the app with your work account and let
the app read your profile. It also allows the app to read basic company information.",
    "userConsentDisplayName": "Sign you in and read your profile",
    "value": "User.Read"
}
],
```

Here's a quick description of each delegated permission listed, per their Value property. Please note that this list does change over time. Funny story: it changed a couple of weeks after I finished writing this chapter—I had to come back and revise much of what follows. In fact, the change is not fully complete, as the ServicePrincipal object shown above still shows some old values. The first four permissions described in what follows are the ones that Azure AD has offered since it started supporting consent as described in this book; the last four are brand-new and likely to be less stable. Wherever appropriate, I will hint at the old values so that if you encounter code based on older strings, you can map it back to the new permissions. Chances are the list will change again: please keep an eye on the permissions documentation, currently available at *https://msdn.microsoft.com/ Library/Azure/Ad/Graph/howto/azure-ad-graph-api-permission-scopes*.

User.Read (was *UserProfile.Read*)

This is the permission that each app needs to authenticate users. Applications created in the Azure portal and Visual Studio are configured to automatically request this permission, which is why you don't see it mentioned in the UI you use for creating apps in either tool.

Besides the ability to request a token containing claims about the incoming user, this permission grants to the app the ability to query the Graph API for information about the currently signed-in user.

As you've experienced, this permission can be granted by nonadmin users. That is confirmed by the type property of value User in the permissions declaration.

Directory.Read.All (was *Directory.Read*)

As the name implies, obtaining this permission allows one application to read via the Graph API (I'll stop saying that; just assume that's what you use to interact with the directory) the content of the directory tenant of the user that is currently signed in.

Here's the first exception. In the general case, `Directory.Read` is an admin-only permission: only an admin user can consent to it. However, if the application is a web app (as opposed to a native client) defined in tenant A, and the user being prompted for consent is also from A, `Directory.Read` behaves like a `User`-type permission, which is to say that even a nonadmin user can consent to it. For the scenario we have been considering until now—app developer and app users are from the same tenant—this is effectively a `User`-type permission. When we consider the case in which the app is available to other tenants, you'll see that an app created in A that is requesting `Directory.Read` and being accessed by a user from B will be provisioned in B only if that user happens to be an administrator.

Directory.ReadWrite.All (was *Directory.Write*)

Once again, the name is self-explanatory: this permission grants to the app the ability to read, modify, and create directory data. No exceptions this time; only administrator users can consent to `Directory.Write`.

Directory.AccessAsUser.All (was *user_impersonation*)

This permission, which today is surfaced in the Azure portal under the label "Access the directory as the signed-in user," allows the application to impersonate the caller when accessing the directory, inheriting his or her permissions. That is a pretty powerful thing to do, which is why for web applications this permission can be granted only by an admin user.

As a side note, for native applications, this permission behaves like a `User` permission instead. A native app does not have an identity per se, and it is already doing the direct user's bidding anyway. It stands to reason that the app should be able to do what the user is able to do, just as happens on-premises when a classic native client (say Word or Excel) can or cannot open a document from a network share depending on whether the user has the correct permissions on that folder.

User.ReadBasic.All

You can think of this permission as the minimum requirement allowing an app to enumerate all users from a tenant. Namely, `User.ReadBasic.All` will give access to the user attributes displayName, givenName, surname, mail and thumbnailPhoto. Anything beyond that requires higher permissions.

User.Read.All

This is an extension of `User.ReadBasic.All`. This permission allows an app to access all the attributes of User, the navigation properties manager, and `directReports`. `User.Read.All` can be exercised only by admin users.

Group.Read.All, Group.ReadWrite.All

These new permissions are still in preview at this point, so I hesitate to give too detailed a description here. The idea is that groups and group membership are important information and deserve their own permissions so that access can be requested and granted explicitly. Group.Read.All allows an app to read the basic profile attributes of groups and the groups they are a member of. Group.Read-Write.All allows an app to access the full profile of groups and to change the hierarchy by creating new groups and updating existing ones. Both permissions alone won't grant access to the users in the groups—to obtain that, the app also needs to request some User.Read* permission.

As usual, it's important to remember that scopes don't really add to what a user can do: an application obtaining Group.ReadWrite.All will only be able to manipulate the groups owned by the user granting the delegation to the app.

Table 8-1 summarizes how the out-of-the-box Azure AD permissions work. I've added a column for the permission identifier, which I find handy so that when I look at the Application object, which uses only opaque IDs, I know what permission the app is actually requesting. Let me stress that there's no guarantee these won't change in the future, so please use them advisedly.

TABLE 8-1 A summary of the Azure AD permissions for accessing the directory.

Permission description in the Azure portal	Identifier	Scope value	Type
Sign in and read user profile	311a71cc-e848-46a1-bdf8-97ff7156d8e6	User.Read	User
Read directory data	5778995a-e1bf-45b8-affa-663a9f3f4d04	Directory.Read.All	Admin (except for users from the tenant where the Application is defined)
Read and write directory data	78c8a3c8-a07e-4b9e-af1b-b5ccab50a175	Directory.ReadWrite.All	Admin
Access the directory as the signed-in user	a42657d6-7f20-40e3-b6f0-cee03008a62a	Directory.AccessAsUser.All	Admin (except native clients)
Read all users' basic profiles	cba73afc-7f69-4d86-8450-4978e04ecd1a	User.ReadBasic.All	User
Read all users' full profiles	c582532d-9d9e-43bd-a97c-2667a28ce295	User.Read.All	Admin
Read all groups	6234d376-f627-4f0f-90e0-dff25c5211a3	Group.Read.All	Admin
Read and write all groups	970d6fa6-214a-4a9b-8513-08fad511e2fd	Group.ReadWrite.All	Admin

Now that you have some permissions to play with, let's get back to the exploration of how consent operates.

Application requesting admin-level permissions

Let's say that your application needs the ability to modify data in the directory. You might be surprised to learn that you can create such an application even with a nonadmin user: you'll simply not be able to use it at run time.

Note If you are keeping track of the identifiers in the JSON, technically I could modify the app we've been working on so far, but for the sake of clarity I'll create a new one.

Go back to the Azure portal, sign in as a nonadmin user, and go through the usual application creation flow. Once the app is created, head to the Configure tab and scroll all the way to the bottom of the page. As of today, you'll find a section labeled Permissions To Other Applications, already containing one entry for Azure Active Directory—specifically, the default delegated permission Sign In And Read User Profile. Figure 8-5 shows you the UI at the time of writing, but as usual you can be sure there will be something different (but I hope functionally equivalent) by the time you pick up the book.

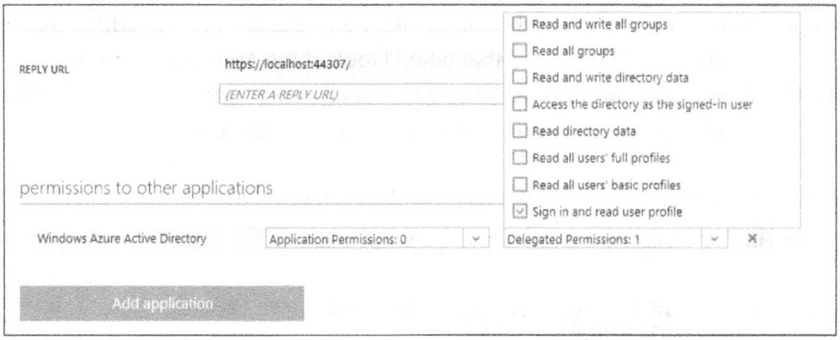

FIGURE 8-5 The application permission selection UI in the Azure portal (fall 2015).

You'll also see an ominous warning: "You are authorized to select only delegated permissions which have personal scope." Today that isn't actually the case. Select Read And Write Directory Data, and then click Save.

You'll receive a warning that the portal was unable to update the configuration for the app, but that's only partially true. If you go take a look at the `Application`, you'll see that it was correctly updated. Here is its `requiredResourceAccess` section:

```
"requiredResourceAccess": [
{
  "resourceAppId": "00000002-0000-0000-c000-000000000000",
  "resourceAccess": [
    {
      "id": "78c8a3c8-a07e-4b9e-af1b-b5ccab50a175",
      "type": "Scope"
    },
    {
      "id": "311a71cc-e848-46a1-bdf8-97ff7156d8e6",
      "type": "Scope"
    }
  ]
}
```

Thanks to our magical Table 8-1, we know those to be the correct permissions.

The part that the portal was *not* able to add was the oauth2PermissionGrant that would allow the current (nonadmin) user to have write access to the directory. If you list the oauth2Permission-Grants of the ServicePrincipal, you'll find only the original entry for User.Read.

That entry is the reason why, if you try to sign in to the app as the user who created it, you will succeed: the directory sees that entry, and that's enough to not show the consent prompt and issue the requested token. However, if after you sign in, your app attempts to get a token for calling the Graph, the operation would fail.

If you launch the application again and try to sign in as any other nonadmin user, instead of the consent prompt you'll receive an error along the lines of "AADSTS90093: Calling principal cannot consent due to lack of permissions," which is exactly what you should expect.

Finally, launch the app again and try to sign in as an administrator. You will be presented with the consent page as in Figure 8-6, just as expected.

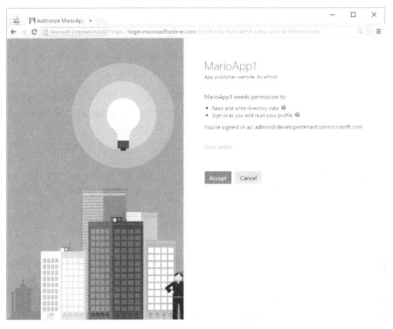

FIGURE 8-6 The consent prompt presented to an admin user.

Grant the consent—you'll find yourself signed in to the application. That done, take a look at what changed in oauth2PermissionGrants:

```
{
    "odata.metadata": "https://graph.windows.net/developertenant.onmicrosoft.com/$metadata#oauth2
PermissionGrants",
    "value": [
        {
            "clientId": "725a2d9a-6707-4127-8131-4f9106d771de",
            "consentType": "Principal",
            "expiryTime": "2016-02-26T18:17:06.8442687",
            "objectId": "mi1acgdnJOGBMU-RBtdx3knIMYJNhOpOkFrsIuF86Y_VUmVPfKg_R6aK4EVKgQSW",
            "principalId": "4f6552d5-a87c-473f-a68a-e0454a810496",
            "resourceId": "8231c849-844d-4eea-905a-ec22e17ce98f",
            "scope": "Directory.Write UserProfile.Read",
            "startTime": "0001-01-01T00:00:00"
        },
        {
            "clientId": "725a2d9a-6707-4127-8131-4f9106d771de",
            "consentType": "Principal",
            "expiryTime": "2016-02-26T00:50:43.3860871",
            "objectId": "mi1acgdnJOGBMU-RBtdx3knIMYJNhOpOkFrsIuF86Y9KENMTkWjSRaS-glgajkZb",
            "principalId": "13d3104a-6891-45d2-a4be-82581a8e465b",
            "resourceId": "8231c849-844d-4eea-905a-ec22e17ce98f",
            "scope": "UserProfile.Read",
            "startTime": "0001-01-01T00:00:00"
        }
    ]
}
```

There's a new entry now, representing the fact that the admin user consented for the app to have `UserProfile.Read` and `Directory.Write` permissions. As discussed earlier, by the time you read this, those scopes will likely have their new values—`User.Read` and `Directory.ReadWrite.All`—but it is really exactly the same semantic.

Note that this did not change the access level for anybody but this particular admin user. If you try to sign in as a nonadmin user (other than the app's creator), you'll still get error AADSTS90093.

Admin consent

If the consent styles you've encountered so far were the only ones available, you'd have a couple of serious issues:

- Each and every user, apart from the application developer, would need to consent upon their first use of the app.

- Only admin-level users would be able to consent for applications requiring more advanced access to the directory, even when a user did not plan to exercise those higher privileged capabilities.

Both issues would limit the usefulness of Azure AD. Luckily, there's a way of consenting to applications that results in a blanket grant to all users of a tenant, all at once, and regardless of the access level requested. That mechanism is known as *admin consent*, as opposed to user consent, which you've been studying so far. Achieving admin consent is just a matter of appending to the request to the authorization endpoint the parameter `prompt=admin_consent`.

Scopes can't grant to the app more power than their user has!

I want to make sure you don't fall for a common misconception here. Scopes are a way of delegating to the app some of the capabilities of their current user. In the most extreme case, this means that an app can be as powerful as its current user (full user impersonation). What can never happen via delegated permissions is that an app can do more than what its user can. If a user cannot write to the directory, the fact that the app obtains `Directory.ReadWrite.All` does not mean that such user can now use the app for writing to the directory! What that scope really means is that if the current user of the app has that capability, the app has that capability, too. If the user does not have that capability, he or she cannot delegate it to the application. As you will see later, applications can have their own permissions (as opposed to delegated permissions) that are independent from their current user and that can be used when the app needs to perform things that would not normally be within the possibilities of its users.

Let's give it a try and see what happens. From Chapter 7, you now know how to modify authentication requests by adding the change you want to the `RedirectToIdentityProvider` notification. In a real app, you would add some conditional logic to weave this parameter in only at the time of first access, but for this test you can go with the brute-force solution in which you add it every time.

Important Here I am adding `Prompt=admin_consent` in the sign-in request for the sake of simplicity, but you would never do that in a production application without at least some conditional logic. In fact, more often than not, you would not include it in the sign-in action but wire it up to a dedicated sign-up action instead. Including `Prompt=admin_consent` in a request will result in the consent being shown to the user, regardless of the past consent history. You want to show this only when needed, and that's only the first time. Wire it up to some specific action in your app, like sign-up, onboarding, or any other label that makes sense for your application.

Here's the code:

```
public static Task RedirectToIdentityProvider(RedirectToIdentityProviderNotification<OpenIdConn
ectMessage,
    OpenIdConnectAuthenticationOptions> notification)
{
    notification.ProtocolMessage.Prompt = "admin_consent";
    return Task.FromResult(0);
}
```

After you've added that code, hit F5 and try signing in. You will be prompted by a dialog similar to the one shown in Figure 8-7.

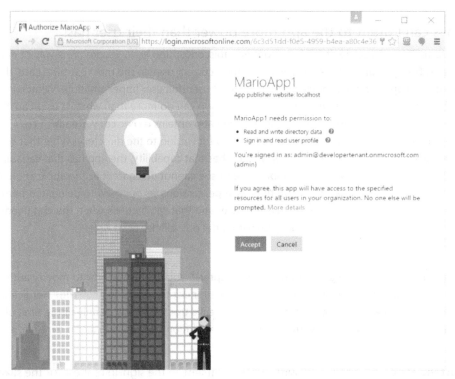

FIGURE 8-7 The admin consent dialog.

Superficially, the dialog in Figure 8-7 looks a lot like the one shown in Figure 8-6, but there is a very important difference! The dialog shown when admin consent is triggered has new text, which articulates the implications of granting consent in the admin consent case: "If you agree, this app will have access to the specified resources for all users in your organization. No one else will be prompted."

Click OK—you'll end up signing in as usual. The app will look the same, but its entries in the directory underwent a significant change. Once again, take a look at the ServicePrincipal's oauth2PermissionGrants:

```
{
  "odata.metadata": "https://graph.windows.net/developertenant.onmicrosoft.com/$metadata#oauth2
PermissionGrants",
  "value": [
    {
      "clientId": "725a2d9a-6707-4127-8131-4f9106d771de",
      "consentType": "AllPrincipals",
      "expiryTime": "2016-02-27T00:38:03.4045842",
      "objectId": "milacgdnJOGBMU-RBtdx3knIMYJNhOpOkFrsIuF86Y8",
      "principalId": null,
      "resourceId": "8231c849-844d-4eea-905a-ec22e17ce98f",
      "scope": "Directory.Write UserProfile.Read",
      "startTime": "0001-01-01T00:00:00"
    },
```

```
    {
      "clientId": "725a2d9a-6707-4127-8131-4f9106d771de",
      "consentType": "Principal",
      "expiryTime": "2016-02-26T18:17:06.8442687",
      "objectId": "mi1acgdnJOGBMU-RBtdx3knIMYJNhOpOkFrsIuF86Y_VUmVPfKg_R6aK4EVKgQSW",
      "principalId": "4f6552d5-a87c-473f-a68a-e0454a810496",
      "resourceId": "8231c849-844d-4eea-905a-ec22e17ce98f",
      "scope": "Directory.Write UserProfile.Read",
      "startTime": "0001-01-01T00:00:00"
    },
    {
      "clientId": "725a2d9a-6707-4127-8131-4f9106d771de",
      "consentType": "Principal",
      "expiryTime": "2016-02-26T00:50:43.3860871",
      "objectId": "mi1acgdnJOGBMU-RBtdx3knIMYJNhOpOkFrsIuF86Y9KENMTkWjSRaS-glgajkZb",
      "principalId": "13d3104a-6891-45d2-a4be-82581a8e465b",
      "resourceId": "8231c849-844d-4eea-905a-ec22e17ce98f",
      "scope": "UserProfile.Read",
      "startTime": "0001-01-01T00:00:00"
    }
  ]
}
```

 Note As I mentioned earlier in this chapter, `Directory.Write` and `UserProfile.Read` will change to `Directory.ReadWrite.All` and `User.Read`.

I highlighted the new entry for you: it has a `consentType` of `AllPrincipals`, as opposed to the usual `Principal`. Furthermore, its `principalId` property does not point to any user in particular; it just says `null`. This tells Azure AD that the application has been granted a blanket consent for any user coming from the current tenant. To prove that this is really the case, sign out from the app, stop it in Visual Studio, comment out the code you added for triggering admin consent, and start the app again. Sign in as a third user from the same tenant, one that you have never used before with this app. Figure 8-8 shows a visual summary of this `oauth2PermissionGrant` configuration.

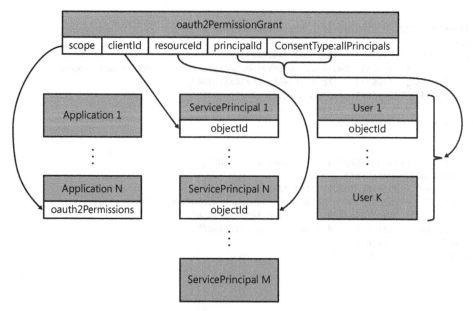

FIGURE 8-8 An `oauth2PermissionGrant` recording admin consent enables the app to operate with the requested scope with all users of a tenant at once.

After the credential gathering, you'll find yourself signed in right away, with no consent prompt of any form.

Application created by an admin user

What happens when you sign in to the Azure portal as an admin user and you create an app in Azure AD? The portal creates the same list of entities: an `Application`, its `ServicePrincipal`, and an `oauth2PermissionGrant`. The difference from the nonadmin case is that the `oauth2Permission-Grant` for an app created by an admin looks exactly like the one you observed as an outcome of the admin consent flow: it includes `consentType allPrincipals`, which means that every user in the tenant can instantly get access to the application.

> **Note** The creation of the `ServicePrincipal` and the associated grant is at the origin of the peculiar behavior of native apps created via the Azure portal by an admin. That is the only case in which a native app does not trigger consent for all users in a tenant. In all other cases, Azure AD today does not record consent for native apps in the directory, storing it in the refresh token instead—which means that each new native app instance running on a different device will prompt its user for consent regardless of its past consent history. This is really out of scope for this book, but given that you have the concept fresh in your mind, I thought I'd share this tidbit.

Multitenancy

How to develop apps that can be consumed by multiple organizations is such a large topic that for some time I wondered whether I should devote an entire chapter to it. I ultimately decided against that. Even if this is going to be a very large section, it still is a logical extension of what you have been studying so far in this chapter.

The first part of this section will discuss how Azure AD enables authentication flows across multiple tenants, and how you can generalize what you have learned about configuring the Katana middleware to the case in which users are sourced from multiple organizations.

The second part will go back to the application model proper, showing you what happens to the directory data model when your app triggers consent flows across tenants.

Azure AD as a parametric STS: The common endpoint

Ironically, if you are a veteran of federation protocols, you are at the highest risk of misunderstanding how Azure AD handles multitenancy. The approach taken here is very different from the classic solutions that preceded it, and I have to admit that I myself needed some time to fully grok it.

In traditional claims-based protocols such as SAML and WS-Federation, the problem of enabling access to one application from multiple IdPs has a canonical solution. It entails introducing one intermediary STS (often referred to as resource STS, R-STS or RP-STS) as the authority that the application trusts. In turn, the intermediate STS trusts all the IdPs that the application needs to work with—assuming the full burden of establishing and maintaining trust, implementing whatever protocol quirks each IdP demands. This is a very sensible approach, which isolates the application itself from the complexities of maintaining relationships with multiple authorities. It is also likely the best approach when you don't know anything about the IdPs you want to connect to, apart from the protocol they implement and the STS metadata they publish. ADFS, Azure Access Control Services (ACS), and pretty much any STS implementation supports this approach.

If you restrict the pool of possible IdPs to only the ones represented by a tenant in Azure AD, however, you have far more information than that, and as you'll see in the following, this removes the need to have an intermediary in the picture. Although each administrator retains full control over her or his own tenant, all tenants share the same infrastructure—same protocols, same data model, same provisioning pipes. Focusing on endpoints in particular (recall their description from Chapter 3), rather than a collection of STSs for each of its tenants, Azure AD can be thought of like a giant parametric STS, where each tenant is expressed by instantiating its ID in the right segment of the issuance endpoint. Figure 8-9 compares the R-STS approach with the multitenant pattern used by Azure AD.

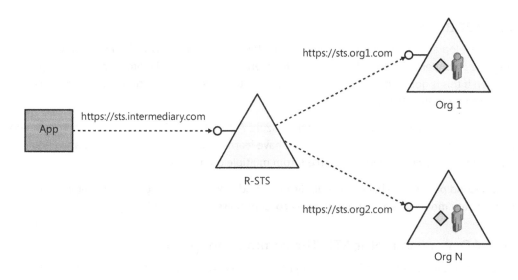

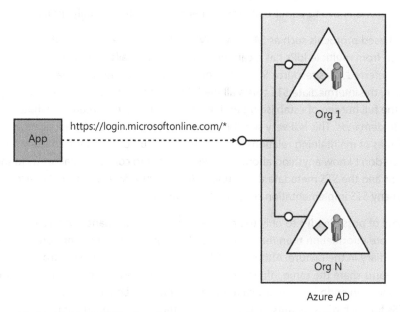

FIGURE 8-9 The R-STS brokered trust pattern and the parametric STS pattern. Besides allowing for directory queries that would be impossible via federation alone, the latter makes it possible to automate application provisioning and trust establishment.

In the hands-on chapters, you've experienced directly how the endpoint pattern https://<instance> /<tenant>/<protocol-specific-path> can be modulated to indicate tenant-specific token-issuance endpoints, sign-out endpoints, metadata document endpoints, and so on. You have also seen how the Katana middleware leverages those endpoints for tying one application to one specific tenant. For example, in Chapter 6 you saw how the metadata document published at https://login .microsoftonline.com/DeveloperTenant.onmicrosoft.com/.well-known/openid-configuration (which, by the way, is equivalent to https://login.microsoftonline.com/6c3d51dd-f0e5-4959-b4ea-a80c4e-36fe5e/.well-known/openid-configuration, where the GUID is the corresponding tenantID) asserts that tokens issued by that tenant will carry an iss(uer) claim value of https://sts.windows.net/6c3d51dd-f0e5-4959-b4ea-a80c4e36fe5e/. In Chapter 7, you saw how that information is used by the Katana middleware to ensure that only tokens coming from that tenant (that is, carrying that iss value) will be accepted. That's all well and good, and exactly what you want for line-of-business applications and single-tenant apps in general.

You can repeat the same reasoning for all tenants: all you need to do is instantiate the right domain (or tenantID) in the endpoints paths.

Azure AD makes it possible to deal with multitenant scenarios by exposing a particular endpoint, where the tenant parameter is not instantiated up front. There is a particular value, common, that can be instantiated in endpoints in lieu of a domain or tenantID. By convention, that value tells Azure AD that the requestor is not mandating any particular tenant—any Azure AD tenant will do.

 Very important: *Common* is not a tenant. It is just an artifact used for constructing Azure AD endpoints when the tenant to be used is not known yet. This is a crucial point to keep in mind at all times when working with multitenant solutions, or you'll end up baking assumptions into your app that will inevitably turn out to be false and create all sorts of issues that are hard to debug.

When the endpoint being constructed is one that would serve authentication UI, as is the case for the OAuth2 authorization endpoints, the user is presented with a generic Azure AD credentials-gathering experience. As the user enters his or her credentials, the account he or she chooses will indirectly determine a specific tenant—the one the account belongs to. That will resolve the ambiguity about which tenant should be used for the present transaction, concluding the role of common in the flow. The resulting code or token will look exactly as it would have had it been obtained by specifying the actual tenant instead of common to begin with. In other words, whether you start the authentication flow using https://login.microsoftonline.com/common/oauth2/authorize or https://login.microsoftonline.com/6c3d51dd-f0e5-4959-b4ea-a80c4e36fe5e/oauth2/authorize for an OpenID Connect sign-in flow, if at run time you sign in with a user from the tenant with ID 6c3d51dd-f0e5-4959-b4ea-a80c4e36fe5e, the resulting token will look the same, with no memory of what endpoint path led to its issuance. That should make it even clearer that common is not a real tenant: it's just an endpoint sleight of hand for late binding a tenant, if you will.

Now comes the fun part. Upon learning about the common endpoint, the typical (and healthy) developer reaction is "Awesome! Let me just change the OpenID Connect middleware options as shown here, and I'll be all set!"

```
app.UseOpenIdConnectAuthentication(
    new OpenIdConnectAuthenticationOptions
    {
        ClientId = "c3d5b1ad-ae77-49ac-8a86-dd39a2f91081",
        Authority = "https://login.microsoftonline.com/common",
```

Let's say that you do just that, and then you hit F5 and, just for testing purposes, use the same account you used successfully earlier—the one from the same tenant where the app was defined in the first place. Well, if you do that—surprise! The app won't work. Sure, upon sign-in you will be presented with your credential-gathering and consent experience, but the app won't accept the issued token. If you dig in a bit, as you learned in Chapter 7, you'll discover that the token failed the issuer validation test.

Recall the id_token validation logic from Chapter 7, and the comment about how the discovery document of each tenant establishes what iss value an app should expect. If your app is initialized with a tenant-specific endpoint, it will read from the metadata the tenant-specific issuer value to expect; but if it is initialized with common, what issuer value is it going to get? I'll save you the hassle of visiting https://login.microsoftonline.com/common/.well-known/openid-configuration yourself: the discovery doc says *"issuer": "https://sts.windows.net/{tenantid}/"*. No real tenant will ever issue a token with that value, given that it's just a placeholder, but the middleware does not know that. That's the value that the metadata asserts is going to be in the iss claim, and the default logic will refuse anything carrying a different value.

> **Note** What about all the other values in the discovery doc? Issuer is the only problematic one, everything else (including keys, as you have seen in Chapter 6) is shared by all tenants.

This simply means that the default validation logic cannot work in case of multitenancy. What should you do instead? You already saw the main strategies for dealing with this in Chapter 7, although at the time I could not fully discuss the multitenant case. I recommend that you leaf back a few pages to get all the details, but just to summarize the key points here:

- If you have your own list of tenants that your application should accept, you have two main approaches. If the list is short and fairly static, you can pass it in at initialization time via TokenValidationParameters.ValidIssuers. If the list is long and dynamic, you can provide an implementation for TokenValidationParameters.IssuerValidator where you accommodate for whatever logic is appropriate for your case.

- If the decision about whether the caller should be allowed to get through is not strictly tied to the tenant the caller comes from, you can turn off issuer validation altogether by setting TokenValidationParameters.ValidateIssuer to false. You should be sure that you do add your own validation logic; for example, in the SecurityTokenValidated notifications or even in the app (custom authorization filters, etc.). Otherwise, your app will be completely open to access by anybody with a user in Azure AD. There are scenarios where this might be what you want, but in general, if you are protecting your app with authentication, that means that you have something valuable to gate access to. In turn, that might call for you to verify whether the requestor did pay his monthly subscription or whatever other monetization strategy you are using—and usually that verification boils down to checking the issuer or the user against your own subscription list.

Now that you know how Azure AD multitenancy affects the application's code, I'll go back to how consent, provisioning, and the data model are influenced.

Consenting to an app across tenants

The section about the `Application` object earlier in this chapter, and specifically the explanation of the `availableToOtherTenants` property, already anticipated most of what you need to know about creating multitenant applications. All apps are created for being used exclusively within their own tenant, and only a tenant admin can promote an app to be available across organizations. Today, this is done by flipping a switch labeled "Application is multi-tenant" on the Configuration page of the application on the Azure portal, and this has the effect of setting the `availableToOtherTenants` app property to true. Also, an app is required to have an App ID Uri (one of the elements in the `identifierUris` collection in the `Application` object) whose host portion corresponds to a domain registered for the tenant. In the sample I have been using through the last couple of chapters, that means that you'd need to set the App ID Uri to something like https://developertenant.onmicrosoft.com/MarioApp1.

Let's say that you signed in to the Azure portal and modified your app entry to be multitenant. Let's also say that you modified your app code to correctly handle the validation for tokens coming from multiple organizations. Let's give the app a spin by hitting F5.

> **Note** If you promote the app you have been using in this chapter until now, be sure to comment out the logic that triggers the admin consent (for now). Consequently, make sure also that the app does not request any admin-only permissions.

In case you did not code your validation logic yet

If you are just experimenting and didn't set up your multitenant validation code yet, here's the code you can use for turning off issuer validation while you play with the walk-through in this chapter:

```
app.UseOpenIdConnectAuthentication(
 new OpenIdConnectAuthenticationOptions
 {
  ClientId = "c3d5b1ad-ae77-49ac-8a86-dd39a2f91081",
  Authority = "https://login.microsoftonline.com/common",
  TokenValidationParameters = new System.IdentityModel.Tokens.TokenValidationParameters
  {
    ValidateIssuer = false,
  },
```

I cannot stress this enough: you should not go into production with the issuer validation logic disabled unless you have also added your own validation.

Once the app is running, click the Sign In link, but this time sign in with a user from a different Azure AD tenant. As explained in Chapter 3, in the section "Getting Azure Active Directory," any Azure subscriber can create a number of Azure AD tenants, create users and apps in them, and so on. If you belong to a big-ish organization, you likely already did this in creating your development tenant, as that's the best way of experimenting with admin-only features. If you already have a second tenant and an account in it, great! If you don't, create one tenant, create a user in it, then come back and pick up the flow from here.

Upon successful sign-in, you'll be presented with the consent page. As you can see in Figure 8-10, the consent page presents some important differences from the single-tenant case. For one, the tenant where the `Application` object was originally created is prominently displayed as the publisher. Moreover, there's now text telling you to consider whether you trust the publisher of the application. This is serious stuff—if you give consent to the wrong application for the wrong permissions, the damage to your own organization could be severe. That's why only admins can publish apps for multiple organizations, and that's why even the simple `Directory.Read` permission requires admin consent when it's requested by a multitenant app.

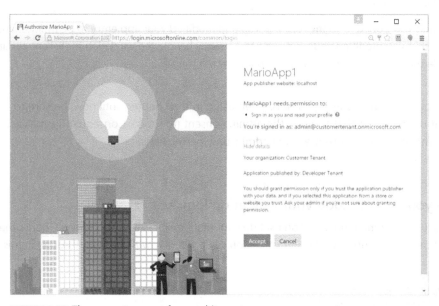

FIGURE 8-10 The consent prompt for a multitenant page.

At the beginning of this chapter, you encountered a description of what happens in the tenants for this exact consent scenario: the `Application` object in the original development tenant is used as a blueprint for creating a `ServicePrincipal` in the target tenant. In fact, if you query the `Applications` collection in the target tenant (you'll learn how to do this in the next chapter), you'll find no entries with the ClientId of your application—but you will find a `ServicePrincipal` with that ClientId. From what you have learned a few pages ago, you know that if you look into the collection of oauth2PermissionGrants for that `ServicePrincipal`, you will find an entry recording the consent of that particular user for this app and the permissions it requires. The principles of admin consent apply here as well: if you want the admin of your prospective customer tenants to be able to grant a blanket consent for all of his or her users, provide a way for your app to trigger an admin consent request.

Changing consent settings

I touched on this earlier, but it's worth stressing that the list of permissions an app requires isn't very dynamic. More concretely, say that your application initially declares a certain list of permissions in its `requiredResourceAccess`, and some users in a few tenants consent to it. Say that after some time you decide to add a new permission. That change in the `Application` object in your development tenant will not affect the existing `oauth2PermissionGrants` attached to the `ServicePrincipals` that have been created at consent time. With this version of Azure AD, the only way of reflecting the new permission set for a given app in a tenant is to revoke the existing consent (typically done by the user visiting myapps.microsoft.com, the Office 365 portal, or any other means that might be available when you read this book) and ask for consent again.

This is less than ideal, especially if you consider that Azure AD offers you no way of warning your users that something changed—you have to handle that in your own app or subscription logic. The good news is that the next version of the Azure AD application model will allow for dynamic consent, solving this issue once and for all.

The last section discussed at length the consent framework used for driving delegated permissions assignment to applications. That is a super important aspect of managing application capabilities, but it is far from the only one. The next section will continue to explore how Azure AD helps you to control how users and applications have access to the directory itself, and to each other.

App user assignment, app permissions, and app roles

This section describes a set of Azure AD features that seem unrelated but are in fact all implemented through the same primitive: the role. Here's the list of features I'll cover.

- **App user assignment**   The ability to explicitly define which users should be allowed to get a token for a certain application, at the exclusion of everybody else.

- **App-level permissions**   The ability to expose (and request) permissions that can be assigned to applications themselves, as opposed to the users of the apps.

- **App roles**   The ability for developers to define application-specific roles, which can be used by administrators to establish in which capacity users can access an application.

All these features give you even more control over who can access your application and how.

App user assignment

By default, every user in a tenant can request a token from any app. Whether the requested token will actually be issued depends on the outcome of user authentication, consent, and considerations of user versus admin permissions, as I've discussed in the preceding sections.

Azure AD offers the possibility for an administrator to restrict access to one application to a specific set of handpicked accounts. In terms of today's experience, an administrator can navigate to the Azure management portal at https://manage.windowsazure.com, select the target tenant, navigate to the appropriate app entry, select the Configure tab, and flip the setting for "User assignment required to access app" to On.

Given that this feature is related to specific instances of the app in specific tenants, the knobs used to control it are not in the Application object but in the ServicePrincipal and associated entities in the target tenant. You already encountered the ServicePrincipal property appRole-AssignmentRequired: flipping the switch in the portal has the effect of setting this property to true.

The Users tab in the application entry in the Azure portal lists all the users that are assigned to the application. From now on, *no user not on that list* can successfully request a token for the application. If you flip the switch for one of the apps you've been playing with in the preceding section, you'll see that all the users that already gave consent for the app are present in the list. Every time a user gives consent to the app, Azure AD adds an entry to a list of AppRoleAssignment, an entity I haven't yet discussed. Here's how one typical entry looks:

```
{
    "odata.type": "Microsoft.DirectoryServices.AppRoleAssignment",
    "objectType": "AppRoleAssignment",
    "objectId": "Bkp-sDgT4kq5a-YB4HMf2q2NyOTf4hpKhVKXXQHxMhA",
    "deletionTimestamp": null,
    "creationTimestamp": "2015-09-06T08:53:30.1974755Z",
    "id": "00000000-0000-0000-0000-000000000000",
    "principalDisplayName": "Vittorio Bertocci",
    "principalId": "b07e4a06-1338-4ae2-b96b-e601e0731fda",
    "principalType": "User",
    "resourceDisplayName": "MarioApp1",
    "resourceId": "725a2d9a-6707-4127-8131-4f9106d771de"
}
```

That entry declares that the user Vittorio Bertocci (identified by its objectId b07e4a06-1338-4ae2-b96b-e601e0731fda) can have access to the app MarioApp1 (object ID of the app's ServicePrincipal being 725a2d9a-6707-4127-8131-4f9106d771de) in the capacity of role 00000000-0000-0000-0000-000000000000.

This is where the role of Role (pun intended) comes into play. As you will see later, Azure AD allows developers to define application-specific roles. The AppRoleAssignment entity is meant to track that a certain app role has been assigned to one user for a certain app. What you are discovering here is that Azure AD uses AppRoleAssignment also for tracking app user assignments—but in this case, Azure AD automatically sets in the AppRoleAssignment a default role, 00000000-0000-0000-0000-000000000000. It's as simple as that.

One notable property of AppRoleAssignment is principalType. The sample entry here has the value User, indicating that the entity being assigned the role is a user account. Other possible values are Group (in which case, all the members of the group are assigned the role) or ServicePrincipal (in which case, the role is being assigned to another client application).

If you use the Azure portal to assign more users to the app, you'll see corresponding new `AppRoleAssignment` entries appearing in the application. By the way, the query I used for getting the list of `AppRoleAssignments` for my app is:

```
https://graph.windows.net/developertenant.onmicrosoft.com/servicePrincipals/725a2d9a-6707-4127-8131-4f9106d771de/appRoleAssignedTo.
```

Just for kicks, try to access your application with a user that has not been assigned. Instead of the usual consent dialog, you'll get back a lovely error along the lines of:

> "error=access_denied&error_description=AADSTS50105: The signed in user 'fabio@ developertenant.onmicrosoft.com' is not assigned to a role for the application 'developertenant. onmicrosoft.com'."

The behavior described in this section is what you would observe if your application didn't define any app roles. In the next section, I'll explore app roles in more depth.

App roles

Azure AD allows developers to define roles associated with an application. Traditionally, roles are handy ways of assigning collections of permissions to a bunch of users all at once: for example, people in a hypothetical Approver role might have read/write access to a certain set of resources, while people in the Reviewer role might have only read access to the same resources. Roles are handy because assigning a user to a role saves you the hassle of adding all the permissions a role entails one by one. Moreover, when a new resource is added to the milieu, access to that resource can be added to the role to enable access to it for all the users already assigned to the role, replacing the need to assign access individually, account by account. That said, roles in Azure AD do not necessarily need to represent permissions grouping: Azure AD does not offer you anything for representing such permissions anyway; it is your app's job to interpret each role. You can use application roles to represent any user category that makes sense for your application, like what is the primary spoken language of a user. True, there are many other ways of tracking the same info, but one big advantage of app roles over any other method is that Azure AD will send them in the form of claims in the token, making it extra easy for the app to consume the info they carry.

After you declare application roles, such roles are available to be assigned to users by the administrators of the tenants using your app. Let's take a look at how that cycle plays out.

The `Application` entity has one collection, `appRoles`, which is used for declaring the roles you want to associate with your application. As of today, the way in which you populate that property is by downloading the app manifest as described in "The *Application*" section at the beginning of this chapter, adding the appropriate entries in `appRoles`, and uploading it back via the portal. Here is what one `appRoles` collection looks like:

```
"appRoles": [
    {
        "allowedMemberTypes": [
            "User"
        ],
```

```
                "description": "Approvers can mark documents as approved",
                "displayName": "Approver",
                "id": "8F29F99B-5C77-4FBA-A310-4A5C0574E8FF",
                "isEnabled": "true",
                "value": "approver"
            },
            {
                "allowedMemberTypes": [
                    "User"
                ],
                "description": "Reviewers can read documents",
                "displayName": "Reviewer",
                "id": "0866623F-2159-4F90-A575-2D1D4D3F7391",
                "isEnabled": "true",
                "value": "reviewer"
            }
        ],
```

The properties of each entry are mostly self-explanatory, but there are a couple of nontrivial points.

The displayName and description strings are used in any experience in which the role is presented, such as the one in which an administrator can assign roles to users.

The value property represents the value that the role claim will carry in tokens issued for users belonging to this role. This is the value that your application should be prepared to receive and interpret at access time.

The id is the actual identifier of the role entry. It must be unique within the context of this Application.

The allowedMemberTypes property is the interesting one. Roles can be assigned to users, groups, and applications. An allowedMemberTypes collection including the entry "User" indicates a role that can be assigned to both users and groups. (In the next section, I'll cover roles assignable to applications.)

Once you have added the roles in the manifest file, don't forget to upload it back via the portal.

Note Sometimes the upload will fail, unfortunately without a lot of information to help you troubleshoot: watch out for silly errors—for example, nonmatching parentheses. I recommend using a syntax-aware JSON editor, which should take care of most issues up front.

If you head back to the Users tab and try to assign a new user to the app like you did in the preceding section, you'll see that you are no longer able to simply declare that you want to assign a user to the app: now you are presented with a choice between the various roles you declared in the manifest. Assign one of the roles to a random user, and then launch the app and try to sign in with that user.

> **Note** Subscribers to Azure AD Premium will also see an experience allowing the assignment of groups.

If you go back to the appRoleAssignedTo property of the `ServicePrincipal` and inspect the role assignments there, you'll find the same user assignments from the preceding section, plus a new entry for the user you just assigned to a role. It should look something like this:

```
{
    "odata.type": "Microsoft.DirectoryServices.AppRoleAssignment",
    "objectType": "AppRoleAssignment",
    "objectId": "9pcRosZaCOa1Oyoa5rOIwZrIr_JYzUxFtCm1WBYn6wO",
    "deletionTimestamp": null,
    "creationTimestamp": null,
    "id": "8f29f99b-5c77-4fba-a310-4a5c0574e8ff",
    "principalDisplayName": "Fabio Bianchi",
    "principalId": "a21197f6-5ac6-460b-b5d3-2a1ae6bd08c1",
    "principalType": "User",
    "resourceDisplayName": "MarioApp1",
    "resourceId": "725a2d9a-6707-4127-8131-4f9106d771de"
},
```

As expected, the `id` property points to one of the roles just defined, as opposed to the default 00000000-0000-0000-0000-000000000000 used during user assignment.

Launch the app and sign in as the user you just assigned to the role. If you capture the traffic via Fiddler (as you learned about in Chapter 6) and peek at the JWT token sent in the id_token, you'll notice a new `roles` claim:

```
{
    "amr" : [ "pwd" ],
    "aud" : "1538b378-5829-46de-9294-6cfb4ad4bbaa",
    "c_hash" : "EOuY-5M5XFxRyNCvRHe8Kg",
    "exp" : 1442740348,
    "family_name" : "Bianchi",
    "given_name" : "Fabio",
    "iat" : 1442736448,
    "iss" : "https://sts.windows.net/6c3d51dd-f0e5-4959-b4ea-a80c4e36fe5e/",
    "name" : "Fabio Bianchi",
    "nbf" : 1442736448,
    "nonce" : "635783335451569467.YzJiYmZjMGUtOWFkMS00NzI3LWJkYjMtMzhiMjE0YjVmNWE0ZDcwZTk3YmY
tNzQ4NC00YjkyLWFiY2YtYWViOWFhNjE0YjFj",
    "oid" : "a21197f6-5ac6-460b-b5d3-2a1ae6bd08c1",
    "roles" : [ "approver" ],
    "sub" : "OpcgG-Rxo_DSCJnuAf_7tdfXp7XaOzpW6pF3x7Ga8YO",
    "tid" : "6c3d51dd-f0e5-4959-b4ea-a80c4e36fe5e",
    "unique_name" : "fabio@developertenant.onmicrosoft.com",
    "upn" : "fabio@developertenant.onmicrosoft.com",
    "ver" : "1.0"
}
```

From your own application's code, you can find out the same information through the usual `ClaimsPrincipal.Current.FindFirst("roles")` or, given that this is a multivalue claim, `FindAll`. Once you have the value, you can do whatever the semantic you assigned to the role suggests that your code should do: allow or deny access to the method being called, change environment settings to match the preferences of the caller, and so on.

If you are using roles for authorization, classic ASP.NET development practices would suggest using `[Authorize]`, `<Authorization>`, or the evergreen `IsInRole()`. The good news is that they are all an option. The only thing you need to do is tell the identity pipeline that you want to use the claim type `roles` as the source for the role information used by those artifacts. That's done via one property of `TokenValidationParameters`, `RoleClaimType`. For example, you can add the following to your OpenID Connect middleware initialization options:

```
TokenValidationParameters = new TokenValidationParameters
{
    RoleClaimType = "roles",
}
```

Azure AD roles are a very powerful tool, which is great for modeling relationships between users and the functionality that the app provides. Although the concept is not new, Azure AD roles operate in novel ways. For example, developers are fully responsible for their creation and maintenance, while the administrators of the various tenants where the app is provisioned are responsible for actually assigning people to them. Also, Azure AD roles are always declared as part of one app—it is not possible to create a role and reuse it across multiple applications. There is no counterpart for this on-premises. The closest match is groups, but those have global scope, and a developer has no control over them. Before the end of the chapter, I will also touch on groups in Azure AD.

Application permissions

All the features you encountered in this chapter are meant to give you control over how users have access to your app and how users can delegate your app to access other resources for them.

In some situations you want to be able to confer access rights to the application itself, regardless of what user account is using the app, or even when the app is running without any currently signed-in user. For example, imagine a long-running process that performs continuous integration—an app updating a dashboard with the health status of running tests against a solution and so on. Or more simply, think about all the situations in which an app must be able to perform operations that a low-privilege user would not normally be entitled to do—like provisioning users, assigning users to groups, reading full user profiles, and so on. Note that, once again, those kinds of permissions come into play when accessing the resource as a web API, so you won't see this feature really play out until the next chapter. Here I'll just discuss provisioning.

While delegated permissions are represented in Azure AD via `oauth2Permission` in the `Application` object and the `oauth2PermissionsGrants` collection in the `ServicePrincipal` table, Azure AD represents application permissions via `Application.appRoles` and `Service-Principal.appRoleAssignedTo`.

The AppRole entity is used to declare application permissions just as you have seen for the application roles case, with the difference that allowedMemberTypes must include an entry of value "Application". To clarify that point, let's once again turn to the Directory Graph API Service-Principal and examine its appRoles collection:

```
"appRoles": [
    {
        "allowedMemberTypes": [
          "Application"
        ],
        "description": "Allows the app to read and write all device properties without
a signed-in user.  Does not allow device creation, device deletion, or update of device
alternative security identifiers.",
        "displayName": "Read and write devices",
        "id": "1138cb37-bd11-4084-a2b7-9f71582aeddb",
        "isEnabled": true,
        "value": "Device.ReadWrite.All"
    },
    {
        "allowedMemberTypes": [
          "Application"
        ],
        "description": "Allows the app to read and write data in your organization's
directory, such as users and groups.  Does not allow create, update, or delete of applications,
service principals, or devices. Does not allow user or group deletion.",
        "displayName": "Read and write directory data",
        "id": "78c8a3c8-a07e-4b9e-af1b-b5ccab50a175",
        "isEnabled": true,
        "value": "Directory.Write"
    },
    {
        "allowedMemberTypes": [
          "Application"
        ],
        "description": "Allows the app to read data in your organization's directory, such as
users, groups, and apps.",
        "displayName": "Read directory data",
        "id": "5778995a-e1bf-45b8-affa-663a9f3f4d04",
        "isEnabled": true,
        "value": "Directory.Read"
    }
],
```

 Note Directory.Write and Directory.Read will follow the same update path as their delegated homonyms and become Directory.ReadWrite.All and Directory.Read.All, respectively.

You can think of each of those roles as permissions that can be requested by applications invoking the Graph API. Although in the case of user and group roles, administrators can perform role assignments directly in the Azure management portal, granting application roles works very much like delegated permissions—via consent at the first token request.

A client application needs to declare in advance what application permissions (that is, application roles) it requires. That is currently done via the Azure portal, in the Permission To Other Application section of the Configure tab. In Figure 8-5 earlier, you can see that the middle column of the screen contains a drop-down labeled Application Permissions, in that case specifying the options available for the Directory Graph API. It is operated much as you learned about for the Delegated Permissions list, but the entries exposed in Application Permissions are the ones in the target resource from its `appRoles` collection, and specifically the ones marked as `Application` in `allowedMemberTypes`.

What happens when you select an application permission, say Read Directory Data, for the Directory Graph API? Something pretty similar to what you have seen in the case of delegated permissions. Take a look at what changes in the `Application`'s `requiredResourceAccess` collection:

```
"requiredResourceAccess": [
{
  "resourceAppId": "00000002-0000-0000-c000-000000000000",
  "resourceAccess": [
    {
      "id": "5778995a-e1bf-45b8-affa-663a9f3f4d04",
      "type": "Role"
    },
    {
      "id": "78c8a3c8-a07e-4b9e-af1b-b5ccab50a175",
      "type": "Scope"
    },
    {
      "id": "311a71cc-e848-46a1-bdf8-97ff7156d8e6",
      "type": "Scope"
    }
  ]
}
```

The resource you want to access remains the same, the Directory Graph API—represented by the ID 00000002-0000-0000-c000-000000000000. In addition to the old delegated permissions, of type Scope, you'll notice a new one, of type `Role`. The ID of this one corresponds exactly to the ID declared in the Directory Graph API's `ServicePrincipal` `appRoles` for the Read Directory Data permission.

As I mentioned, granting application permissions takes place upon successful request of a token from the app and positive consent granted by the user at authentication time. The presence of an entry of type `Role` in a `RequiredResourceAccessCollection` introduces a key constraint, however: only admin consent requests will be considered. This means that every time you develop an app requesting application permissions, you have to be sure that the first time you request a token from it, you append the `prompt=admin_consent` flag to your request.

If you actually launch the app and go through the consent dance, you'll find that after provisioning, the directory has added one new `AppRoleAssignment` entry to the `appRoleAssignedTo` property of the app's `ServicePrincipal` entry in the target tenant. Or better, you would find it if your app had requested permissions for *any* resource other than the Directory Graph API. As I am writing this chapter, the Directory Graph API is the only resource that received special treatment from

Azure AD: whereas every other resource has its consent settings recorded in the entities described in this chapter, as of today clients accessing the Graph API record the application permissions consent for it elsewhere. I won't go into further details for two reasons. One, it would not help you understand how application permissions work in general, given that each and every other resource does use appRoleAssignedTo. Two, there is talk of changing the Directory Graph API behavior so that it will start acting like any other resource—it's entirely possible that this will already be the case once the book is in your hands, but given that it's not for sure, I am not taking any chances.

With their permission/role dual nature, application permissions can be confusing. However, they are an extremely powerful construct, and the possibilities their use opens up are well worth the effort of mastering them.

Groups

In closing this chapter about how Azure AD models applications, I am going to show you how to work with groups. Groups in Azure AD can be cloud-only sets of users, created and populated via the Azure portal or the Office 365 portal, or they can be synched from on-premises distribution lists and security groups. Groups have been a staple of access control for the last few decades. As a developer, you can count on groups to work across applications and to be assigned and managed by administrators: all you need to know is that a group exists and what its semantic is and then use that information to drive your app's decisions regarding the current user (access control, UI customization, and so on).

By default, tokens issued by Azure AD do not carry any group information: if your app is interested in which groups the current user belongs to, it has to use the Directory Graph API (cue the next chapter).

Just as with application roles, you can ask Azure AD to start sending group information in issued tokens in the form of claims—simply by flipping a switch property in the Application object. If you download your app manifest, modify the groupMembershipClaims property as follows, and then upload the manifest again, you will get group information in the incoming tokens:

```
"groupMembershipClaims": "All",
```

If you are interested in receiving just the security groups, enter "SecurityGroup" instead of "All".

After changing the manifest as described, I used the portal to create in my test tenant a new group called "Hippies," and assigned to it the test user Fabio. That done, I launched the app and signed in as Fabio. Here's the token I got:

```
{
    "amr" : [ "pwd" ],
    "aud" : "c3d5b1ad-ae77-49ac-8a86-dd39a2f91081",
    "c_hash" : "zit-F66pwRsDeJPtjpuzgA",
    "exp" : 1442822854,
    "family_name" : "Bianchi",
    "given_name" : "Fabio",
    "groups" : [ "d6f48969-725d-4869-a7a0-97956001d24e" ],
```

```
    "iat" : 1442818954,
    "iss" : "https://sts.windows.net/6c3d51dd-f0e5-4959-b4ea-a80c4e36fe5e/",
    "name" : "Fabio Bianchi",
    "nbf" : 1442818954,
    "nonce" : "635784160492173285.ZmIyMTM5NGYtZDEyNC00MThmLTgyN2YtNTZkNzViZjA1MDgxMzljZDA1OWMtNjV
hOC00ZWI1LThkNmQtZDE4NGJlOTU2ZGZj",
      "oid" : "a21197f6-5ac6-460b-b5d3-2a1ae6bd08c1",
      "sub" : "OvmQvSCoJqTYby1EE0XR94PgRuveuOWUbAHNkmf0xTk",
      "tid" : "6c3d51dd-f0e5-4959-b4ea-a80c4e36fe5e",
      "unique_name" : "fabio@developertenant.onmicrosoft.com",
      "upn" : "fabio@developertenant.onmicrosoft.com",
      "ver" : "1.0"
}
```

You can see that there is indeed a groups claim, but what happened to the group name? Well, the short version of the story is that because Azure AD is a multitenant system, arbitrary group names like "People in building 44" or "Hippies" have no guarantee of being unique. Hence, if you wrote code relying on only a group name, your code would often be broken and subject to misuse (a malicious admin might create a group matching the name you expect in a fraudulent tenant and abuse your access control logic). As a result, today Azure AD sends only the objectId of the group. You can use that ID for constructing the URI of the group itself in the directory, in this case that's:

```
https://graph.windows.net/developertenant.onmicrosoft.com/groups/d6f48969-725d-4869-a7a0-
97956001d24e.
```

In the next chapter, you'll learn how to use the Graph API to use that URI to retrieve the actual group description, which in my case looks like the following:

```
{
  "odata.metadata": "https://graph.windows.net/developertenant.onmicrosoft.
com/$metadata#directoryObjects/Microsoft.DirectoryServices.Group/@Element",
  "odata.type": "Microsoft.DirectoryServices.Group",
  "objectType": "Group",
  "objectId": "d6f48969-725d-4869-a7a0-97956001d24e",
  "deletionTimestamp": null,
  "description": "Long haired employees",
  "dirSyncEnabled": null,
  "displayName": "Hippies",
  "lastDirSyncTime": null,
  "mail": null,
  "mailNickname": "363bdd6b-f73c-43a4-a3b4-a0bf8b528ee1",
  "mailEnabled": false,
  "onPremisesSecurityIdentifier": null,
  "provisioningErrors": [],
  "proxyAddresses": [],
  "securityEnabled": true
}
```

Your app could query the Graph periodically to find out what group identifiers to expect, or you could perform queries on the fly as you receive the group information, though that would somewhat defeat the purpose of getting groups in the form of claims.

Consuming groups entails more or less the same operations described for roles and `Claims-Principal`. You can even assign groups as the `RoleClaimType` if that's the strategy you usually enact for groups (traditional `IsInRole` actually works against Windows groups on-premises, often creating a lot of confusion).

One last thing about groups. There are tenants in which administrators choose to use groups very heavily, resulting in each user belonging to very large numbers of groups. Adding many groups in a token would make the token itself too large to fulfil its usual functions (such as authentication and so on), so Azure AD caps at 200 the number of groups that can be sent via JWT format. If the user belongs to more than 200 groups, Azure AD does not pass any group claims; rather, it sends an overage claim that provides the app with the URI to use for retrieving the user's groups information via the Graph API. Azure AD does so by following the OpenID Connect core specification for aggregated and distributed claims: in a nutshell, a mechanism for providing claims by reference instead of passing the values. Say that Fabio belonged to 201 groups in our sample above. Instead of the groups claims, the incoming JWT would have contained the following claims:

```
"_claim_names": {
    "groups": "src1",
},
"_claim_sources": {
    "src1": {"endpoint": "https://graph.windows.net/developertenant.onmicrosoft.com/users/
a21197f6-5ac6-460b-b5d3-2a1ae6bd08c1/getMemberObjects"}
}
```

In the next chapter, you'll learn how to use that endpoint for extracting group information for the incoming user.

Summary

The Azure AD application model is designed to support a large number of important functions: to hold protocol information used at authentication time, provide a mechanism for provisioning applications within one tenant and across multiple tenants, allow end users and administrators to grant or deny consent for apps to access resources on their behalf, and supply access control knobs to administrators and developers to fine-tune user and application access control.

That's a tall order, but as you have seen throughout this chapter, the Azure AD application model supports all of those functions—though in so doing, it often needs to create complex castles of interlocking entities. Note that little of that complexity ever emerges all the way to the end user, and even for most development tasks, you don't need to dive as deep as we did in this chapter. However, as a reward for the extra effort, you now have a holistic understanding of how applications in Azure AD are represented, provisioned, and granted or denied access to resources. You will find that this skill will bring your proficiency with Azure AD to a new level.

CHAPTER 9

Consuming and exposing a web API protected by Azure Active Directory

The emphasis on API-centric scenarios is probably the characteristic that most of all sets modern authentication apart from classic federation approaches that focus on single sign-on.

The first part of this chapter explores what it takes for one app to gain access to a web API protected by Azure AD. I will explore the phases of the OpenID Connect hybrid flow that come after the authentication phase, picking up the discussion about OAuth2 where I left it back in Chapter 2, "Identity protocols and application types," and filling in the remaining details. In the code samples, you'll learn how to use ASP.NET OWIN middleware and the Active Directory Authentication Library (ADAL) to implement those flows. In the process you'll also get a quick introduction to the Directory Graph API. As usual, the discussion will be peppered by architectural considerations and gotchas.

The second part of this chapter will discuss how to use Azure AD for protecting your own API. You'll find out that if you squint, the implementation details aren't too different from those used to secure a web app, but the lack of a user experience (UX) and the need to address nonbrowser clients introduce important differences you need to be aware of.

Consuming a web API from a web application

Nearly every Microsoft cloud service API today requires a client to present an Azure AD token to gain access. And the things you can do with that token! You can read a user's calendar to integrate scheduling functions into your app. You can send email on behalf of the user, or you can crunch through the user's inbox for insights. You can deploy an app automatically to Azure websites. You can start and stop virtual machines. You can perform queries against SQL Server instances in the cloud, or you can play with Azure Table storage, Redis caches, and many other storage types. You can track contacts and opportunities in a CRM system. You can crawl through an organizational tree. Although it sounds clichéd, the possibilities are endless.

In Chapter 2, you learned about a number of different ways in which an application can use OAuth2 to obtain an access token for accessing a resource (which from now on you can consider equivalent to "invoking a web API"). In this section I'll examine in detail the code-flow portion of the

OpenID Connect hybrid flow as the main method for obtaining tokens for an API. Once done with that, I'll build on your new knowledge of the protocol and libraries to present the other methods.

Redeeming an authorization code in the OpenID Connect hybrid flow

Say that you want to enable our sample web app to query the Azure Active Directory Graph to find out more information about the current user. How would you go about it?

You have already configured the sample app to handle sign-in via the OpenID Connect hybrid flow. Although you've so far focused only on the authentication aspects of the hybrid flow, the use of it means that you are already getting an authorization code, as described in Chapter 2 and shown in the Fiddler traces of the authentication response in Chapter 6, "OpenID Connect and Azure AD web sign-on." Specifically, look back at legs 4 and 5 in Figure 2-8 from Chapter 2: you just need to retrieve that code from the response and redeem it.

To clarify things further, let's pick up the swim-lane diagram in Figure 6-4 from Chapter 6, in the section "Sign-in sequence diagram." That diagram focused on the sign-in legs of the process and omitted the ones pertaining to acquisition and redemption of the authorization code. Figure 9-1 expands the response phase of the flow originally shown in Figure 6-4, adding the calls handling the authorization code.

Unlike all the old calls, which were always originating from the browser, the call performed for redeeming the authorization code is a server-to-server call. The application (in our case, the middleware) POSTs to the Azure AD tenant's token endpoint the code and the application's credentials. In return, it gets the desired access token and a refresh token. In the case of Azure AD, it also gets an id_token, which will be used for caching purposes. The rest of this section will cover those two legs in fine detail.

That's what you should observe once you implement the authorization-code redemption flow. Before you do that, however, you need to verify whether the application entry in Azure AD has the correct permission for accessing the resource you are targeting.

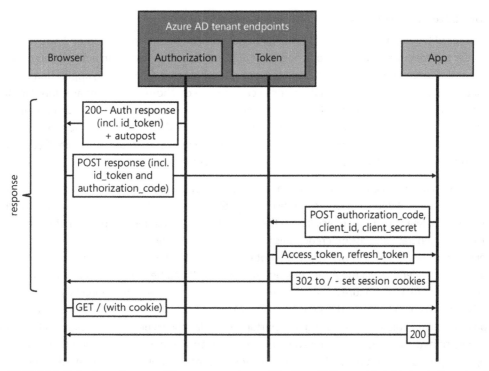

FIGURE 9-1 Swim-lane diagram of the response phase of the OpenID Connect hybrid sign-in flow, showing all the authorization-code acquisition and redemption legs.

Permissions

As you learned in Chapter 8, "Azure Active Directory application model," an application that needs access to an Azure AD–protected resource must explicitly ask for the necessary permissions in its Application object. That will allow the directory to prompt the user for the proper permissions at authentication time. For simplicity, here I am choosing a call that requires a permission that is always automatically granted as part of authentication. If I had chosen a more advanced task, like reading or writing directory entities, you would have had to request the appropriate permissions. Conversely, the permission used for authentication, "Sign in and access the user's profile," also gives the app the right to request an access token for the Directory Graph (from now on just "the Graph"), which allows it to query the user's profile. (That means that even if you are still digesting the information in Chapter 8, you'll be able to perform the tasks described in this chapter.)

Application credentials

If you recall the description of the OAuth2 authorization-code grant from Chapter 2, you know that in order to redeem an authorization code, your application must perform an authenticated request against the token endpoint. Applications authenticate with Azure AD by using application credentials that are assigned directly through their Application object. Those credentials are stored in the properties passwordCredentials and keyCredentials, which you encountered in Chapter 8. A more precise description would say that those properties provide references to the actual credential values: for security reasons, once assigned, those values can never be retrieved again. If you lose track of them, your only recourse is to create and assign new credentials.

How do you assign credentials to an application? One very easy way is to let Visual Studio do the work for you. If you created the app using the ASP.NET project templates in Visual Studio 2015, selecting the Read Directory check box in the authentication management portion of the project wizard will generate and assign credentials for your app automatically. However, for existing applications and for all the cases in which you are not using Visual Studio, the most common way is to assign application credentials via the Azure management portal. If you head to the Configure tab of the application entry in the Azure AD area of the portal, you'll find a section labeled Keys. Here you can add a new key by selecting a duration (choices vary from one to two years of validity) and saving the application. Immediately after saving, the portal will display the value of the autogenerated string key. As I mentioned, this is the only time you have to save it. Your application will need to access it later on, during the authorization-code redemption flow and, as you will see later in the chapter, for any flow requiring the app to talk to the Azure AD token endpoint.

> **Note** It is worth stressing that those instructions refer to the "old" Azure management portal, at the URL https://manage.windowsazure.com/, which was the only management portal available for Azure AD at the time of writing. The step-by-step instructions will likely change, but you can expect any new management portal to keep offering the same functionality.

As counterintuitive as it might seem, this newly minted credential does not end up in the keyCredentials property but in the passwordCredentials property of the Application object. If you take a look at the application manifest after having saved the app, you'll find the new element, as shown here:

```
"passwordCredentials": [
    {
        "customKeyIdentifier": null,
        "endDate": "2016-10-12T18:06:53.0931896Z",
        "keyId": "91edc961-4689-4979-84bc-66badbe1b109",
        "startDate": "2015-10-12T18:06:53.0931896Z",
        "value": null
    }
],
```

This naming stems from the way in which this credential type is meant to be used: the key string is simply included in the request in the `client_secret` property of the request, kind of like a password.

The `keyCredentials` property, conversely, is meant to work with the private/public key pairs from X.509 certificates. Azure AD stores a certificate holding the public portion of the key pair. The application uses the corresponding private key to sign a JWT assertion, which is attached to the request to the token endpoint. Azure AD uses the public key to verify that the assertion was signed by the private key owner, and if everything checks out, the application is considered authenticated. From a security standpoint, this method has clear advantages over the shared-secret model. Those advantages come at the price of more complexity in the app (the certificate must be stored and used for signing) and in provisioning. Although, for the application side of things, the Azure AD libraries can keep things simple by taking care of handling signatures and request management transparently, as of today provisioning a certificate as an application credential in Azure AD is possible only via Office 365 PowerShell cmdlets.

For the sake of keeping things simpler, in this chapter I will work with key-string credentials. If you want to follow along, use any of the techniques described previously to get a key string assigned to your application and be sure to save the string's bits somewhere—you'll need them in the code soon enough.

Handling *AuthorizationCodeReceived*

Without further ado, let's go ahead and add code to retrieve and redeem the authorization code (no pun intended). In Chapter 7, "The OWIN OpenID Connect middleware," you learned about the existence of `AuthorizationCodeReceived`, a notification in the OpenID Connect middleware that is invoked in case the authorization response from the authority includes an authorization code. That's where we are going to place our code-redemption logic.

This is where the Active Directory Authentication Library (ADAL) comes into play. As you learned in Chapter 4, "Introducing the identity developer libraries," the ADAL can transparently take care of handling communications with Azure AD and cache tokens. You are about to see that in action.

 Important I am going to use ADAL's default cache settings for a good portion of the following explanations. However, such default settings are *not* suitable for web applications. In the section "ADAL cache considerations for web applications" later in the chapter, I will share guidance on how to use the ADAL cache properly with web applications.

Start by adding a reference to the ADAL .NET NuGet package. As I showed in Chapter 5, "Getting started with web sign-on and Active Directory," I like to use the NuGet package management console because it ensures that I'll end up with the correct version. At this time (fall 2015), the released version of ADAL is v2.*. Open the NuGet package management console and enter the following command:

```
Install-Package Microsoft.IdentityModel.Clients.ActiveDirectory -Version 2.19.208020213
```

That is the latest package at the time of writing. However, updates and bug fixes are released all the time, so be sure you also run the following to get the latest 2.* release:

```
Update-Package Microsoft.IdentityModel.Clients.ActiveDirectory
```

Once you've done that, you are ready to add the implementation of AuthorizationCode-Received:

```
AuthorizationCodeReceived = (context) =>
{
    Debug.WriteLine("*** AuthorizationCodeReceived");
    string ClientId = "c3d5b1ad-ae77-49ac-8a86-dd39a2f91081";
    string Authority = "https://login.microsoftonline.com/DeveloperTenant.onmicrosoft.com";
    string appKey = "a3fQREiyhqpYL10006hfCW+xke/TyP2oIQ6vgu68eoE=";
    string resourceId = "https://graph.windows.net";
    var code = context.Code;
    AuthenticationContext authContext = new AuthenticationContext(Authority);
    ClientCredential credential = new ClientCredential(ClientId, appKey);
    AuthenticationResult result = authContext.AcquireTokenByAuthorizationCode(code,
        new Uri(HttpContext.Current.Request.Url.GetLeftPart(UriPartial.Path)),
        credential,
        resourceId);
    return Task.FromResult(0);
},
```

Remember, the goal of that code is to redeem the authorization code you got during the sign-in via the OpenID Connect hybrid flow. To understand in detail how that is accomplished, you need to brush up on the high-level description of how ADAL works, and specifically the diagram in Figure 4-4 in Chapter 4. ADAL is a token-requestor library, which helps you to obtain tokens from Active Directory to access resources. It does so by offering you primitives that model the main actors and artifacts involved in such transactions.

Ignore the various declarations at the beginning of the method and consider the line initializing AuthenticationContext. AuthenticationContext is a class meant to represent in your code the directory tenant you want to work with. Here it is initialized with "https://login.microsoftonline .com/DeveloperTenant.onmicrosoft.com", the same tenant I've been using for initializing the OpenID Connect middleware. From now on, whenever I need something from my tenant, I know I can use authContext to access the tenant's authentication capabilities.

The main primitive offered by AuthenticationContext is the method AcquireToken and all its variants. Its function is simply to do whatever is necessary to obtain a token from the tenant modeled by AuthenticationContext, complying with the requirements represented by the parameters passed to AcquireToken. There are as many AcquireToken overloads and variants as there are supported scenarios. All you need to do is pass everything you know about your scenario (for example, the client_id of your app, the resource you need a token for, and so on), and AcquireToken will do its best to retrieve a suitable token, while minimizing user prompts and network traffic.

In this specific case, we know that we want to get a token by redeeming an authorization code, we know that redeeming a code requires application credentials, and we know that we want that token for accessing the Graph API. In that light, the rest of the code is easy to understand:

- The `ClientCredential` initialization instantiates a class meant to represent application credentials. Note that it takes the app's client_id and the string key I discussed early on. In actual production code you would not hardcode the key but retrieve it from a secure place (such as encrypted storage or a service such as Azure Key Vault).

- The intent of the call to `AcquireTokenByAuthorizationCode` is self-explanatory, and so is the use of the code and `credential` parameters. The second parameter represents the redirect_uri registered for the client (although it won't be used in this flow, Azure AD expects that in the request). The `resourceId` is the identifier of the resource we want a token for, in this case the Graph API. This can be the value you find in the App ID URI field in the application entry in the Azure portal, but in more general terms, it can be any of the entries in the `servicePrincipalNames` property of the `ServicePrincipal` representing the resource, or the union of the `identifierUris` list and `appId` properties of the corresponding `Application` object.

Note that the call can result in one exception, so you should plan your code accordingly.

The outcome of the operation is recorded in one instance of `AuthenticationResult`. Figure 9-2 shows what it looks like.

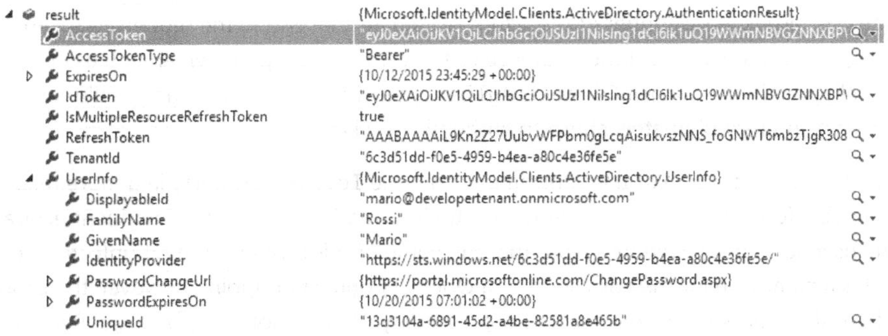

FIGURE 9-2 A typical `AuthenticationResult` instance.

Before I go into the details of the main properties of `AuthenticationResult`, I want to highlight a key point: *you can ignore most of the properties shown here.* As you will see in a few pages, ADAL automatically and transparently takes care of storing tokens and keeping sessions fresh without requiring any explicit action from you. Developers who are used to operating at the protocol level or who use lower-level libraries expect to have to use some of those properties to write logic for handling token expiration, refreshes, and so on, but that is not necessary when you use ADAL. ADAL will do that for you, and given that Azure AD offers some special tricks, ADAL will do it better than you possibly could. In fact, to remove all temptation, properties such as RefreshToken are poised to disappear from `AuthenticationResult` in ADAL v3! That clarified, here's a cursory description of the main properties:

- `AccessToken` is really the main result you are after—it is the `token` referenced in `AcquireToken*`. We'll use it for securing our call to the Graph API later on.

- **AccessTokenType** declares the type of token usage and verification meant to be applied to the returned access token. Today it is always "Bearer"; you'll see in a few pages what that means.

- **ExpiresOn** indicates the instant at which the access token will no longer be valid. Today all Azure AD–issued access tokens last one hour from the instant of issuance, but that will likely become configurable in the future.

- **IdToken** contains information about the authentication that had to take place to lead to the issuance of the access token. In this particular case, the user signing in to the web app and the user obtaining the access token happen to be the same, but in generic OAuth2 scenarios that is not the case. I'll explore that scenario more in depth later.

- **IsMultipleRefreshToken** is an Azure AD–specific property of the refresh token, which signals whether the current refresh token can be used for obtaining access tokens for multiple resources in the same tenant. More details later.

- **RefreshToken** holds the bits of the actual refresh token, whose function I will describe shortly. Don't get too attached to this property. As I mentioned, ADAL automatically uses it behind the scenes, and in ADAL v3 it will no longer be returned here.

- **TenantId** carries the identifier of the Azure AD tenant that issued the requested token. In Chapter 8 you learned about the existence of the common endpoint: when you use common to initialize **AuthenticationContext**, **AuthenticationResult.TenantId** tells you which tenant the end user ultimately chose to authenticate with.

- **UserInfo** presents some of the information from the **IdToken** property in a more readily consumable format, plus some occasional extra information (such as the imminent expiration of the user account's password). Note that the name of this property is a bit unfortunate, given that it is a namesake for the corresponding OpenID Connect endpoint; however, the property predates the spec, so short of breaking compatibility, it could not really be fixed. Remember that the two have nothing to do with each other.

That's it! Before using the resulting access token, however, let's take a look at the traffic our code generated.

Protocol flow of the authorization code redemption

Fire up Fiddler, and capture the traffic generated during the execution of AuthorizationCode-Received. The request should look similar to the following trace, apart from the newlines I added to make the trace more readable:

```
POST https://login.microsoftonline.com/DeveloperTenant.onmicrosoft.com/oauth2/token HTTP/1.1
Content-Type: application/x-www-form-urlencoded
client-request-id: 172e30f9-54f9-4770-b61b-3aadcbbb8892
return-client-request-id: true
x-client-SKU: .NET
x-client-Ver: 2.19.0.0
x-client-CPU: x64
```

```
x-client-OS: Microsoft Windows NT 10.0.10240.0
Host: login.microsoftonline.com
Content-Length: 994
Expect: 100-continue

resource=https%3A%2F%2Fgraph.windows.net&
client_id=c3d5b1ad-ae77-49ac-8a86-dd39a2f91081&
client_secret=a3fQREiyhqpYL10006hfCW%2Bxke%2FTyP2oIQ6vgu68eoE%3D&
grant_type=authorization_code&
code=AAABAAAAiL9K [..SNIP..] PPf7ErO6oDyZSeiD_UgAA&
redirect_uri=https%3A%2F%2Flocalhost%3A44300%2F
```

In the POST, you can identify all the parameters passed in. The POST recipient is the token
endpoint of the authority passed in AuthenticationContext; the body indicates the resource,
client_id, client_secret, code, and redirect_uri as passed to AcquireTokenByAuthorizationCode.

Just for kicks

What would this trace look like if you used a certificate instead of a string key? Instead of a
ClientCredential, you would have used a ClientAssertionCertificate. And the body
of the request would have looked slightly different:

```
resource=https%3A%2F%2Fgraph.windows.net&
client_id= c3d5b1ad-ae77-49ac-8a86-dd39a2f91081&
client_assertion_type=urn%3Aietf%3Aparams%3Aoauth%3Aclient-assertion-type%3Ajwt-bearer&
client_assertion=eyJhbGciOi[...SNIP...]-j5UBo1A&
grant_type=authorization_code&
code=AAABAAAAiL9K [...SNIP...] PPf7ErO6oDyZSeiD_UgAA&
redirect_uri=https%3A%2F%2Flocalhost%3A44300%2F
```

The main difference lies in the absence of client_secret, replaced by client_assertion
(the signed JWT described earlier) and client_assertion_type. If you want more details on
this, please take a look at the proposed standard "Assertion Framework for OAuth 2.0 Client
Authentication and Authorization Grants" at *https://tools.ietf.org/html/rfc7521*.

One important thing to notice here is the use of the resource parameter, which you encountered
earlier in Chapter 6. Other providers implementing this flow would likely not specify anything, given
that the resource is almost always colocated with the authorization server itself, or they would specify
scopes. Please take a moment to go back to Chapter 6, to the section "Parameters omitted in the
default request," and refresh your memory on why the current version of the Azure AD model uses
resources instead of scopes.

The response from the token endpoint is also not particularly surprising, especially after our peek
into AuthenticationResult.

```
HTTP/1.1 200 OK
Cache-Control: no-cache, no-store
Pragma: no-cache
Content-Type: application/json; charset=utf-8
```

```
Expires: -1
Server: Microsoft-IIS/8.5
x-ms-request-id: e551a34e-a2a5-4989-b537-cdb828830269
client-request-id: 172e30f9-54f9-4770-b61b-3aadcbbb8892
x-ms-gateway-service-instanceid: ESTSFE_IN_153
X-Content-Type-Options: nosniff
Strict-Transport-Security: max-age=31536000; includeSubDomains
P3P: CP="DSP CUR OTPi IND OTRi ONL FIN"
Set-Cookie: flight-uxoptin=true; path=/; secure; HttpOnly
Set-Cookie: x-ms-gateway-slice=productionb; path=/; secure; HttpOnly
Set-Cookie: stsservicecookie=ests; path=/; secure; HttpOnly
X-Powered-By: ASP.NET
Date: Mon, 12 Oct 2015 20:44:09 GMT
Content-Length: 3809
```

```
{
"token_type":"Bearer",
"expires_in":"3599",
"scope":"User.Read",
"expires_on":"1444686250","not_before":"1444682350",
"resource":"https://graph.windows.net",
"pwd_exp":"641813","pwd_url":"https://portal.microsoftonline.com/ChangePassword.aspx",
"access_token":"eyJ0eX [...SNIP...]HWE8aMjw",
"refresh_token":"AAABA [...SNIP...] OIuMXIAA",
"id_token":"eyJ0eXAi [...SNIP...] gZdORQ"
}
```

That's all it takes to get a token for calling an API protected by Azure AD for which your app requested permissions. Next, you'll see what's required to actually use the token to gain access to a protected API.

Using the access token for invoking a web API

It's not very likely that you'll perform your API calls from the Startup class, but I know you are eager to use the access token you just got back, so I'll go over the code used for accessing a protected API right away. Later, I'll come back to key considerations such as where to perform API calls, how OAuth2 uses refresh tokens for establishing a session of sorts, and how ADAL helps to handle token life cycle and sessions. Those considerations are super important, so please be sure that you read this section in its entirety.

Invoking an API according to OAuth2 bearer token usage

One of the specifications from the OAuth2 constellation, "The OAuth 2.0 Authorization Framework: Bearer Token Usage" (available at *https://www.rfc-editor.org/rfc/rfc6750.txt*), details how you can leverage tokens for accessing protected resources—for us, that means a web API.

The specification presents various techniques, but the most popular one entails including the token in the request by embedding it in the Authorization HTTP header, following the form shown here:

```
GET /resource HTTP/1.1
Host: server.example.com
Authorization: Bearer <token>
```

The idea is that the resource will expect the token in such a header and validate it before granting access. As is the tradition for OAuth2, no details are given in the spec about the format of the token. As a result, there is no prescriptive guidance on what validation looks like. Every provider and protected resource will privately negotiate the details. In the second part of this chapter, you will learn how that works for Azure AD, when you set up the validation logic for your own web API.

A client should NEVER look inside an access token

I made this point in Chapter 4 while describing token-requestor libraries, but it is worth stressing it here again. Clients requesting an access token for accessing a protected resource should treat that token as an opaque blob. It is extremely tempting to peek into that token from the client app's code, given that it often contains interesting info, but that is truly a recipe for disaster. From the client's perspective, the token's only function is to gain access to a protected resource. Details such as token format, what claims it contains, and so on are a contract between the resource and the token issuer, a contract in which the client plays no role. If you write client code that takes a dependency on the content of the access token, as soon as that content changes (for example, if the issuer starts encrypting the token so that only the target API can access its content), your client code will be broken with no recourse. This is one of the worst antipatterns I have seen in my years working in the identity space, and it often leads to the unrecoverable loss of functionality. Don't give in to the temptation to parse the access token from the client.

The term "bearer" here hints at the only aspect of the token-validation logic that the spec does provide. To use a bearer token, a client is simply required to attach it to the request. This is a bit like money: to use a banknote, all you need to do is hand it over—the recipient does not need to do any verification other than knowing the authenticity of the banknote. Incidentally, that's why you need to be very careful when handling money and bearer tokens alike, because if somebody else gets ahold of them, they can use them with no limitations. Think about it the next time you are tempted to forgo setting up HTTPS for your web apps!

Let's add some simple code in AuthorizationCodeReceived to call the Graph API just after the call to AcquireTokenByAuthorizationCode:

```
//...
string callOutcome = string.Empty;
HttpClient httpClient = new HttpClient();
httpClient.DefaultRequestHeaders.Authorization =
    new AuthenticationHeaderValue("Bearer", result.AccessToken);
HttpResponseMessage response =
    httpClient.GetAsync("https://graph.windows.net/me?api-version=1.6").Result;

if (response.IsSuccessStatusCode)
{
    callOutcome = response.Content.ReadAsStringAsync().Result;
}
//...
```

I'll ignore the Graph API calling syntax for now. At a high level, the code appears to be doing exactly what I described was necessary for accessing a protected resource in accordance with the OAuth2 bearer token usage spec. You add the access token in the Authorization HTTP header right after the Bearer keyword, and then you perform your call (in this case a simple GET of the profile of the account that was used for obtaining the token).

This is what the request looks like on the wire:

```
GET https://graph.windows.net/me?api-version=1.6 HTTP/1.1
Authorization: Bearer eyJ0eXAiOiJKV1Q[..SNIP..]jWxB3LG4UtyQ
Host: graph.windows.net
```

That's as simple as it gets. The response looks like the following:

```
HTTP/1.1 200 OK
Cache-Control: no-cache
Pragma: no-cache
Content-Type: application/json;odata=minimalmetadata;streaming=true;charset=utf-8
Expires: -1
Server: Microsoft-IIS/8.5
ocp-aad-diagnostics-server-name: +u3G9g5PWpdX413WhNwPLKppymwjckPFROXoe0Q7+kA=
request-id: e260d0b6-b26a-4753-bf02-1f12df4eb85d
client-request-id: c613119a-20b4-45d4-82e3-67b89772c1a4
x-ms-dirapi-data-contract-version: 1.6
x-ms-gateway-rewrite: false
ocp-aad-session-key: qBZHXeGGhx-rPXPzvx5G98D9srmgVjZj5IIUGG5IbqpEH4mlKTgCEw
i57NIrmxzeWHkpHMa2NPthk-EtanVYysWnzBU2Dpp34zvBDbyk1TkuEl_59avaoX5TjW9xgqMN.
s8OcJFO7Gg7AXspmlJ3OlXI4vbHaot1g4bUl5Zcka5U
X-Content-Type-Options: nosniff
DataServiceVersion: 3.0;
Strict-Transport-Security: max-age=31536000; includeSubDomains
Access-Control-Allow-Origin: *
X-AspNet-Version: 4.0.30319
X-Powered-By: ASP.NET
Duration: 2036141
X-Powered-By: ASP.NET
Date: Tue, 13 Oct 2015 19:50:06 GMT
Content-Length: 2083
```

{"odata.metadata":"https://graph.windows.net/myorganization/$metadata#directoryObjects/
Microsoft.DirectoryServices.User/@Element","odata.type":"Microsoft.DirectoryServices.Us
er","objectType":"User","objectId":"13d3104a-6891-45d2-a4be-82581a8e465b","deletionTime
stamp":null,"accountEnabled":true,"assignedLicenses":[{"disabledPlans":["bea4c11e-220a-
4e6d-8eb8-8ea15d019f90","0feaeb32-d00e-4d66-bd5a-43b5b83db82c","e95bec33-7c88-4a70-8e19-
b10bd9d0c014"],"skuId":"6fd2c87f-b296-42f0-b197-1e91e994b900"}],"assignedPlans":[{"assigne
dTimestamp":"2014-03-24T06:36:17Z","capabilityStatus":"Enabled","service":"exchange","ser
vicePlanId":"efb87545-963c-4e0d-99df-69c6916d9eb0"},{"assignedTimestamp":"2014-03-24T06:36:17Z"
,"capabilityStatus":"Enabled","service":"SharePoint","servicePlanId":"5dbe027f-2339-4123-9542-
606e4d348a72"},{"assignedTimestamp":"2014-03-24T06:36:17Z","capabilityStatus":"Enabled","service
":"MicrosoftOffice","servicePlanId":"43de0ff5-c92c-492b-9116-175376d08c38"}],"city":null,"compan
yName":null,"country":null,"department":null,"dirSyncEnabled":null,"displayName":"Mario Rossi",
"facsimileTelephoneNumber":null,"givenName":"Mario","immutableId":null,"jobTitle":null,"lastDirSy
ncTime":null,"mail":"mario@developertenant.onmicrosoft.com","mailNickname":"mario","mobile":null
,"onPremisesSecurityIdentifier":null,"otherMails":[],"passwordPolicies":null,"passwordProfile":n
ull,"physicalDeliveryOfficeName":null,"postalCode":null,"preferredLanguage":"en-US","provisioned

Plans":[{"capabilityStatus":"Enabled","provisioningStatus":"Success","service":"exchange"},{"ca
pabilityStatus":"Enabled","provisioningStatus":"Success","service":"MicrosoftOffice"},{"capabil
ityStatus":"Enabled","provisioningStatus":"Success","service":"SharePoint"}],"provisioningError
s":[],"proxyAddresses":["SMTP:mario@developertenant.onmicrosoft.com"],"sipProxyAddress":null,"s
tate":null,"streetAddress":null,"surname":"Rossi","telephoneNumber":null,"thumbnailPhoto@odata.
mediaContentType":"image/Jpeg","usageLocation":"US","userPrincipalName":"mario@developertenant.
onmicrosoft.com","userType":"Member"}

Promptly, you get back a nice JSON representation of Mario's profile in the directory. Congratulations! You just successfully concluded your first REST API call protected by Azure AD.

If you compare this trace with the ones you studied earlier for web apps, one thing should jump out: here, there's not a trace of cookies. Each and every call is expected to present a suitable bearer token, which the client obtained before performing the call. For the fun of it, comment out the lines adding the access token in the header and run the app again. Here's what you'll get as a response:

```
HTTP/1.1 401 Unauthorized
Cache-Control: private
Content-Type: application/json;odata=minimalmetadata;charset=utf-8
Server: Microsoft-IIS/8.5
ocp-aad-diagnostics-server-name: JOcOImGbsHySgKlAQbtemgj5KuX+mrNNzouN4cLWfY8=
request-id: 8bb21bef-13bd-401a-87dd-b96b7cd6bfb0
client-request-id: 73eebaa6-e588-472a-98c5-215cba480c42
x-ms-dirapi-data-contract-version: 1.6
Strict-Transport-Security: max-age=31536000; includeSubDomains
Access-Control-Allow-Origin: *
WWW-Authenticate: Bearer realm="myorganization", error="invalid_token", error_
description="Access Token missing or malformed.", authorization_uri="https://login.
microsoftonline.com/common/oauth2/authorize", client_id="00000002-0000-0000-c000-000000000000"
X-AspNet-Version: 4.0.30319
X-Powered-By: ASP.NET
Duration: 328488
X-Powered-By: ASP.NET
Date: Wed, 14 Oct 2015 18:14:52 GMT
Content-Length: 143

{"odata.error":{"code":"Authentication_MissingOrMalformed","message":{"lang":"en","value":"Acce
ss Token missing or malformed."},"values":null}}
```

Get it? Whereas you get a 302 in the case of web sign-on against a redirect-based web app, here you get a cold 401. In the web sign-on case, the authentication happens in the context of the browser, hence an unauthenticated request can be handled by redirecting the user to the place where he or she can authenticate. However, in the case of a web API, the client is responsible for obtaining the necessary token out of band: furthermore, the client isn't really a browser (here the call is performed from the app's code-behind on the server), so the 302 cannot be used to prompt some kind of action.

Using cookies for protecting a web API is a very common antipattern. People often use it when performing AJAX calls: they secure the entire web app by using redirect-based mechanisms such as the OpenID Connect or WS-Federation middlewares, and then they simply make AJAX calls that leverage the fact that the browser automatically attaches cookies to requests and that the cookie middleware validates them. It is an antipattern because it does not work very well. When cookies expire, the AJAX calls receive 302s, but those can't be exploited directly. As soon as you try to access the API from a different client (a back end or a mobile app), you suddenly discover that there is no mechanism to obtain suitable cookies. As soon as you need to call the API from different domains, you find out that you don't have suitable cookies for those domains, no mechanism for obtaining them, and so on. I'll talk more about this in the sections about exposing your own API.

The Directory Graph API

Although the Azure AD Graph API is not strictly an authentication feature, it plays such a pivotal role in all things related to Azure AD that I cannot avoid giving you at least a quick overview. For more details, I recommend that you refer to the comprehensive online documentation pages at *https://msdn.microsoft.com/en-us/Library/Azure/Ad/Graph/api/api-catalog*.

The Graph API is an OData API that offers programmatic access to the entities that constitute an Azure AD tenant and all that it contains. By "programmatic access," I mean performing HTTP GET, POST, PUT, PATCH, and DELETE requests against directory entities, accompanied by a suitable access token. (Nearly) every resource in the directory can be represented as a URL by using the Graph API—as long as you structure the URL according to the base template:

```
https://graph.windows.net/<tenant>/<resource path>?<api version>[odata parameters]
```

Throughout this book, and especially in Chapter 8, I have been providing paths for the entities I've described. All those paths match the common URL template. Here's a quick explanation of its components:

- `<tenant>` represents the tenant you want to query. Just as with Azure AD protocol endpoints, `<tenant>` can be either one of the domains associated with the tenant of choice or the GUID representing the tenantId.

- `<resource path>` represents the entity you want to reach. The Graph hosts a hierarchical structure, where the top-level features are containers for all the basic entities you'd expect in the directory: users, groups, applications, service principals, and so on. If you want to list all the users in your tenant (ignoring results pagination), `users` is the value you'd use in `<resource path>`.

  Individual entities can be selected directly by appending one of their identifying properties in the path. The exact property depends on the entity type; for example, users can be identified by their user principal name, whereas objectId works across the board.

  For example, if I wanted to get the directory entry for Mario, our test user, I could use "https://graph.windows.net/developertenant.onmicrosoft.com/users/mario@developertenant.onmicrosoft.com" or "https://graph.windows.net/developertenant.onmicrosoft.com/users/13d3104a-6891-45d2-a4be-82581a8e465b".

  Resource paths can get deeper still. Alongside the classic declared properties, entities feature so-called navigation properties—properties that refer to other entities to which the target entity is tied through some kind of relationship. If I wanted to know who Mario's manager is, I could simply GET the corresponding directory entry via "https://graph.windows.net/developertenant.onmicrosoft.com/users/mario@developertenant.onmicrosoft.com/manager". As another example, if you go back to the discussion in Chapter 8 about app user assignment, you'll see that I used "https://graph.windows.net/developertenant.onmicrosoft.com/servicePrincipals/725a2d9a-6707-4127-8131-4f9106d771de/appRoleAssignedTo" for establishing which users were assigned to the sample app. The `appRoleAssignedTo` property is an example of a navigation property (of the `ServicePrincipal` entity) that can yield multiple results.

- The `<api version>` value indicates what version of the Graph API you want to use. It is mandatory and is there for your protection: different versions will introduce new behaviors, and you should be able to opt in explicitly by changing the version number or stick with the version you coded against. For reference, the current value is `api-version=1.6`.

- The `odata parameters` are an extremely handy way of refining your queries so that the work takes place on the server instead of having your app download large amounts of data and filtering it on the client side. For example, say that I want to get the entry for one `Application`, but I only know its client_id—that is to say, its declared property `appId`. Unlike with `objectId`, the `appId` property is not indexed as an identifier that I can use in the path. But thanks to the $filter feature of OData, I can still craft a single URL that will yield the `Application` entry I seek: "https://graph.windows.net/developertenant.onmicrosoft.com/applications?$filter=appId+eq+'e8040965-f52a-4494-96ab-0ef07b591e3f'".

You might have noticed that the sample code you write for accessing the Graph did not really match the URL template. Graph API features two special aliases, /me and /myorganization, which resolve to the signed-in user and his or her tenant, respectively. Those are resolved from the access token that accompanies the request to the Graph. Those aliases are superhandy for writing more reusable queries and provide very useful adaptive functionality because they resolve contextually and result in very readable queries.

If you are not a fan of REST and prefer to work with client libraries, you are in luck: the Graph API team offers a client library that automates most of these operations for you, wrapping them through a nice proxy interface. It is, of course, available via NuGet: the package ID is Microsoft.Azure.ActiveDirectory.GraphClient.

Chapter 8 dedicated a large section to permissions for the Graph API, so I won't repeat that here. My hope is that you now better understand how the permissions map to entities. Once again, I invite you to check out the online documentation. Now that you have learned how to perform a REST call secured by Azure AD, it's time to retrace our steps and make things a bit more realistic.

ADAL session management and refresh tokens

Your app will likely need to sprinkle API calls through its entire codebase, as opposed to making a call right after redeeming the authorization code. You might be tempted to save `result.AccessToken` somewhere in your code and retrieve it whenever you need to make a call, but that would not take you very far. The problem is that access tokens are short-lived: once the token expires and your API call fails, what would your remediation be? OAuth2 defines a nice mechanism for extending the time in which you can access a protected API by providing an artifact—the already mentioned refresh token—that can be used for obtaining fresh access tokens without requiring more user prompts. Refresh tokens last significantly longer than access tokens, which makes it possible to maintain long-running sessions. Azure AD builds on that mechanism, adding Kerberos-like features to it. I'll give you details about both of those aspects in just a minute, but the key point I want to make is the following: Implementing those OAuth2 features in your own code is hard. Luckily, you don't have to! ADAL maintains a cache with all the access tokens and refresh tokens you obtained through an instance of `AuthenticationContext`. When you call one of the flavors of `AcquireToken*` to obtain an access token that happens to already be in the cache, ADAL will return the cached copy without hitting the network. If the cached token is expired, about to expire, or absent, but the cache contains a suitable refresh token, ADAL will automatically use that refresh token to obtain a new access token, cache it, and return it to you. That process is exceptionally handy and one of the reasons that the ADAL has been so well received—token life-cycle management is historically one of the hardest things to do.

To take advantage of this feature, you have to make sure that every time you need a token, you always use ADAL to get it. Whereas a local copy of an access token could hold an expired token, asking ADAL (that is, calling `AcquireToken*` passing the parameters defining the token you want) guarantees that the caching and refresh logic have a chance to run and do their magic.

As a practical example, say that you want to display the user's profile from the About action of the home controller of your application (remember, we are using the default ASP.NET MVC template here). Remove the API invocation code from the `AuthorizationCodeReceived` notification, head to HomeController.cs, and modify `About()` as shown here:

```
public ActionResult About()
{
    string ClientId = "c3d5b1ad-ae77-49ac-8a86-dd39a2f91081";
    string Authority = "https://login.microsoftonline.com/DeveloperTenant.onmicrosoft.com";
    string appKey = "a3fQREiyhqpYL10006hfCW+xke/TyP2oIQ6vgu68eoE=";
    string resourceId = "https://graph.windows.net";

    ClientCredential credential = new ClientCredential(ClientId, appKey);
    AuthenticationContext authContext = new AuthenticationContext(Authority);
    AuthenticationResult result = authContext.AcquireTokenSilent(resourceId, credential,
UserIdentifier.AnyUser);

    HttpClient httpClient = new HttpClient();
    httpClient.DefaultRequestHeaders.Authorization =
        new AuthenticationHeaderValue("Bearer", result.AccessToken);
    HttpResponseMessage response =
        httpClient.GetAsync("https://graph.windows.net/me?api-version=1.6").Result;
```

```
    if (response.IsSuccessStatusCode)
    {
        ViewBag.Message = response.Content.ReadAsStringAsync().Result;
    }
    return View();
}
```

The code is nearly the same as what you wrote earlier. The main difference is that you invoke `AcquireTokenSilent` instead of obtaining a token via an authorization code. `AcquireToken-Silent` is a method that attempts to retrieve the requested token only by using the artifacts already present in the ADAL cache. It has the suffix "silent" because the method is guaranteed not to throw up any UI, which is somewhat moot in this particular scenario because no flavor of `AcquireToken*` shows any UI on the server side. However, ADAL works both with web apps on the server and native clients on devices, and the latter can interactively prompt the user when requesting a token.

`AcquireTokenSilent`'s parameters can be thought of as conditions that must hold true for the requested token. It has to be scoped for the resource specified (in our case, the Graph API), it has to be issued for the specified client_id (passed indirectly through the `ClientCredential` instance), and it has to have been issued for the specified user account (in our case, we declare that any user is fine, via the `UserIdentifier.AnyUser` constant).

By default, ADAL uses an in-memory cache. When the code in `About()` executes, that cache has already been primed by the code in `AuthorizationCodeReceived`. The call to `AcquireTokenBy-AuthorizationCode` has the effect of saving in the cache a token for accessing the Graph. Hence, assuming that the call to `About()` takes place within an hour from initialization and that the process does not recycle, the call to `AcquireTokenSilent` will find a matching access token in the cache and return it right away. Go ahead, try this yourself. Start Fiddler, and then start the app, sign in, and click About. You'll see that the call to `AcquireTokenSilent` correctly returns the desired token, but Fiddler will show no network traffic toward Azure AD for that call.

This functionality is pretty handy, but the serious return of investment from using ADAL emerges when refresh tokens come into play. Allow me to spend a moment to describe how refresh tokens work in OAuth2 and Azure AD. After that, I'll come back to the code and describe how it all fits together.

Access tokens are short-lived for security reasons. Say that you issue an access token for Mario, who can now use it to access your company resources. Imagine that you discover that Mario is stealing and you decide to terminate him. Given that access tokens have no revocation mechanism, Mario will still be able to access resources with that access token until it expires; clearly, it is in your interest to issue access tokens with a short validity period. At the same time, forcing Mario to go through the credential-gathering dance to obtain a new token every time the old one expires leads to unacceptable experiences, or to antipatterns such as clients caching user credentials (defeating OAuth2's purpose). How do you reconcile those seemingly contrasting requirements? Enter the refresh token.

The refresh token is an artifact that is issued alongside the access token. Whenever an access token expires, the client can use the refresh token to go back to the authorization server's token endpoint (without requiring any user interaction) and ask for a new access token. If the conditions are right (the user still exists in the system, consent has not been revoked, and so on), the client will be issued a new access token. Problem solved. The flow, dubbed a "refresh token grant" in the OAuth2 core specs, is shown in Figure 9-3.

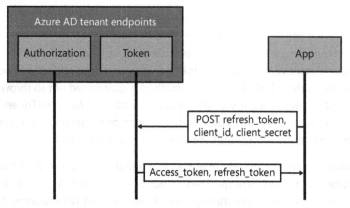

FIGURE 9-3 Swim-lane diagram of the refresh token grant for a confidential client.

That's all that OAuth2 has to say on the matter. That is, of course, not enough for fully specifying how a refresh token behaves in a real-life solution. In the following, you can find more details on how refresh tokens work in Azure AD. Please note that this information describes the situation at the time of writing. Things are almost guaranteed to change in the coming months, as Azure AD introduces features granting you finer control over token validity times.

- At issuance time, a refresh token is valid for 14 days.

  If you use the refresh token within those 14 days, together with the new access token, you receive a new refresh token with a new validity window of 14 days, starting from the new issuance instant. This process can be repeated for up to 90 days of total validity from the very first issuance. After those 90 days, the user has to reauthenticate.

- Refresh tokens issued for guest Microsoft accounts last only 12 hours.

- Refresh tokens can be invalidated at *any* time for reasons independent of your app; the deprovisioning of the user is an extreme example, but there are far more common circumstances that have that effect, too. For example, as of today, refresh tokens will be invalidated whenever a user changes his or her password.

You should not take a dependency in your code on the expected validity times of refresh tokens. Your logic should always assume that the refresh token can fail at any time.

I'll tackle the case in which the refresh token itself has expired shortly, but for the time being let's pause and go back to the code. Now we know what should happen in case the cached access token expires: ADAL should automatically use the cached refresh token to get a new access token (and a new refresh token with updated validity). Here's a little trick you can use to see the flow in action if you don't want to wait one hour (actually 55 minutes, given that ADAL will trigger renewal within 5 minutes from the projected access token expiration time). Place a breakpoint right after the `AuthenticationContext` creation in `About()`, start Fiddler as usual, and then start the app. Sign in and click About. Once you hit the breakpoint, go to the Locals window in Visual Studio. Open `authContext.TokenCache`, go to the nonpublic members, and expand `tokenCacheDictionary`. You'll see that it has one entry. Expand the value, and then right-click ExpiresOn and choose Edit Value. Change the value to something like **DateTime.Now.AddDays(-1)**. Then go ahead and let the execution go past the breakpoint. Fiddler will display something similar to the following:

```
POST https://login.microsoftonline.com/DeveloperTenant.onmicrosoft.com/oauth2/token HTTP/1.1
Content-Type: application/x-www-form-urlencoded
client-request-id: 5bbaccbb-82d6-483a-b224-14301c9bfbd7
return-client-request-id: true
x-client-SKU: .NET
x-client-Ver: 2.19.0.0
x-client-CPU: x64
x-client-OS: Microsoft Windows NT 10.0.10240.0
x-client-last-request: 8ef2acec-c8a8-481e-a1f3-fdd43c0c0059
x-client-last-response-time: 424
x-client-last-endpoint: token
Host: login.microsoftonline.com
Content-Length: 971
Expect: 100-continue
Connection: Keep-Alive

resource=https%3A%2F%2Fgraph.windows.net&
client_id=c3d5b1ad-ae77-49ac-8a86-dd39a2f91081&client_secret=a3fQREiyhqpYL10006hfCW%2Bxke%2FTyP
2oIQ6vgu68eoE%3D&
grant_type=refresh_token&
refresh_token=AAA[...SNIP...]MIAA
```

As you can see in the request, the application must authenticate with the token endpoint by presenting its credentials alongside the refresh token bits. That explains why `AcquireTokenSilent` required a `ClientCredential` parameter. Note that overloads of `AcquireTokenSilent` that do not require application credentials exist, but they are meant to be used with public clients (that is to say, native and mobile apps). Web applications are modeled as confidential clients in Azure AD and can act autonomously; hence, they are required to authenticate.

The response is equivalent to the one received from the authorization-code grant flow, although here we don't get an id_token:

```
HTTP/1.1 200 OK
Cache-Control: no-cache, no-store
Pragma: no-cache
Content-Type: application/json; charset=utf-8
Expires: -1
Server: Microsoft-IIS/8.5
x-ms-request-id: 05af78be-c6fd-44aa-95b2-42ab4ee77b5d
client-request-id: 5bbaccbb-82d6-483a-b224-14301c9bfbd7
x-ms-gateway-service-instanceid: ESTSFE_IN_226
X-Content-Type-Options: nosniff
Strict-Transport-Security: max-age=31536000; includeSubDomains
P3P: CP="DSP CUR OTPi IND OTRi ONL FIN"
Set-Cookie: flight-uxoptin=true; path=/; secure; HttpOnly
```

```
Set-Cookie: x-ms-gateway-slice=productionb; path=/; secure; HttpOnly
Set-Cookie: stsservicecookie=ests; path=/; secure; HttpOnly
X-Powered-By: ASP.NET
Date: Wed, 14 Oct 2015 22:43:50 GMT
Content-Length: 2371

{"token_type":"Bearer","expires_in":"3599","scope":"User.Read","expires_on":"1444866230","not_be
fore":"1444862330","resource":"https://graph.windows.net","pwd_exp":"461833","pwd_url":"https://
portal.microsoftonline.com/ChangePassword.aspx","access_token":"eyJ0e [...SNIP...]
XAoUPJPqYQ","refresh_token":"AAAB[...SNIP...]MOIAA"}
```

The nice thing about this exchange is that it all happens transparently within the call to `Acquire-TokenSilent`. Technically, as long as you use ADAL, you don't even need to know that refresh tokens exist—you reap the benefits of long sessions without having to deal with the associated complexity.

> **Note** Like the access token, the refresh token is also completely opaque to the client. The only entity meant to consume it is Azure AD itself, hence there's no point for anybody else to peek at it. And, of course, the refresh token is protected against tampering. The only thing a client can do with it is to haul it back and forth with Azure AD.

The advantage of this approach becomes even more evident when you consider another special property of Azure AD refresh tokens—their ability to be used to get access tokens for multiple resources.

Multiresource refresh tokens   As you have learned throughout this book, and in particular in Chapter 8, Azure AD models very precisely the relationships between applications and resources. Requests for access tokens need to specify the resource for which the desired token is meant, and the resulting access token is scoped down so that it can be used only against the resource it has been issued for. In the section "Exposing a protected web API," you'll learn in detail how that takes place.

In the sample app we are calling only the Graph API. But what if you want to also call Office 365 and the Azure API? You already know how you'd handle that from the permissions-configuration perspective—you'd just add the required resources and permissions in the client's `Application`. In turn, that would cause the consent prompt to ask for all the required permissions at once. But here's the important part: the refresh token you receive from Azure AD knows about all the resources you granted consent for. As a result, it doesn't matter what resource you ask for on your first `Acquire-Token*` call. Once ADAL gets the refresh token, it can use it to obtain access tokens for any of the other resources your client is configured to have access to.

In practice that means that you can make new calls to `AcquireTokenSilent`, each time passing the resourceId of any of the other resources you want. ADAL will transparently use the refresh token grant to obtain and cache the requested access token. This nice property earns for Azure AD–issued tokens the moniker *multiresource refresh tokens*, or MRRTs. In a sense, you can think of MRRTs as the OAuth2 equivalent of ticket granting tickets (TGTs) in Kerberos: they are artifacts that allow a user to obtain tokens to access the resources the directory decides she or he has access to.

Note that even for those new resources, refresh tokens remain tied to a particular client ID and user: refresh tokens can only be used together with the client ID of the application that is used to obtain the refresh token in the first place, and the user will always be the one that granted the consent recorded or referenced by the refresh token itself.

Just a closing note on the topic: Until recently, the use of MRRTs was also limited to the tenant that originally issued the first refresh token. Thanks to a recent change in Azure AD, however, now you can use MRRTs to ask for access tokens from any tenant in which the user has a guest account and has already granted consent for the client app originally used to obtain the first refresh token. In practice, say that I have an Microsoft account user who is an administrator for an Azure subscription. All Azure AD tenants created under that subscription will have a guest account for that user. Say also that I have tenant A and tenant B and a multitenant web app that needs Graph API (or any other API) access for which I consented with the same Microsoft account user in both tenants. I can now obtain a token for the Graph API of tenant A and then use the refresh token so obtained to request an access token for the Graph API in tenant B. All I need to do is repeat the AcquireTokenSilent call, but against an instance of AuthenticationContext initialized for tenant B, and ensure that the token cache in the new AuthenticationContext is the same as the one that was primed with tokens from tenant A. Clear as mud? That's a good segue to the next section.

ADAL cache considerations for web applications   ADAL began its existence as a library for native applications, apps meant to be run on devices and operated by a user engaged in an interactive session. The default ADAL cache is aligned with that original mission: it is an in-memory cache that relies on a static store, available process-wide. That means that by default, each and every AuthenticationContext instance you initialize within a process will read and write against the same token cache.

However, what works for native clients doesn't work too well for applications meant to be executed on midtiers and back ends. Namely:

- These applications are accessed by many users at once. Saving all access tokens in the same store creates isolation issues and presents challenges when operating at scale: many users, each with as many tokens as the resources the app accesses on their behalf, can mean huge numbers and very expensive lookup operations.

- These applications are typically deployed on distributed topologies, where multiple nodes must have access to the same cache.

- Cached tokens must survive process recycles and deactivations. Think of the scenario I already mentioned in Chapter 2, in which you connect your Facebook account to Twitter so that every time you tweet your Facebook Wall posts the same update. That is only possible if Twitter saves in persistent storage the access tokens necessary for calling the Facebook API—or you'd have to reauthenticate to Facebook to reacquire the delegated token every time you sign in to Twitter.

For all those reasons, when you are implementing web apps, it is a good idea to override the default ADAL token cache with a custom implementation. Unfortunately, the library's developers cannot predict at design time what persistent storage you'll use at run time, hence they can't provide a default cache for midtier applications, but the good news is that implementing a custom cache in ADAL is surprisingly easy.

ADAL's cache extensibility model isolates you from all the details of its internal structure, which is always maintained in memory: its primitives are meant to allow you to persist the token cache on an arbitrary store; hence, they are mostly concerned about warning you when a read or write operation is about to happen or just concluded. That gives you an opportunity to update the private ADAL in-memory copy of the cache from your custom storage right before a read, or to reflect in persistent storage any changes that just occurred in the in-memory copy. And, of course, by controlling how the token cache is instantiated, you can also control its scope: for example, you can enforce that every web application session have its own cache instance so that the content of the cache is limited to all the access tokens that a given web app user accumulated for calling the web API. This breaks down individual caches into manageable chunks, instead of having to save potentially millions of sessions in a flat store as the default cache would.

For completeness, here's a super quick explanation of how the main cache primitives operate. However, I would recommend that you study the custom-cache-classes feature in the .NET samples at *https://github.com/azure-samples?utf8=%E2%9C%93&query=openidconnect*.

You create a custom cache by deriving from TokenCache. You tell `AuthenticationContext` that you want to use your custom cache by passing an instance of your cache class at construction time, as shown in the following. Note that you have to pass the same cache instance, or instances designed to work against the same store, to all the `AuthenticationContext` occurrences that you want to share the cache. In our current sample, that means passing the same custom cache to the `AuthenticationContext` constructor calls both in `Startup` and in `About()`.

```
AuthenticationContext authContext = new AuthenticationContext(Authority, new CustomADALCache
(whateverInitDataINeed));
```

TokenCache features three notifications—`BeforeAccess`, `BeforeWrite`, and `AfterAccess`—that are triggered at specific moments at which ADAL works against the cache.

Say that you make a call to `AcquireTokenSilent` asking for a token for resource 1. ADAL needs to check the cache to see whether there is already an access token for resource 1 or if there is a valid refresh token for obtaining such an access token. Right before it reads the cache, ADAL calls the `BeforeAccess` notification. Here you have the opportunity to retrieve your persisted cache blob from your persistent store and pass it to ADAL's in-memory cache. You do so by passing that blob to `Deserialize`. Note that you can apply all kinds of heuristics to decide whether the existing in-memory copy is still okay and skip the deserialization to reduce the time in which you access your persistent store.

Now consider a case in which you are invoking `AcquireTokenByAuthorizationCode`. Once ADAL obtains a new token, it needs to save it in the cache. But right before that, it invokes the `BeforeWrite` notification. That gives you the opportunity to apply whatever concurrency strategy you want to enact: for example, you might decide to place a lock on your blob so that other nodes in your farm that are possibly attempting a write at the same time would avoid producing conflicting updates.

After ADAL adds the new token to its in-memory copy of the cache, it calls the AfterAccess notification. That notification is in fact called every time ADAL accesses the cache, not just when a write takes place. However, you can always tell whether the current operation resulted in a cache change because in that case the property HasStateChanged will be set to true. If that is the case, you will typically call Serialize() to get a binary blob representing the latest cache content—and save it in your storage. After that, it will be your responsibility to clear whatever lock you might have set. Please note that ADAL never automatically resets HasStateChanged to false. You have to do it in your own code after you are satisfied that you handled the event correctly.

Other areas you might want to modify in your class concern the basic life cycle. You'll likely want to populate the cache from your store at construction time, you'll want to override Clear and Delete-Item to ensure that you reflect cache state changes, and so on.

To make things a bit more concrete, here's a naïve implementation of a custom cache that persists tokens in the HTTP session. This comes straight from one of the Azure AD samples online:

```
public class NaiveSessionCache: TokenCache
{
    private static readonly object FileLock = new object();
    string UserObjectId = string.Empty;
    string CacheId = string.Empty;
    public NaiveSessionCache(string userId)
    {
        UserObjectId = userId;
        CacheId = UserObjectId + "_TokenCache";

        this.AfterAccess = AfterAccessNotification;
        this.BeforeAccess = BeforeAccessNotification;
        Load();
    }
    public void Load()
    {
        lock (FileLock)
        {
            this.Deserialize((byte[])HttpContext.Current.Session[CacheId]);
        }
    }
    public void Persist()
    {
        lock (FileLock)
        {
            // reflect changes in the persistent store
            HttpContext.Current.Session[CacheId] = this.Serialize();
            // once the write operation took place, restore the HasStateChanged bit to false
            this.HasStateChanged = false;
        }
    }
    // Empties the persistent store.
    public override void Clear()
    {
        base.Clear();
        System.Web.HttpContext.Current.Session.Remove(CacheId);
    }
```

```
    public override void DeleteItem(TokenCacheItem item)
    {
        base.DeleteItem(item);
        Persist();
    }
    // Triggered right before ADAL needs to access the cache.
    // Reload the cache from the persistent store in case it changed since the last access.
     void BeforeAccessNotification(TokenCacheNotificationArgs args)
    {
        Load();
    }
    // Triggered right after ADAL accessed the cache.
    void AfterAccessNotification(TokenCacheNotificationArgs args)
    {
        // if the access operation resulted in a cache update
        if (this.HasStateChanged)
        {
            Persist();
        }
    }
}
}
```

The main thing I'll point out about this implementation is that the store is initialized per user, so every session with the web app has its own cache instance. If you want to see a more complete implementation, based on the Entity Framework, you can look at the more advanced samples (such as the multitenant ones). Alternatively, you can simply create a new project in Visual Studio 2015 and be sure to select the Read Directory check box in the authentication settings wizard. Visual Studio will automatically generate a custom cache class for you, also based on the Entity Framework.

What to do when a refresh token expires   The call to AcquireTokenSilent can fail, and your code needs to be prepared for that.

Excluding the obvious case in which the cache is empty, there are two main reasons that AcquireTokenSilent will fail for the scenario we've examined so far:

- There are multiple cached tokens that can satisfy the requirements imposed by the parameters of the call.

- Both the access token and all the suitable refresh tokens have expired.

Let's get the first case out of the way because it's the simplest. You recognize that you are in this situation from the fact that AcquireTokenSilent fails with an AdalException warning you that "multiple_matching_tokens_detected: The cache contains multiple tokens satisfying the requirements. Call AcquireToken again providing more requirements (e.g. UserId)". How did you end up with multiple tokens in the cache for the same client ID, meant for the same resource? Sometimes that's intentional: our scenario so far expects the user of the web application and the user calling the web API to be the same, but that's definitely not the only valid scenario. Think of an app showing you multiple Exchange Online calendars: an administrative assistant might sign in to the web app with his or her own account and then proceed to get an access token for his or her own calendar and another access token for his or her boss's calendar. I'll examine similar scenarios more closely later on.

In our sample app, having multiple tokens is more likely the result of a mistake. For example, if you did not override the default cache with one that has better user isolation, this is your punishment: multiple concurrent users access your app and all get an access token for themselves via the call to AcquireTokenByAuthorizationCode in Startup. Once the execution reaches the Acquire-TokenSilent call in About(), the cache will contain as many access tokens for the Graph API as there are concurrent users. Given that in our call we don't specify for which user we want the token (we pass UserIdentifier.AnyUser), ADAL does not know which token should be returned and errors out.

For this specific case the solution is to use a better cache, but in general you deal with this situation first by inspecting the cache to see whether you indeed have multiple entries for multiple users. For this task I like to use Visual Studio's Immediate window and perform LINQ queries against the cache to see how many tokens matching my requirement (same client ID for the same resource) are stored. For example:

```
var usrz = authContext.TokenCache.ReadItems().Where(p => p.Resource == "https://graph.windows.net" && p.ClientId == "c3d5b1ad-ae77-49ac-8a86-dd39a2f91081");
```

This will return an IEnumerable of entries—if there's more than one, the error message is accurate, and your recourse is to specify in AcquireToken* which user you want a token for. Before looking at how that's done, let's take a look at one of those entries. If you type **usrz.First();** in the Immediate window, you'll get something like the following:

```
{Microsoft.IdentityModel.Clients.ActiveDirectory.TokenCacheItem}
    AccessToken: "eyJ0eX[...SNIP...]aohJ6LA"
    Authority: "https://login.microsoftonline.com/DeveloperTenant.onmicrosoft.com/"
    ClientId: "c3d5b1ad-ae77-49ac-8a86-dd39a2f91081"
    DisplayableId: "mario@developertenant.onmicrosoft.com"
    ExpiresOn: {10/15/2015 8:47:54 PM +00:00}
    FamilyName: "Rossi"
    GivenName: "Mario"
    IdToken: "eyJ0eX[..SNIP..]oMQ"
    IdentityProvider: "https://sts.windows.net/6c3d51dd-f0e5-4959-b4ea-a80c4e36fe5e/"
    IsMultipleResourceRefreshToken: true
    RefreshToken: "AAA[..SNIP..]XIAA"
    Resource: "https://graph.windows.net"
    TenantId: "6c3d51dd-f0e5-4959-b4ea-a80c4e36fe5e"
    UniqueId: "13d3104a-6891-45d2-a4be-82581a8e465b"
```

The fields DisplayableId and UniqueId are the ones that you can use for indicating to AcquireToken* which user you want a token for. The former can contain the user's UPN or email address, depending on what Azure AD sends. The latter can contain the users' ObjectId in the directory when available, or the NameIdentifier in case it is not. You pass one of those values to a new instance of the UserIdentifier class, and then you pass that instance in AcquireToken*. For example:

```
authContext.AcquireTokenSilent(resourceId, credential, new UserIdentifier("mario@developertenant.onmicrosoft.com",UserIdentifierType.OptionalDisplayableId);)
```

If you want to use the UniqueId value—a great idea given that it is nonreassignable—you'd use UserIdentifierType.UniqueId. If, as I am doing in the snippet, you want to use the DisplayableId, you can use either UserIdentifierType.OptionalDisplayableId or UserIdentifierType.RequiredDisplayableId.

Note On the midtier, UserIdentifierType.OptionalDisplayableId and UserIdentifierType.RequiredDisplayableId are fully equivalent. If you were using them with an interactive flavor of AcquireToken* in a native client, that call might trigger a dialog box in which the user can enter credentials. RequiredDisplayableId would enforce that the resulting token match the ID that was passed when calling AcquireToken*, so it would error out if the end user enters different credentials; OptionalDisplayableId would instead accept the outcome of entering new user credentials, as the UserIdentifier instance would be used only as a way of inspecting the cache and prepopulating the username field.

The case of the refresh token expiration is more complicated and, of course, far more frequent.

The assumption that the signed-in user in the web app and the user who obtains the tokens for calling the API are in fact the same user makes the remediation very clear: that user must be used in the context of a new authorization request to get a brand-new refresh token, and in the OpenID Connect hybrid flow, that can be accomplished by triggering the sign-in flow again.

Before I jump to the code, however, I'd like to offer a few words on what that means for the experience. A refresh token might expire while the web session with the app (that is, the session cookie that the cookie middleware emitted at sign-in time) is still valid. If the nature of your application is such that the user can still do something useful with your pages even if she or he is not able to perform the API call you need the refresh token for, then you should be careful with how you handle reauthentication. Triggering a blind redirect at a random moment in your app will disorient your user and disrupt the experience. My favorite pattern for handling this situation is the one that you can observe when using the Klout (*klout.com*) web application. Klout integrates with many web APIs to aggregate your activity over social networks. Occasionally the tokens for invoking those APIs expire. Klout does not kick you out of your session, however; rather, it informs you that there are features you don't have access to until you go through the authorization flow again—and gives you an opportunity to do so in the form of a link. You can see an example in the top banner in Figure 9-4.

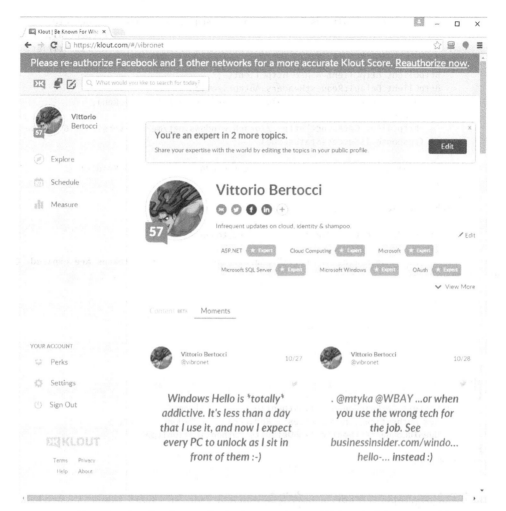

FIGURE 9-4 How Klout handles the reauthorization experience with the APIs it integrates with.

Now here's a quick-and-dirty way of modifying the About() action to achieve a similar effect. Again, the "same user" assumption is of huge help here. I've highlighted the new and interesting bits:

```
public ActionResult About(string reauth)
{
    if (reauth == null)
    {
        string ClientId = "c3d5b1ad-ae77-49ac-8a86-dd39a2f91081";
        string Authority = "https://login.microsoftonline.com/DeveloperTenant.onmicrosoft.com";
        string appKey = "a3fQREiyhqpYL10OO6hfCW+xke/TyP2oIQ6vgu68eoE=";
        string resourceId = "https://graph.windows.net";
        try
        {
            ClientCredential credential = new ClientCredential(ClientId, appKey);
            AuthenticationContext authContext = new AuthenticationContext(Authority);
```

```
                AuthenticationResult result = authContext.AcquireTokenSilent(resourceId,
                                                                            credential,
                                                                            UserIdentifier.
                                                                            AnyUser);

            HttpClient httpClient = new HttpClient();
            httpClient.DefaultRequestHeaders.Authorization =
                new AuthenticationHeaderValue("Bearer", result.AccessToken);
            HttpResponseMessage response =
                httpClient.GetAsync("https://graph.windows.net/me?api-version=1.6").Result;
            if (response.IsSuccessStatusCode)
            {
                ViewBag.Message = response.Content.ReadAsStringAsync().Result;
            }
        }
        catch (AdalException ex)
        {
            if (ex.ErrorCode == "failed_to_acquire_token_silently")
            {
                Response.Write("<a href=\"./About?reauth=true\">Your tokens are expired. Click
here to reauth</a>");
            }
            else
            {
                // more error handling
            }
        }
    }
    else
    {
        HttpContext.GetOwinContext().Authentication.Challenge(
            new AuthenticationProperties { RedirectUri = "/Home/About", },
            OpenIdConnectAuthenticationDefaults.AuthenticationType);
    }
    return View();
}
```

The token acquisition and API call logic is wrapped in a try-catch block. In the case in which the app fails because AcquireTokenSilent does not succeed in obtaining a token, we crudely display a message and provide a link to the same action—but with an extra parameter (of nullable type, so that nothing happens when the action is invoked without parameters, as is usually the case). If the end user clicks that link, we know that he or she intends to perform the reauthentication flow, hence the redirect won't be a surprise and won't disrupt the experience.

At the beginning of the method, the code checks for the presence of that parameter. If we find it, we trigger a sign-in, specifying that we intend to come back to the original action once we're done. Assuming that the sign-in goes well and that the AcquireTokenByAuthorizationCode runs successfully to seed the cache, this time around the AcquireTokenSilent call will succeed. Back to business as usual.

You can experience that flow in action by signing in, placing a breakpoint right after the AuthenticationContext construction, and then using the Immediate window for cleaning up the cache (via authContext.TokenCache.Clear();). That will also show you that if there's still a valid session with the web app, token acquisition will take place without throwing any UI—the user will only experience a quick flash as the redirect goes through.

Let me stress that the preceding snippet truly is quick and dirty—it's meant to make the flow as clear as possible, with the expectation that once you understand the gist of it, you'll write the proper error-management code, break down functionality across multiple actions if it fits your app, and so on.

Other ways of getting access tokens

The OpenID Connect hybrid flow is the one that gives you the most bang for the buck, thanks to its sign-in and authorization-code flow integration. That said, it does not cover all the possible topologies of interest for a web application that needs to access a web API. Two notable examples are the case in which you want to access an API as the application itself, with no user involvement, and the case in which you want to access the API as a user other than the one with which you are signed in.

Accessing an API as an application: Client credentials

As I briefly mentioned in Chapter 2, the OAuth2 core spec defines a grant in which a client can obtain access tokens directly by presenting its credentials to the token endpoint. The flow is summarized in Figure 9-5.

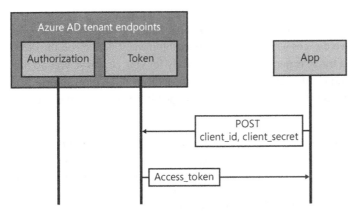

FIGURE 9-5 Swim-lane diagram for the client-credentials grant. Azure AD requires an extra parameter in the request, not shown in the figure: it's the identifier of the resource to access.

In Chapter 8 you learned about the existence of application permissions. Specifically, you learned how to configure your client app to request them (via the portal or by adding the right entry in `RequiredResourcesAccess` in the `Application` object/manifest) and how to handle consent for obtaining them (`prompt=admin_consent` is required). After you have done that, requesting a token via client credentials with ADAL is very easy:

```
result = authContext.AcquireToken(resourceId, clientCredential);
```

The credentials are passed through the same `ClientCredential` class you encountered while studying `AcquireTokenByAuthorizationCode`. ADAL will cache the resulting access tokens to minimize network traffic. The flow does not result in any refresh token because there's no need for one: when you want a new access token, you can always use the client credentials again. Note that ADAL does that automatically when necessary—that is to say, within five minutes from the cached access token's expiration or if there's no cached token yet.

Accessing an API as an arbitrary user: Raw OAuth2 authorization grant

The vast majority of the OAuth2 flows you observe in the wild are cross-provider, as making that integration possible is OAuth2's main raison d'être. You sign in to Twitter's web app with your Twitter user, and the Twitter back end can call the Facebook and LinkedIn APIs on your behalf. You sign in to Tumblr with your Tumblr user, and the Tumblr back end can call the Facebook and Twitter APIs on your behalf. And so on. One has to assume that the Twitter web app can access the Twitter API on behalf of the user currently signed in, of course, but for all other APIs, the identity used has to be different.

In Azure AD land, different providers means different tenants. Or one can consider scenarios such as for the admin and boss, where a single web session needs to access the API as two distinct users from the same tenant. Allowing a web application to acquire and use an access token on behalf of a user that is not related to the currently signed-in user requires you to implement an OAuth2 authorization grant flow.

I'll be honest with you: this is one of the toughest flows to implement with today's libraries. But you are not totally left to your own devices—far from it. ADAL caching will still save you tons of lines of code, and most of the protocol traffic is generated automatically for you. However, you do need to write code in your app for handling identity-specific details, such as receiving authorization code and validating messages. Those things could be taken care of by a library, but ADAL is simply not at that point yet.

You can find a detailed code sample demonstrating this scenario at *https://github.com/Azure-Samples/active-directory-dotnet-webapp-webapi-oauth2-useridentity*, so I won't give complete end-to-end instructions, but I want to be sure that you understand what's going on in this topology.

At a high level, you can think of this as a variant of the logic you studied in the hybrid flow for handling the case in which the refresh token expires. You still attempt to get the token you need via `AcquireTokenSilent`, and you still react to a failure to do so by providing the end user with a link for going through reauthorization. However, the reauthorization logic is no longer a simple trigger to sign in: this time it entails constructing an OAuth2 authorization-code request, tailored to the specific tenant and user you wish to engage. There's more. You can no longer rely on the OpenID Connect middleware notifications for redeeming the code, which means you need to provide something (such as a controller) that waits for the authorization code to come back, validates the message, redeems the code for a token via ADAL (so that it ends up in the cache), and redirects to the controller from where this all originated. It sounds worse than it actually is, but it is definitely more work than all the other flows we have discussed so far.

Exposing a protected web API

The counterpart of consuming APIs is, of course, offering your own API for consumption—from your own clients and from third parties.

From the project perspective, this is even simpler than setting up web sign-on for a redirect-based application. Whereas web sign-on entails orchestrating a dance of redirects and handling sessions, verifying a web API call simply requires you to expect a bearer token in the request and to validate it against the requirements advertised by the trusted authority's metadata. ASP.NET offers specialized middleware for that, which I'll show you in detail.

Web APIs are provisioned in Azure AD through the same application type used for web apps with a UX. Whether your app serves pages to be rendered by a browser or JSON to be parsed by a client process is a private matter you decide in your own code—after you add a web app entry, Azure AD is ready to support both scenarios at all times. Web APIs do have extra configuration requirements, though. As you learned in Chapter 8, web APIs have to declare what delegated and application permissions a client can request at consent time. At request time, those permissions will be expressed in different ways in the incoming token. You'll see how you can tap into that information from your code and make access decisions.

The following section will walk you through the process of creating a web API project, protecting it with Azure AD, and consuming it from our sample application. As usual, I will use the scaffolding offered by that process to contextualize Azure AD and developer library features, protocol considerations, and gotchas.

Setting up a web API project

Let's start by creating a Visual Studio project for our API. Feel free to add a new project to your existing solution or to start a new instance.

Visual Studio offers a specialized template for a web API protected by Azure AD, just like the one you used in Chapter 1 for creating your very first Azure AD application. You gain access to it by clicking the Change Authentication button in the project creation wizard and selecting the Work And School Account section. Notably, the web API templates in Visual Studio 2013 and Visual Studio 2015 are very similar—the middleware for handling the OAuth2 bearer token usage specification is the first protocol-oriented middleware Microsoft shipped.

Using the template is very handy because it automatically provisions the app in Azure AD, adds all the necessary NuGet references, and weaves in boilerplate authentication code. In Chapter 5 you had the opportunity to become familiar with all the moving parts the template adds, so there's not much educational value to going through the manual route again here. The main difference from the process shown in Chapter 5 is the protocol middleware being added. In Chapter 5 you added the OpenID Connect and cookie middlewares, but here you'll add middleware that takes care of the OAuth2 bearer token validation (more details below). Furthermore, in Chapter 8 you studied how applications can declare permissions in the Application object/manifest file, so you already know how to handle that part, and it's okay at this point to let Visual Studio do the work for you.

Go ahead and create a new ASP.NET 4.6 Web API project, either standalone or in the same solution. As you go through the creation wizard, select Change Authentication, and then Work And School Account. Very important: in the domain drop-down, be sure to select or enter the same Azure AD tenant you used for the sample web app you want to use for consuming the new API. Cross-tenant API calls are possible, but they require some extra steps I will introduce a little later.

NuGets

Once the project is ready, you can take a look around. First, head to packages.config. If you compare the list of NuGet packages with the list from the web app project, you'll see that whereas the latter references Microsoft.Owin.Security.Cookies and Microsoft.Owin.Security.OpenIdConnect, the protocol middleware components used for web API are these:

- Microsoft.Owin.Security.ActiveDirectory

- Microsoft.Owin.Security.Jwt

- Microsoft.Owin.Security.OAuth

As of today, they are all at version 3.0.1.

At first you might find it strange that the middleware implementing the OAuth2 bearer token usage lives in an Active Directory–specific NuGet package. But think of what you know about that flow, and the reason will become immediately obvious. The function of a middleware implementing that protocol is to validate access tokens, but the format of such access tokens (hence their validation logic) is left as an exercise to the reader. When you connect to Azure AD (or ADFS), it is well known in what format the tokens will be and where to retrieve the metadata containing the validation coordinates. Hence, we can enshrine such knowledge in ready-to-use components. Validation for other providers will follow the same rough functional steps (retrieve the token from the message, validate it, manufacture a `ClaimsPrincipal` with the content) but will have to differ in the actual validation bits.

Let's see what this all means in concrete terms.

Middleware initialization code and API controllers

Head to the Startup.Auth.cs. Here's the interesting bit:

```
public void ConfigureAuth(IAppBuilder app)
{
    app.UseWindowsAzureActiveDirectoryBearerAuthentication(
        new WindowsAzureActiveDirectoryBearerAuthenticationOptions
        {
            Tenant = ConfigurationManager.AppSettings["ida:Tenant"],
            TokenValidationParameters = new TokenValidationParameters {
                ValidAudience = ConfigurationManager.AppSettings["ida:Audience"]
            },
        });
}
```

The middleware pipeline is decisively simpler in the case of a web API. You add only one middleware, through what must be the extension method with the longest name in ASP.NET's history: `UseWindowsAzureActiveDirectoryBearerAuthentication`. (I played no part in picking the name! True story, when that name was picked I was on a tiny Fiji island, 30 minutes by boat from where they shot the movie *Castaway*.)

The job of this middleware is very simple: it examines incoming calls, and if it finds a bearer token in the Authorization header, the middleware extracts it, validates it, manufactures a `Claims-Principal` out of it, and marks the current user as authenticated. That's it. There is no session creation, proactive interception of 401s to be turned into 302s, or anything else.

Before I can properly explain the meaning of the properties used to initialize the middleware, I need to introduce you to how Active Directory chose to represent access tokens. I have been putting off this explanation as long as possible to avoid creating the temptation to examine the content of the access token from the client. But at this point, you are implementing the intended recipient of the access token, so here you are expected to look into it to validate it and consume its content.

Both Azure AD and ADFS represent access tokens as JWTs, which closely resemble the ones you encountered in the form of id_tokens. The rationale for choosing an actual format, one that anybody with the correct metadata can validate, is right here in the custom web API scenario we are studying. If AD would allow you to call only Microsoft-owned APIs—as Facebook issues tokens only for its own Graph API—then the format would be irrelevant to you. But AD can also be used for securing your own API, so you need a mechanism for examining incoming tokens and deciding whether they are good for you or should be rejected. Given that we already have logic for validating tokens in the web sign-on case, it just makes sense to reuse it here—plus some extra checks the scenario calls for.

You validate the JWTs used as access tokens by using the same metadata-driven logic you saw in action for id_tokens in Chapters 6 and 7. That is the function performed by the `Tenant` parameter in the `WindowsAzureActiveDirectoryBearerAuthenticationOptions` initialization: it contains a string representing a domain associated with the tenant you want tokens from, or the corresponding tenantId, which the middleware uses for constructing the URL of the metadata document from which the validation coordinates should be retrieved. In our sample, the value in `Tenant` (saved by the project wizard in web.config) is "developertenant.onmicrosoft.com". The tenant is automatically considered to be associated with the Azure AD instance https://login.microsoftonline.com. If you need to connect to a different Azure AD instance, you can omit the `Tenant` property in the options and directly specify the metadata document's URL via the property `MetadataAddress`. The twist you might not expect is that for this middleware, you need to specify Azure AD's WS-Federation metadata. For example, in our case the equivalent of specifying "developertenant.onmicrosoft.com" in the `Tenant` property would be to set `MetadataAddress` to "https://login.microsoftonline.com/developertenant.onmicrosoft.com/federationmetadata/2007-06/federationmetadata.xml".

Note Why the WS-Federation metadata instead of the OpenID Connect discovery document? Simple. When the web API middleware came out, Azure AD did not support the OpenID Connect discovery document yet.

Remember how in the OpenID Connect options you had to specify the `ClientId` of the application? The OpenID Connect middleware uses the `ClientId` for two purposes—to identify the client app when generating the sign-in request to the provider and to validate the audience claim in incoming tokens—to be sure that the caller isn't simply replaying a token stolen from someone else. If you need a refresher, head to Chapter 6 and search for the aud claim in the section "The JWT format."

Access tokens are different. Whereas id_tokens are tokens meant to be consumed by the requesting app itself—so the audience of the token is the requestor itself—access tokens are requested by a client that is (most of the time) distinct from the resource it is requesting a token for. You already saw this in action, albeit indirectly, in the calls to `AcquireToken*` for gaining access to the Graph API. You had to pass in the call the identifier of the resource you wanted, which in our case is "https://graph.windows.net". What you have not seen yet is that the same resource identifier is placed by Azure AD in the aud claim from the access token it issues back. The OAuth2 bearer middleware needs to check that incoming tokens carry the correct audience, which is why you are required to set that value in the `ValidAudience` property at initialization. The value you want to put in there has to be one of the identifiers that Azure AD uses for representing your web API app as a resource—that is to say, as a potential recipient of a token. In most of the developer guidance, the value put there is the App ID URI, the value you find in the Azure portal on the Configure tab of the app entry. That corresponds to one of the values from the `identifierURIs` property of the corresponding `Application` object. In our case, the project template generated a unique URI (https://developertenant.onmicrosoft.com/SimpleWebAPI) and used it both while creating the app and for initializing the corresponding value in web.config. Another possible value is the ClientId of the app itself, as you have seen in the OpenID Connect case, or the `appId` property of the `Application` object. In general, all the acceptable audience values for the app are listed in the `servicePrincipalNames` property of the `ServicePrincipal`, which normally is the union of the `identifierURIs` and `appId` property.

> **Important** Azure AD will accept in the token request any of the valid resource identifiers, and will reflect that in the audience. This means that the client must request the exact resource ID that the middleware will set in its `ValidAudience` property; otherwise, the incoming token will be rejected!

From the code generated by the project template wizard you can already see that `ValidAudience` is a property of `TokenValidationParameters`, a class you should already be very familiar with thanks to the detailed analysis of its usage in Chapter 7. The things you learned there about valid values, validation flags, and validators can be applied here as well. That includes what you learned in Chapter 8 about how to use `TokenValidationParameters` for manipulating issuer validation in the case of multitenant apps.

> **Note** One interesting thing is that you don't really need to initialize an entire `TokenValidationParameters` class just to set the audience, because `WindowsAzureActiveDirectoryBearerAuthenticationOptions` offers an equivalent

property directly. You could successfully set a web API without ever knowing that TokenValidationParameters even exists. Why did the template end up using it instead? Long story. Ask me about it if you see me at some conference!

Here's one last thing I want to point your attention to. If you take a look at the sample API controller generated by the template, ValuesController, you'll see that there's a blanket [Authorize] on the entire class. That means that any caller better be authenticated, or they will be denied access. You'll see in a few pages what that means in terms of bits on the wire.

Directory entries

The Application object for the web API contains a default entry in oauth2Permissions, just like you have seen for portal-created web apps in Chapter 8. It's worth taking another quick look at that property here:

```
"oauth2Permissions": [
        {
          "adminConsentDescription": "Allow the application to access SimpleWebAPI on behalf of
the signed-in user.",
          "adminConsentDisplayName": "Access SimpleWebAPI",
          "id": "f41d8346-0715-4728-83f2-6ee1d817167c",
          "isEnabled": true,
          "type": "User",
          "userConsentDescription": "Allow the application to access SimpleWebAPI on your
behalf.",
          "userConsentDisplayName": "Access SimpleWebAPI",
          "value": "user_impersonation"
        }
    ],
```

You've already seen that those are the permissions (in this case permission, singular) that a client can ask for when requesting access to your API. Without an entry in oauth2Permissions, your app could not operate as a web API, which is why Azure AD provides a default one. One thing I have not yet mentioned is that if you want your app and permissions to show up in the drop-down list of potential clients, your application must already have a ServicePrincipal in the same tenant. This is why the web API template provisions one ServicePrincipal for the app directly at creation time.

The value property of an oauth2Permissions entry is especially interesting when you're developing a web API because it holds the value of the scope that a token will carry to indicate it has been granted the corresponding permission. As a web API developer, it is your responsibility to verify the scope values in incoming tokens and decide whether they grant to the caller the right to do with your API what they are attempting to do at the moment. Just to make that operation a bit more interesting, I downloaded the manifest of my web API via the Azure portal, added a new entry, and then uploaded it again. Now it looks like the following:

```
"oauth2Permissions": [
    {
        "adminConsentDescription": "Allow the application to use SimpleWebAPI in write mode.",
        "adminConsentDisplayName": "Use SimpleWebAPI in write mode",
        "id": "ae08ca44-4241-449a-abbf-a9a0e0ce2730",
        "isEnabled": true,
        "type": "User",
        "userConsentDescription": "Allow the application to use SimpleWebAPI in write mode.",
        "userConsentDisplayName": "Use SimpleWebAPI in write mode",
        "value": "SimpleWebAPI.Write"
    },
    {
        "adminConsentDescription": "Allow the application to access SimpleWebAPI on behalf of
the signed-in user.",
        "adminConsentDisplayName": "Access SimpleWebAPI",
        "id": "f41d8346-0715-4728-83f2-6ee1d817167c",
        "isEnabled": true,
        "type": "User",
        "userConsentDescription": "Allow the application to access SimpleWebAPI on your
behalf.",
        "userConsentDisplayName": "Access SimpleWebAPI",
        "value": "user_impersonation"
    }
],
```

I added a new scope, SimpleWebAPI.Write, which is meant to represent the permission one client needs to have to invoke the sample API controller with PUT, POST, and DELETE verbs. You'll see how to do that shortly.

Web APIs and consent

If you are writing a multitenant app, or if you are creating apps as a nonadmin user, you will have to deal with consent. A web API is just like a web app; in fact it *is* a web app from the Azure AD standpoint, but without the benefit of a UX. And without a UX, there's no real opportunity to present the caller with a consent prompt. Technically, you could set up a web sign-in flow just for the purpose of provisioning the ServicePrincipal for the web API . . . but most of the time that's unnatural. The more common approach is to have the user consent for the web API in the context of the consent prompt they are already engaging for provisioning the client application that needs to call the API. In Chapter 8 you encountered the Application property knownClientApplications. If you want the consent for a given client to be capable of prompting for consent for your API as well, be sure to list that client in the knownClientApplications property of the Application object of your API.

Handling web API calls

If you want to see our web API in action, you need to set up a client for it first.

Let's go back to our original sample web application. You need to let Azure AD know that you want the web app to access our web API. In today's portal (https://manage.windowsazure.com/) that's easily done by navigating to the app entry, selecting the Configure tab, scrolling to the section Permissions To Other Applications and clicking the Add Application button.

As I mentioned, I am reluctant to include screenshots in this book because I am nearly certain that screens will change. In today's experience, clicking that button brings up a dialog in which you can choose whether you want your client app to request permissions to access a Microsoft app (Office 365, Power BI, Azure management, Directory Graph API, and so on) or all apps (any web app with a `ServicePrincipal` in your tenant and a nonempty `oauth2Permissions` section). Choose the latter, and locate your web API project. Visual Studio names the app entry in the same way in which you named the Visual Studio project, plus some numeric identifier to avoid collisions: in my case the entry is SimpleWebAPI. Once you find it, select the entry and close the dialog.

The Permissions To Other Applications section now includes an entry for your web API. You might notice that it is displayed in purple because the new setting hasn't been saved yet. Open the corresponding Delegated Permissions drop-down: here you'll find all the permissions defined in the web API manifest. Select them all, and click Save.

Now comes the fun part. I want the web app's permission in the directory to reflect the new requirements. Chapter 8 taught you that if you make the changes while you're signed in to the portal as a directory admin, all the changes are automatically applied to the `ServicePrincipal` as well. If I were signed in as a standard (nonadmin) user, we might need to revoke consent (by visiting myapps. microsoft.com and revoking consent for the web app) before going through the consent experience again.

For simplicity, let's assume that I did everything as an admin and we are good to go. The way to be sure that this is the case is to retrieve the list of grants associated with the app's `Service-Principal` and verify that the right entries are there. The entity I need is "https://graph.windows. net/developertenant.onmicrosoft.com/servicePrincipals/b128da6c-5570-43fa-ab2e-6bc5abb8e6e1/ oauth2PermissionGrants", where b128da6c-5570-43fa-ab2e-6bc5abb8e6e1 is the `objectId` of the `ServicePrincipal`. Here's what I have in there:

```
{
  "odata.metadata": "https://graph.windows.net/developertenant.onmicrosoft.com/$metadata#oauth2
PermissionGrants",
  "value": [
    {
      "clientId": "b128da6c-5570-43fa-ab2e-6bc5abb8e6e1",
      "consentType": "AllPrincipals",
      "expiryTime": "2016-04-09T11:52:54.8020064",
      "objectId": "bNoosXBV-kOrLmvFq7jm4UnIMYJNhOpOkFrsIuF86Y8",
      "principalId": null,
      "resourceId": "8231c849-844d-4eea-905a-ec22e17ce98f",
      "scope": "User.Read",
      "startTime": "0001-01-01T00:00:00"
    },
```

```
{
    "clientId": "b128da6c-5570-43fa-ab2e-6bc5abb8e6e1",
    "consentType": "AllPrincipals",
    "expiryTime": "2016-04-14T23:56:39.9710775",
    "objectId": "bNoosXBV-kOrLmvFq7jm4Ye5XNQ8LzhPkSsr0-GWByM",
    "principalId": null,
    "resourceId": "d45cb987-2f3c-4f38-912b-2bd3e1960723",
    "scope": "SimpleWebAPI.Write user_impersonation",
    "startTime": "0001-01-01T00:00:00"
  }
 ]
}
```

That's exactly what we want. The first entry is the old permission, which allows every user on the tenant to get a token for signing in and for accessing the profile. The second is the permission establishing that every tenant user will also be able to access SimpleWebAPI through the web app, with both permissions granted.

Let's add a bit of code to the web app to make a vanilla call to our web API. In fact, you can reuse the code for invoking the Graph API; you just need to change a couple of lines. Here's the relevant fragment:

```
{
    string ClientId = "c3d5b1ad-ae77-49ac-8a86-dd39a2f91081";
    string Authority = "https://login.microsoftonline.com/DeveloperTenant.onmicrosoft.com";
    string appKey = "a3fQREiyhqpYL10006hfCW+xke/TyP2oIQ6vgu68eoE=";
    //string resourceId = "https://graph.windows.net";
    string resourceId = "https://developertenant.onmicrosoft.com/SimpleWebAPI";
    try
    {
        ClientCredential credential = new ClientCredential(ClientId, appKey);
        AuthenticationContext authContext = new AuthenticationContext(Authority);
        AuthenticationResult result = authContext.AcquireTokenSilent(resourceId,
                                                                     credential,
                                                                     UserIdentifier.AnyUser);
        HttpClient httpClient = new HttpClient();
        httpClient.DefaultRequestHeaders.Authorization =
            new AuthenticationHeaderValue("Bearer", result.AccessToken);
        HttpResponseMessage response =
            //httpClient.GetAsync("https://graph.windows.net/me?api-version=1.6").Result;
            httpClient.GetAsync("https://localhost:44301/api/values").Result;

        if (response.IsSuccessStatusCode)
        {
          //..more stuff
```

The only items that changed are the resource ID of the token we are requesting and the URL of the web API itself (which I got from the property pages of the project in Visual Studio). As expected, the refresh token cached from the Startup invocation of AcquireTokenByAuthorizationCode is a MRRT, capable of obtaining access tokens for any resource the app has been configured to gain access to. If you set up Fiddler and take a look at the traffic, you'll see the same pattern you observed with the calls to the Graph. The only thing that changes is the recipient of the REST call.

Note By default, Fiddler won't capture traffic generated by HttpClient, especially when directed to localhost. There's an awesome trick you can use to fix that: when you initialize your request, instead of passing plain `https://localhost:44301/`, try passing `https://localhost.fiddler:44301/`. Fiddler will now trace that traffic, too. Don't forget to change the address back, or your API calls will fail when Fiddler isn't running.

Before I get to how to handle scopes on the web API side, let's simulate a couple of error situations you are likely to encounter while working with a web API.

First, comment out the client code that adds the Authorization header and try the call again. The API call is going to come back with a 401; the response object will carry a StatusCode 401, and the ReasonPhrase will be the dreaded "Unauthorized." Just as expected, the middleware won't let through any calls not carrying a valid token from the intended issuer.

Let's try something else. Add back the lines that include the token in the request headers, and then go to the web API project. In the web.config file, locate the audience value in AppSettings, and change the value somehow (for example, add some trailing characters). Now go through the call flow again. You'll end up with the same error.

That gives you a taste of a hard truth: diagnosing issues with a web API on the client side is hard. When the bearer token middleware encounters issues, it doesn't usually send back errors; rather, it lets the call proceed without adding to it the identity of the caller. The error message is generated when the execution reaches the controller decorated with [Authorize], and at that point the reason that you weren't able to get a ClaimsPrincipal for an authenticated user is lost. All you know is that the caller is unauthorized, and the message returned to the client reflects that. This means that troubleshooting issues with a web API is best done statically through a series of checks that in my experience catch the vast majority of the issues:

- Does the aud claim in the incoming token match *exactly* (down to casing, trailing slashes, HTTP vs. HTTPS) the value used to initialize ValidAudience (or Audience in the options) in the middleware initialization?

- Does the iss claim in the incoming token match exactly the issuer indicated in the metadata referenced by Tenant or MetadataAddress in the middleware initialization logic? Special attention should be reserved for a multitenant case, as discussed in Chapter 8.

- Is the API route correctly configured for using the OAuth2 bearer middleware, or is it being protected by some other middleware? More about this a bit later.

When all those static checks fail, it's time to turn on tracing or implement some of the validators in TokenValidationParameters just to place some breakpoints.

Another thing that you already know but is worth stressing is how a web API protected via OAuth2 bearer tokens doesn't do much to help you get a token. Whereas a failed request against a web app results in a 302 and a web sign-on request—in other words, an attempt to remediate the situation—here you get a cold 401, an invitation to get your act together in your own client logic. It is up to your code to decide how to react to the 401, and if the reaction entails obtaining a new token, it's up to your code to drive all the token-request work.

> **Note** The OAuth2 bearer token usage specification provides a mechanism for sending back in the 401 response some information that a client can use to understand what the authentication and authorization requirements of the web API are and attempt to comply. The information is sent back in a WWW-Authenticate header and mostly pertains to what scopes the API requires and from which authority. ADAL has some features meant to make it easier for a client to make sense of the WWW-Authenticate header, but it's still up to your code to work with it. Also, you should always be wary of entities suggesting an authority to authenticate against—phishing and token forwarding are constant threats. For more details, see *http://www.cloudidentity.com/blog/2013/11/04/call-a-web-api-without-knowing-in-advance-its-resource-uri-or-what-authority-it-trusts/.*

Processing requests

Let's now take a look at how to process incoming requests, from dealing with scope-driven authorization to performing some common customizations.

Scopes are, as you might imagine, represented as claims. If you fire up Fiddler again and capture an access token (you learned in Chapter 6 how to extract JWTs and their claims content from traces), you should see something such as the following:

```
{
    "acr" : "1",
    "amr" : [ "pwd" ],
    "appid" : "c3d5b1ad-ae77-49ac-8a86-dd39a2f91081",
    "appidacr" : "1",
    "aud" : "https://developertenant.onmicrosoft.com/SimpleWebAPI",
    "exp" : 1445208111,
    "family_name" : "Rossi",
    "given_name" : "Mario",
    "iat" : 1445204211,
    "ipaddr" : "73.169.211.13",
    "iss" : "https://sts.windows.net/6c3d51dd-f0e5-4959-b4ea-a80c4e36fe5e/",
    "name" : "Mario Rossi",
    "nbf" : 1445204211,
    "oid" : "13d3104a-6891-45d2-a4be-82581a8e465b",
    "scp" : "SimpleWebAPI.Write user_impersonation",
    "sub" : "wrFY8NpHyppkDsmTbQVOZXRkkAtT2sIhnU1LoJYvYZU",
    "tid" : "6c3d51dd-f0e5-4959-b4ea-a80c4e36fe5e",
    "unique_name" : "mario@developertenant.onmicrosoft.com",
    "upn" : "mario@developertenant.onmicrosoft.com",
    "ver" : "1.0"
}
```

This does look remarkably similar to the id_token you saw in Figure 6-3 in Chapter 6. The differences I've already mentioned are the audience value (though technically you could use the client_id of the web API, provided that you use it consistently in the token request on the client and in the audience setting on the API) and the presence of a scope (scp) claim. The id_token also has some extra cryptography tricks used for validation (nonce and c_hash), but the middleware takes care of low-level validations, so for our current purposes we can ignore those.

The bearer middleware validates that token and uses it to create a ClaimsPrincipal. However, you might be surprised by how different the two look. To see that, go to the ValuesController class on the API, find the parameterless overload of Get, and add the following line to it:

```
ClaimsPrincipal cp = ClaimsPrincipal.Current;
```

Now place a breakpoint on that line and run the solution again. Once the execution reaches the breakpoint, take a look at the ClaimsPrincipal's Claims list as shown in Figure 9-6.

FIGURE 9-6 The list of claims extracted by the middleware from the incoming access token.

The claim types used in the ClaimsPrincipal are much longer than the ones found in the actual token. In Chapter 1 you learned that this normalization is performed for the purpose of helping you write code that queries claims without worrying about which protocol or token format was used.

Checking the scopes in the API means ensuring that for each of the methods offered, the caller possesses the necessary scopes representing the permissions for accessing the feature. Here's a brute- force example:

```
public IEnumerable<string> Get()
{
    string [] scopes = ClaimsPrincipal.Current.FindFirst(
        "http://schemas.microsoft.com/identity/claims/scope").Value.Split(' ');
    if (scopes.Contains("user_impersonation"))
    {
        return new string[] { "value1", "value2" };
    }
    else
    {
```

```
            throw new HttpResponseException(new HttpResponseMessage {
                StatusCode = HttpStatusCode.Unauthorized,
                ReasonPhrase = "The Scope claim does not contain 'user_impersonation' or scope claim
    not found"
            });
        }
    }

    // ...

    // POST api/values
    public void Post([FromBody]string value)
    {
        string[] scopes = ClaimsPrincipal.Current.FindFirst(
            "http://schemas.microsoft.com/identity/claims/scope").Value.Split(' ');
        if (scopes.Contains("user_impersonation")&& scopes.Contains("SimpleWebAPI.Write"))
        {
            // do stuff
        }
        else
        {
            throw new HttpResponseException(new HttpResponseMessage
            {
                StatusCode = HttpStatusCode.Unauthorized,
                ReasonPhrase = "The Scope claim does not contain 'user_impersonation' and
    'SimpleWebAPI.Write' or scope claim not found"
            });
        }
    }
```

In this case, we impose a rule that every call to any of our actions be performed by applications that have full faculty for impersonating the user, as confirmed by the presence of the user_impersonate scope. For example, this means that calls coming from a web app that acquired tokens through a client-credentials flow would not be able to invoke any actions. Moreover, we impose a rule that all actions that can alter the API's state (here represented by the Post method) can be performed only by a caller presenting the scope SimpleWebAPI.Write as well. If you want to test this, create a new client app and ask only for the user_impersonate permission. You'll see that users going through the new client app will not be able to perform Post calls.

Repeating the scope-verification logic in each and every method might not be the most efficient way of handling the problem. You might consider adding that logic in an AuthorizeAttribute.

Customizations As I mentioned, the presence of TokenValidationParameters in the bearer middleware means that you can apply to a web API all the tricks it enables for web apps. That includes everything described in the "*TokenValidationParameters*" section in Chapter 7 and the features mentioned through Chapter 8 (such as the use of RoleClaimType).

One thing that the bearer middleware lacks is the rich notifications delegates pipeline you encountered studying the OpenID Connect middleware. That's mostly because the idea wasn't fully fleshed out when the bearer token middleware came out—and, in fact, in ASP.NET 5 the new bearer middleware sports notifications as well. However, not everything is lost in Katana 3: there is a mechanism that can be used for injecting your code in the validation flow, and that's by specifying a

Provider. A Provider is an artifact used in the bearer middleware to supply a rudimentary counterpart for notifications. I am reluctant to go too deeply into the details, given that this has already changed in ASP.NET 5, so I hope you'll forgive me if I for once do a bit of cargo cult programming. Suffice to say that specifying a Provider as shown in the following code gives you an opportunity to use `OnValidateIdentity` to make any last-minute changes you want to make to the identity about to be passed to the application. For example, here I am using it to add a custom claim—an analogy with what I did in Chapter 7 in the `SecurityTokenValidated` notification of the OpenID Connect middleware:

```
app.UseWindowsAzureActiveDirectoryBearerAuthentication(
    new WindowsAzureActiveDirectoryBearerAuthenticationOptions
    {
        Tenant = ConfigurationManager.AppSettings["ida:Tenant"],
        TokenValidationParameters = new TokenValidationParameters {
            ValidAudience = ConfigurationManager.AppSettings["ida:Audience"],
        },
        Provider = new OAuthBearerAuthenticationProvider()
        {
            OnValidateIdentity = async context =>
            {
                context.Ticket.Identity.AddClaim(
                    new Claim("http://myclaimtypes/hairlength", "pretty awesome"));
            }
        }
    });
```

Exposing both a web UX and a web API from the same Visual Studio project

Imagine that you have a web application that is meant to be consumed both through a web browser and by active clients such as mobile apps or the code-behind of other web apps.

You can see how this presents an interesting challenge. From the pure REST perspective, all resources are kind of the same, regardless of whether the representation sent back from a given route is meant to be rendered by a browser or parsed programmatically. If you consider the identity angle, however, there are important differences. Consuming a resource through a web browser entails the usual dance of 302s, token requests and responses performed by jerking the browser around, and session cookies. Conversely, consuming a web API entails sending an access token every time, obtaining that token out of band, and dealing with 401s and 403s when the API isn't satisfied with the token it receives. Say that an unauthenticated user requests a given route. Should you trigger a 302 with a sign-in request? That wouldn't make sense for a programmatic client. Should you send back a 401? That would cut the navigation experience short.

Very well. Maybe having individual routes that work for both consumption models is problematic; however, you should at least be able to partition your app into routes meant to serve back UX and routes meant to expose an API. This is the moment for which all the deep study of the Katana pipeline you did in Chapter 7 pays off! Consider the following middleware initialization pipeline:

```
public void ConfigureAuth(IAppBuilder app)
{
    app.SetDefaultSignInAsAuthenticationType(CookieAuthenticationDefaults.AuthenticationType);
    app.UseCookieAuthentication(new CookieAuthenticationOptions());
    app.UseOpenIdConnectAuthentication(
        new OpenIdConnectAuthenticationOptions
        {
            ClientId = "c3d5b1ad-ae77-49ac-8a86-dd39a2f91081",
            Authority = "https://login.microsoftonline.com/DeveloperTenant.onmicrosoft.com"
        }
    );
    app.UseWindowsAzureActiveDirectoryBearerAuthentication(
        new WindowsAzureActiveDirectoryBearerAuthenticationOptions
        {
            Tenant = ConfigurationManager.AppSettings["ida:Tenant"],
            TokenValidationParameters = new TokenValidationParameters {
                ValidAudience = ConfigurationManager.AppSettings["ida:Audience"]
            },
            AuthenticationType = "OAuth2Bearer",
        });
```

This pipeline includes the cookie, OpenID Connect, and OAuth2 bearer middlewares. The first two are initialized as usual, and coupled together by the same AuthenticationType. The highlighted line shows that you change the AuthenticationType of the bearer middleware to a unique value, OAuth2Bearer. You can use that value from resources to elect to work with this specific middleware. For a web API, this is done through the HostAuthenticationFilter attribute.

HostAuthenticationFilter lives in the Microsoft.AspNet.WebApi.Owin NuGet package. You can use it for decorating the actions or controllers you want to use as an API. Passing to it a specific AuthenticationType will cause the user's principal to be set from the corresponding middleware. Assuming that your app has a ValueController like the web API we've been playing with so far, you'll want to decorate it as follows:

```
[HostAuthentication("OAuth2Bearer")]
[Authorize]
public class ValuesController : ApiController
{
//...
```

All the other routes with [Authorize] alone will keep working with a browser as usual.

A web API calling another API: Flowing the identity of the caller and using "on behalf of"

It is exceedingly common for an API to have to call another API as part of implementing its functions.

The client credentials grant is an option, although it has the shortcoming of creating a trusted subsystem: the client API accesses the resource API always with the same rights regardless of the user accessing the client API—so enforcing what that user can or cannot do is left to the client API instead of relying on the directory. Another limitation of the client credentials approach is that granting consent for application permissions always requires administrator consent, which might not be ideal if you want to maximize the reach of your solution.

The section "More API consumption scenarios" in Chapter 2 introduced another approach to address this scenario, the on-behalf-of flow defined by the OAuth2 Token Exchange extensions (which you can find at *https://tools.ietf.org/html/draft-ietf-oauth-token-exchange-02*). If you want to refresh your knowledge of the approach, turn back to Chapter 2 and refer to Figure 2-9.

Let's take a look at the code required to make the on-behalf-of flow work. Ultimately, the client API needs to send to the authority the access token it receives from its caller, along with the client API's credentials and the resourceId of the API it wants to access. The authority is expected to examine the request and issue a new access token scoped for the new API, which the client API can use for gaining access. The operation is summarized in the diagram in Figure 9-7.

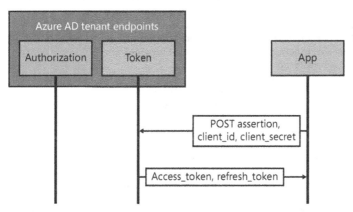

FIGURE 9-7 Swim-lane diagram of the token request call in the on-behalf-of flow, as detailed in the OAuth2 Token Exchange extensions specification.

Let's modify our sample API to perform a call to the Graph on behalf of the caller. The first step is to retrieve the bits of the access token that our client sent to our API so that our API can use the original access token to request a new access token for accessing the next layer. We already know that the content of the incoming access token is deserialized in ClaimsPrincipal.Current, but that's not good enough: we need the original, unmodified token bits so that the authority can examine them (and possibly recheck signatures and so on). Since .NET 4.5, the .NET Framework features a mechanism for preserving the bits of tokens used for gaining access to the current app: it is simply an option in the authentication pipeline. In the Katana middleware, that option is driven by the SaveSigninToken property of TokenValidationParameters. You activate it by setting it to true, as shown here:

```
app.UseWindowsAzureActiveDirectoryBearerAuthentication(
    new WindowsAzureActiveDirectoryBearerAuthenticationOptions
    {
        Tenant = ConfigurationManager.AppSettings["ida:Tenant"],
        TokenValidationParameters = new TokenValidationParameters {
            ValidAudience = ConfigurationManager.AppSettings["ida:Audience"],
            SaveSigninToken = true,
        },
```

SaveSigninToken is false by default. That does not have much of an impact on web API scenarios, but for web sign-on cases (in the OpenID Connect hybrid flow, the token to save would be the id_token), the token bits would increase the session cookie size, so we keep ahold on the original token only when needed.

Now take a look at the code you might add to the Get action of our sample API for enabling it to invoke the Graph API on behalf of the original caller:

```
public IEnumerable<string> Get()
{
    string [] scopes = ClaimsPrincipal.Current.FindFirst(
        "http://schemas.microsoft.com/identity/claims/scope").Value.Split(' ');
    if (scopes.Contains("user_impersonation"))
    {
        var bootstrapContext = ClaimsPrincipal.Current.Identities.First().BootstrapContext
                            as System.IdentityModel.Tokens.BootstrapContext;
        string userName = ClaimsPrincipal.Current.FindFirst(ClaimTypes.Upn) != null ?
            ClaimsPrincipal.Current.FindFirst(ClaimTypes.Upn).Value :
            ClaimsPrincipal.Current.FindFirst(ClaimTypes.Email).Value;
        string userAccessToken = bootstrapContext.Token;
        UserAssertion userAssertion = new UserAssertion(
                                        bootstrapContext.Token,
                                        "urn:ietf:params:oauth:grant-type:jwt-bearer",
                                        userName);
        ClientCredential clientCred = new ClientCredential(
                ConfigurationManager.AppSettings["ida:ClientID"],
                ConfigurationManager.AppSettings["ida:Password"]);
        AuthenticationContext authContext = new AuthenticationContext(
                    "https://login.microsoftonline.com/DeveloperTenant.onmicrosoft.com");
        AuthenticationResult result =
            authContext.AcquireToken("https://graph.windows.net", clientCred, userAssertion);

        // ...more stuff
```

As usual, the code is pretty rough—for example, I am not setting up a persistent cache as I should, given that we're on the server side—but it should clarify how to deal with this flow.

The token is saved in the BootstrapContext property of ClaimsIdentity: this allows your code to gain access to the token bits in a fashion that's independent of protocol and token format, instead of you having to worrying about whether you should search for the token in a header or in the body of a POST. That's what the statement assigning boostrapContext is about.

Once you have the original token, you need to use the ADAL object model to manufacture a UserAssertion. This class is meant to wrap the bits of the original token to be sent to the authority, augmenting them with some extra information such as the token type and the user to which the token was issued in the first place. The information about the user is important. Given that ADAL is a token-requestor library, it does not know anything about access token formats, so it cannot inspect the original token content—however, ADAL needs to know for which user you are requesting a new token so that it can look up the cache in case a suitable token that fits the bill already exists.

The request to the authority must pair the UserAssertion with the client API's own credentials: if that was not required, any rogue obtaining one access token would be able to mint new access tokens at will. The credentials are represented by the usual ClientCredentials class.

Finally, the call for retrieving the new access token is a simple overload of the AcquireToken method. As soon as you get the result back, you can extract the access token from it and use it as shown earlier in the chapter. Moreover, the cache is now primed with both the new access token and a new refresh token for the client_id of the client API, so subsequent calls don't necessarily need to hit the network again.

Now let's take a look at the generated traffic. Fire up Fiddler and run through the scenario. As soon as execution hits the AcquireToken call, you'll capture something along the lines of the following:

```
POST https://login.microsoftonline.com/DeveloperTenant.onmicrosoft.com/oauth2/token HTTP/1.1
Content-Type: application/x-www-form-urlencoded
client-request-id: a97cd78d-f147-45d0-b64b-59ea4a99b916
return-client-request-id: true
x-client-SKU: .NET
x-client-Ver: 2.19.0.0
x-client-CPU: x64
x-client-OS: Microsoft Windows NT 10.0.10240.0
Host: login.microsoftonline.com
Content-Length: 1626
Expect: 100-continue
Connection: Keep-Alive

resource=https%3A%2F%2Fgraph.windows.net&
client_id=fdb34bf3-74e6-4da7-bf97-de4cb664e261&
client_secret=z5qE%2Bs2gnDkA8R8TGzisjh4EfSP1ZPjCw9EU7ZVtp7Y%3D&
grant_type=urn%3Aietf%3Aparams%3Aoauth%3Agrant-type%3Ajwt-bearer&
assertion=eyJ0eXA[...SNIP...]YBWg&
requested_token_use=on_behalf_of&
scope=openid
```

The parameters that are sent are pretty much what you'd expect: client_id, client_secret, the assertion itself, the grant_type, and requested_token_use=on_behalf_of as dictated by the OAuth2 Token Exchange spec. The scope parameter is perhaps the only surprise. It is included so that the token endpoint will also send back an id_token—an id_token containing user information that ADAL uses for creating the correct cache entry for the resulting tokens.

And now look at what you find in the response:

```
HTTP/1.1 200 OK
Cache-Control: no-cache, no-store
Pragma: no-cache
Content-Type: application/json; charset=utf-8
Expires: -1
Server: Microsoft-IIS/8.5
x-ms-request-id: bbfbc87c-4dd0-43e6-a32f-d7c5f9c5e0e1
client-request-id: a97cd78d-f147-45d0-b64b-59ea4a99b916
x-ms-gateway-service-instanceid: ESTSFE_IN_228
X-Content-Type-Options: nosniff
Strict-Transport-Security: max-age=31536000; includeSubDomains
```

```
P3P: CP="DSP CUR OTPi IND OTRi ONL FIN"
Set-Cookie: flight-uxoptin=true; path=/; secure; HttpOnly
Set-Cookie: x-ms-gateway-slice=productiona; path=/; secure; HttpOnly
Set-Cookie: stsservicecookie=ests; path=/; secure; HttpOnly
X-Powered-By: ASP.NET
Date: Mon, 19 Oct 2015 02:43:57 GMT
Content-Length: 3017
```

```
{"token_type":"Bearer","expires_in":"3898","scope":"Directory.Read User.Read","expires_
on":"1445226536","not_before":"1445222337","resource":"https://graph.windows.net","pwd_
exp":"101826","pwd_url":"https://portal.microsoftonline.com/ChangePassword.aspx","access_
token":"eyJOeXA[...SNIP...]IvNq4w","refresh_token":"AAABA[...SNIP...]wtyAA","id_token":"eyJ0[...
SNIP...] CJ9."}
```

As predicted, you get back a new token triplet. But how do you know that the token you get back is actually for the Graph? Well, using it successfully would be a pretty good indication, but just to be on the safe side, let's decode the access token and verify that it's what we expected:

```
{
    "acr" : "1",
    "amr" : [ "pwd" ],
    "appid" : "fdb34bf3-74e6-4da7-bf97-de4cb664e261",
    "appidacr" : "1",
    "aud" : "https://graph.windows.net",
    "exp" : 1445226536,
    "family_name" : "Rossi",
    "given_name" : "Mario",
    "iat" : 1445222337,
    "ipaddr" : "73.169.211.13",
    "iss" : "https://sts.windows.net/6c3d51dd-f0e5-4959-b4ea-a80c4e36fe5e/",
    "name" : "Mario Rossi",
    "nbf" : 1445222337,
    "oid" : "13d3104a-6891-45d2-a4be-82581a8e465b",
    "puid" : "10037FFE894016DA",
    "scp" : "Directory.Read User.Read",
    "sub" : "VD3MBzqKX_DFcJjwq5K9xa1ODW5AXYNgnci589pLLb8",
    "tid" : "6c3d51dd-f0e5-4959-b4ea-a80c4e36fe5e",
    "unique_name" : "mario@developertenant.onmicrosoft.com",
    "upn" : "mario@developertenant.onmicrosoft.com",
    "ver" : "1.0"
}
```

The token does carry the information for the original user, the one who invoked the web app that invoked our web API, which in turn is about to invoke the Graph as the same user. The appid corresponds to the client_id of the client API, so we are good there. To be extra certain about distinguishing the various tokens, I changed the resources and permissions requested by the client API to include Directory.Read, an extra permission with respect to the other project in the solution. Sure enough, the extra entry appears in the scope.

The on-behalf-of flow is an extremely powerful one. This is a simple sample, probably the simplest you can encounter. I encourage you to experiment with different combinations of APIs, permissions, client types, and consent models to explore the boundaries of what can be accomplished with it.

Protecting a web API with ADFS "3"

As you learned in Chapter 3, "Introducing Azure Active Directory and Active Directory Federation Services," ADFS "3" introduced the ability for native clients to obtain access tokens for invoking web APIs. ADFS happens to be using JWT as the format for its access tokens too, which means that most of the infrastructure of the bearer middleware can be used for securing tokens coming from ADFS as well.

It might come as a surprise to you that, in fact, despite the extension method `UseWindows-AzureActiveDirectoryBearerAuthentication,` there is no such thing as a specialized Azure AD OAuth2 bearer token middleware. That extension method provides Azure AD–specific ways to supply the authority metadata, but the validation coordinates are fed to another extension method, `UseOAuthBearerAuthentication`. That method ultimately instantiates a more generic OAuth2 middleware, `OAuthBearerAuthenticationMiddleware`, which implements a generic JWT-based OAuth2 bearer token interceptor and validator.

Something similar applies to ADFS. There is a different extension method, `ActiveDirectory-FederationServicesBearerAuthentication`, which is typically initialized with an `Audience` and a `MetadataAddress`, the latter pointing to the WS-Federation metadata document of the ADFS instance you work with. Something like the following:

```
app.UseActiveDirectoryFederationServicesBearerAuthentication(
    new ActiveDirectoryFederationServicesBearerAuthenticationOptions
    {
        Audience = "https://myservices/myAPI",
        MetadataEndpoint = "https://sts.contoso.com/federationmetadata/2007-06/
federationmetadata.xml"
    });
```

That's all you need to do to configure the OAuth2 bearer middleware to validate tokens from ADFS. In fact, you can do this even more quickly—all you need to do is choose the on-premises option of the authentication settings when using the web API project template in Visual Studio 2013 or 2015. The template will generate this code for you.

One area where ADFS is stiffer than Azure AD is how applications are provisioned. They both strictly require an app to be registered before any token can be issued for it, but whereas Azure AD has API and consent flows for that process, ADFS mandates that every app be created by an administrator. That can be done through the management console or with PowerShell. Just to give you an example, here's a command you can use for provisioning a web API:

```
Add-ADFSRelyingPartyTrust -Name MyWebAPI -Identifier https://myservices/myAPI
-IssuanceAuthorizationRules '=> issue(Type = "http://schemas.microsoft.com/authorization/claims/
permit", Value = "true");' -IssuanceTransformRules 'c:[Type == "http://schemas.xmlsoap.org/
ws/2005/05/identity/claims/emailaddress"] => issue(claim = c);'
```

In plain English, this command creates a new relying party trust, which is to say it tells ADFS about one new app to issue tokens and claims for. As part of that, it also establishes that tokens for that app should contain one single claim, http://schemas.xmlsoap.org/ws/2005/05/identity/claims/emailaddress.

ADFS "3" OAuth2 support is limited to public clients—native and mobile apps that do not have their own credentials. As such, I cannot adapt the web app sample we've been using in this chapter to give the web app a test run—the web app is a confidential client and must use its credentials when going through the code grant flow, but ADFS "3" won't accept it. The good news is that ADFS in Windows Server 2016 will work with confidential clients, too.

Summary

The ability to invoke an API is a feature of paramount importance for modern web applications. For the same device, making your resources available to all sorts of clients via the REST API, while maintaining robust and flexible authentication capabilities, is table stakes in today's mobile-first, cloud-first market.

This chapter walked you through some of the most fundamental topologies involving web APIs and Azure AD. To understand how things unfold, you had to recall many of the topics you've studied throughout the book: how protocols work; how OWIN middleware extensibility operates; and how Azure AD represents applications, grants and denies permissions, and exposes its own capabilities in the form of the Graph API. I hope you've started to reap a good return for your hard work so far!

CHAPTER 10

Active Directory Federation Services in Windows Server 2016 Technical Preview 3

In the summer of 2015, Microsoft released the third technical preview of Windows Server 2016. That version comes with a special present—a new and improved ADFS, which offers support for OpenID Connect and the full gamut of the OAuth2 grants you've been learning about in this book.

In this chapter I am going to give you a quick overview of the new ADFS, focusing mostly on the modern authentication functionalities. I will not go very deep into anything, given that Windows Server 2016 is still a preview (so prone to breaking changes before reaching general availability). However, I will at least walk you through one concrete scenario, showing you how to implement web sign-on with ADFS via OpenID Connect. Not surprisingly, the code used with ADFS is nearly identical to the code you wrote against Azure AD.

Setup (for developers)

From Chapter 3, "Introducing Azure Active Directory and Active Directory Federation Services," you know that ADFS is a Windows Server role, which augments Active Directory with higher-level protocol capabilities. That means that before you can set up ADFS, you have to set up Active Directory itself.

Giving detailed Active Directory and ADFS deployment guidance goes well beyond the scope of a book for developers, but I don't think it's a good idea to put in printed form the cowboy setup process I go through. I am not an administrator: I somehow stumble through the Active Directory setup and end up with something that works well enough to code against, but I am sure that in the process I make all sorts of horrible mistakes that would be unacceptable on a production system. Add the fact that Windows Server 2016 is still in preview and things are likely to change.

I could always point you to the official deployment documentation, which is guaranteed to be correct, but that is not always practical for nonadmins such as myself, and possibly you. Here's a compromise: back in August I wrote a blog post that contains step-by-step instructions for setting up a Hyper-V virtual machine with Windows Server 2016 Technical Preview 3, Active Directory, and ADFS.

You can find it at *http://www.cloudidentity.com/blog/2015/08/21/openid-connect-web-sign-on-with-adfs-in-windows-server-2016-tp3/.* I still advise you to refer to the official documentation, but if you get lost and want something simpler for nonproduction systems, take a look at my blog.

The new management UX

Traditionally, ADFS has operated with two primitives: identity provider trust (defining which identity providers can send tokens to the ADFS instance) and relying party trust (defining which apps can be a recipient of tokens issued by the ADFS instance).

ADFS "3" introduced a new entity, the client. A client was defined as one particular entity, entitled to perform a single operation: engaging with ADFS "3"'s OAuth2 endpoints to obtain an access token for an application provisioned in ADFS as a relying party trust. However, the new primitive didn't make it to the management console, which remained largely the same as the one in ADFS 2.x (besides new features such as device registration and access, which added new knobs for existing protocol flows).

ADFS in Windows Server 2016 changes all that, introducing an all-new UX section dedicated to modern authentication topologies. Figure 10-1 shows the new UX.

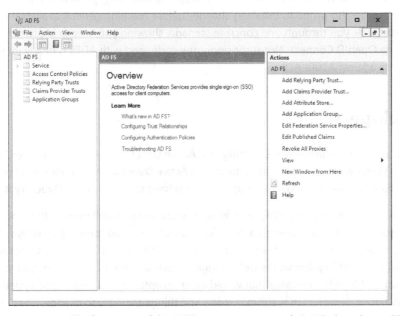

FIGURE 10-1 The first screen of the ADFS management console in Windows Server 2016 Technical Preview 3.

The notable new entry here is the last folder, Application Groups. You can think of application groups as templates, representing typical application topologies used in modern authentication. To see the groups offered by ADFS at this time, click Add Application Group in the Actions pane on the right. Figure 10-2 shows the available options.

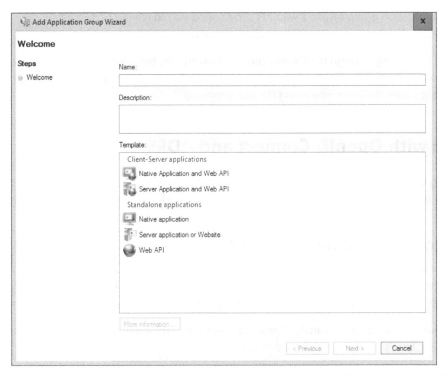

FIGURE 10-2 The application group types available in ADFS in Windows Server 2016 Technical Preview 3.

Perhaps a tad démodé in its terminology, the Client-Server Applications section provides you with a way to create in a single swoop one entry in ADFS for a token-requestor app and an entry for a resource app. ADFS will be configured out of the box to allow the token-requestor app to ask for tokens for the resource app in the same application group.

The two available templates have self-explanatory names. Native Application And Web API creates a public client and a corresponding API; Server Application And Web API creates a confidential client and a corresponding API. Given that this book is about web applications, you might expect us to work with the latter, but, in fact, we'll use neither here. For the sake of clarity, I will separate my description of setting up web sign-on from a discussion about enabling a web app to invoke a web API.

The standalone application templates help you to create single nodes of solution topologies. I'll ignore the Native Application template and focus on the other two. Server Application Or Website is your classic confidential client, be it a website or a daemon application. You'll see that ADFS introduces a special flavor of this that makes sense only on-premises. The Web API template is kind of an incomplete web application—at least if you only use the UX. It is designed to be a recipient of requests secured via OAuth2 bearer token, and the setup constrains the settings you can add to that use case. I'll go into this in reasonable detail.

It's important to note that the applications provisioned via old relying party trust are separate and distinct from the ones created via application groups. In the preview there is no easy way of having a client from an application group invoke a web API provisioned via old relying party trust. It is perfectly possible that such behavior will be maintained once Windows Server 2016 ships.

I could keep spelunking through the UX and comment on entries, but my bias for action pushes me to get to work right away. Let's set up a web app to use ADFS for web sign-on via OpenID Connect; we'll encounter the most interesting UX along the way.

Web sign-on with OpenID Connect and ADFS

As usual, setting up an app to rely on an external provider for authentication entails two steps: working on the app's code and provisioning the app with the provider.

OpenID Connect middleware and ADFS

The code necessary to hook up a web app to ADFS for performing OpenID Connect–based web sign-on is practically the same as you have already internalized for working with Azure AD. The main differences lie in from where you obtain the values you pass to the middleware at initialization time.

Assuming that you are using the vanilla OpenID Connect sign-on sample web app from Chapter 5 as a starting point, here's what you need to do in the code:

Head to App_Start/Startup.Auth.cs and work on the first few basic properties initialized in OpenIdConnectAuthenticationOptions.

Delete the assignment to Authority, given that here our authority will be an ADFS instance as opposed to an Azure AD tenant.

Next, change the assignment of PostLogoutRedirectUri to an assignment for RedirectUri, using the same value (the root URL of the application). ADFS does not support sign-out in this preview release, so you can get rid of that part. However, you do need to specify a value for RedirectUri. Although Azure AD will accept requests without a redirect _uri (and use one that was preregistered for that client_id), ADFS decided to go the other way and always mandate the presence of one explicit redirect_uri. That certainly eliminates ambiguity (if your app has many redirect_uri values, you can never be certain of which one Azure AD will pick up), but it does require just a bit more work.

You can keep the current ClientId value or change it, it's up to you. Whereas Azure AD assigns you a client_id at provisioning, ADFS allows you to override the self-generated client_id at registration time with your custom client_id value.

That takes care of storing the application's coordinates; now it's time to provide information about the ADFS instance you want to work with. ADFS is equipped with the usual arsenal of OAuth2 and OpenID Connect endpoints. You can find the complete list through the UX by using the left side navigation pane to reach the ADFS/Service/Endpoints folder. If you scroll all the way to the bottom of the endpoints list, you'll notice the OAuth2 endpoints (or endpoint) at the end of the token issuance section and the OpenID Connect endpoints under the section with that name. For your reference, those endpoints normally look like the following:

https://<hostname>/adfs/oauth2/ (applies to both token and authorization endpoints)

https://<hostname>adfs/.well-known/openid-configuration

https://<hostname>/adfs/discovery/keys

https://<hostname>/adfs/userinfo

From Chapter 7, "The OWIN OpenID Connect middleware," you know that you can initialize the OpenID Connect middleware by passing the address of the discovery endpoint; here, we are going to pick from the preceding list the URL of this ADFS instance's discovery document and assign it to the MetadataAddress property.

Your initialization code should look like the following:

```
app.UseOpenIdConnectAuthentication(
    new OpenIdConnectAuthenticationOptions
    {
        ClientId = "98ff52e2-6deb-4029-99e4-6c15486d9c56",
        RedirectUri = "https://localhost:44320/",
        MetadataAddress =
            "https://ws2016tp3.vibrodomain.net/adfs/.well-known/openid-configuration",
//..more stuff
```

It is worth stressing that functionally this is nearly equivalent to what you did for connecting Azure AD. Instead of using Authority for communicating data about the trusted issuer, here you specify the discovery document location directly via MetadataAddress. You don't include a sign-out URL because it isn't supported yet.

Those are all the code changes you need, apart from disabling all the gestures for sign-out or adapting them to use only the cookie middleware.

Setting up a web app in ADFS

Eventually, we want to have a web app that handles web sign-on and invokes an API. As mentioned earlier, ADFS provides a template that depicts that exact topology—however, I don't want you to have to do too many things before seeing the app work. For that reason, we'll start with a standalone application group representing just the web app. We'll extend it appropriately later on.

Head to the Application Groups section. In the Actions section in the right pane you should see the Add Application Group link. Click it, and then choose Server Application Or Website from the Stand-alone Applications section. You'll notice that the left side of the dialog now displays a list of steps, and the dialog buttons become wizard controls. Let's see what you need to do screen by screen.

 Note In this chapter I have relaxed my self-imposed rule against screenshots. Although the ADFS version I am describing here is still in preview and the screens can still change,

I felt that the more freeform layout of the ADFS UX would have been too awkward to describe without any visual aids.

On the welcome page, shown in Figure 10-3, enter one application name that you'll remember. I am calling my app "Simple ADFS web app." Once you've done that, click Next.

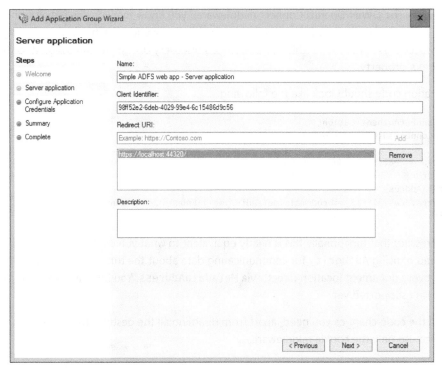

FIGURE 10-3 The first screen of the web application creation wizard gathers essential protocol coordinates of the application.

The Server Application screen shown in Figure 10-3 gathers all the information about your app that's required to perform the sign-in protocol dance. The Client Identifier field holds the client_id, discussed earlier. If you were following the instructions, here you have to paste the value you used in the middleware initialization code.

The Redirect URI field holds the list of the URLs to which ADFS is allowed to return tokens. A typical rookie mistake here is to paste the address in the text box and not click Add; your job isn't finished until you have at least one URL in this list. Once you are done, click Next. You'll see the Configure Application Credentials screen, shown in Figure 10-4.

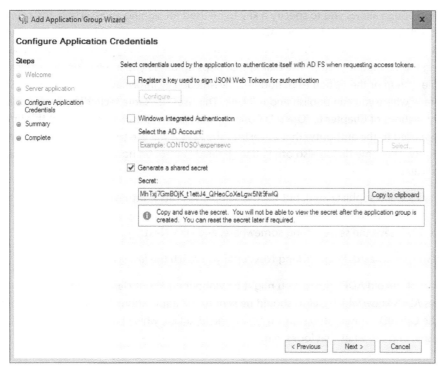

FIGURE 10-4 The application credentials screen offers you various options to provision credentials for your web app.

The Configure Application Credentials screen is one of the areas where the difference between Azure AD and ADFS is the most significant. You can see this in Figure 10-4.

You don't need to assign an application credential for supporting web sign-on, but you will need it later on for calling the web API. But because we are already here, we can just as well explore the options now.

At the bottom of the page you can see the section dedicated to the generation of a shared secret. This is the near-perfect analogy to the corresponding functionality in the Azure AD portal. The approach you are expected to follow for dealing with secrets is the same, too: you are able to see the secret bits only at creation time, and then they're invisible forever. If you don't save the secret or if you lose it, your only recourse is to create a new secret.

In the middle of the page you are offered the option to define a type of application credential that is unique to ADFS, Windows Integrated Authentication. If your app's process is running as a given account—as might be the case for a Windows service, for example—you can use that fact to fulfill the credential obligations of OAuth2 and OpenID Connect flows for confidential clients. Very neat.

Finally, the top option allows you to specify a key to be used for signing an assertion, the counterpart of the certificate credentials in Azure AD. Although in Azure AD using this credential requires you to use PowerShell cmdlets and X.509 certificates, ADFS offers a full range of options that you can reach by clicking the Configure button. The dialog that pops up offers you a selection of certificate files from the file system or the option to periodically download key information from a JWKS (JSON Web Keys set) feed where you can publish and roll keys. This uses the same technology you studied in the discovery sections of Chapter 6, "OpenID Connect and Azure AD web sign-on," but this time it is the app (as opposed to the authority) that advertises the keys it will use to sign tokens to prove its application identity. The same dialog also offers fine-grained control on how to perform revocation checks on certificates.

That's all very nice and sophisticated, but for this sample we'll stick with what's simple. The shared secret is the credential type we'll use in the next section: select the corresponding check box, as shown in Figure 10-4, save the secret string somewhere, and click Next.

We're done with the wizard. Keep clicking Next until you reach the last screen.

If you are part of the old ADFS guard, you might be wondering about claim issuance rules at this point. How does ADFS know which claims should be sent to the application? The answer is that the token sent in the OpenID connect web sign-on flow is the id_token, which has a fixed structure. Let's give the app a spin and see what that looks like.

Testing the web sign-on feature

Fire up Fiddler, go back to Visual Studio, and hit F5. Click the Sign In link as usual. You'll be led through the ADFS credential-gathering experience, which at this point in time has a very similar look and feel to the one served by Azure AD. Enter the credentials of one of the users from the Active Directory instance where ADFS is set up. You'll see that the sign-in concludes just like the one you experienced with Azure AD.

> **Note** If you are on an intranet and are using Internet Explorer or Microsoft Edge, your credential-gathering experience might be different because the DNS will resolve to the ADFS authentication endpoints using Kerberos. An easy way of taking that aspect out of the equation is to debug by using Chrome or Firefox.

If you take a look at the traffic captured in Fiddler, you'll see the usual dance: middleware reaching out to the discovery document, retrieval of the keys, authorization request to the authorization endpoint, automatic POST to the app with the id_token and code, a 302 for setting the session cookies, and finally a 200. Business as usual.

If you peek at the `id_token`, however, you'll find it significantly skinnier than the one issued by Azure AD:

```
{
    "aud" : "98ff52e2-6deb-4029-99e4-6c15486d9c56",
    "auth_time" : 1445677071,
    "c_hash" : "5h5QGlrTWmSUxVHO9sf5AQ",
    "exp" : 1445680671,
    "iat" : 1445677071,
    "iss" : "https://WS2016TP3.vibrodomain.net/adfs",
    "nonce" : "635812738685261506.MDczY2RkYzAtMzEyNyO0YjRiLWJkZDUtZTdjNTMxNjZlZjkzNm Y4ZDc3OTTctN2
QOMCOOYzYxLWJlOGYtMzdhZGUwMmRlZjk2",
    "sub" : "/P6RGnF6Q9FbVfyjFY6whvkQIbzQR4z2WurnPHfUSME=",
    "unique_name" : "VIBRODOMAIN\\mario",
    "upn" : "mario@vibrodomain.net"
}
```

That is pretty bare-bones, but it's all it takes to sign on with the web application. Very easy!

Protecting a web API with ADFS and invoking it from a web app

Let's complete our topology by adding a web API to our solution.

Setting up a web API in ADFS

Head back to the ADFS management UX, and specifically to the Application Groups section.

Double-click the entry for the application group you created in the earlier section. ADFS will display a dialog with the list of all the applications in the group, which at the moment includes only the sample web application we worked on. At the bottom of the dialog you'll find the Add Application button. Click it, and you'll land on a dialog that looks just like the first screen of the wizard we used earlier for creating the web app; the only difference is that the list of templates here is limited to the standalone app types. Select Web API, and then click Next.

The first screen, shown in Figure 10-5, gathers the essential protocol coordinates describing your web API.

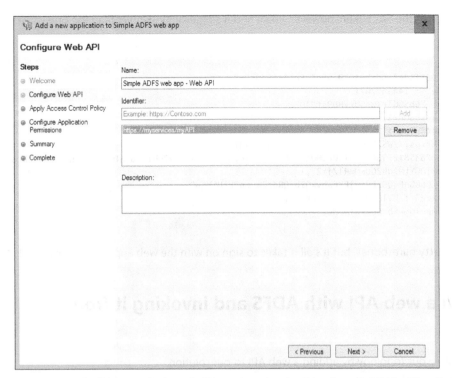

FIGURE 10-5 The first screen in the web API creation wizard gathers the web API identifiers that will be used to request tokens and populate the audience claim in tokens issued for the API.

The only setting of notice here is the Identifier list. That holds the strings that ADFS will use for recognizing that a token request is meant to grant access to this particular API. That is also the string that will end up in the audience claim of the issued token, that the actual web API (or better, its middleware) will have to validate. Given that I am fundamentally lazy, I plan to reuse the web API project described in the ADFS section of Chapter 9, "Consuming and exposing a web API protected by Azure Active Directory," so here I need to specify the same audience value, https://myservices/myAPI.

One interesting note is that ADFS does not ask you to specify a URL for the web API. It is true that such a URL doesn't really come into play when you implement the OAuth2 bearer token usage flow. At the same time, in Chapter 9 we considered the possibility of web apps exposing both API and browser-ready routes serving back UX. In this preview, ADFS does not allow you to create a single app to fulfill both the web API and web app roles, as the latter would require you to specify a URL (and a client_id, too). There is an easy workaround: you can simply create two different entries in ADFS, one for the API and the other for the UX.

Once you have added at least one identifier, click Next. You'll come to a page that offers you the chance to define who can access your API and how. Figure 10-6 has the scoop.

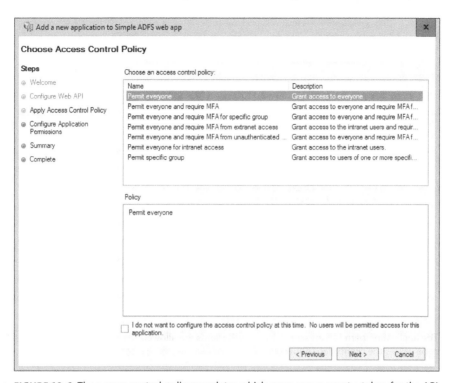

FIGURE 10-6 The access control policy regulates which users can request a token for the API.

All the access policies offered out of the box are quite self-explanatory. Given that most options there would require more setup work, I am just going to go with Permit Everyone. That applies only to the token-issuance operation, of course. The API is still responsible for inspecting incoming tokens for validation and authorization purposes.

After you select Permit Everyone, click Next. You'll reach the application permissions section, shown in Figure 10-7.

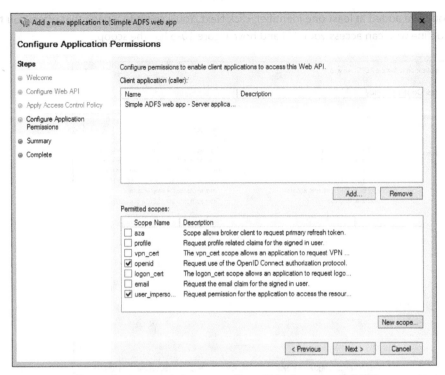

FIGURE 10-7 The application permissions screen lists which clients are allowed to request tokens for the API and the possible scope values the clients can request.

This screen summarizes which client apps are allowed to request this ADFS instance for the web API we are provisioning and what scopes clients are allowed to request.

I will defer the discussion about callers to the end of the chapter. Here it should be enough to say that given we are creating this API in the same application group, the sample web API is automatically listed as an allowed client.

The Permitted Scopes section lists all the scopes that a client is allowed to request. Note that a client is free to request a subset of these. Here I am picking up both openid and user_impersonation.

If your web API has its own scopes, it is easy to add them as custom ones. Click New Scope. You will be prompted to add a scope through the dialog shown in Figure 10-8.

FIGURE 10-8 The dialog used for creating new scopes.

Here I am adding a fictitious scope, representing the ability of calling the API with HTTP verbs that can change its state. This is the same approach discussed in Chapter 9, and on the web API side the code validating the presence of the required scopes looks just like the code you used against Azure AD. Once you create the new scope, you'll find it in the Permitted Scopes list.

Click Next all the way to the end of the wizard. As you exit, you'll see that your application group now counts a new member—your web API.

Code for obtaining an access token from ADFS and invoking a web API

The code for requesting an access token for our web API from ADFS is different from the code used with Azure AD in a couple of small but important ways.

First, ADFS requires that you have already provided information about the resource you want to access at the time of the web sign-on request, the one against the authorization endpoint. Here's how the basic initialization code changes:

```
app.UseOpenIdConnectAuthentication(
    new OpenIdConnectAuthenticationOptions
    {
        ClientId = "98ff52e2-6deb-4029-99e4-6c15486d9c56",
        RedirectUri = "https://localhost:44320/",
        MetadataAddress =
            "https://ws2016tp3.vibrodomain.net/adfs/.well-known/openid-configuration",
        Resource = "https://myservices/myAPI",
        Scope = "openid profile user_impersonation MyService.Write",
//..more stuff
```

In a nutshell, you need to specify which resource you want an access token for, and you need to specify which scopes your client app needs. Note that given you want to also get an id_token for signing the user in to the web app, you always want to specify the openid scope. That will have the (not always fully intentional) effect of including the openid connect scope in the access token, too. The need to specify up front the resource you want a token for might concern you, especially if your client needs to call multiple APIs. The good news is that with the new ADFS, refresh tokens are multiresource, too. That means that as soon as you redeem the resulting authorization code, you'll get an access token for the resource you specified in the request and a refresh token that can be used for any of the resources your client is configured to have access to. Take note that here there's no concept of consent: if the administrator wrote in the ADFS settings that a certain client can access a certain API with a certain set of scopes, that just happens for all users—no questions asked. It's like the use of admin_consent described in Chapter 9, but it is in effect all the time and right after the settings have been saved via the management UX.

Next, you need to actually redeem the authorization code. For the sake of simplicity I will do that right in AuthorizationCodeReceived, as I did in the first sample in Chapter 9; all the considerations and techniques about how to move that code to actual controllers apply here, too.

```
AuthorizationCodeReceived = context =>
{
    string code = context.Code;
    AuthenticationContext ac = new
        AuthenticationContext("https://ws2016tp3.vibrodomain.net/adfs/", false);
    AuthenticationResult ar = ac.AcquireTokenByAuthorizationCode(
                                code,
                                new Uri("https://localhost:44320/"),
                                new ClientCredential(clientId, secret),
                                "https://myservices/myAPI");

    string callOutcome = string.Empty;
    HttpClient httpClient = new HttpClient();
    httpClient.DefaultRequestHeaders.Authorization =
        new AuthenticationHeaderValue("Bearer", ar.AccessToken);
    HttpResponseMessage response =
        httpClient.GetAsync("https://localhost:44324/api/values").Result;

    if (response.IsSuccessStatusCode)
    {
        callOutcome = response.Content.ReadAsStringAsync().Result;
    }
    return Task.FromResult(0);
}
```

I highlighted the interesting code in bold—everything else is just like you've seen.

ADAL's `AuthenticationContext` is initialized passing the URL of the ADFS instance. It is important to include the trailing /adfs/ with the authority as that tells ADAL that this is an ADFS instance, and in turn that determines whether it is necessary to tweak how the requests are made.

The other interesting thing about `AuthenticationContext`'s initialization is that the authority validation is set to false. Normally, `AuthenticationContext` verifies that the URL passed as authority complies with the template describing valid Azure AD tenants—as advertised by a discovery document. At the time ADFS came out, comparable functionality wasn't yet available in ADFS, so authority validation with ADFS and ADAL 2.x is impossible. If you don't set the corresponding flag to false, requests will fail. You might wonder why the developer experience team did not automatically shut down validation when the library detects that it's ADFS. The team working on the library did think about that long and hard, but it concluded that a decision of this potential impact (with a malicious authority, people can trick users into surrendering their credentials to evil endpoints) has to be made explicitly.

The other interesting part is the secret used for manufacturing the `ClientCredential`. That has to come from the secret you generated when you were provisioning the web application earlier in this chapter.

Finally, the resource identifier passed to `AcquireTokenByAuthorizationCode` is the same as you added to the web API entry in ADFS.

If you have followed the steps I've described so far, your web app will be wired to call the web API from the project discussed in the last section of Chapter 9—the one about ADFS. All you need to do is ensure that the `MetadataEndpoint` used to initialize the OAuth2 bearer token middleware points to the correct URL for your ADFS instance. In my case, the code looks like the following:

```
app.UseActiveDirectoryFederationServicesBearerAuthentication(
    new ActiveDirectoryFederationServicesBearerAuthenticationOptions
    {
        Audience = "https://myservices/myAPI",
        MetadataEndpoint =
            "https://ws2016tp3.vibrodomain.net/FederationMetadata/2007-06/FederationMetadata.xml"
    });
```

If you don't want to code this manually, it is also worth stressing that you can ready up a web API project that's hooked up to ADFS in less than 30 seconds if you use the ASP.NET project templates in either Visual Studio 2013 or 2015. Just create a new web API project, click Change Authentication, choose Organizational Accounts (if using Visual Studio 2013) or Work And School Accounts (in Visual Studio 2015), select On-Premises, paste in the ADFS metadata address and the desired audience value, and you're done. Figure 10-9 shows you the Visual Studio 2013 dialog box; the one in Visual Studio 2015 looks nearly the same.

Don't forget that ADFS does not offer any API for automating the app provisioning from Visual Studio; the template can only emit the right configuration code and add the right NuGet references for you, but you still need to have access to the ADFS management UX and provision the web API manually before being able to call it.

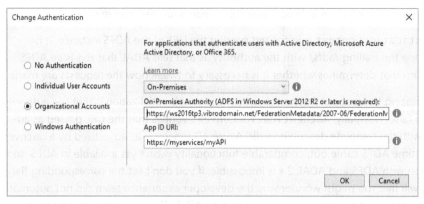

FIGURE 10-9 The dialog you use to set authentication preferences for ASP.NET projects in Visual Studio 2013. Visual Studio 2015 projects offer a similar dialog box.

We're finally ready to test our scenario end to end.

Testing the web API invocation feature

Let's start by firing up Fiddler. To test this scenario, we must be sure that both the web app and the web API are running. If you added the web API as a project under the same Visual Studio solution, you can simply go to the Startup Project settings, select the Multiple Startup Projects option, and set both projects to perform the action Start. Alternatively, you can launch each instance separately by right-clicking the project in Solution Explorer and starting a new debug instance.

Once both projects have started, sign in as usual. Here's the request in Fiddler:

```
GET https://ws2016tp3.vibrodomain.net/adfs/oauth2/authorize/?
client_id=98ff52e2-6deb-4029-99e4-6c15486d9c56&
redirect_uri=https%3a%2f%2flocalhost%3a44320%2f&
resource=https%3a%2f%2fmyservices%2fmyAPI&
response_mode=form_post&
response_type=code+id_token&
scope=openid+profile+user_impersonation+MyService.Write&
state=OpenIdConnect.AuthenticationProperties%3dF[...SNIP...]_rO_ &
nonce=.NGZ[...SNIP...]jh iMzkxOTUy HTTP/1.1
```

As expected, the core set of parameters we observed in the web sign-on sample are now extended by the extra settings we injected for telling ADFS about the resource we want to access and the scopes we want to be granted.

I am assuming that your call to AcquireTokenByAuthorizationCode succeeds and the subsequent web API call fires correctly. If you extract the token from the trace of the web API call and decode it, you'll see something like the following:

```
{
    "_sso_data" : "D3Qox[...SNIP...]gLpeeP1xAm ",
    "appid" : "98ff52e2-6deb-4029-99e4-6c15486d9c56",
    "apptype" : "Confidential",
    "aud" : "https://myservices/myAPI",
    "auth_time" : "2015-10-24T23:29:50.181Z",
    "authmethod" : "urn:oasis:names:tc:SAML:2.0:ac:classes:PasswordProtectedTransport",
    "exp" : 1445733204,
    "iat" : 1445729604,
    "iss" : "http://WS2016TP3.vibrodomain.net/adfs/services/trust",
    "scp" : "MyService.Write user_impersonation openid",
    "ver" : "1.0"
}
```

Note I learned from the development team that the _sso_data claim is only present in Technical Preview 3 and will be removed in upcoming preview refreshes.

Once again, the token issued by ADFS is quite bare-bones, but it contains everything required for authenticating the call. Issuer, audience, scopes . . . it's all there. In fact, the OAuth2 token bearer middleware should be happy with it and allow the API to be invoked. You can apply to this ADFS-based scenario the same considerations about scope validation and middleware customization you studied in the Azure AD case, with the obvious differences (for example, multitenancy for on-premises AD does not really apply).

Additional settings

I hope this chapter has provided you with guidance for solving the core modern authentication scenarios with ADFS and given you a solid scaffolding as you decide to leverage new ADFS features. ADFS in Windows Server 2016 Technical Preview 3 is chockful of new features, but many of them are still very fluid, and I don't want to mislead you about their stability by describing them in detail here. Instead, I'll just mention a couple of additional features that are especially important for developers— adding arbitrary claims to access tokens and exercising finer control over which clients can call the API.

The screens in the application creation wizard tend to ask for little more than the essential settings ADFS needs to create a functional entry for the application. The management UX you can access after creation gives you some more interesting options that are worth exploring.

Open the application group of your solution, and double-click the entry for the web API. You'll see a classic multitabbed properties dialog (visible in the background in Figure 10-11). Go to the Issuance Transform Rules tab. This screen allows you to specify more claims for ADFS to add to access tokens issued for this API. Click Add Rule, and you'll be presented with the dialog in Figure 10-10.

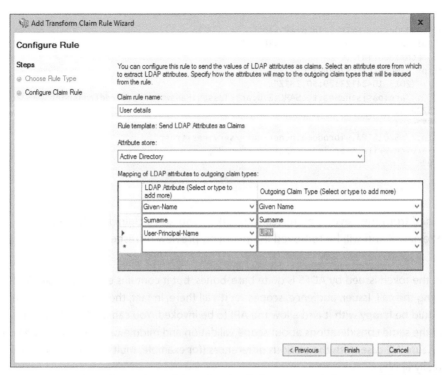

FIGURE 10-10 The Add Transform Claim Rule Wizard allows you to define more claims to be included in the token for the web API.

If you have used ADFS before, you are probably familiar with these settings. You can choose from where to source the claims values you want to issue: those typically range from Active Directory itself to custom stores you hook up to ADFS. Once you have done that, you have a simple tabular interface where every row determines the attribute you want to retrieve and what claim types you want to use for representing that value in the token. In Figure 10-10 you can see that I chose a few user attributes, just to show something new in the token. Be sure that you give a name to your rule, and then click Finish. You'll see the new rule listed on the Issuance Transform Rules tab.

Claims or attributes?

After about 300 pages of subtleties and fine points, allow me to bother you with (seemingly) philosophical matters one last time. People often confuse the concept of attribute with the concept of claim. The two things are very tightly related, but they are not the same. Whereas an attribute is a free-floating piece of information, a claim is information stated by a verifiable source (as in it travels in a token signed by the source). This is the same difference that applies to your name written on a random Post-it note and your name printed on your passport. The string is the same, but the uses you can make of it change dramatically—the latter carries all the strength that its source's credibility can lend. For many conversations, the two terms might be used interchangeably without immediate bad consequences, but occasionally the difference *will* be relevant, and misunderstandings are often hard to troubleshoot. I always try to use the correct term.

I know you are itching to try the flow that will issue new claims in the token, but given that we have the app properties dialog open, I want to show you one last thing. Go to the Client Permissions tab: you'll see a screen similar to the one shown in Figure 10-11.

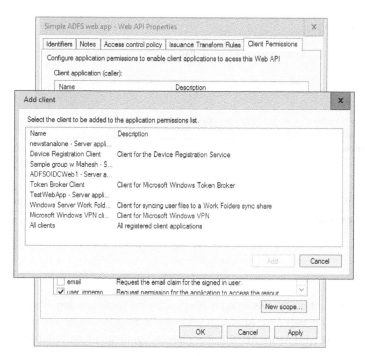

FIGURE 10-11 The web API property dialog allows you to extend the list of clients that are allowed to request a token for your web API.

That property page allows you to edit the list of scopes that your sample web client can request for this API, as we have seen at creation time.

More interestingly, this page allows you to manage the list of known clients that can access the web API. By default, only client apps within the same application group can access the API. If you click Add, you will be presented with a list of potential new clients. That list includes clients you created in this instance under different application groups and some built-in clients. I won't describe the built-in clients here, as they mostly come with heavy infrastructural considerations; please refer to the ADFS online documentation for that. The main built-in setting I want to be sure you are aware of is All Clients, which allows you to drop the restriction for specific clients and opens up ADFS to issue tokens for this API to any registered requestor. That's analogous to how ADFS "3" operated.

Let's not change the client list right now. Click Cancel to get back to the main properties dialog. Here, click OK.

Make sure that Fiddler is still running, go back to Visual Studio, and hit F5 again.

Looking at the web API call and decoding the token, you should see something like the following:

```
{
    "_sso_data" : "D3QoxP[..SNIP..]W_o6VBCA",
    "appid" : "98ff52e2-6deb-4029-99e4-6c15486d9c56",
    "apptype" : "Confidential",
    "aud" : "https://myservices/myAPI",
    "auth_time" : "2015-10-24T23:29:50.181Z",
    "authmethod" : "urn:oasis:names:tc:SAML:2.0:ac:classes:PasswordProtectedTransport",
    "exp" : 1445737813,
    "family_name" : "Rossi",
    "given_name" : "Mario",
    "iat" : 1445734213,
    "iss" : "http://WS2016TP3.vibrodomain.net/adfs/services/trust",
    "scp" : "MyService.Write user_impersonation openid",
    "upn" : "mario@vibrodomain.net",
    "ver" : "1.0"
}
```

As shown in the highlighted lines, ADFS applies our rule and has injected the claims we wanted in the access token, ready for the web API to consume.

Summary

This chapter gave you a quick introduction to leveraging ADFS directly for implementing modern authentication with your web apps and web APIs. Although there are some differences with respect to the code you write when you work with Azure AD, those are largely syntactic sugar. What you have learned through the book applies nearly verbatim to ADFS, which is what made it possible to cover so much functionality in a relatively short chapter.

Please remember that the version of ADFS discussed here is a preview, and it is very likely that some of the instructions provided here will no longer apply. If you try something and it doesn't work as expected, before you add breakpoints and traces take a quick look at *http://www.cloudidentity .com/blog/books/book-updates/* to see if there is a known change.

Further reading

The chapters in this book went deep into one specific scenario, modern authentication for web applications and web APIs. All the code samples were presented in C# and developed in Visual Studio (although apart from the Visual Studio wizards, you could have used any other IDE). Many scenarios and technologies are just as important, but they didn't make it into the book for various reasons—sometimes because they are still too early in the development cycle, but more often because of a lack of time. This appendix is meant to ensure that you are aware of these important topics and give you pointers if you want to know more.

If you follow just one link, be sure it's *http://aka.ms/aaddev*, which is the entry point for the online developer guide for Azure AD and offers the most comprehensive set of links you can find on identity and development for Active Directory. For keeping up with changes affecting what the book covers, please refer to *http://www.cloudidentity .com/blog/books/book-updates/*.

- **Other platforms**   The Azure AD developer experience team produces development libraries for an ever-growing list of popular platforms. You have explored .NET in depth in this book, but there are counterparts in the pipeline for popular server stacks such as Node.JS, Java, Ruby, Python, and more. All the libraries are open source and can be found at *https://github.com/azuread/*. Feel free to explore the libraries themselves and the test cases. The site I mentioned earlier, *http://aka.ms/aaddev*, has various quick starts that can get you up and running. Finally, *https://github.com/azure-samples?query=active-directory* has a very comprehensive list of samples. The convention is that the sample repo name includes the platform being demonstrated—for example, active-directory-node-webapp-openidconnect indicates a sample showing how to do web sign-on via OpenID Connect with Node.JS.

- **Single-page applications**   Single-page applications, or SPAs, are a very popular application development style I touched on in Chapter 2, "Identity protocols and application types." Azure AD offers comprehensive support for this style of development, from the protocol features necessary to implement the token flow to a handy JavaScript library (ADAL JS; source at *https://github.com/AzureAD /azure-activedirectory-library-for-js*) and accompanying samples (*https://github*

.com/azure-samples?utf8=%E2%9C%93&query=singlepage). I originally considered adding a chapter on SPAs, but as I started writing, it became clear that the chapter would have been too much of a detour from the main flow of the book. You can find more information on this scenario on my blog (*http://www.cloudidentity.com/blog/tag/adaljs/*) and, as usual, in the guide at *http://aka.ms/aaddev*. Finally, on the web you can find many samples and labs published from Office, as SPAs are a very popular way of consuming the Office API.

- **Native clients**   Modern authentication for native clients, as mentioned in Chapter 2, is a topic that deserves an entire book (or two) of its own. The Azure AD team supports lots of platforms through dedicated libraries: you can find .NET, iOS, Android, Xamarin, Cordova, Windows Store, Universal Windows Platform, and others at *https://github.com/AzureAD*. There are lots of samples at *https://github.com/azure-samples* and comprehensive guidance at *http://aka.ms/aaddev*.

- **Business to consumer (B2C)**   The flavor of Azure AD I discussed in this book is meant to address classic business-organization scenarios, such as internal app portfolios, cross-organization collaboration, or software developer vendors targeting the business world.

  As I write, Azure AD has announced an entirely new offer, dubbed B2C, or business to consumer, which is meant to help businesses handle authentication for their customer-facing applications and assets. The new offer makes use of the same infrastructure as classic Azure AD and is based on the same protocols (OpenID Connect, OAuth2); however, it tweaks the offer to support the features that B2C scenarios require. Simple sign-up, fully customizable authentication experiences, social identity provider integration, and profile management are examples of new features B2C offers. At this point, B2C is still in preview, but you can experiment with it by developing web apps with the same middleware you learned about in this book. Head to *http://aka.ms/b2c* for more details.

- **Azure AD vNext and convergence with Microsoft accounts**   The Azure AD team is hard at work to deliver a new version of Azure AD, which will introduce some key features currently missing. In the new system, the team is aiming at allowing you to get tokens from Azure AD or from Microsoft accounts by using the same protocol and developer libraries. Furthermore, you will no longer be strictly bound by the static permissions and consent rules described in Chapter 9—you will be able to ask for scopes on the fly. This is going to open up scenarios that are impossible or really hard to achieve today, and members of the identity team are all very excited about it. The new endpoints and libraries are in preview: you can read about them at *http://aka.ms/aadconvergence*.

Index

A

C

O

About the author

VITTORIO BERTOCCI is principal program manager on the Azure Active Directory team, where he works on the developer experience: Active Directory Authentication Library (ADAL), OpenID Connect and OAuth2 OWIN components in ASP.NET, Azure AD integration in various Visual Studio workstreams, and other things he can't tell you about (yet).

Vittorio joined the product team after years as a virtual member in his role as principal architect evangelist, during which time he contributed to the inception and launch of Microsoft's claims-based platform components (Windows Identity Foundation, ADFS 2.0) and owned SaaS and identity evangelism for the .NET developers community.

Vittorio holds a masters degree in computer science and began his career doing research on computational geometry and scientific visualization. In 2001 he joined Microsoft Italy, where he focused on the .NET platform and the nascent field of web services security, becoming a recognized expert at the national and European level.

In 2005 Vittorio moved to Redmond, where he helped launch the .NET Framework 3.5 by working with Fortune 100 and Global 100 companies on cutting-edge distributed systems. He increasingly focused on identity themes until he took on the mission of evangelizing claims-based identity for mainstream use. After years of working with customers, partners, and the community, he decided to contribute the experience he had accumulated back to the product and joined the identity product team.

Vittorio is easy to spot at conferences. He has spoken about identity in 23 countries on four continents, from keynote addresses to one-on-one meetings with customers. Vittorio is a regular speaker at Ignite, Build, Microsoft PDC, TechEd (US, Europe, Australia, New Zealand, Japan), TechDays, Gartner Summit, European Identity Conference, IDWorld, OreDev, NDC, IASA, Basta, and many others. At the moment his Channel 9 speaker page at *https://channel9.msdn.com/events/speakers/vittorio-bertocci* lists 44 recordings.

Vittorio is a published author, both in the academic and industry worlds, and has written many articles and papers. He is the author of *Programming Windows Identity Foundation* (Microsoft Press, 2010) and coauthor of *A Guide to Claims-Based Identity and Access Control* (Microsoft patterns & practices, 2010) and *Understanding Windows Cardspace* (Addison-Wesley, 2008). He is a prominent authority and blogger on identity, Azure, .NET development, and related topics: he shares his thoughts at *www.cloudidentity.com* and via his twitter feed, *http://www.twitter.com/vibronet*.

Vittorio lives in the lush green of Redmond with his wife, Iwona. He doesn't mind the gray skies too much, but every time he has half a chance, he flies to some place on the beach, be it the South Pacific or Camogli, his home town in Italy.

Now that you've read the book...

Tell us what you think!

Was it useful?
Did it teach you what you wanted to learn?
Was there room for improvement?

Let us know at http://aka.ms/tellpress

Your feedback goes directly to the staff at Microsoft Press,
and we read every one of your responses. Thanks in advance!